The College of Idaho Campus, April, 1991.

THE COLLEGE OF IDAHO

1891-1991:

A CENTENNIAL HISTORY

by

Louie W. Attebery

Louie W. Attebery

Photographic Editor, Jan Boles
Design & Typography by M. Lane Thomas

**The College of Idaho
Caldwell, Idaho
1991**

First Printing 1991

Copyright 1991 by

THE COLLEGE OF IDAHO

Library of Congress Catalog Card Number: 91-73929
ISBN 0-9630028-0-5

Endsheets Left: *Nine-foot sculpture of Dr. William Judson Boone.*
Right: *Display of memorabilia in the Margaret Boone Alumni House.*
Inset: Margaret Boone with students, c. 1954.

Printed and bound in the United States of America by
The CAXTON PRINTERS, Ltd.
Caldwell, Idaho 83605

Dedication

This book is dedicated to one who has served as organist for countless weddings, solemnized innumerable funerals, accompanied other performers without number, provided the unifying structure for illimitable church services, and taught a great many old and young fingers to play piano. Most of all she has filled and surrounded our home with music. Modest and self-effacing, she views her musicianship as her ministry. Although it will make you uncomfortable, Barbara, to be thus held up for admiration and love, this book is for you.

Acknowledgements

It is appropriate in the first place to acknowledge with deep gratitude the debt owed to those who dug the wells from which we now drink. To call them sturdy and selfless is accurate, but hardly adequate. I hope we are worthy of that deep devotion of which this campus is the symbol (or objective correlative).

I include in this acknowlegement the first and subsequent administrators, donors, staff and workers, students, and faculty. Respecting the latter, although I have included many names, I have had to omit many more. It may seem to the reader that whim has dictated the appearance or non-appearance of favorite teachers: The writing of history is selective.

Thus it is that I hold up for acknowlegement many who served and waited: Bob Post, former Director of Admissions, loyal beyond the call of duty; Alice Dennerline, who ran the mail room with patience and good will; Mr. Judd, who mowed the campus lawns with two good horses and an old-fashioned reel mower up to and even after the middle of this century; Mas Yamashita, judo instructor for many years; Wendy MacLaren, former alumni secretary; Midori Furushiro, so helpful to the Admissions Department and then to the Regional Studies Center; Norma Allen, June Domek, and Lee Lenuson, all of whom served as executive secretaries of the highest order. Here, too, I should acknowledge the hard and patient work of Rudy Rickenbach, Glenn Weed, and Phil and Betsy Eldredge, and Sylvia Hunt, and.... But this list must end even though many remain unacknowledged. Individually and collectively you are recognized.

Churlish would I be indeed if I did not thank Jan Boles and Lane Thomas, C of I '65 and '76 respectively, for their help with this book and Robin Kothman '92, for her patient processing of words.

Table of Contents

Every generation, looking backward, is apt to remember its time of wine and roses with the nostalgic certainty that "Those were the days!" Thus it is with us who were here fifty years ago; and so I suspect it will be with those who will look backward from the year 2036 to the spring of this very special senior year.

Governor Robert E. Smylie '38
Annual Spring Convocation Address
February 27, 1986

Map of Idaho, 1891.
Inset: Glass plate negative, Caldwell First Presbyterian Church in 1891, the first location
of The College of Idaho

FOREWORD

This book sets before the reader the story of one institution, which, by any reasonable analysis, is both like and yet quite unlike any other institution in the world. If the reader can grasp paradox, the story of The College of Idaho will make sense. To reverse the Wordsworthian purpose, one of the reasons for this book is to find dissimilitude—particularity—in similitude or sameness.

I see no reason to take refuge in the third person, and I have reservations about the imperial or editorial first person. Much of the time pronouns are not necessary, but when such use is unavoidable the reader should know that it is I speaking, not some remote investigator or indifferent writer. Even so, the personal pronoun ought not be overused. Aside from problems of vanity vs. humility associated with the first person is the more serious problem of perspective. Should the writer of such a chronicle as this one be an outsider—critical, dispassionate, objective—or an insider—warped in favor of the institution, convinced of its merit, committed to its enduring life and values?

When I was asked to undertake this chore, aware of my own limitations and knowing the constraints upon my time, I demurred and mentioned people who I thought were much better equipped for the task—Bob Smylie, Margaret Boone, and others. But the invitation persisted, and so it is that the book develops from my perspective, one who is a passionate supporter of private higher education, who has had this special private college very near the center of his consciousness since 1938 (the year my oldest brother matriculated), who was a student here from 1946 to 1950, and who returned to teach full time in 1961. The perspective is that of a partisan.

As for the readership for whom the work is intended, most readers will likely be College of Idaho family, those who already know something of the institution. Such readers are dangerous, in a sense, because their notions of the facts surrounding the institution may not always coincide with information identified as factual in the book. These kinds of problems are usually resolved through the standard scholarly practice of documentation, provided that the authorities cited are indeed reliable. As for interpretations of facts, ground for debate may well exist, and any such debate may be productive when the debating teams are aware of the provisional nature of their knowledge. The debate teams could profitably re-read chapter eleven of Bronowsky's *The Ascent of Man*, the one on certainty.

But I have omitted mentioning one important reader for whom this book is intended, and that reader must be identified as posing special problems. She or he may well be a member of a foundation's board of trustees, the executive secretary or executive vice president of some philanthropic organization. This reader is the one who might glance at the prospectus for such a book as this and observe that closets are full of institutional histories that nobody reads. Aside from the questionable accuracy of such an observation, the attitude behind the observation is unfortunately cynical.

Let me be a bit more specific. When the executive of an educational philanthropy located in New York but Idaho-based was approached about underwriting publication costs for this history, his reply was the one given above. But the cynicism does not stop there. The College of Idaho representative was not easily cowed, and he did not wish the interview to conclude with the rejection of this request which was, after all, minor in the larger story of The College of Idaho. So the College's representative replied that might be so, that perhaps histories of institutions are not widely read, but he intended to return to the foundation with other requests for other and perhaps more important projects. Fine, said the foundation, but we shan't fund them. We are restricting our philanthropy to such institutions as...and here he named some Northwestern institutions—none in Idaho—that would receive the largess of this foundation. He said, in effect, that his foundation was content to support those institutions whose strength was already proved and to ignore the institutions that had not quite arrived. "Everything supports what is already strong" might be a fair synopsis, an unfortunate philosophical position for institutions struggling to arrive. Those with, get.

Unfortunate but not atypical, as the next anecdote reveals. Another fundraiser had managed to make an appointment with the Mellon Foundation, and when the Foundation officer asked why in the world his organization should be interested in assisting a college in a part of the world so remote from any ties with the Mellon family, the representative of the College could only blink. Did the officer in his comfortable suite not know that millions of dollars had been added to Mellon wealth from mines in the Owyhee Mountains not 60 miles from The College of Idaho? Did he not know that Caldwell, Idaho, had been named after Andrew Mellon's brother-in-law, Sen. Alexander Caldwell of Kansas? Did these facts not establish a connection?

Thus it is for the reader who knows the College *and* for the reader who should know it that this book is written.

As for methodology, the conventional sort of research in primary and secondary sources is predominant, with anecdotal material appearing here and there as seems appropriate. I have tried to avoid footnotes; when documentation is required, the Modern Language Association style is used. A bibliography with comments on sources is included.

The genesis of the work is the celebration of our one hundredth year of life. It was done because a history of the College seemed both appropriate and necessary, there being no other chronicle of our hundred years. It was done so that the individuals responsible for the ongoing life of the institution could pause for a moment and, by drawing hope and inspiration from the record of the past, find resolution for plowing the fields whose next harvest will be gleaned in another one hundred years when the present generation has been gathered to its forebears. The reader may not be surprised to find references to and comments upon the status of American higher education, upon the essentiality of private education to that scene, and to the private sector which cries for a level playing field in international trade and finance.

As for the organization of the book, when my old and respected English department chairman at the University of Montana, Harold G. Merriam, wrote the story of that institution—whose founding was nearly parallel to ours—he organized it according to the administrations of its various presidents. Merriam's scheme worked. Hence this book (strange how lines from literature come unbidden, as Whitman's "Whoever you are, holding me now in hand") has nine parts, since the College has had only nine presidents: William Judson Boone, Raymond Hotchkiss Leach, William Webster Hall, Jr., Paul Marsh Pitman, Tom E. Shearer, Warren Barr Knox, William C. Cassell, Arthur H. DeRosier, Jr., and Robert L. Hendren, Jr. There are many who have known them all: Dr. Boone was presiding officer from the founding in 1891 until his death in 1936, creating a tenure unmatched for longevity among his contemporary college presidents. As a matter of fact, I have known them all except Dr. Boone and his replacement, who lasted almost a year. There is a minor problem of proportion here, for how should Dr. Boone's nearly fifty percent of the College's life be weighted respecting the no more than ten percent of any of his successors? The book shows how the problem was managed if not solved.

On one matter, I crave the reader's indulgence. I want to say a brief word about style, about the conventions governing capitalization. The popular press seldom capitalizes "the" unless it begins a sentence or appears as the first word in the title of a book, play, poem, or the like which is cited. The name of this institution is The College of Idaho, because when it was founded it was, indeed, the college of the state, the one and only, and the definite article is part of the Articles of Incorporation. In spite of the fact that there are other equally good institutions whose proper names include the definite article—The College of Wooster, The College of William and Mary, The Colorado College, The Citadel— the popular press does not recognize the article. But then neither has the popular press to my knowledge admitted that there are such things as brackets, so useful in inserting editorial comments or clarifications in someone's speech or press release. Throughout this narrative, the full name of the institution appears as The College of Idaho. When it is referred to by its shortened form, then only "College" is capitalized and when it functions adjectivally—a College of Idaho student—the article disappears. Refinements of this practice can be observed throughout the book, as various typographic conventions have been silently modernized.

The continuing story of The College of Idaho reads like a fairy tale, not in the shallow sense of narratives about unreal or immaterial beings but in the very structure of its life. The parallels are so real that I considered analyzing them as a folklorist would, using the "functions" of Vladimir Propp to make the similarities clear. A few sentences will clarify this matter: anyone offended by this strategy may skip to the last two paragraphs of the foreword.

The gender of the protagonist is quite clearly feminine as the chronology reveals a pattern of growth from the humble (though noble) birth of an unpretentious infant to alma mater. How appropriate. The Presbyterian parentage or sponsorship provides the nobility and humility of the Christian tradition, and so the church-parent monitors the infancy of the College. The hero or heroine of the fairy tale must undergo a series of trials in order to secure the appropriate role and identity in adulthood. So also does the College encounter trial after trial in her quest for role and identity. In the life of the College there have been four major trials, each one negotiated with great distress. The first of these was the Panic of 1893. Would the institution survive? The second was the Depression. The 1930s seemed to endure forever, and the life of the College was in grave danger. And the Depression had hardly ended when World War II caused such a reduction of student body (The class of 1945

xiv

consisted of five graduates!) that the prognosis was grave indeed. The final trial, though more difficult to analyze, occurred in the post-Viet Nam era when enrollment plummeted from nearly 950 students to a figure nearer 450, a time when the consequences of over-building, continuing indebtedness, inflation, and a grossly inadequate endowment coincided with national and regional shifts of philanthropy away from private education and toward tax-supported institutions. In this connection it is illuminating to note that as late as 1950, fifty-three percent of students enrolled in American colleges were taking their work at private institutions (McGrath, *Values, Liberal Education, and National Destiny*, 1975, p. 54). But thereafter public institutions either initiated or intensified efforts to corral more students, and much financial support formerly assured to private institutions found its way into the treasuries of tax-supported universities, creating a field of competition anything but level.

In the structure of the simplest kind of fairy tale and many other sorts of folk tales, the following "functions" or structural elements appear: a lack, an interdiction, a violation of the interdiction, a consequence of the violation, the appearance of one or more helpers, the liquidation of the lack, and the restoration of order. Without requiring too much of our imaginations, it is easy to see the size of the endowment and the student body as a lack. In view of these, the traditional admonitions to be thrifty, to count pennies, can be viewed as an interdiction, violated when the institution comes up short in pennies and students. An unbalanced budget violates an interdiction and general anxiety and institutional distress result. Both are only temporarily and unsuccessfully relieved by dipping into the endowment. At crucial times, one or more helpers—Proppian "functions"—have appeared to provide the gifts through which ultimate disaster is forestalled, and further admonitions about thrift and increasing the size of the endowment have been forthcoming. The lack has not yet been liquidated, and until it is, order cannot be restored.

But I chose not to put the book together using these functions as chapter titles, tempted though I was by the remarkable parallels. Instead, the book develops diachronically or chronologically, as the table of contents indicates. Even so, I cannot escape the conviction that like the protagonist of a *märchen*, The College of Idaho is growing into her destiny partly through the presence of helpers most clearly apparent in times of greatest need.

Other elements also bear a significant role in her growth, and the character or quality of the protagonist herself is important: after all, the heroine must be worth saving in order for salvation to be forthcoming. If something of that character is elucidated in this book, then another useful purpose will have been served. History must, after all, mean something.

J. R. R. Tolkien once observed that he entertained wild heraldic preferences for blue, Oxford University's color. I hope that readers of this history have a similar taste for purple and gold.

The Snake River Plain, southwest Idaho.

Part I

The Boone Years and the Establishment 1891-1936

Blaine Street to the northwest, from College Heights, or "the Hill."

CHAPTER ONE

The College of Idaho

Our claim to be the oldest college in the state rests upon fairly solid documentation. A brief look at our beginnings is therefore appropriate in order that the claim may be sustained.

In the College's yearbook of 1908 (*Renaissance*), Dr. Boone refers to the traditional division of history into "three periods, Ancient, Medieval, and Modern" (5). The ancient history of the College is "the time between September 19, 1884, and April 29, 1893, or from the dates of the first agitation to the date of the legal incorporation" (5). In Shoshone, Idaho Territory, on the day following the formation of Wood River Presbytery, that organization's committee on education reported to it as follows:

> Having examined the cause of higher education in Idaho we find that in all our sister states and territories schools of academic and collegiate powers are being established. As money has already been placed in the hands of your committee toward the establishment of a college in the Territory of Idaho we...recommend a committee...be appointed to take the subject under advisement and report at the next meeting of the Presbytery (5).

On April 15, 1887, when Wood River Presbytery met in Boise, the minutes report that "the committee on the establishment of a Presbyterian College in Idaho reported progress and was continued" (6). Two years later when the Presbytery met in Montpelier, a report informed the group that publicity about the proposed college had been widely disseminated, that parental support for a college "near their homes" was strong indeed, that energies of people along the Oregon Short Line Railroad needed to be consolidated and directed toward such an establishment, and that "Rev. W. J. Boone be requested to canvass for the erection of an academy with a boarding department at Caldwell" (7).

All of this is consistent with the Presbyterian concern for education which resulted in the founding of colleges on the edge of settlement as population generally moved from a more populous East to a thinly settled West.

Dr. Boone continues his essay on the founding of the College—its ancient history—by citing the Minutes of the 1890 meeting of the Presbytery of Wood River, whose committee on establishing a Presbyterian College in Idaho reported that the town of Caldwell had a proposition to make. Since the meeting of the Presbytery was in Caldwell, it was possible to arrange for a committee of citizens to appear before the church body with a resolution that Kimball Park be reserved for the institution and that if the Presbytery accepted, the legal work be done to transfer the property. The resolution was signed by Montie B. Gwinn, Chairman of the Caldwell Town Trustees, and Chas. B. Reed, Clerk (8). The proposal was accepted at about three o'clock in the afternoon of April 19, 1890, and the committee of the Presbytery was instructed to discuss details with the local citizens, reporting back to the Presbytery a day and a half later (8).

Caldwell, c. 1895.

4

So far, the way seemed clear. The College committee, however, had not finished its work, and subsequent meetings generated additional reports. These reports contained word of promises for $2,000 for the College from the citizens of Caldwell, a Presbyterian pledge to increase that amount to $10,000, and rather specific instructions to the trustees of the Presbytery representing the acquisition of real estate, the contracting of debts (none were to be contracted!), and the continuation of the committee (9). Additionally, a board of managers was identified to make plans for the school and the naming of a building committee was requested (9).

The next year, on April 18, 1891, the education committee of Wood River Presbytery reported that the town of Caldwell had in the meantime prepared a substitute proposition, since a good title to the Kimball Park land could not be secured although the $2,000 cash gift was retained. Under the new proposal certain other lands and permanent water rights to them were pledged by H. D. Blatchley, Henry W. Dorman, Montie B. Gwinn, Chas. A. Hand, Frank Steunenberg, and Howard Sebree. The Rev. J. H. Barton, chairman, matter-of-factly closed his report thus: "Other places have also asked the privilege of making propositions to Presbytery with a view of securing the location of the college" (10).

One of those other places was Nampa, and parliamentary maneuvering by the Rev. J. D. Black of that town managed to bring up yet once again the whole issue of where the college should be located in response to the best offers of land. The ensuing debate was not without "right hot personal retorts"; but the result was consistent with earlier action, as the following resolution was passed:

> Resolved, that we accept the new offer of the people of Caldwell respecting the locating of a college to be established by the Presbytery of Wood River (11).

The Rev. Mr. Black was granted permission to withdraw from membership on the college committee (11).

Indeed the way was clear, and plans were made for the opening of school in the fall of 1891.

So the question recurs: How old is The College of Idaho? Does it date, as H. H. Hayman says, from April 19, 1890 (*That Man Boone*, Caldwell, Idaho: The College of Idaho, 1948, p. 85)? From April 20, 1891, when the Nampa Gambit was declined and the Caldwell location reconfirmed? From the day classes began: 2 pm, Wednesday, October 7, 1891? Or should the date be set according

5

to the signing of the Articles of Incorporation of April 1, 1893? This April Fool's date would be painful to accept. The Articles were filed with Secretary of State James Curtis on April 12, 1893, and this is the date ordinarily assigned for the execution of the Articles of Incorporation.

But it is well known that the first years of the College's life found no students prepared for the intellectual rigors of a college curriculum; therefore, those first students were enrolled in the preparatory or Academic department. The reader acquainted generally with western history will remember that there were then few public high schools in this part of the world. The academy met this need. Dr. Boone's words are appropriate:

> The school was incorporated as a college and it was expected to do college work; for three years college courses were outlined in the catalogs, but no students were prepared to enter, so the secondary school work was all that was attempted.

The first class from the academy graduated in 1894 (13-14).

At the last session of the Idaho territorial legislature late in 1888, Latah County legislator John Brigham introduced Council Bill 20, which, when signed on January 30, 1889, by Governor Edward R. Stevenson, became the law by which a university was to be established at Moscow (Keith C. Petersen, *This Crested Hill: An Illustrated History of the University of Idaho.* Moscow, Idaho: University of Idaho Press, 1987, p. 20). The sites of few tax-supported universities in the United States are spelled out in their states' constitutions; Idaho's public university is so located by virtue of the approval of the Idaho constitution in 1889, its translocation possible only by constitutional amendment (Petersen 21). When Idaho became a state in 1890 through congressional action, it had its state university on the books. If being on the books is the same as being a university, then the school at Moscow can point to 1890 as the year of its birth; as a state university its existence could not precede the existence of the political unit of which it is a part. Otherwise, it would have been the University of the Territory of Idaho.

But the matter is not that simple. Aside from excavation work in 1889, nothing was accomplished until 1891 when the penurious legislature made funding available for construction (Petersen 25). By autumn of 1892, only a wing of an administration building could be called completed (25), but "On October 3, 1892, the University of Idaho opened its doors" (27). Two faculty (one of whom was the president) met the first students—about forty—of whom none was eligible to do college work, according to entrance examinations (27).

"The University would operate for a dozen years before students in the collegiate department consistently outnumbered those in prep school" (27-28).

In this respect the foundings of the University of Idaho at Moscow and The College of Idaho parallel one another. Much friendly rivalry, though little recrimination, has developed as to which is entitled to boasting rights about being the older. The University was established by constitution in 1890, but a supine legislature failed to appropriate adequate money for its construction and operation. It did not begin to serve students until 1892. The College was given a board of managers, a promise of $2,000 and a building committee in April 1890, capitalizing upon committee work and Presbyterian conviction on 1887. Both institutions found a dearth of young people prepared to do college-level work. It was a familiar pattern. Whitman College in Walla Walla, Washington, although chartered earlier than the University in Seattle, still had not offered college courses by 1877 (G. Thomas Edwards, "Pioneer President: Alexander Jay Anderson and the Formative Years of the University of Washington and Whitman College," *Pacific Northwest Quarterly*, vol. 9, no. 2, April 1988, p. 67); it opened for its fall session in 1882 with sixty students, most of whom were placed in elementary school classes, but by spring of 1883, with ninety-one students enrolled, Whitman could in good conscience place four as college freshmen (Edwards, 71). The C of I, in operation since October 7, 1891, had to confine its instruction to preparatory classes until the fall of 1906 when the first freshman class matriculated (Boone, 14). The University began offering college level courses to six students by the end of 1893 (Petersen 28). These facts about the founding of the two institutions prompted Stanford University scholar W. H. Cowley to make the following observations about The College of Idaho in a report of October 8, 1949:

> In point of operations you are the oldest college in Idaho. The State [Territory would have been a better choice of words] chartered the University at Moscow in 1889, but it did not offer instruction until a year after your chartering and opening in 1891 (*Report* 4).

I suppose that if one wished to urge the case semantically it might be said that we are the oldest four-year college in the state. Nobody can dispute that. But my inclination is to insist upon the oldest institution of higher learning in the state. College courses were available in 1891; the College was *in situ* then. And anyone knowing Presbyterian determination and wishing to urge the issue stridently could say that the will of a presbytery in 1884 in reporting funds available "toward the establishment of a college in the territory of Idaho" carries far more weight than the inclination of a legislative body. Thus it might even be argued that The College of Idaho was established in 1884.

The two institutions, having grown up together, share a historical fact, perhaps unique. Idaho's first Rhodes Scholar, Lawrence Henry Gipson, was prepared for college by the Academic Department of The College of Idaho, he matriculated at the University in Moscow, and from there he won his Rhodes' distinction, as a product of both establishments, returning to Caldwell to take charge of the department of Literature and History for 1908 after his work at Oxford.

In their very nature, most beginnings are exciting—a marriage, a birth, the first grandchild—and the beginning of an institution is a particularly exciting thing, I should think. No such institution as this was ever started with the idea of its ultimate demise, yet it is a sad fact that a great number of promising

Lawrence Henry Gipson

educational institutions have gone under. Gooding College and the experimental Intermountain Institute of Weiser serve as examples of the shocking national statistic of the many private schools forced, or allowed, to die.

In southern Idaho on those bright April mornings in the last decade of the century when hope and good cheer and belief in progress were almost palpable, the founders of The College of Idaho must have walked to their committee meetings with lightness in their feet. A town hardly eight years old; a railroad; water, both irrigation water that was beginning to change the desert into a garden and orchard, and domestic water of indescribable good taste and purity; and in the midst of all this, a new college: of course the institution would endure, grow, and triumph.

The Boone home, Belmont Street, during the Academy years.

Academy chemistry lab prior to 1910.

CHAPTER TWO

The Curriculum, the Faculty,

and the Students 1891-1903

Because we are watching the creation of a new thing, *Ecclesiastes* to the contrary notwithstanding, it seems appropriate to ask what was created back there in April of 1891, whose doors opened to students in October of the same year. But that question is answered in part, at least, by the whole book. A more basic one is "What is a college?"

A college is an institution of higher learning devoted to instruction in a particular field or fields of learning. Unlike a university, which divides its energies between teaching and research, that is, between dealing with known knowledge and generating new knowledge a college is primarily the agency for developing critical thinking, perfecting skills in some academic enterprise or other, exciting students about the known, and pointing the way toward the yet-to-be-known. Liberal arts colleges are, within this definition, devoted to instruction in particular fields of learning called by that name. The liberal arts, however they are defined, provide a curriculum whose purpose is analytic and synthetic and integrative. Knowledge and the fields of knowledge are analyzed, broken down into their component parts, assessed, and described; then those pieces are re-integrated—synthesized—into wholes, perhaps familiar, perhaps new. The process of education—and a college is part process—is intended to shape beings who are as fully human as it is possible to be in the present light of what full humanity means. The point here is that there is a difference between a liberal arts college, which emphasizes education broadly conceived, and some other kind of college—medicine, law, pharmacy, animal husbandry—in which the emphasis is on detailed mastery of a specific subject.

In the beginning, the College curriculum was classical. That curriculum was in the hands of a corps of teachers, including Frank Steunenberg, John T. Morrison, John C. Rice, E. E. Maxey, Carrie S. Blatchley, Chas. A. Hand, and W. J. Boone (Boone 12). Two members of that first faculty served the state as governors—Steunenberg and Morrison—and Rice sat on the Supreme Court. Although only two students were present at that first meeting, during the year their number increased to nineteen (Boone 12). No students were found eligible for work in the Collegiate Department, although the College was prepared to offer such a course of study.

The Preparatory Department for the academic year 1891-92 offered a course of study for the junior, the "middle," and the senior years. From the perspective of academic indulgence that crept into American college instruction following the 1960s, it appears formidable—English, mathematics, and Latin each year; considerable history, natural science, Greek, and German. The *Announcement*—the early equivalent of the catalog—goes on to say that "these

Academy students and faculty, 1902.

courses are preparatory to the collegiate courses—Classical, Philosophical, and Literary—leading to the following degrees: A.B., Ph.B., and Lit.B. Those who expect to enter the higher department and study for a degree must have completed the preparatory course, or the equivalent, leading up to the course which they intend to pursue."

This institution was no academic pushover. The infant institution sought guidance from more mature establishments about the curriculum and about other matters. Writing in the *Caldwell Tribune* of September 14, 1892, Dr. Boone makes this point clear:

> To inquiring friends we wish to say for our course of study in the academic department that it was not arranged by us without consultation with men of more experience. So, recognizing the fact that Leland Stanford University is by far the best school west of the Mississippi, we submitted our course to the faculty of that institution asking them to make any changes or make a new outline of study as they saw fit; also to name the best text-books for the various subjects in the course.

> . . . .

> President Jordan's faculty assure that the students who successfully pursue this course of study will have no conditions to make up as entering freshmen in Leland Stanford.

> Inquiry has been made as to why the Roman method of pronouncing Latin is used in this school. We answer: Because the instructors in Cornell, Michigan, Chicago, Leland Stanford Universities, and in nearly all of the other first-class schools and colleges in this country use this method, and it is very discouraging to a student on entering a first-class school to have a change in method of pronouncing Latin.

So it was Kikero and Kaiser, not Sisero and Seezer, at The College of Idaho: that was how first-rate institutions did it with Cicero and Caesar.

Readers may need to be reminded of the ordinary circumstances prevailing in American elementary and high school education in the last quarter of the nineteenth century and into the second or third decade of the twentieth. In rural areas district schools provided eight years of elementary instruction, broken, usually, into segments of instruction called "terms." A teacher was hired to teach during the terms the school was in session, the length of which was decided by the school board in consultation with the county superintendent, taking into account the funds available for the teacher's salary and other expenses, the number of pupils who would likely be in attendance for that period of time, and the availability of a teacher. Sometimes winters made attendance difficult, and a fall and spring term would be established. Summer terms were rare because children were essential to the farm work force. Even if the district were fortunate enough to afford three terms, some pupils might attend only one or two, depending upon home conditions.

Since the construction of public high schools was usually far behind the demography, growing needs were often met instead by tuition schools, that is, private academies or other kinds of college preparatory enterprises. The Intermountain Institute at Weiser was something of an exception: although it represented the non-tax-supported philosophy, it also sought to provide two things many such tuition-supported schools could not—domiciliation and work in exchange for expenses. Both of these provisions were extremely attractive to a potential high school student who might live fifty miles away, a considerable distance in a time when distance was measured by days of travel by horse. The Academy of The College of Idaho was such a tuition-based enterprise, born out of the absence of area tax-supported preparatory training in the 1890s and early 1900s. So even though a college was in place with its curriculum on the books, necessity and educational integrity said that students needed to be prepared for college work.

Dr. Boone's descriptions of the opening services that Wednesday morning, October 7, 1891, are printed elsewhere and need not be repeated here. But readers with moral imaginations will cast their minds back across the years to try to feel what those first two timid students felt as they faced the faculty across the lecture room in the Presbyterian church, the College's first home. What was it all about, this new thing under the sun? What business have I here? Can I make the grade? Is it worth the sacrifice? In addition to presenting a Stanford-approved curriculum, as more students enrolled the College encouraged the organization of an extra-curricular literary group, named the Lowell Society after the American poet, essayist, and editor James Russell Lowell, who had died that year. The rivalry between this group and the later-established Columbian Society (1895) shed both heat and light for a number of years.

That first academic year ended on June 15, 1892. With one solid year to its credit, the Board of Managers, acting on orders from the Presbytery of Wood River, advanced toward legal incorporation and set about planning the construction of a new building (Boone 13). The names and amounts involved in that original pledge by citizens of Caldwell are memorable: Howard Sebree, $500; Montie B. Gwinn, $500; The Coffin-Northway Co., $300; Isador Mayer, $100; William Cupp, $100; Central Lumber Co., $100 (Boone 13). Completed and furnished for $2,401.68, the new building was occupied by the College on Monday, October 10, 1892. The same year, the Board of Managers was replaced by a Board of Trustees and this group led the way to legal incorporation under the laws of the three-year-old state. The actual incorporators who "voluntarily associated [themselves] together for the purpose of forming a corporation, under the laws of the State of Idaho" certified that the name of the corporation was The College of Idaho (Articles of Incorporation). Twelve trustees besides the president, an ex-officio member of the Board, were named, two-thirds of whose membership "shall always be members of the Presbyterian Church in the United States of America," although the corporation was owned solely by the Board. Thus, from its incorporation, The College of Idaho was its own creature, inspired by the Presbytery of Wood River, presided over by a Presbyterian minister, but owned by its Board of Trustees. Later, that two-thirds membership requirement would be replaced by the following: "...Board of Trustees, said members to evidence a continuing desire to relate The College of Idaho to The United Presbyterian Church in the United States of America or the latter's successor..." (p. 1 Amended Articles June 1969). Connected by history and related by affection, The College of Idaho and the church are traditionally identified together. It is not, however, a church college but an independent liberal arts institution as is typical of colleges with a Presbyterian connection.

Academy campus, c. 1900.

With the Act of Incorporation, Dr. Boone said, the period of "ancient history closes and medieval begins" (13).

William Judson Boone, who had come to Caldwell to serve the new Presbyterian communion in 1887, continued to serve that church until 1893, when he resigned the pastorate in order to devote himself wholeheartedly to The College of Idaho. He had been minister **and** college president for about three years. He continued to minister, however, nearly all the rest of his life, preaching, marrying young couples, and conducting funeral services throughout the Boise River Valley.

In that first decade, a college had begun with a curriculum, students, and faculty. Soon it had three buildings. It is difficult for us today to imagine what that first campus must have looked like there in the north part of town, east of 10th Street along Albany, parallel with the railroad tracks (then a dynamic and respected symbol of American entrepreneurialism).

The 1893-94 Catalog shows that the classical curriculum developed through four departments identified as Academic (Preparatory), Collegiate, Music, and Art. In 1894 the first class finished and graduated from the Academic Department. Prominent faculty members during this decade include Mrs. Grace D. Morrison in music; Edith Perkins, Art; Lawrence Hemphill, Ph.D., German, Natural Science, and Latin, a tubercular who came in 1893 and died in 1894; Miss Abby F. Hull, who taught from 1895 to 1899 and founded the Columbian Society, arch-rival of the Lowell Society; Edward Ernest Maxey, M.D., Physiology; Carrie S. Blatchley, Elocution; John Campbell Rice, Economics; John Tracy Morrison, Practical Ethics; Rev. Joseph Hughes Barton, Bible Study and Greek; A. P. Haydon, Greek and German; Elma Brown, Painting and Drawing; David Andrew Clemens, Greek, Latin, and Mathematics; Julia V. Finney, English, German, and History; and of course, William Judson Boone, Natural Science, Latin, and Mathematics.

This classically trained faculty came from institutions like The College of Wooster, Cornell, Chicago, Washington and Jefferson, London, Drury, Maryville, Oberlin, Carleton, Washington, and Oshkosh. They were men and women of intelligence and probity, whose intellects were honed by the superb education that prevailed then. I have found no evidence that would suggest they were chosen by a committee; rather, they were, apparently, picked by Boone, who seemed to have a gift for selecting the best.

While it would prove tedious to catalog the home towns of all the students who matriculated at The College of Idaho during this first decade of its life, it is nevertheless a valuable exercise in the local history of southwestern Idaho and eastern Oregon to note some of them. The following Oregon towns were represented: Huntington, Jordan Valley, Carlton, Westfall, Baker City, Pleasant Valley, Ontario, Owyhee, and Portland. Idaho towns included the following— and it is difficult not to raise the query of medieval poets, *ubi sunt?* Where are they now? as some of these names appear—Falk's Store, Silver City, Placerville, Caldwell, Banner, Middleton, Idaho City, Boise City, Emmett, Reynolds, Malad City, Payette, De Lamar, Roseberg, Lower Boise, Star, Parma, Roswell, Mountain Home, Horseshoe Bend, Salubria, Van Wyck, Nampa, Meridian, South Boise, New Plymouth, Weiser, Council, Garden Valley, Quartzburg, St. Anthony, Hagerman, Hailey, Cambridge, Lemp, and Sweet.

In the first dozen years of its life, the College had graduated ten classes from its Academic Department. Enrollment showed a steady, if not meteoric increase. Clearly, Dr. Boone's school meant something to this part of the world.

Academy dining room, c. 1900.

First Academy graduating class, 1894.

CHAPTER THREE

A New Campus

The Caldwell *Tribune* of June 22, 1907, offered perhaps the first public inkling of plans for a new campus:

This year's [fifteenth annual] commencement will witness the graduation of one of the largest classes in the history of the school. It will be a pleasure as well as some worry on the part of the officers to know that the school has assumed such proportions that the institution is crowded for room and has arrived at the point where it is absolutely necessary that larger buildings be erected and more and better facilities be provided in order that the school may continue to hold its present enviable position.... The Tribune understands that there is a proposition pending whereby The College of Idaho can get an endowment of $200,000 providing that $50,000 additional be raised by the friends of the College.... The Tribune has no hesitation in predicting, that Caldwell...will respond with the usual liberality.

On page one of this number of the *Tribune* appeared a four-column-by-seven-inch teaser in the form of a drawing by J. E. Tourtellotte and Co. of the projected new twenty-acre campus, with ten buildings, a horseshoe drive into the campus from Cleveland Boulevard, and an athletic field. Page eight, the last page, was devoted nearly exclusively to the College. Clearly a cordial connection had developed between gown and town, between the publisher of the *Tribune* and President Boone.[*] The cordiality extended beyond Canyon County. Boise's

---

[*] It is both gratuitous and vain to observe that Caldwell's fourth estate has in these latter days abandoned her and moved east. The thought arises that of all the local enterprises—excluding churches and fraternal organizations—begun at about the same

Evening Capital News for Saturday, June 29, 1907, featured Caldwell, The College of Idaho, and Dr. W. J. Boone, "President of The College of Idaho, Located at Caldwell," on page seven. The Boise paper was unstinting in its praise of all three subjects.

The president was his institution's best press agent. Writing in the 1908 *Renaissance*, Dr. Boone said the following:

> During the past year the faculty has been increased by the following members: F. W. Barr, in charge of the Greek department; M. Hawkes, in charge of the English department; L. H. Gipson, in charge of the department of Literature and History; and J. Barr, librarian and assistant in Mathematics. The school now outlines courses in regular collegiate work, and efficient teachers are in charge of the same.

> The campaign for the "New College of Idaho" is now on. The College is engaged in the task of raising the endowment and equipment fund of $125,000. Of this amount $25,000 has been donated by the citizens of Caldwell, $25,000 by two Canyon County patrons of the school and $25,000 by Dr. A. [D.] K. Pearsons of Chicago. In all something over $76,000 has been raised up to date. A financial agent is now in the East, and it is hoped that in the near future the school will be established on the 20-acre campus on Washington Heights (15-16).

The twenty acres cited above carry the legal description as "being in Sec. 27, Tp. 4, N. of R. 3 W. of B. M., together with a permanent water right therefor." H. H. Hayman in *That Man Boone* (1948) identifies the foregoing legal description as the "site of the present campus except in dimensions. The original [Washington Heights] campus lay between Twentieth and Twenty-Third Avenues, extended one half block across the Boulevard and lacked one half block of Fillmore Street" (97).

Dr. Boone continues:

> Some 750 persons have been enrolled as students in the school, 135 have graduated and 49 persons have been cataloged as instructors and

---

time as The College of Idaho, few survive with her. Time does not permit a thorough investigation, but I would hazard a guess that Caxton Printers comprises the list. Indeed, the College newspaper of May 12, 1925, carried an advertisement stating that Caxton's was incorporated in 1907 but had been doing job printing since 1896. The reader is reminded that Canyon County is only from March to April older than The College of Idaho and Caldwell is about seven years senior, using the date given by H. H. Hayman (see Chapter 1). Canyon County was formed March 7, 1891, according to Robert I. Vexler and William F. Swindler, *Chronology and Docmentary Handbook of the State of Idaho*, (6).

lecturers. Whatever success the school has had may be attributed to three facts: the people of the town and community have always given it hearty support, the trustees have kept it free from debt, and the College Board has come up with an appropriation every year since its legal incorporation (14-15).

There is familiar stuff here: avoidance of debt (a condition that has not always prevailed, as subsequent chapters will show), gratitude for support, and steady but strong growth. The prospect of a new college and a new campus, however, is unfamiliar. The old college was not old. The classroom building was finished and occupied in 1892; in 1899 a dormitory was constructed; in 1901 an Assembly Hall was added to the back of the first structure (Boone 14; Hayman 118). But a move to Washington Heights was impelled by the conditions cited in the *Tribune* story. This part of town quickly became College Heights; old-timers still refer to it as "the Hill," as did Dr. Boone in entries of his diary, for September 20, 24, and 26 of 1910, although it is only a modest lump on the landscape.

Science demonstration equipment, Assembly Hall stage.

As daunting as the undertaking must have been, I find no indication of reluctance in Dr. Boone's diary. Indeed, it is not until September 16, 1910, that the institution's first president confided to the privacy of his diary that at the

> Meeting of Trustees at 3 P.M. not much [was] done. A Quorum but no good for school. We are **chumps** [Boone's emphasis].

Two years after the first indication that a new College of Idaho was a-borning, the Caldwell *Tribune* of March 13, 1909, published the financial outlook for the College as outlined by Professor Julia V. Finney in a report to the Boise Valley Presbytery meeting in Caldwell that year.

By early May of 1909, the official organ of the Associated Student Body of The College of Idaho, with the forthright name *The College Critic*, was preaching the word of a new College of Idaho. This broadside featured a three-column-by-nine-inch spread with the following headlines:

THE NEW C. OF I.

A College of the People, for the People and by the People of all Southern Idaho

ONLY $10,000.00 MORE NEEDED FOR THE $175,000

Every City, Town, and Hamlet; Homesteaders, Farmers, Ranchers, Stockman = All Join Hands and Rally Round the College in its Hour of Need. Caldwell Proud to be Home of object of such Universal and Unselfish Support. Buildings to be Ready for Next School Year.

In the fifth paragraph, the reader learns that "there now remains something less than $10,000 to raise in order to satisfy all conditions and bring to the College three splendid buildings, costing not less than $25,000 each, and an endowment of $100,000. The grounds, most admirably situated, were donated by Mr. Blatchley and consist of a twenty-acre tract." Two motifs are introduced here that help characterize the life of this and most other independent educational institutions: fund raising for the very life of the place and the need for an endowment.

A closer look at the raising of this hoped-for $175,000 is necessary, partly because it belongs in the record and partly because the crucial venture was fraught with anxiety as it launched President Boone into the role of mendicant, soliciting funds principally from eastern wealth—a task he disliked.

Two entries in Boone's diary for July of 1907 catch the eye. On July 5 the reader is introduced to a Dr. H. B. Knight, "our new financial agent from Tacoma.... Knight is a fine man and knows his job." Four days later, July 9, this information appeared: "Dr. D. K. Pearsons writes Miss Finney that when we get $75,000 endowment he will give us $25,000. On November 6 he wrote, "Mr. and Mrs. Kirkpatrick give us $20,000 towards a new building for the College.... Mr. Howard Sebree signs up for $5,000 for the College...." On November 8, "Dr. Knight sets out for New York. He will run the College Board and others for the Endowment money for the school." The year 1908 was only three days old when Dr. Boone wrote the following optimistic entry:

> Day fine. I do some work in College. [Remember: this was the old College down town.] Evening at 8 p.m. mass meeting in Opera House to enthuse for the College. A good meeting and leave no doubt but that $25,000 will be a go in short order and that we will land the $125,000.

On January 27 the optimism was still there:

> The $25,000 Endowment fund now about $21,000. Mr. Blatchley at the wheel. He will make it go. Dr. Knight will be back soon, then the wheels will go round.

But it was Boone who attended to the wheels, for a couple of reasons: he was one who, entrusted with ultimate responsibility for the institution, was not constitutionally able to shirk that responsibility; and philanthropy generally does not wish to talk with vice presidents, deans, and functionary fund-raisers, however good they are. Philanthropy wishes—and is in a position to expect—to see the head man. So after attending the 120th General Assembly of the Presbyterian Church in Kansas City, Dr. Boone left "the green and lively country on the Missouri River" on June 1, 1908, for Chicago. By June 3 he was oriented to the metropolis, visiting the

> city library, Montgomery Wards, and the art museum. Then go out to Hinsdale on the C. B. and Q. See Dr. D. K. Pearsons, have a talk with him. Back to town. Sleep at the New Waldorf at $.50.

For the next thirty-seven days Boone was on the road, visiting and seeking funds and advice in Chicago; Pittsburgh and western Pennsylvania; Wooster and Cleveland, Ohio; Denver, Colorado Springs, and other Colorado cities; Salt Lake City, Utah; and on July 7, 1908, "hit home 3:35 A.M. All well." He was not to travel east again until December 7, 1908, a trip which would require his absence from Caldwell for more than six months.

The record is a bit confusing: a $25,000 gift from a philanthropist when an endowment of $75,000 was reached. That much is clear. But how did that target of $100,000 become $125,000 which Dr. Boone hoped to land? And how did that figure become the $175,000 of the school paper? Dr. Hayman's understanding of the matter is the clearest account I have found.

> The Pearsons' offer of July, 1907, was simply that he would pay $25,000 toward endowment if $25,000 more for endowment could be raised by July 1, 1908. This would give the College an endowment of $100,000 but nothing for buildings.
>
> Complications set in. In the Caldwell drive of January, 1908, for $25,000 the pledges were made on condition that the endowment would be secured by July 1 [1908]. As the weeks passed it was becoming evident that the time would have to be extended to May 1, 1909. This necessitated making over the old pledge to conform. So read Boone's comment of July 17, 1908: "Dr. Knight is getting extension on College notes." Further difficulties arose. On January 20, 1909, Boone's work in New York came to a climax (143-44).

We pick up the story from Boone's diary:

New campus construction, Sterry Hall prior to 1913.

> 20 January 1909:...Get a note...that our application to Mr. Carnegie had succeeded, $25,000 for endowment but the condition is big. $75,000 for buildings and when $150,000 is paid in he will pay the last $25,000 on a grand total of $175,000. Good news. I write to friends all morning and do not get much else done but scheme to make the race for the last $66,000 needed to make all good.

Dr. Hayman's account continues:

> The Carnegie foundation...stated that it would make a gift of $25,000 to the endowment if the amount for the **buildings** would be settled at $75,000, making the entire amount to be raised $175,000. So what started out as $100,000 for endowment in 1907 now included $75,000 more for buildings—$125,000 of which was to be raised by May 1, 1909 and the remaining $50,000 to be secured by July 1, 1909. Notwithstanding these complications, the entire campaign was successfully concluded (144).

With funds available, construction on two buildings on the Hill began: Sterry Hall, named for Christopher W. Sterry, father of Mrs. E. M. Kirkpatrick of Parma, and Finney Hall, named for longtime faculty member and college champion Julia V. Finney. She was given credit for securing the challenge gift from Dr. Daniel Kimball Pearsons, a wealthy real estate magnate in Chicago who distributed more than $4,000,000 to colleges and other non-profit institutions and withheld the money until those establishments had secured larger sums than he had promised (Hayman 143). His form of donation must have been among the earliest of the "challenge" grants, the hope and sometimes the despair of fundraisers for charitable institutions.

An entry in Boone's diary for July 29, 1909, reads as follows: "We finally get the Buildings settled. The Sterry to cost $30,000 and the woman's [Finney] $20,000." However, by the time the buildings were completed and furnished, Sterry Hall had cost $45,000 and Finney $35,000, according to the "President's Book"—a looseleaf notebook of faculty and other information about the College used for fund raising.

But the new campus was a reality. Within two years of the move, three impressive brick buildings lorded it over the alkali flats surrounding the Hill and must have caused more than one passenger on the Oregon Short Line to look across at the structures in amazement. And it is difficult for us today to sense the pride that Caldwell and the region took in this place. It was, indeed, a new thing under the sun.

C. of I. Faculty 1913-14

Faculty in front of Sterry Hall, 1913. Left to right: H. H. Hayman, F. E. Springer, Helen Case, Sara Scheckner (Rankin), O. J. Smith, Payne Boulton, Margaret Nichol, Julia Finney, Mrs. William Case, The Reverend William Case, Carrie Blatchley, Paul Murphy, Joseph Rankin, Dr. William Judson Boone.

CHAPTER FOUR

The Faculty, Students,

Curriculum...

and the Extra-Curricular

So Boone's new college was off and if not running, at least walking steadily. By 1901 the institution consisted of two buildings and an "L."[*] The first graduates from the old school were Julia Matilda Cooper, Nellie Hargrave Gilbert, Edna Little, and Lillian Potter, names to be remembered. Classes in the collegiate department began in the fall of 1906, initially with two freshmen—Cleve Groome and Boyd Kreider, both products of the preparatory department. The first collegiate graduating class, in the spring of 1911, consisted of Daniel Banks, Cleve Groome, Fannie Kimbrough, and Ralph Trowbridge.

---

[*] Incidentally, it was this year—1901—that the College Club was organized consisting of wives of college faculty. In 1911 it became the College Clan. Dr. Boone often spelled it with a "K."

Some things that happened at the College in its first incarnation—those nineteen years on the old campus—seemed to establish a pattern for the future. One of these was the success Boone had in attracting quality faculty who, in most cases, either were or soon became loyal to the institution and to its first president. How he was able to accomplish this may always remain a mystery, one of those impenetrable unknowns of personality and character, but part of Boone's success must have resulted from his capacity to lead rather than his ability to drive; he was a model of hard work, integrity, wisdom, and intelligence. Then, too, there was a vulnerability to the man, never more strongly stimulated (though you might have had to look carefully) than when he ministered to bereaved family and friends of those received into death's dateless night.

When the Boones' bright and talented daughter Marie died of a ruptured appendix on June 30, 1911, grief flooded in that was never totally relieved. For twe[nty-five years every June 30, in Boone's diary] there appears a memorial of tha[t] mi[ ] nin[ ] de[ ] Wh[ ] up[ ] ne[ ] mo[ ] tee[ ] buggy to perform a wedding that evening, radiating comfort and assurance at the one and showing joy and affirmation at the other, great indeed were the demands on his own spiritual and emotional resources. I suppose this was especially true following Marie's death. But those resources were equal to the task, Boone suffering quietly inside as they were renewed.

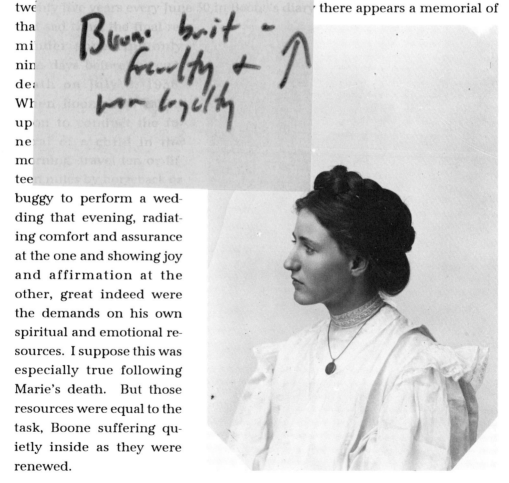

Marie Boone, 1911.

There was a quality about him that I can only identify as integrity. I say this even though I never knew him; I have, however, come to appreciate the legacy of the superb teachers he left behind. I will be forgiven, I know, if I mention only these and their years of service and let them stand for all the others it was not my good fortune to know: H. H. Hayman, 1909-1947; Paul Murphy, 1908-1953; Orma J. Smith, 1910-1948; J. H. Roblyer, 1923-1966; J. M. Rankin, 1912-1956; Sara Sheckner Rankin, 1913-1916, 1919-1952; F. F. Beale, 1911-1947; Ancil K. Steunenberg, 1921-1961; Anna S. Eyck, 1924-1949. These were teachers who would have dignified any campus. Classically educated, they were produced by a philosophy of education which inculcated a graceful and sound use of English and imparted a knowledge of Western civilization. They took their work seriously, and nowhere did one find a supercilious or blase cast of mind.[*] It is not surprising that one finds this legacy in those students nurtured by Boone's college. Carl Tappan, who died on October 11, 1989, at 103 was this sort of person, as are W. Paul and Eleanor French Tate. And here belong Harold Tucker and Lyle Stanford. From Margaret Sinclair's impassioned policing of stray beer cans, Rhodes Scholar Jim Roelofs' impulse toward social responsibility and a desire for a clean campus took inspiration. The list is long, but it is not inappropriate to point the way back from these to their source, Dr. Boone.

On both the old and new campuses, Dr. Boone worked like a hired hand. If it occurred to him that there might be an academic proscription against cleaning litter, painting woodwork, repairing toilets, shovelling coal, preparing blackboards, unpacking crates and boxes of books, planting clover and alfalfa, and cleaning out furnaces, he did not let on that he knew it. It was all work and work simply had to get done.

If sacrifice seems to be the topic addressed above, I suspect Dr. Boone might chide just a bit by saying something about the joy of work, the satisfaction of watching a young and growing mind ignite, of knowing that what good one does is never lost but adds to the total good of the universe.

The early faculty were bright and devoted to teaching, the kind Boone was able to attract with remarkable consistency. Among them was Lawrence Alexander Hemphill, Ph.D., *magna cum laude*. Dr. Hemphill was elected to the

> Professorships of German, Natural Science, and Latin...by the trustees
> of the College at their regular annual meeting, Tuesday, June 6th, 1893.

---

[*] There seems to be something humanizing and civilizing about the study of Greek and Latin.

> It was a bright day for the College when word came that he would accept the position (obituary in pencil in Boone's writing).

Hemphill's career glowed with promise, but it was a short-lived career, for he died of tuberculosis in 1894. Like several other later College of Idaho teachers, he died in the harness.

Another gifted scholar and promising teacher was Lawrence Henry Gipson, a product of The College of Idaho Academic Department, the University of Idaho, Oxford University, and Yale. Idaho's first Rhodes Scholar and a member of the first class of Rhodes Scholars, Gipson returned from England to join the faculty in September of 1907, after being released from obligations at McMinnville, Oregon, or so I interpret the following entry in Boone's diary for September 2, 1907:

> Lawrence Gipson in from Middleton. He is in a dilemma. Seems he is not going to get off from McMinnville [Linfield College] so very easy as he had hoped.

Gipson taught for the College from 1906 to 1909, after which he pursued the Ph.D. degree at Yale and settled finally at Lehigh University. He became the world authority on Britain's eighteenth century empire, winning a Pulitzer Prize for history for volume ten of his remarkable fifteen-volume series. Volume eleven was dedicated to Dr. Boone.

Julia V. Finney, Carleton College and the University of Minnesota and Chicago, had a long and significant tenure at the College, teaching English and German from 1898 to 1925 and serving as vice president of the school for part of that time.

While this chronicle of the College is not a biography of Dr. Boone, that man's character was such a rich one that aspects of it keep appearing, sometimes in a startling and even refreshing way. In recognizing Julia Finney's work with Dr. Pearsons, for instance, Boone wrote College treasurer L. S. Dille May 31, 1909, as follows:

> ...Will look in on Dr. Pearsons. Am going to offer him Miss Finney for an additional $25,000.... Then we will put the buildings on Miss Finney's forty and call the whole plant Pearsons-Finney.... I have turned clear around and see that to boast of finishing the year "free of debt" and keep within our income is poor policy in College building...(Hayman 144-45).

In 1912 another of those remarkable, loyal young faculty members arrived to teach home economics or domestic science, as it was then called. Her name was Margaret Nichol, and she continued to teach until 1939, producing many public school teachers of that subject as well as preparing many young women for life in their own homes.

H. H. Hayman came to the Academy from Roswell, Idaho, taught at the Academy from 1905 to 1907, reversed the footsteps of his great teacher and friend Boone **back** to Wooster for his degree, went to Princeton for his theological training, and returned to teach at the College from 1909 to 1947. Another of those loyal and self-sacrificing teachers to whom the College was an institution worth almost unlimited sacrifice, Hayman, like Boone, helped keep the campus clean, helped mend what was broken, irrigated the lawn (when a lawn was established), cut the hay (when the campus produced alfalfa), helped tend the potatoes (when during WWI the campus aided the war effort to the extent of producing food), and devoted years to excellent work in the classroom and in the supervision of forensics.

Like Boone, over the course of his busy ministry he conducted a multitude of funeral and wedding services. I recall being mildly shocked one time when he came to class and said, "Well, we planted old Mrs. So and So today." He was wearing a black suit and had obviously conducted a funeral service, and to a sophomore it seemed disrespectful of the dead, if not sacrilegious, to describe a burial as a planting.

Another familiar Haymanism had to do with the family meat supply, and to understand the witticism requires a bit of knowledge of social history. He might say upon concluding a lecture that he would like to stay to visit after class, but he had to go take care of his Townsend Plan Steer. For the benefit of those who did not know the name Townsend Plan* and who did not realize that careful attention to the provisioning process would help reduce grocery bills (the early faculty tended gardens, picked and canned fruit, kept a milk cow, and often fattened a veal, a steer, or a pig) Dr. Hayman would say, "Yes, I need to look after my Townsend Plan Steer: I supported him for a while, and now he's going to support me."

Long after Dr. Hayman retired and while his health permitted, he would be the first to rise on a winter morning to clear the snow from his sidewalk and probably from that of his neighbors. It was a thoughtful and responsible act

---

*   Proposed by Dr. Francis Townsend, this plan called for strategy to take care of retirement at age sixty—$150 (later $200) per month to all who retired at that age and agreed to spend the money in thirty days. A "transaction" tax would finance the plan.

of a good citizen and added to the upper Dearborn Street understanding of what neighborliness means.

Professor Paul Murphy was at various times an officer of the Caldwell Kiwanis Club, and when he was secretary the membership could expect to receive mailings of what he called "Paul's Epistle to the Kiwanians." Throughout his long career, he was the College's resident classicist, preparing many future high school teachers to conduct classes in Latin and many pre-theology students for divinity school Greek. His two ancient history classes, one in Greek civilization and one in Roman, were popular with students.

In addition to his work as Director of Strahorn Library, Professor Murphy was institutional faculty representative to the Northwest Athletic Conference, an obligation he did not take lightly. He was undoubtedly committed to Juvenal's maxim (on grounds of manner **and** matter), "Orandum est ut set mens sana in corpore sano." An efficient and responsible intercollegiate athletic program was one way of meeting the sound body part of the truism which spoke also of a sane mind.

Orma J. Smith, B.S. Ohio University, M.A.S. Iowa State, Iowa, was a virtuoso teacher and could have become an outstanding administrator. He served as acting president of the institution on two different occasions, the first at Boone's death, the second at the conclusion of Raymond Leach's brief tenure (1938-39). He was Dean of the Faculty 1931-1941. It is unarguable that this giant intellect, devoted scientist, and faithful Methodist started the College on the road to her significant reputation for accomplishments in science and the healing arts professions. Coming to the College as a teacher of chemistry and biology, Professor Smith soon attracted and produced students of the highest caliber. Among those who took their pre-professional scientific training at The College of Idaho while Dean Smith was confirming students in the wisdom of their choice, the following names appear: H. Corwin Hinshaw, Manley B. Shaw, Charles Ferguson, and William H. Chisholm.

Dean Smith is remembered by many students of embryology as the teacher who made the mysteries of the transformations of the fertilized egg considerably less mysterious, less difficult to conceive, through the apt use of modeling clay. Thus the budding embryologists could see the cell undergoing its amazing metamorphoses as Dean Smith shaped the changes in clay.

Some also remember him as asthmatic and opposed to tobacco smoke. When he and Mrs. Smith rented apartments to college students, one of their first questions asked was, "Do you smoke?" Their renters were assured the pleasure of a smoke-free environment at 1822 Dearborn.

One of Smith's brightest students—indeed, he was the College's nominee for the Rhodes Scholarship competition his senior year—was Lyle Stanford, Class of 1933. More will be said of Stanford in the chapter on the College's third president, Dr. William W. Hall, but here it may be appropriate to suggest that Dean Smith was in actuality grooming his successor. Although Smith was hopeful that young Stanford would go on to medical school and encouraged him in that direction, fortune decreed otherwise, and the mantle in the succession of brilliant department headship would indeed pass to Lyle Stanford.

Dean Smith was Boone's kind of man, a scientist who saw in the orderly processes of nature the design of the designer and thus no conflict between science and religion. The theories of Darwin, which offered reasonable explanations for so many biological phenomena in a systematic, observation-based epistemology, could not gainsay the insights into spiritual matters and ethics of the Bible. Those who thought they saw conflicts probably knew neither subject adequately, although the aging Dean Smith I knew was too gentle a Christian to argue very much about the matter. Even in what we perceive as randomness in the universe Dean Smith might have chuckled in his high-pitched asthmatic voice and said something about the design containing apparent disorder and anomalous phenomena so that it might also contain an element which in human terms is called freedom. If it were not so, the universe might well be an absolutely closed system with all events—human and non-human—either absolutely prearranged or absolutely determined by previous events.

Joseph M. Rankin served the College from 1912 to 1956, as noted earlier. Together the Rankin husband-and-wife team invested eighty years of life in this institution, Joe serving forty-four and Sara thirty-six (1913-1916 and 1919-1952): a remarkable testimony of loyalty and affection.

Joe's gifts were not confined to mathematics, for he had strong talents in music as well and was a gifted narrator of what folklorists call memorates—first-person accounts of memorable occurrences. From Tennessee and a graduate of Maryville College (also Presbyterian), Professor Rankin commented upon what it was like to conduct a country school where an outsider was observed by unseen eyes, some of which may well have been squinting through the sights of "rifle guns," when the stranger first walked into the district where he was to teach. Whether he spoke of his own or another's experience I cannot be sure.

Sara Scheckner Rankin came to the College in its second decade to begin a long and remarkably successful tenure as a teacher of German and Spanish.

She too had a genuine gift of music and left a legacy of lyrics, some of them published, celebrating various aspects of the region including its great Snake River.

Others will remember her skill as a teacher of foreign languages, a bright-eyed wren of a woman who customarily told her students to let her know if some emergency or unexpected happening had not permitted the preparation of an assignment so that she would not embarrass anyone by expecting oral participation when the assignment was unprepared. Her Spanish classes will remember her eight columns of pronouns, her attention to the naming of the parts of *el cuerpo humano*, and the time and attention she paid to enriching the textbook assignments by reading Spanish legends. As long as they can recall anything, these students will remember the story of Juan Cintron, the folktale of the grape farmer in Estremadura who forgot the wind, and the singing of Spanish-language art and folk songs. Some will remember *El Sombrero de tres Picos*, *El Coloquio de Los Perros*, *La Vida de un Picaro*, and the exciting *Noche Oscura en Lima*.

F. F. Beale was Idaho's most capable and best known figure in music. He and his wife, Mary Meyer Beale, started a school of music—The Frederick Fleming Beale School of Music—which was formally affiliated with and accredited by The College of Idaho in 1925, although Beale had been teaching for the College and serving as Dean of the Department of Music. Not all aspiring musicians saw the necessity to hold the B.A. degree and could study music in the Beale school without taking science, mathematics, literature, and other impediments on their road to musicianship.

A Kansan by birth, Beale studied with, among others, Jessie L. Gaynor, serving at the age of seventeen as organist and choirmaster at the Westminster Presbyterian Church of St. Joseph, Missouri. At the American Conservatory of Music in Chicago, he studied with the well-known and respected Adolph Weidig and Wilhelm Middelschulte, taking his Bachelor of Music degree and returning to teach at the Gaynor Studios in St. Joseph. From there he moved west to Seattle where he served as Head of the Department of Piano for two years before leaving the University, coming to Caldwell in 1911. Mary Beale, a graduate in piano of the Gaynor Studios, specialized in piano and Frederick taught organ, piano, theory, history, and harmony in the Beale School of Music (Soran, "The Frederick Fleming Beale School of Music," 2).

Frederick Beale was a superb performer at the piano and organ; the quality of his teaching is attested by his fine legacy of teachers and performers of those same instruments even today, some 42 years after his retirement and death. Another legacy is the music he created, his art songs, his operettas, his orchestral pieces. In his program notes for the Frederick Fleming Beale Memorial Concert (Caldwell, Idaho December 7, 1965), Dr. Richard Skyrm wrote the following:

> Mr. Beale's best writing is exemplified in his art songs. Many...were performed by famous artists of the day including Anna Kansas, George Hamlin, Charles W. Clark, Wilbur Evans, Nelson Eddy, and Albert Jampolski (Soran 3).

The Skyrm program notes cite an early orchestral success, "Dance Caprice" (c1909), performed in Seattle by the Seattle Symphony Orchestra, to an audience so appreciative that the composer was given a great ovation and called to the stage, and modestly—or shyly, perhaps—declined to take a bow (Soran 3). A popular formulation among Beale's former students about his gifts runs, "If he couldn't find a production he liked, he'd write his own operetta." And he did precisely that, "Fatima" probably the best known. This two-act work received its world premiere in Boise at the request of the Boise Independent

F.F. Beale at the organ of the Caldwell First Methodist Church, c. 1912.

School District in December of 1933. In 1937 a second production was staged, this time in Caldwell (Soran 4).

Correspondence between Beale and C. C. Birchard music publishers, Beale and the Max Factor Make-up Studios—yes, the Hollywood people—and Beale and costume and scenery rental agencies is interesting because it shows that Beale wanted to do things with a flair. However, the following letter regarding Beale's candidacy for a position at UCLA reveals the professional standing of the man and the esteem in which Beale was held by the American musical world of 1936. Music major Mimi Soran obtained this copy in the spring of 1989:

March 20th '36

My dear Frederick Fleming Beale—

Your letter came nearly a month ago, and every day I have planned to write you in regard to its contents.

. . . .

I was in a difficult position as to the recommendation you suggested; for I have been offered as a candidate for the same position, for some time; thro the urgent request of Mr. Cecil Frankel (a pupil of mine) of the Women's Committee (Pres) of the Symphony; Mrs. Leiland Atherton Irish, also of the Symphony Ass'n; several of the Southern Regents, and many others. I was also recommended for the position , when Mr. Stearns was appointed; but Dr. Moore's reply to them, has been that "altho I hold Mrs. Moore to be the best on the Coast, in her line, I must have a man."—This has been his text, to several which has [sic] been handed on to me, within the last few days.

I had been hoping, since he felt that way about the matter, that you might be the man—but the news has filtered through, just now, that Arnold Schönberg has been engaged.

. . . .

I hope you will let me know when next you come South, and I shall be so glad to see you. It would give me real pleasure, were you to be appointed, at UCLA, for I believe you would obtain results; which I doubt will be obtained under the present regime, unless there is a plan for assistance, in teaching capacity.

Yours with all good wishes,

[signed] Mary Carr Moore

Dr. Francis E. Springer came to the College in 1911, according to Hayman (48) or 1910, according to Bess Steunenberg's 1959 *Directory* teaching philosophy, psychology, and education classes until 1939. Others with lengthy tenures were Carl Salomon, English (1916-1942) and Elford C. Preston (1925-1943), who taught history.

This ramble has taken us from the move to the new campus in 1910 up to the 1920's, with special reference to the fine faculty Boone was able to hire and keep. Some accounting must now be forthcoming of the students, their activities, their accomplishments; and of what watersheds, or perhaps what crises in the growth of the institution occurred.

In September of 1910, Dr. Boone wrote Robert Mackenzie, Secretary of the College Board of the Presbyterian Church in the U.S.A., asking about the Board's wishes respecting synodical government of colleges in view of "[our] desire to make our school a synodical rather than presbyterial college." Boone then outlined his understanding of what Mackenzie had said on this matter the previous autumn.

On October 21, Mackenzie replied as follows:

> The Board is instructed by the Assembly to cooperate with three classes of colleges: those (1) organically connected with the Presbyterian Church in the United States of America, or (2) required by charter to have at least two-thirds of their Boards of Control members of said Church, or (3) actually under Presbyterian approval at the time of receiving assistance.

Mackenzie continued by saying that the Board made no distinctions between the first two classes, assisting them with equipment, current expresses, and endowment, whereas the Board assisted the third class only "in the matter of equipment and endowment." After identifying the College as belonging to class 2 because of the requirement that two-thirds of the Board of Trustees belong to the Presbyterian Church, Mackenzie quoted Boone's letter to him in which Boone mentioned a by-law that, by courtesy, asked "the Presbytery of Boise to take part in the election of trustees." Mackenzie pointed out a conflict between the self-perpetuating nature of the College's board and the participation in the election of trustees by the Presbyterian of Boise. He suggested that Dr. Boone get a legal opinion on the matter:

> If the Board is self-perpetuating, should any other men or body of men take part in the election of trustees? If, one of these days, someone

should leave a bequest to your College, and some interested party should contest the bequest, as is often the case, he would look closely and technically into the legality of the election of your trustees.... It may be that the laws of Idaho permit you, under your charter, to make and act upon the by-law under which the Presbytery elects two-thirds of your trustees, but still I think you should submit the question to your lawyer for his written opinion, and send copy to me for our files.

The connection with the church needed clarification, for there was a kind of restiveness in it. It is safe to say that the College always needed more financial support than was forthcoming from the College Board, although, as stated earlier, President Boone attributed part of the College's continued success to the Board's consistent support. But still,

> Dr. Boone's relation with the old Board of Aid for Colleges...was not always satisfactory.... The earlier members of that board would not see any prospects for a college here in Idaho. It looked to them just like desert, and that was that. This might have been the basis of their slogan "Keep out of debt," so that when the school disbanded there would be no financial scandal...(Hayman 154).

Out of this not-always-satisfactory connection, this negative capability, some saw opportunity—specifically the Methodist Episcopal Church. A story in the Caldwell *Tribune* of February 9, 1912, was headed "METHODISTS SAID TO BE FIGURING ON THE COLLEGE." A subheading said "Negotiations Are in Progress for the Sale of the Institution," followed by "COMMITTEE PAYS VISIT." The third subheading offered an abstract of the ensuing story: "The Rumor of Purchase is Afloat but Cannot be confirmed—The Commission Pays Visit to Magic City in Order to Look Over the Situation—Appears Pleased." The abstract is accurate although it fails to include an extensive (about a third of the item) recital of community reluctance to accept such a change. One paragraph near the end of the story mentions that "Dr. Boone...is in the east now on business connected with the school. Exactly the nature of the business is not known." The business, of course, was the one with which he became so familiar over time—holding out his hat, begging for money so that this institution might survive.

While he was in New York at the Chelsea Hotel (January 27, 1912: "Get to N.Y. at 9 am.... Go over to Continental Hotel but lo! It is closed...get good room [at] Chelsea Hotel on 23rd St."), he received a long letter from the Reverend Bruce J. Giffen of the First Presbyterian Church of Parma, in which Giffen explained "the steps taken by some of us last week at Boise with regard to the College." It is difficult to excuse his adding to Dr. Boone's burden, for the letter not only presents Giffen's advocacy of putting the College under interdenominational control, but it also states that "Mr. and Mrs. Blatchley have wished for some such arrangement." Was there, indeed, a falling off of support in these two stalwarts? Giffen mentions a meeting of Presbyterian ministers and conversations with leading laymen—Presbyterian, I suppose—"all of whom favored it except Ex-Governor Morrisson [sic]." Some of Giffen's comments and analysis were close to the mark, as, for instance, when he called attention to Presbyterian reluctance

> to come out and claim the College as a denominational agency and solicit from our own people the support that they should give.... I would have it that the Presbyterian church have a yet closer relation to the College than it now has. I would like to see a new charter which would give the Synod the right to elect trustees direct for the College. I would have it put before the people of southern Idaho as most emphatically a denominational school.

Synod group, Voorhees Hall, after 1912.

But then the Reverend Mr. Giffen suggested that the College should be a multidenominational school with the Methodist church a logical co-sponsor.

In a letter to the Blatchleys at the same time, Giffen pressed the same paradox of stressing the potential denominational relationships while at the same time making the College more Presbyterian than ever. He even had a formula by which the composition of the faculty would reflect denominational control: "It would become the duty of each denomination to furnish a certain number of instructors.... I anticipate that the quota of the Presbyterian church would be at least as many as are now members of the faculty from our church."

The next missive from Caldwell was a note from L. S. Dille, stating:

> The Methodist scare does not alarm me as it did though there is undoubtedly a growing sentiment that in some way the Presbyterians are not equal to the situation and if other denominations do not come to our assistance we are bound to remain a poorly equipped and poorly supported school. The general public will not be patient indefinitely. We are likely to lose its good will from this time on.

It is fair to wonder whether the Presbyterian establishment—the General Education Board, as Boone identified the agency in his diary—had heard premonitory rumbles from the West. Indeed, a historian of a certain cast of mind might argue that if there was a genuine Methodist threat, Boone and his associates certainly exploited it fully in their efforts to coerce the Board into providing greater support. A thoroughgoing cynic would carry the matter further by suggesting that the whole Methodist bugaboo was a fabrication intended to force the Board to take a more active role and adopt a more generous policy of providing financial aid. I doubt these interpretations, for I am convinced that Boone was too forthright a person to conceive let alone execute such a boardroom ploy. I suspect, however, that Boone was tremendously agitated by the whole matter of the College's destiny, whether it lay in Presbyterian or non-denominational hands and, if in the former, then with what kind of governance. I suspect, moreover, that this agitation was a tremendous source of energy for Dr. Boone and that he pursued his mendicant mode with renewed energy and effectiveness.

On February 16, for instance, he wrote:

> Day was fine. A red letter day for me....got check for $10,000 from Ellen G. James. Wonderfully fine. I go to Gen-Ed. Board at White Hall. Am very cordially received and am made to take off my coat and stay.

James's was a substantial gift: a helper had emerged at just the right time. How characteristically Boone, though, to conclude this day's entry with, "C of I debaters won at home and at Albion. Great." After all, the wellbeing of the tiny school was the only reason for the trip east. Naturally he cared about what was going on in Caldwell and at Albion.

A like note was sounded on February 19:

> I went to Gen. Ed. lunched, very fine.... Stay about 3 hours. One of the red letter days of my life. I give to Dr. [Russell] Sage my own desire as to The College of Idaho.

The entry for the next day includes the following:

> Day was fine. I go down to Gen. Ed. Bd. at about 3 p.m. Take down all the Idaho information on the M. E. situation in Idaho. Do not see any other persons. Nothing new.

Eleven days later—March 2, 1912—an arresting diary entry highlighted something new:

> Go to Ben Haven (Pa) [home of some of Boone's family], find all well. Get $10,000 by mail from Clinton, N.J. Fine.

That would build Voorhees Dormitory! Another helper had appeared at just the right time.

Surely one of the critical events in the teens and in the life of the College was an act of the legislature recognizing the rights of graduates of The College of Idaho to teacher certification. This feather in her cap came to the College in

Carnegie check, $25,000, the first large cash contribution to The College.

the Twelfth Session in 1913. Graduates of the College were placed on equal status with university graduates and were no longer compelled to go to universities or normal schools for training.

Another historical watershed was World War I and the terrible flu epidemic. The College of Idaho *Bulletin* for December of 1979 featured Sara Rankin remembering some of her long tenure here:

> During World War I there were only four men left on campus. The faculty agreed to take whatever salary was left over after expenses were met (3).

Times, she commented, have always been frugal. Indeed they have, and this frugal time might have witnessed the dissolution of the College. For the academic year 1918-1919, the year of the Armistice and the most serious for the College, the number of students dropped from 134 to 83 (data sheet McCormick). This decline of about 41 percent was unprecedented and would not be approximated again until the abyss of World War II. Boone's diary for September 19, 1918, said, "Only 3 boys in school to date" and for September 25, discussed attempts to get involved in military instruction for the College but "no results. We are too small and too poor and it is really not patriotic to urge our Government to take us on." On October 13, 1918, "at least one case of SP. influenza in town"—a foreshadowing of sickness that would involve town and gown, faculty and students, and lead to quarantine as health officers tried to control this serious problem.[*]

But the College survived, the Academic Department was phased out (1919) and that next academic year (1919-1920) enrollment soared to 141, at that point the second largest student body ever. Before we look at that magic decade of the 20's, though, it is well to be reminded of what the school and its setting were like in the teens. There were few dwellings in the neighborhood, and they may well not have any lawns; certainly the vernacular houses would be simple and small. There were few trees and shrubs over eight (or ten or twelve) feet high, except those growing on the riparian (littoral) margins. Much of the land was dry, with shoestrings of green paralleling the streams and representing pre-Reclamation Act irrigation districts. What roads were there were likely

---

[*] So far as I have been able to discover, one College of Idaho student out of the 101 who served in the Great War lost his life. He was Andrew Thompson, killed in action at Vimy Ridge on Easter Sunday of 1917.

as not tracks through the sagebrush. This was the country from which students who desired an education came to Caldwell, the cultural center for eastern Oregon and southwestern Idaho, beginning in 1891.

Imagine the thrill with which a bright youngster from that environment began to experience the moment of intellectual growth. Here at this College of Idaho were men and women who spoke English correctly, who could read and write German, Spanish, French, Latin, Greek, and Hebrew! Here were learned people who had read and could actually explain Shakespeare. Plants and animals could be coaxed into revealing their true identities, and the properties of chemicals and laws of nature were no longer hidden.

Even though work in the classroom, the laboratory, and the library was—and remains—central to the College, activities of one sort or another were conducted so as to approach the ideal of the sane mind in the sound body. The Lowell Society had been founded in 1891, and the rival Columbian Society was founded by Miss Libby F. Hall in 1895. A fascinating social and cultural history of the College from 1895 to 1929 could be written solely in connection with the rivalry between these two literary societies. This chronicle must be content with only a few observations, the first of which is that the *Coyote* of November 1, 1929, announced the death of the two societies as of that year. Before that death, much of the emotional energy of the College swirled about these two organizations that sponsored competition primarily in forensic and creative endeavors. To generations of folk nurtured on "talkies," radio, and television, it may be difficult to imagine that people of the last decade of the nineteenth

Columbian Society float, Founders Day Parade, c. 1920.

century and first thirty years or so of this century found such things exciting; but both commercial and student publications devoted as much space to Lowell-Columbian set-tos as to athletics.

The activities of the societies, however, included more than debates and public-speaking contests with one another. At their respective meetings they studied the finer points of forensic art, discussed literature and philosophy, held dinners and picnics, went on outings, and conducted raids on one another's memorabilia. Many C of I students found that one or the other of these two organizations claimed their loyalty, and perfervid partisanship developed.

At the meeting of March 11, 1912, the Lowell Society and guests enjoyed the following program: a musical selection by the Lowell Quartet; a debate on the proposition "Resolved, that a system of compulsory voting should be adopted in the U.S."; essays; orations; and a declamation.

Playbills, posters, and other announcements of cultural events—all chosen at random—suggest something of the flavor of the place. For instance, a faded blue card announces the Blatchley Oratorical Contest on Tuesday, May 26, 1908, at the Assembly Hall (old campus). The program consisted not only of oratory but of songs and instrumental performances as well.

Commencement was an occasion for young people to show what they had learned. The printed program for the seventeenth commencement, June 4, 1908, at the Opera House, lists twenty-two separate events, including "Remarks by Presiding Officer" and "Presentation of Diplomas." The program was varied enough for everyone's taste—vocal renditions, orations, essays, orchestral selections—and that year the Chorus performed the prize-winning "College Loyalty Songs."

For the season of 1910-11 the Department of Music offered "A Musical Soiree" over two days, June 13 and 14. It was an ambitious program, with twenty-four numbers performed on June 13 and eighteen on the next day. A wide range of instrumental and vocal music, solo and ensemble, was offered, some still familiar, others reading like messages from a time capsule—"The Scarf Dance," "Oh, Divine Redeemer," "Rustle of Spring (Sinding)," "Little Pictures from Toneland," "Scenes from Childhood," "Welcome Pretty Primrose," "Down in the Deep," and many more.

Another Blatchley Oratorical Contest, this one held on March 21, 1913, featured a piano duet by Mrs. Murphy and Mr. Rankin (he also coached basketball) and three orations, and concluded with a vocal solo by Edgar Oakes, a classmate of James Boone and longtime friend of the Boone family.

On December 9, 1914, at 8:30 p.m. in the Huree Theater, The College of Idaho Men's Glee Club gave a concert, including the "Barcarolle" from *Tales of Hoffman*, "Last Night," and "It's a Long Way to Tipperary," among others. Professor Beale played three piano solos.

The College of Idaho Alumni Association was established in 1899, representing six classes (including that of 1899) (166). By 1914 the organization was sponsoring an annual banquet, that year's meeting in Finney Hall on June 12. The menu consisted of iced fruit, salmon croquettes, cold sliced tongue, mint jelly, mashed potato with parsley, pickles and olives, pineapple salad, wafers, orange sherbet, cake, and coffee, a bill of fare that is still attractive. A yell master put the graduates through their paces, not in the manner of today's strange solo performances by the appointed cheerleaders—the spectators silent—but acting in concert under the direction of the leader to raise the roof.* On June 7, 1915, the twenty-third annual College of Idaho Declamation Contest took place. Two divisions—serious and humorous—were separated by a musical interlude.

The next evening—the appetite for cultural enrichment was immense—the College short story contest (again with musical interludes) took place in Sterry Hall.

On Friday of that same week, June 11, 1915, the Alumni Association held its banquet. John J. Plowhead, '95, served as toastmaster; E. H. Plowhead, '95, told the alums what the College expected of them; Mrs. John C. Rice, '95, made reference to the second generation; Cleve Groome, '05, spoke of the first college class; Jesse Ragsdale, '15, spoke of untried pinions; the Rev. F. E. Springer (he who in 1930 would perform a wedding ceremony in an airplane!) talked about the spirit of the College, and Prof. Beale concluded the program as he discussed music in everyday life. All were listed on the program as "Toasts."

At least one program detailing a Lowell-Columbian Contest must be included. Since our theme year is 1915, let us have a look at the sixteenth of these annual fracases. At 8:15 p.m. in the College auditorium (in Sterry Hall) the hostilities began...but they were civilized hostilities. The first event was a debate on the topic "Resolved: that Congress should establish a central bank."

---

*   Professor Murphy once, in an aside to his class in Greek Civilization, remarked that it was the chorus of frogs from Aristophanes' great comedy of the same name that inspired some Harvard boys to create the taunt against Yale, "Brek-kek-kek-kex/ko-ax/ko-ax" becoming "Give 'em the axe, the axe, the axe."

The next event consisted of two orations, a Lowellite on "America's Defense" and a Columbian on "Our National Destiny."

Partisans then wrapped themselves in the virtues of their societies and awaited the beginnings of the second half, which consisted of essays and declamations. For this contest, six judges were selected, three assessing delivery and three judging composition and thought.

College of Idaho
1 9 2 2
ANNUAL OPERA PERFORMANCE
by the
GLEE CLUBS

Samson and Delilah
Opera in 3 Acts
by
Camille St. Saens
(In concert form)

AMERICAN THEATRE
Caldwell, Idaho.

Monday and Tuesday Nights
May 29-30

F. F. BEALE, Director

CAXTON PRINTERS, CALDWELL 24696

Two events the next year deserve some attention because they further show that The College of Idaho was doing a brisk business in the cultural stock market. F. F. Beale and the College Glee Clubs presented a musical extravaganza in the form of an operetta with dances titled "Contest of the Nations." Part of Commencement Week, this production was the very sort of thing Beale did so well. Fifty-four people, including Marjorie Beale as pianist and Elbert Rice as organist, brought the program to an audience of college students and townspeople.

The last cultural event that should be mentioned here was a presentation by the Expression Class in recognition of Shakespeare's Tercentenary (1616-1916). The lengthy program offered both the serious and silly (appropriate since the Swan of Avon could also quack like Donald Duck). Part I was entitled "Shakespeare Burlesque"; one can only imagine how the four speakers—Juliet, Portia, Ophelia, and Lady Macbeth—engaged themselves and the audiences in the projection of these serious females in a burlesque manner. Part 2, "Henry Fifth's Wooing," the Forest Scene from *As You Like It*, the Balcony Scene from *Romeo and Juliet*, and the Tent Scene from *Julius Caesar*, was a serious presentation of these strong vignettes. Part 3 was titled "Midsummer Dance Dream," with a cast of nine well known Shakespeare female characters plus Justine, a college girl. The synopsis of this last appears here as it was printed on the program:

> Justine falls asleep over her graduating thesis, "The Heroines of Shakespeare" and thru the mischievousness of Puck and the modern dance music, dreams the following:

> Hermione and Perdita have fallen upon hard times. Proud of having taught Hamlet the Hesitation, Perdita opens a dancing school. Hermione objects, but finding Shakespearean heroines flocking to the school, her complaint of "My Daughter" finds the satisfied addition of "My ducats."

The campus—the new campus—was an active place, and this small college in an appropriately small college town was by far the liveliest cultural center for hundreds of miles in any direction. It was, indeed, the place to send your children.

As late as June of 1911 the College was still offering work in four departments—Collegiate, Academic, Music, and Art. By October of that same year, Art had been dropped. Collegiate work led to either of two baccalaureate degrees, arts or science. The Bachelor of Philosophy degree had been dropped.

The catalog of 1919-20 shows that the curriculum leading to the baccalaureate degree was organized around five groups, analogous to our present arrangement of departments into divisions: Language Group - English, Greek, Latin, French, Spanish, German; Philosophical Group - Bible, Ethics, History, Psychology, History of Philosophy, Logic, Education, Economics, Political Science, Sociology; Science Group - Chemistry, Biology, Geology, Zoology, Botany, Physics; Mathematical Group - Algebra, Trigonometry, Astronomy, Descriptive Geometry, Analytic Geometry, Calculus, Mechanics; Vocational Group - Home Economics, Music, Public Speaking, Commercial Subjects, Surveying.

Of the foregoing categories of courses, only the Vocational Group might be vulnerable to criticism as inappropriate to a liberal arts education. However, the general graduation requirements served well to protect the A.B. or B.S. degrees from charges of vocationalism, for the A.B. candidate could select a major only in courses in Groups I and II, with minors from Groups III and IV. Candidates for the B.S. degree could select majors from Groups III and IV, with minors from Group I and II. All candidates had to prepare two majors and two minors. Majors and minors are carefully defined in the Catalog, and "year courses," "semester courses," and "semester hours of college work" are clarified.

In addition to the majors and minors, other general graduation requirements included Bible study, "satisfactory personal conduct and compliance with school requirements such as classroom and assembly attendance," and enough elective hours to total at least 128 semester hours.

College catalogs are invariably and probably inevitably dull. They are sources of objective fact and ought to be the most reasonably accurate description of the curriculum—the heart of a college—that can be assembled. The 1919-20 Catalog is a fairly typical one, and it may well be that application for accreditation by the Northwest Association was already planned. Two citations from this catalog may be instructive. The first is a statement of aims and objectives:

> The aim of the school is to furnish young men and women with the opportunity of obtaining a liberal arts education in the arts and sciences. It is hoped that the institution and moderate expenses will induce many young people to secure that higher education which fits them to appreciate and perform the duties devolving upon them as American citizens. This is not a theological school, as some infer, and no sectarian instruction will be given, yet it aims to be strictly Christian in its character and influence. The common principles of Christianity and good morals will be taught and insisted upon in the daily lives of instructors and students.

The second is the course description of Philosophy 2: Epistemology:

> This course is open to all who have had introductory psychology. This course embraces a study of the laws of thought and knowledge. The relation between thought and knowledge is investigated from the standpoint of various authorities upon the subject, and the aim is to lead the student to form his own conclusions. Prerequisite, Course 1 - Second Semester.

The aim of the school then and the aim today are not so very far apart; the course in epistemology reads as if it were a fairly serious study of how we come to know what it is we think we know.

The life span of student-centered college organizations is likely to be unpredictable, tastes and whims being what they have ever been. For example the Walking Club of 1911, which celebrated the feat of its female membership trekking six miles, had a very short life. And in the 1908-1909 Catalog appears an announcement for the following year about membership in the Zaonian Society, a literary and social club that for three years challenged the ascendancy

Men's championship basketball team, 1913, posing on the top floor of Sterry Hall. Note the structural cable, above right.

of the Lowell-Columbian hegemony. After the 1910-1911 Catalog, there is no further mention of the society.

The College has always had a strong interest in intercollegiate athletics, and from time to time her teams and individual performers have acquitted themselves with distinction. Indeed, this whole topic deserves a much fuller treatment than can be given here. Boone himself had been an athlete, and his interest in and support of the College's athletic program can be detailed through reading the entries in his diary. He attended all the games he could get to and watched for scores from games he could not attend.

He was also sensitive to the capabilities of the coaches—David Harold Cramer (1906-07), H. R. Cleaver (1907-1916), Ralph Kyle (1908-1912)—and the highest praise of a coach I have found in the diaries was extended on Saturday, November 22, 1919, as follows:

> Our men at Pocatello successful 28-0 for college. First football game we
> ever won at Pocatello. Good team and Anson Cornell the greatest coach
> in Northwest. Some jubilation here.

In closing this story of the second and third decade of The College of Idaho (about 1900 to about 1919), I wish to concentrate for a brief moment upon two students. These two from the early years stand for all the students whose lives were affected by the Academic Department and the early Collegiate Department of The College of Idaho. To represent the Academy, I have chosen Bertra Cupp, Class of 1907, and to represent the College, James L. Boone, Class of 1913.*

This history does not presume to duplicate the work of the four College of Idaho directories. It might be appropriate, therefore, for the reader to have a directory at hand so that when a name appears in the history with no class year,

---

*   It is appropriate to say something here about identifying a graduate or a one-time student with that person's class year. Since the history develops chronologically with each chapter encompassing about a decade, an approximation of the class year is built in. When a class year is identified, it may be that I simply followed the source utilized at the moment. At other times I may have supplied a class year to convey a sense of venerability: this or that student may be presumed to represent a sense of the past. Or it may be that I have supplied the class year because the person had been either a student with me or a student of mine. Finally, I must confess that it is possible the class year was given or withheld because it seemed the right thing to do at the time. If the reader wishes to criticize on the grounds of inconsistency, I can take refuge in Emerson or his disciple Whitman...or I can plead *mea culpa*.

the reader may make that determination. None of these directories, however, is entirely free of errors.

Bertra comes to mind because she was a member of a family long identified with the establishment and early years of the College. Indeed eight Cupps came to the Academy between 1901 and 1910 from the Cupp ranch in the Squaw Butte country above Emmett, a favorite place of Boone's where he could botanize and perhaps stir up a sagehen now and then. An additional reason for paying her some special regard was her winsome and honest photograph as a member of the graduating class of 1907 whose school pictures dominated the last page of the Caldwell *Tribune* for Saturday, June 22, 1907. The photograph is that of a very pretty girl.

James was a scholar, graduating with honors and going on to earn a degree in law from one of the nation's finest law schools. He was a leader, serving as editor-in-chief of *The College Coyote*, student body president, Lowell Society president, captain of the football team. "One of the fastest and most sensational football players in the state," he galvanized spectators time after time as "an adept at receiving the forward pass"; in the game against Pocatello he made a ninety yard run on a pass. When the "All-Time Team" was named in 1912, he was the right end, the fastest player ever on a C of I team. As noted further in the *Coyote* of June 1912, in the four years he played, the Coyotes won two

Bertra Cupp, '07.

James L. Boone, '13.

championships straight out and tied another. On the basketball squad he played center and served as captain, and in baseball he was first baseman. He was also, to use a favorite word of the *Coyote* columnist, an "adept" at debate, declamation, oratory, and creative writing.

He may have felt the eyes of the community on him, for he was the president's son; but whatever consequences that visibility caused him, he put his best self forward and triumphed in spite of them, as the children of faculty who stayed in Caldwell for their undergraduate education have done ever since.

Perhaps one of the reasons he is so appealing is that he worked in the hay and harvest; he drove a team and rode horses; he fished for trout and hunted grouse and pheasants; he spent time in a sheep camp; he worked in stores in town. These things bind many of us into a silent and boyish fraternity. But all of this does not explain why, as one looks at photographs of folk of an earlier time, his face so arrests one's gaze. As was the case with Bertra Cupp, 1907, the face of Jim Boone stretches the limits of the two dimensional medium of photography and the life-closing limits of time to say that here was a rare human being whom we were fortunate to have with us for awhile.

After a time in the Army in World War I, and after a career in law in the Boise Valley, he moved to Great Neck, New York, where he served as a corporation lawyer and became a member of the College's Board of Trustees, serving from 1933 until his death in 1961. It cannot be said of him that he was a typical College of Idaho student, but what an ideal he was for College of Idaho students to emulate—James Loudon Boone, Class of 1913.

The new campus, on the hill, viewed from the southeast.

*Academy
library, prior
to 1910.*

Administrators in a hurry: Vice President Chalfant and Field Secretary Robert McCormick, c. 1925.

CHAPTER FIVE

Canis latrans Rampant

As America generally roared and soared in the 1920s, so too did the fortunes of the school in the dusty West. Thus the heraldic device of a Coyote rampant on a field of gold and purple is not an inappropriate icon. Problems with the endowment did not go away; they are omnipresent. But that fund which is so basic to the health of all independent institutions of higher learning continued to grow. Numbers of students also indicate the health of a young school, and in this critical area the College improved. But perhaps the clearest justification for the image of a coyote upreared with front paws in an attitude of bellicosity and teeth gleaming ferociously was the accreditation extended in 1922. A college lives or dies on its accreditation (or, more accurately, accredited schools may live, but the failure to win accreditation is nearly always a death warrant).

Other aspects of the life of the College in the 1920's show remarkable progress and a basic good health: excellent additions to the faculty, continued access to the campus for Boise Valley students by way of flourishing interurban electric transit, and athletic and other extracurricular activities of a very high order indeed.

In his unpublished *The Excitement of Building a College*, Robert McCormick, longtime Field Secretary and former Vice President of the College, presents the following meticulous statistical record for the years 1914-15 through 1932-33:

THE COLLEGE OF IDAHO

Year	Endowment Growth	Total Endowment	Income from Endowment	Number of Students	Income per Student from Endowment
1914-15	—	$ 25,000	$1,750	86	$20
15-16	—	44,000	2,338	116	20
16-17	—	85,000	4,500	154	29
17-18	—	105,000	5,580	134	42
18-19	$32,000	137,000	7,280	War-83	88
19-20	32,000	169,000	8,981	141	64
20-21	—	182,000	10,295	164	63
21-22	40,600	222,600	13,006	202	64
22-23	—	240,500	13,940	286	49
23-24	—	250,200	13,941	363	44
24-25	40,300	290,500	15,739	400	45
25-26	56,500	347,000	18,396	432	48
26-27	—	365,000	20,308	437	49
27-28	—	370,000	21,134	414	47
28-29	—	385,000	23,566	420	54
29-30	44,000	429,000	24,805	424	54
30-31	—	455,000	23,578	429	59
31-32	58,000	513,000	23,707	443	54
32-33	—	513,000	22,715	413	55

The record is one of generally impressive growth, with anomalies here and there: the war's impact in 1918-19, the phenomenal increases in numbers of students from 1921 to 1925, and the decline in 1927-28 and in 1932-33—not surprising in view of the Depression.

In the Catalog of 1922-23, containing the announcements for the next year, the following words appear: "The College of Idaho is a member of the American Association of Colleges, The Inland Empire Teachers' Association, the National Education Association of the United States and the **Northwest Association of Secondary and Higher Schools.**" The bold-type words appear for the first time, significant because it is this organization which extends or denies accreditation to us. The College has been accredited continuously since...but sometimes with considerable anxiety.

That the College was planning to apply to the Northwest Association for accreditation is apparent in 1921. That year the catalog made explicit reference to the policies of Columbia Chicago, and Berkeley in dividing the curriculum into upper- and lower-division courses and called attention to the dangers of students foreshortening the four-year curriculum and attempting to take part of their preparation outside the classrooms; these ploys, said the catalog, might handicap the student applying for admission to graduate school.

Accreditation means that close and critical examination of a college by experts certifies that the institution is accorded recognition by its peers as meeting standards appropriate to it. The process is initiated by a year's self-study, during which the institution seeking accreditation turns a critical eye upon itself and minutely analyzes its faculty, its curriculum, its library, its campus life, its bookstore—in short, its institutional self—writes up the results of that analysis in a document of sometimes fearsome magnitude, and sends the document to the offices of the accrediting association. In the meantime, the officers of the association have developed a list of faculty and administrators from other accredited member institutions to whom the self-study will be sent. These dozen or so individuals study the documents supplied by the postulant institution to see whether what the school has said about itself is true and whether standards appropriate to an institution of higher learning have been met. It is, in a sense, trial by jury of peers.

The Northwest Association of Secondary and Higher Institutions was organized in 1918 and accredited six colleges and universities at its first meeting, according to the College of Idaho Bulletin for January 1949. The College was accredited in 1922, the tenth institution of higher learning in the Northwest to be thus recognized. At that time, accreditation was extended or denied on the basis of Association reaction to documents submitted. Only occasionally did a member of the Association choose to visit the school.

Thus the carefully prepared Catalog of 1922-23 "with Announcements for 1923-24" which contained considerably expanded and detailed course descriptions, was part of the documentation to assist the accrediting agency in its task.

The carefully wrought descriptions of "English 31-32. Shakespeare" and "33-34. History of English Literature" show the quality of mind of Dr. Carl Salomon as he helped to prepare his department and his college for the examination for accreditation. (In order to major in English then, a student had to take Old English or Anglo-Saxon. The school was no academic patsy.)

UPPER DIVISION

31-32. SHAKESPEARE. Development of early drama in England, with special emphasis on the basis literature has in answering the needs of man, and in affording a medium for the communication of thought and emotion; technique of poetry with stress on its satisfying for man the physiological demands and at the same time meeting the general demands of art; considerations of literary causes and results as founded upon operation of life-truths; study of the origins of tragic effects and of comic effects, and study of the functions of various units in literary composition, especially in dramatic composition; consideration of the importance of moral and historical perspective in appreciating the interest manifested in the various forms of literature in their respective areas of greatest influence; interpretive analyses of significant parts of ten plays selected to emphasize the formative period of Shakespeare's literary activity. Numerous references to those laws of the artistic drama which are satisfied in various phases of the fine arts. Through the course runs an exposition of the operation of Divine Law in the noblest conceptions of man, the value and the beauty of which are genuine only in the degree with which they lead us to a better acquaintance with God.

Lectures, readings, class reports, drama study based on questions concerning the plays considered in the course. Three hours per week. Six semester credits.

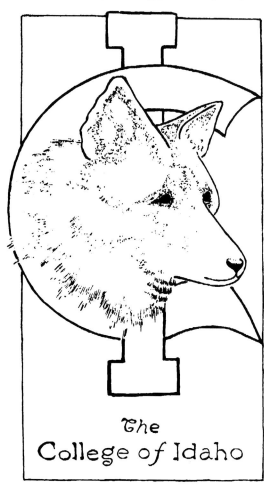

A Coyote logo drawn by Dr. Carl Saloman.

The History of English Literature requires nineteen packed lines.

In this 1921-22 Catalog, it was noted that Professor of Education and Romance Languages Payne Augustin Bolton (b. 1864), who headed those departments from 1910-1921, passed away April 10, 1921, another of the faculty who died in the harness.

Although there are standards galore for the curriculum and for the qualifications of the instructional staff, the Northwest Association wisely lays down no laws respecting how an institution should select its president or what the qualifications for that office should be. There is no one mold in which college presidents are cast. The history of higher education is replete with wise and foolish, effective and ineffective ones who held the Ph.D. degree. Indeed, The College of Idaho has had only two presidents who held the Ph.D., and its first president—longest tenured—held no Ph.D. but two honorary doctorates. What truly matters is getting the job done.

Part of a President's task involves hiring good faculty, and at this Boone was remarkable. Without utilizing a search committee (such committees at the College have been wrong about as frequently as right) Boone got the job done. The following additions to the faculty in the 1920's merit further mention: Ancil K. Steunenberg, Joseph J. Smith, J. H. Roblyer, and Anna S. Eyck.

Ancil K. "Buck" Steunenberg graduated from the Academic Department in 1915 and from the College in 1919. He returned to teach physics at his alma mater in 1921 and taught until retirement in 1961. He died in 1969. Plagued by eye problems which campus folklore in my day attributed to graduate work in physics in which harmful rays were emitted, Buck amazed his physics students with feats of memory. What he could not read—and he could see but little in his mature years—was read to him and promptly filed in its proper place in his prodigious mental storage vault. He was one of several Steunenbergs identified with the College, beginning with the martyred governor (his uncle) who was listed by Boone as a member of the first faculty in 1891, as a member of the board of Managers in 1892, and as a member of its Board of Trustees upon the legal incorporation in 1893.

The College of Idaho Directory, published in 1959, was the handiwork of Bess Steunenberg, Academy 1909, The College of Idaho 1914, Registrar Plenipotential and Extraordinary from 1921 until 1956. Miss Steunenberg (I could never call her "Bess" even when I returned as a faculty member) was a figure of authority whose sometimes austere and brisk manner concealed a love for the institution and a fondness for its students that would lead her to such tasks as that of embroidering the names of Founders Day royalty on the purple coronation robe, a chore the queens were supposed to do but seldom found time for.*

Joseph J. Smith joined the College music faculty in 1921 and brought to Beale's program many varied talents. He had studied violin with a Minneapolis Symphony performer and flute with Professor Guibert of the Grand Opera

---

* I suppose in some musty storage room somewhere on campus the queen's robe with the names of those lovely young women is gathering dust. It and the Elks Honor Award plaque deserve better treatment.

House of Paris and Carl Woempner of the Minneapolis Symphony. Bill Rankin, son of the Professors Rankin and a musician of more than just regional reputation, commented, "He was great. He was a fine musician...a man with no patience...for frivolity—none" (Soran 6). When as his high school student, Rankin congratulated Mr. Smith on the state broad jump record recently set by son Arthur Smith, J. J. characteristically replied, "Any jackrabbit can jump" (6). Rankin asserted categorically that "J. J. Smith was literally the father of instrumental music in this whole Boise Valley, and his influence carries on to this day" (6). Under his leadership The College of Idaho Symphony was developed, as were The College of Idaho Band and The College of Idaho Pep Band.

> What alumnus of The College of Idaho [asks Robert R. McCormick '15, in the typescript Excitement of Building a College] has had his name on the movie screens and TV screen, for music credit, more times surely than Bernstein and yet can be mentioned to a considerable percentage of well informed people without their knowing of whom you are speaking?

> When I was in Los Angeles just after Walt Disney had built a new studio a generation ago, I was invited to lunch at this fine lay-out...by Paul Smith from The College of Idaho. By this time Paul had written the continuity music for "Snow White" and was writing lyrics for other Disney productions....

Ancil Steunenberg, '15.

When Paul went to Hollywood to try his luck getting a job, he was invited to come for a try-out. The director said, "What instrument do you want to play?"

Paul replied, "Oh, hand me a sax." With complete indifference and some skepticism the man gave Paul the saxophone and began with a bored expression to leaf through a magazine.

Paul started to play, and suddenly the director looked up, then stood up in amazement. "Where," he asked, "did you learn to play that kind of sax?"

"In Idaho," said Paul.

"In Idaho?" the director asked in disbelief.

"Who is there in Idaho that can teach that wonderful sax?"

"My father," said Paul quietly...(109-110).

Another fine scientist who soon became a dominant figure in both teaching and research was J. H. Roblyer, who came to the College in 1923 and taught until he retired in 1966. Four decades of chemistry students remember Robyler's classes in General Chem., "Qual. and Quant.," and Organic, with the ten-point quizzes anticipated each week.

He attracted fine students, many of whom rose to positions of significant responsibility in industry and in the classroom. Indeed, a history of the activities of chemistry majors of The College of Idaho would be a fascinating monograph. Broadened to include the history of science at the College, such a study would provide more than enough material for a monograph of surprising accomplishments.

A cursory glance at the roster of Robyler's majors would support these claims, but two names are sufficient for purposes of illustration. Milton Jewett, of the Class of 1928 (d. October 14, 1979), worked as a chemist for C and H. for 36 years and invented a method of making sugar used by the company today (The College of Idaho Bulletin, Dec. 1979). Ray Dunlap (d. July 30, 1989), of the Class of 1939, invented the methods of freezing French fries used by the Simplot Company. Add to these the number of pre-professional health science students who learned their chemistry from Dr. Robyler and the stature of the man is further magnified.

But of all the appointees of the twenties the one I knew best and surely a fine teacher was Anna Smyth Eyck, who taught from 1924 to 1949.

Her academic background reflects the linkage between the College's history and some other similar institutions: The College of Wooster, Boone's and Hayman's alma mater; Carleton College, the alma mater of the never-to-be-forgotten Julia V. Finney and a source of great energy to President Hall; and Cornell College, of Mt. Vernon, Iowa. Professor Clyde Tull of the Cornell College Department of English helped prepare Anna S. Eyck and maintained sufficient interest in her and The College of Idaho to conduct a series of classes here in the summers of the mid-1940s. Tull was a rare teacher, ever alert to the fine balancing between hysterical interest in contemporary literary comets and the abiding concern literate and sensitive readers feel for enduring literary constellations. Another of his students was David Fuller Ash, who taught at the College during the late '40s.

Anna Smyth Eyck must have been one of Tull's star students, for she was a virtuoso teacher: demanding, willing to invest of her energies and wisdom, but not terribly sympathetic to the immature, the dawdler, the student unwilling to spend time in the library on a three-to-one ratio to classroom time. In her later years she frequently wore dresses or suits of bright blue, which she set off with silver necklaces or brooches. With her snow white hair and aquiline profile, she was a commanding presence, one who would not meet the expectations of some of today's generation who are all for "caring" and "sharing" and "nurturing" but who was always prepared to move a person on toward maturity. She was a superb model for many young men and women who became English teachers. Indeed, one of my best high school teachers (Muriel Dudgeon) had been prepared by her, and it was a delight when it became my good fortune to have Professor Eyck for my major professor.

We visited occasionally about the early trials of the College and about Dr. Boone, and she remarked that in those years—the 1920s and '30s—the faculty

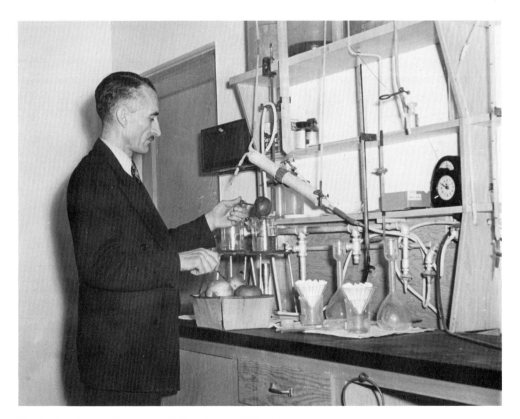

Dr. J. H. Roblyer, Professor of Chemistry, 1923-1966, in the new Covell Hall, 1941.

never had contracts. Boone would let those know whom he expected back, tell them what he hoped he would be able to pay, and thank them for their good work heretofore. One can imagine the shock a devoted member of A.A.U.P. would register at such paternalism. Still, there is something refreshing about a time and place where mutual respect, affection, and above all an overmastering will to see a new thing under the sun succeed that there were few demurrals and no litigation. I don't mean to suggest there were no disagreements, but whatever differences of opinion developed, the good of the institution was never subordinated to passion.

The editorial comment in the *Coyote* of October 1, 1919, is eloquent in its sentiment for high standards:

> In accordance with [the national movement for higher standards in educational institutions] the faculty and Trustees of The College of Idaho are demanding more in all lines of school activities; class work literary and social events, and athletics....
>
> They have set the standards. It remains for us of the Student Body to maintain them....

The next issue of the paper (October 22; by this time the staff had increased to fifteen) identified three forward steps toward the goal of reaching and maintaining those higher standards: first, the recognition of the College as one of two standard colleges in Idaho (the University at Moscow was the other); second, the approval of the College by the Rockefeller General Education Board as one of five approved colleges west of the Rocky Mountains to receive endowment contributions; and in the third place, admission to the competition for Rhodes Scholarships.

In 1919 the College had parties, not dances. The same sophisticated students who today read E. B. White's "Once More to the Lake" with disbelief that there really was a time in American college life when undergraduates ate sugared doughnuts, drank cider, and sang sentimental songs in the twilight, modulating their harmonies to the larger cosmic melodies, sensed rather than heard, all around them—these students find it hard to believe in the innocence of games, stunts, and refreshments of those earlier times.

As observed before, college organizations often have a life even briefer than that of the mayfly. Like opportunistic life forms, such groups seem called into existence by some ecological niche, occupy that niche for a time, and then quietly disappear, unnoticed and unmourned. The Philathea Ecclesia, for example, was organized in 1919 with the following statement of purpose: "to increase interest in philosophy by means of open and untrammeled discussion of philosophical topics." For several years it flourished and provided a forum useful in bringing to the attention of students and faculty ideas from the world outside the region.

News items of February 18 and March 3, 1920 catch the eye: a new building is being discussed, and the reporter hopes it will be Boone Science Hall; freshmen attend a party at the home of Lucy Miller where the evening was spent in dancing, and College of Idaho people enjoy an evening of dancing at George's. The item dealing with a projected science building is interesting in that it deals with a reality that cast its shadow as a coming event; the second and third are interesting since they indicate that although some C of I students did indeed know how to dance, they did not do so on campus. That will come...but not yet.

A senior writes in the *Coyote* of May 19, 1920, that the graduating individual would like to see a Dean of Women, a new heating system, a campus

> beautiful with gymnasium and science buildings adorning it. I should like to see more students stay for the full four years.... it is too bad when a freshman class of sixty or more dwindles to twenty-five or thirty their second fall. So although I wish for change, it is not in the spirit of discontent.... The College is on the way to larger life than it has ever known.

The tune is familiar.

On October 6, 1920, the *Coyote* noted that among the football prospects was "Eastman, a new man, on the right end." Who was this new man? How would he work in with those other players whose names today read like a roster from

Founders Day fete, 1921.

64

Tintagel of yore: Blake Lowell, fullback; Wade Lowell, quarterback; John and Jim Walsh; Sam Foote; Witteborg; Gardner and Huett; Murphy and Tolles; Jim Hawkes? Why was he nearly invariably referred to as "Chief"?

His is an interesting story.

In 1858 a Santee (Eastern) Sioux boy was born. Given the name Ohiyesa (The Winner) because of his successes in Indian games, the boy fled with his people to Canada after the Sioux Uprising of 1862 and was separated from his father and two brothers, according to Raymond Wilson in *Ohiyesa: Charles Eastman, Santee Sioux* (15-16). When he was re-united with his father, Ohiyesa's introduction to Christianity and acculturation began. A bright lad, Ohiyesa finally gravitated to Dartmouth College for undergraduate work and took an M.D. degree from Boston University in June of 1890. He was physician for the Indian Agency at Pine Ridge Reservation during the massacre at Wounded Knee, and in that traumatic place and time served as surgeon, translator, and suffering servant of the United States government. He went on to an association with the YMCA and helped found the Boy Scouts of America (see Chapters 1-3, Wilson). But it is as a writer who detailed the boyhood of a non-reservation Sioux in book after engaging book that most people remember the name Charles Eastman or Ohiyesa I. Married in 1891 to Elaine Goodale, a white teacher at Pine Ridge, Eastman, by 1905 was well enough known to be invited to a party honoring Mark Twain's seventieth birthday (Wilson photographic interchapter, p.10). To this union of the Indian athlete (he excelled in athletics at Dartmouth), writer, physician, humanitarian, and white New England-born teacher of Sioux were born six children, five girls and a boy. Ohiyesa Eastman II was graduated from The College of Idaho.

The question of why a graduate of Kimball Union Academy of Meriden, New Hampshire, would cross the continent to seek the baccalaureate degree at a small and unknown western college is fairly easily answered: because he had met a gifted Idaho athlete, Wade Lowell, whose travels had taken him to New Hampshire. One must assume that the son's decision was approved by his father; Ohiyesa I visited his son in Caldwell late in 1923, stopping off while on an inspection tour requested by the National Advisory Committee of seventeen western reservations (Wilson, 172-173).[*]

---

[*] The National Advisory Committee, which included Eastman "as the most famous Indian," read like a Who's Who: General John J. Pershing, Bernard Baruch, William Allen White, Ray Lyman Wilbur, and Alfred L. Kroeber, among others. On the occasion of his visit, Boone's diary entry describes Eastman as a "wise man."

It may have been on this visit that Eastman left two of his inscribed books for the College library.

Raymond Wilson, whose detailed and scholarly biography of Charles Eastman is the most extensive work on this interesting figure, cites an Eastman grandson, Dr. Herbert B. Fowler, as saying that Eastman and his son were not close, that Ohiyesa II did not really like the outdoors, and that Ohiyesa II was a "mama's boy." The recollections of two of Ohiyesa's contemporaries at The College of Idaho paint a different picture. Thurlow "Stub" Bryant '24 and Edwin "Josh" Lowell '24 remember "Chief," as he was nearly universally called, as a good citizen who was highly regarded by his peers. Both informants had been active in athletics—it was Edwin's older brother who had recruited Chief—and both remembered him as a fine football player who held down the position of right end for four years. He was, moreover, a good student, taking a respectable academic load and doing well, with a particular flair for language and English (Bryant and Lowell Interviews September 25, 1989).

Chief's mother left her memoirs in book form (*Sister to the Sioux*), and although the recollections deal principally with her time at Pine Ridge, she says in the Epilogue, "I was conscious, half proudly, half with regret, of deserting literature for life. Yet my own son [Chief] calls that 'impossible'!"

> "You've always been a poet," he writes, "whether you put the words down on paper or not" (173-174).

"Chief's" mother visited the College October 5, 1925, a guest of Mrs. Lowell.

As far as I have been able to discover, this bit of filial praise is the only literary remnant of Ohiyesa II "Chief" Eastman, right end, The College of Idaho 1920-1924. His contributions as a writer of copy in the advertising department of Kelvinator are, apparently, completely unknown (Wilson 165). He died on January 16, 1940.

Stories other than those about football can be found in the 1920 *Coyote*. In the same number that mentioned the new man at end, considerable space was devoted to improvements. The unidentified reporter noted that the front lawn, which was used for football, had a heavy sod and that the football field behind the Administration

Ohiyesa Eastman II, '24.

Hall had been leveled and was ready for use. Moreover, the cleaned and re-finished dormitories "are among the most pleasant and homelike seen in any school however large." A cement sidewalk from Voorhees to Finney was wide enough for three to walk abreast. The item concludes: "Dr. Boone tells us that Professor Hayman is solely responsible for the improvements on the campus."

Dancing was still not part of college life, as an item of November 3, 1920, indicates, for at a Halloween masque participants **played** [my emphasis] the Virginia Reel to the accompaniment of a five piece orchestra. Folklorists have long recognized that some sections of the country differentiated between **playing** and **dancing**. Thus the American play party developed, in part, at least, as a ploy to circumvent charges of dancing.

If the twenties were beginning to roar as early as November of 1920, some campuses appeared not to hear, for in that issue of the *Coyote* there appeared a pledge to which colleges were subscribing. Emanating from Teachers' College of Maryville, Missouri, and subscribed to by Drury College of Springfield, Missouri, the pledge was submitted to the students of The College of Idaho. It reads as follows:

We will never bring disgrace to this, our College, by any act of cowardice or dishonesty. We will fight for the ideals and sacred things of the College. We will revere and obey the College laws, and do our best to incite a like respect and reverence in others. We will strive unceasingly to widen the students' sense of duty. We will transmit this college to those who come after us greater, better, and

Dr. H. H. Hayman carring water for new trees on campus, Sterry Hall in background.

more beautiful than it was transmitted to us.

As 1920 came to an end, only two sources of disquietude bothered the *Coyote* staff: a 21-14 loss to Whitman (otherwise the record was unblemished, and the College was champion of the Southern Idaho Conference) and a bothersome college debt of $28,000.

The chronicle of 1921 began with a terse note that "Mr. Boulton is on the sick list" and included a plea for civic pride in the appearance of the campus. The anti-rubbish campaign called for collegians to show the same concern for their campus that the decent citizens of any city or town show for their community. Litter seems to be an ever-during problem.

Another problem that had to be settled involved an answer to the legitimate question faced by schools caring about their accreditation: What is a college student? Dr. Boone answered the problem forthrightly by issuing regulations appropriate for accredited institutions that distinguished between regular and special students. A regular student was defined as a student passing in at least twelve hours of work each semester. Special students could take fewer. Moreover, a sophomore was a student having 24 hours of credit; a junior, 56; and a senior, 92; and these "must pass in eighteen or more hours of work each semester." The regulations further declared that

> students who register for regular work and then remain in school only long enough to take full advantage of an athletic season will not be enrolled again.... The College is not hiring men and women to represent it in contests with other schools.

In this same issue (February 16, 1921) appeared a statement of purpose for the College newspaper that could easily provide reasonable guidelines for college newspapers through the years: it was to be an organ for the students, published by them, but ever-jealous of its obligation to truth as the only full record of the life of the institution.

That life, of course, included both the curricular and the extracurricular. In the *Coyote* of March 16, the front-page lead story called attention to the College's debate team: S.I. Conference Debate Champs. These debates had been held since 1911 and starting in 1912 a silver trophy was awarded annually. The C of I won it that year and kept it until Gooding College won it in 1920. But this year the College won it back "and intends to keep it."

On April 10, 1921, as reported in the *Coyote* of April 20, one of those sad events that seem to happen too often in the life of a college occurred: Professor

Payne Boulton died. The terse announcement scarcely four months earlier was in reality Professor Boulton's death knell.

Boone's diary for Friday, April 1, 1921, reads that "Mrs. Boulton has word that Mr. Boulton has cancer and will be operated on tomorrow...very sad...not much hope." The entry for Saturday, April 2, records:

> Mrs. Boulton gets great good news near noon. Operation showed Mr. Boulton had **gall stones** only...no cancer. A great relief to all of us.

On Monday, April 4, although Boone's diary notes Mr. Boulton was doing well and was expected home in three weeks, the optimism was not justified. He died at 3 p.m. in the hospital in Portland where the surgery had been done. Boone, the College, and the Caldwell community were devastated, for Boulton was a respected civic leader and educator who had served as superintendent of the Caldwell schools before joining the College faculty. So once again Boone was called on to help conduct the funeral services for a beloved faculty member who died in the service of the College they both loved.

To read Boone's remarks in the *Coyote* of April 20, 1921, is to be reminded of both his personal grief and his sense of institutional loss on another sad occasion, the earlier death of Dr. Hemphill. Boone's eulogy was alluded to by the *Coyote* editor:

> It has been truly said...he so lived that his character and ideals will be reflected forever in the hearts and lives of all those with whom he came in contact. He spent his life in service for others. He helped to make our college one of high ideals and purposes, a place where young people might come and learn how to live in the best sense of the word: how to make their lives count most for others.

> It remains for us, his pupils, to continue his work, to live true to his high ideals and help others as he has helped us.

Boone used the words "esteemed" and "beloved" as he called attention to Boulton's intense suffering before death released him. But the universe has its way of reminding the survivors that life must go on. For the Caldwell community those reminders, some of them, at least, came in the form of news about what was going on on the campus. We learn from this same April 20 *Coyote* that an idle plot of ground behind Sterry Hall was to become the new athletic field and would accommodate football, baseball, and track and that it might even be turfed!

At the regular meeting of the Ecclesia, student C. Elliot Smith presented a paper entitled "The Mind in the Making." This event might seem a piece of trivia; it is not. The title clearly refers to a book published that same year, a book that seems destined to endure, because it is "mortised and tenoned in granite." Written by historian James Harvey Robinson of Columbia, it is a virtuoso exposition of thinking about thinking; that it had come to the attention of an undergraduate at a small liberal arts college in the West is evidence that the school and its students were alive intellectually.

They were also alive artistically and musically, for Professor Beale was about to present "The Wizard of the Nile," done by the College Glee Clubs with sixty in the chorus and ten principals. J. J. Smith's "splendid orchestra" would provide musical accompaniment. This was one of those blockbuster performances for which Beale was famous, taking his troupe off campus for performances at local commercial theaters and eventually over to the Boise High School Auditorium, for at this time Boise had nothing remotely like Beale and The College of Idaho.

The academic year of 1920-21 ended with Commencement about a month after Founders Day, the latter a time of festivity that included maypole winding, a picnic, and usually a high school track meet or a baseball game. Founders Day this year was celebrated as the 12th annual opportunity established by Trustees to honor the founders of the C of I. The celebration dates, then, from 1909.

The academic year of 1921-22 began, the *Coyote* of October 5 tells us, with enrollment of 181 in regular college courses; as the C of I began its thirty-second year, dormitories and classrooms were "taxed to capacity." Moreover, the financial outlook was especially good, with $5,000 from the General Education Board, $17,500 from the Presbyterian Board, nearly $12,000 from individuals, an additional $25,000 from the Carnegie Corporation, and $25,000 for the endowment from the General Education Board, representing half of the $50,000 pledged by this board for the endowment. To get the remainder, the College was obliged to stay free of debt and collect all money pledged by subscribers.

This same issue of the *Coyote* mentions a party (given on September 21, 1921) to honor Julia V. Finney, "once a teacher and always a friend of The College of Idaho," now in California and busy. The hall bearing her name was planned and furnished under her direction. Students, faculty, and alumni all felt it should carry her name. She had demurred until a petition was submitted to her "signed by every student and the faculty." She could no longer resist. At the party, an enlarged photograph of her, courtesy of Professor and Mrs. Paul

Murphy, was presented with the following inscription: "Miss Julia V. Finney, Friend of Girls. For Twenty Years a Teacher in The College of Idaho." (If this figure is accurate it brings into question Bess Steunenberg's 1959 Directory, which gives Finney's service as 1898-1925. I suspect Bess confused the date of Finney's retirement with that of someone else.)

The *Coyote* of October 19 is full of news, this edition giving a comprehensive graph of the heartbeat of the institution. We learn, for instance, that O. J. Smith was asked to help explore the "Valley" of the Moon, as the Craters of the Moon National Monument was then called, and we learn further that it had not heretofore been completely explored. It is also in this issue that we learn that "the plot of ground adjoining Triangle Park and Cleveland Boulevard between 23rd and 24th has recently been added to the campus," thanks to the generosity of M. B. Gwinn. Moreover, this autumn J. J. Smith's Pep Band made its debut, creating a tradition of performance at games, dedications of buildings, and other public occasions that persisted for a very long time indeed, certainly down to the post-WWII years.

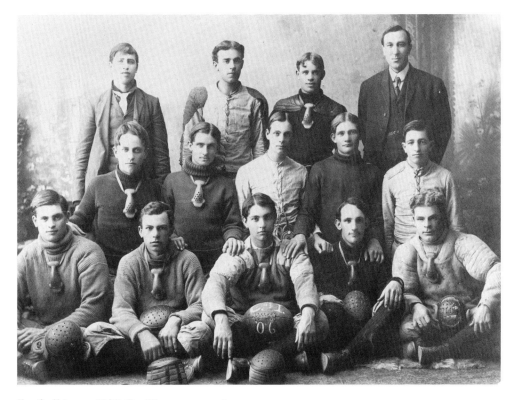

Football team, 1906, Dr. Hayman, coach.

Letters from graduates featured in this issue indicate that Fay Tolles, who had graduated in the spring, was working at the YMCA in Spokane, that Anne Clemens of the same class was teaching in Caldwell, and that Ardath Scarth, also class of '21, was in Roberts, Idaho, some seventeen miles from Idaho Falls, teaching cooking, history, and agriculture!

In all of this, football was not forgotten. Whitman, which had beaten the University of Idaho 13-0, defeated the College 17-13, even with Blake Lowell's dropkicks from the fifteen- and thirty-yard lines. Idaho Tech of Pocatello defeated the Coyotes 13-7, and to redeem themselves the team from Caldwell held Utah State to a 20-20 tie. The remainder of the season was all C of I, as they defeated Montana Wesleyan of Helena 28-7 and Gooding College 56-0, with Blake Lowell scoring four touchdowns and his brother Wade scoring three. All of this was accomplished with a roster of eighteen men.

The year 1921 ended on a high note with J. J. Smith's ringing declaration that all good bands attended punctiliously to the three T's: (Good) Tune, (Clear) Tone, and (Perfect) Time.

Boone's diary and the *Coyote* both describe Vachel Lindsay's appearance in 1922 in glowing terms. The *Coyote* writer dwelt on the fact that the poet was recognized by Oxford and Cambridge as well as by American colleges and universities, that more than a hundred people had to be turned away from the lecture-reading, that the poet had had eight books published by Macmillan, and that Lindsay read his works "The Congo" and "General William Booth Enters Heaven" in a "wonderfully resonant and musical voice." Boone mentioned having "a cracker and milk with him" and noted that the gate for the reading came to $136.00, from which the poet received $75.00, with other expenses amounting to $61.30. The College only broke even but was able to excite the community by sponsoring this apostle of beauty who was an extremely popular lyceum performer.

The *Coyote's* editors commented February 1, 1922, that a $300,000 gift from a Mrs. Linfield of Spokane had changed the name of a small college in Oregon from McMinnville College to Linfield College in memory of her late husband. Such recognition of donors is a fact of life for the independent college. Indeed, early catalogs of The College of Idaho printed the following offers: "I. To the person giving $10,000 toward the erection of suitable buildings, the privilege of naming the institution,—which name will be the legal name; II. To the person who gives $5,000 toward the endowment of one Chair, for example the Chair of Natural Sciences, shall have the privilege of naming the Professorship." It would appear that The College of Idaho continued to be called that for two reasons: it was the college of Idaho, the first one;[*] and nobody advanced $10,000 with a request for a name change.

From the *Coyote* of March 15, 1922, we learn that a Science Club had been organized—the beginning of Philo Tech, which is still flourishing.In the same issue, Robert McCormick gives a brief summary of the outstanding achievements of C of I men in the Yale School of Law:

> Wayland Prizes for Excellence in Debate (Yale Kent Club) 1915; 1st prize, James Louden Boone, B.A., College of Idaho, 1913; 2nd prize, Jno. Francis Collins, B.A., Yale University, 1911; 3rd prize, Sidney Kinney Backus, B.A., Dartmouth 1911.

> Wayland Prizes, 1916; 1st prize, Sherman Minton, Ll.B., Indiana university 1915; 2nd prize, Edward Waldo McGhee, Ll.B., Washington University, 1915; 3rd prize, James Louden Boone, B.A. College of Idaho '13.

> Munson Prizes (Wayland Club) 1919; 1st prize, Hugh Nelson Caldwell, B.A. College of Idaho, '17; 2nd prize, Carl Peter Cline, B.A., Univ. of Colorado, 1916; 3rd prize, Morris Blumer, B.A., Wesleyan University, '16.

> Munson Prizes (Wayland Club) 1920: 1st, Ralph Howard King, B.A. College of Idaho, 1917; 2nd, Hugh Nelson Caldwell, B.A., College of Idaho, 1917; 3rd, John Harold Williams, B.A. Yale University, 1917.

> Three firsts in the four contests were won by C. of I. men.

> Honors in the School of Law, (among 35 graduates six honors granted) Degree of Bachelor of Laws, Cum Laude, 1920:—Ralph Howard King[**], College of Idaho 1917; Roscoe Bernard Turner, B.A., College of Idaho 1916.

> Yale Law Journal; 1918-19, Ralph H. King, B.A., C. of I. '17, Member Board of Editors.

---

[*] Even its northern rival sometimes acknowledged the superior age of the College: the *Coyote* of February 15, 1922, mentions a visit from Dean Eldridge of the University of Idaho, a longtime member of the U of I faculty. He brought, he said, greetings from the "younger, larger sister to the older, smaller sister."

[**] In addition Mr. King was elected to the law honor fraternity, the Order of the Coif, upon graduation.

1919-1920, Ralph H. King, B.A., C. of I. '17, Member Board of Editors.

Roscoe B. Turner, B.A., College of Idaho, Member Board of Editors.

Only men of high scholarship are honored by election to the Board of Editors of the Yale Law Journal.

———————————

Dean Thomas W. Swan of Yale Law School writes: "All of these students have done good scholarship work and have been men of fine standards and ideals."

An editorial in the same issue documents the need for a gymnasium and notes that tuition and fees pay about a third of the cost of running the school.*

The College of Idaho was accredited April 6, 1922, the same time, according to the *Coyote* of April 19, 1922, as the College of Puget Sound. The reporter noted that Whitman College was the only other private school in Washington that had been accorded accreditation.

Three items of information from the May 3, 1922, *Coyote* catch the eye: the campus consisted of 25 acres, a student body numbering 500 was considered the maximum for a small college, and *Samson and Delilah* was presented by the glee clubs. Publicity for this production included a host of photographs which failed to identify the subjects.

The fall of 1922 began in a fine way. The October 11 *Coyote* informs us that Dan Banks, class of 1911—the first class graduated from the collegiate department—is state treasurer, that Fay Tolles and Anne Clemens were married August 15, and that Fay is now teaching in Meridian. We also learn that in football the University of Utah defeated the Coyotes 16-12. And the school newspaper of October 25 makes it clear that the proper name of the school is The College of Idaho and informs us that the science club—PhiloTech—is the newest organization on campus. The Parthenian Forum, organized in 1917 as a debating society and the feminine equivalent of the all-male Senate, was flourishing in 1922. Neither organization is here today.

The spring semester in 1923 began with a student body of 284. Although lists become tedious, it is nevertheless instructive to learn where these students

———————————

* According to the annual Report for 1989-90, tuition and fees accounted for 58.2 percent of the school's income for that year.

came from: Caldwell, 112; Boise, 26; Nampa, 25; Meridian, 10; Parma, 10; Wilder, 10; Huston, 9; Middleton, 8; Emmett, 6; Star, 6; Payette, 5; Twin Falls, 5; New Plymouth, 4; Roswell, 3; Notus, 3; 2 each from Ontario, Greenleaf, McCall, Mountain Home, Bellevue, Castle Creek, St. Anthony, and Idaho Falls; 1 each from Midvale, Weiser, Fruitland, Cascade, Cabarton, Smith's Ferry, Kuna, Melba, Homedale, Bliss, Hagerman, Wendell, Moore, Jerome, Anacortes, Washington; Juntura, Oregon; Canyon City, Oregon; Brownsville, Oregon; Los Angeles, California; Amherst, Massachusetts; Minneapolis, Minnesota; Morrisville, Montana; Hugo and Crawford, Colorado.

What did these students believe? What was their church connection, if any? Eighty-three were Presbyterian, 71 Methodist, 34 Baptist, 18 Christian (Disciples), 11 Friends, 8 Episcopal, 6 Catholic, 5 Congregational, 4 United

Philo Tech field trip, 1935.

Presbyterian, 4 Christian Science, 3, Free Methodist, 2 Mormon, and 1 each Lutheran, Church of God, Church of Christ, Advent Christian, Mennonite, and Seventh Day Adventist. Twenty students had no preference.

The College of Idaho was broadly represented at the dedication of the $75,000 Caldwell Odd Fellows Temple, an indication of the closeness between institution and community. Prof. Hayman prayed, the orchestra under the baton of J. J. Smith played, and Dr. Carl E. Salomon sang the Bach-Gounod "Ave Maria" to which he had written an original dedication ode. The *Coyote* of February 7, 1923, says that Salomon's song was so well received that in response to the audience's demand he sang the second verse of his composition. So the College itself came to be thought of as a resource giving back to the community some of what the school had received from it.

Unlike the men's Senate, the women's Parthenian Society, and a host of other organizations that perished, the Ring Sorority, organized October 23, 1922, with eight charter members, is still a presence on the campus, (albeit a shadowy one), giving credence to the statement that appeared in the *Coyote* of February 7: "This organization is permanent and will be heard from frequently in the future." Mrs. Helen M. Scatterday of the Expression Department was the sponsor.

Scarlet Masque, organized this semester, proposed "to study modern drama and the technique of presenting entertainments" and launched into a series of one-act plays—"'Suppressed Desires' (amusing satire on psychoanalysis) by Susan Gospel [sic] and P.P. Cook; 'The Wonder Hat' (harlequinade); 'The Finger of God' (a drama): place: Sterry Hall, date: Wednesday, February 28; Price: right." This according to the *Coyote* of February 7.

In the next issue of the *Coyote* (March 7) the plays were hailed as a success and "a brilliant future for this dramatic organization" was predicted. Although the first performance was held in the auditorium of Sterry Hall, public demand called for a second production at the downtown American Theater. Some corrections crept into the story: "Suppressed Desires," by George C. Cook and Susan Gladspell [sic]; "The Finger of God," by Perceval Wilde; "The Wonder Hat," by Ben Hecht and Kenneth S. Goodman.

A significant part of the College's cultural growth was the development of the College museum. Just when the museum was begun is impossible to say, but according to the 1909-1910 Catalog "The College is gradually accumulating a valuable collection of mineral, plant, and animal specimens. A portion of these are to be found within the glass cases in the museum room...." When O. J. Smith became its guardian and curator, the museum's growth accelerated;

the *Coyote* of March 21, 1923, reports that the College museum "has several finely etched and sealed stones over 4,000 years old from Jokha, Dreben, and Warha." The story continues:

> These specimens are small, ranging from one inch square to three or four inches square. Several of the pieces contain temple records dating from 2,100 B.C. to 2,300 B.C. and the inscriptions are well preserved.

> There are nine of the tablets...given to the museum by Edgar J. Banks. Such rare pieces are indeed an asset to a museum that contains a number of interesting collections.

A story in the *Coyote* of March 5, 1925, contained a comprehensive list of items and categories of items to be found there.

As noted earlier, the national economy of the 1920's flourished (making allowances for the lagging agricultural component) and The College of Idaho likewise flourished. An exception must be noted. It was announced in April of 1923 that a science hall and a gymnasium were to be erected after a $140,000 fund-raising campaign. Both structures were clearly needed, for the school was growing and the total assets, according to The College of Idaho *Bulletin* of June 1941, increased dramatically from the first decade to 1921: 1909-$10,000; 1913-$177,000; 1917-$250,000; 1921-$328,000. Anticipating further growth, the

Scarlet Masque players at the American Theater, Caldwell.

author of a story in the *Coyote* of April 4, 1923, described the gymnasium as what today is called a multi-purpose structure that could be used as an auditorium seating 1500, an athletic facility, and a music building, and would also house a central heating plant. The College had enjoyed a 31 percent average growth rate increase since the war, and it was time to build. The proposed science hall was to be of brick, to be three stories high, and to feature, in addition to classrooms and laboratories, a science reading room, a large lecture and demonstration room, and space for the museum—all at a cost of $75,000. The gymnasium, with a stage, lockers, showers, dressing rooms, and other facilities would cost $65,000.

A promotional flyer of 1923 declares the financial plans of the College are "1. To keep out of debt. 2. To secure adequate endowment funds. 3. To secure buildings to house properly [property ?] and maintain proper academic standards for the College." The flyer, featuring one of Boone's panoramic shots of the student body and faculty with the three majesties (Sterry, Finney, and Voorhees) behind them, is impressive. Also impressive are the statistical data: Idaho's area is equal to New York, New Hampshire, Vermont, Massachusetts, Connecticut, and Rhode Island—85,000 square miles, with a population of 432,000. There is more:

> The field of The College of Idaho is situated in the Snake River Basin, a comparatively narrow valley, in which all lines of travel are in an easterly and westerly direction. To the east is Gooding College, 125 miles distant. To the west one must travel 294 miles to Whitman College. [Eastern Oregon at La Grande was about 200 miles in that direction.] To reach our own state university at Moscow by rail, one must travel through the states of Oregon and Washington, a distance of 429 miles.

This still reads well; and although Idaho's population now exceeds a million, there is still space, and Owyhee County, Idaho, and Malheur and Harney counties in Oregon can still make the pilgrim shudder with the pleasure or discomfort of the intimidation of space and distance.

Things were also bright around the *Coyote* office. A course in journalism was added to the curriculum for the fall of 1923, and the *Coyote* was to appear weekly and in a format quite similar to, if not identical with, the format in which it appears today.

Even though a drama club had been formed—the one established in 1911 languished, Scarlet Masque taking its place—the production of plays continued to be principally a function of the YWCA and the YMCA, active on campus since 1910 and 1912, and the junior and senior classes. Indeed, any groups that wished could present a play. One of the bright presentations of 1923 was another production by F. F. Beale's glee clubs, "Naughty Marietta," by Victor Herbert. This operetta was so well done that it was performed on two nights (May 17-18) at the downtown American Theater and on the night of May 21 in the Boise High School Auditorium.

Interest in and support of forensics continued as debates were scheduled with, among other opponents, the University of Wyoming and the University of Southern California. In respect to the growth of the College's reputation in academic matters and a further validation of its uniqueness in filling a genuine regional need, summer sessions had been launched in 1922 or 1923.

A final note for the calendar year of 1923 was sounded by the *Coyote* in an editorial of December 19. At the conclusion of a successful football season (the Coyotes had tied Willamette, lost to Idaho, lost to Pacific University, tromped Albion 114-0) the editor presciently called for the establishment of a "Little Northwest Conference," to be comprised of schools like Pacific, Willamette, the College of Puget Sound, and the C of I. This suggestion was a prelude to the very sort of conference that was eventually developed.

Portable promotional exhibit, c. 1922.

Whether or not this was a gag, the participants were enjoying themselves.

CHAPTER SIX

Still Rampant

Those who choose such important elements as school colors, institutional mottos, and college totems are sometimes almost eerily percipient in their decisions. Is there under the sun a better totemic animal for this school than the coyote, *Canis latrans*? The College has had to claw, go hungry, subsist on the leavings of others, adjust its diet, and watch from the sagebrush while other more powerful organisms collected the bounty.

And still, the coyote remains. And extends it range. And perfects its survival skills. The institution has had to remain cautious, at times timid, ever conscious of the cost of a new program, an additional faculty member, a departure from tradition. The College has never had the luxury that its models have come to enjoy—the luxury of money with which to purchase time. When funds have been inadequate to the task, budgets have been frozen. Student enrollment dare not dwindle. There is no fat on the coyote's bones to sustain him through times of bleakness and want, no marvelous endowment which might be drawn upon as time and circumstance dictate. But still he survives. So it is that if any one word expresses the will of the institution imprinted upon it by its first president it is the verb in the imperative mood, "Survive!" Coyotes understand.

The first *Coyote* of the new year (January 16, 1924) mentioned a school Christmas dance at the IOOF Hall. Sponsored by the Bachelors Club, whose initials would be transliterated into the Greek letters "Beta" and "Chi" in 1929, this may well be the first **school** dance, though it was held off campus.

For a number of years the great rivalry on campus was the one between the Beta Chi and the Orion fraternities. In one sense it filled the void left by the dissolution of the Lowell-Columbian societies.

Nineteen twenty-four was the year the Orian—the spelling used by the *Coyote* until the January 15, 1925, issue—Society was granted a charter, under the sponsorship of Professor John D. Bell.

It was earlier noted that college organizations tend to be short-lived creatures. This truth was not lost on the *Coyote* in its reporting of club news, for the March 19, 1924, issue carried a story of a new club called "Bob Co." Its members held their first meeting under the weeping willow at the corner of Arthur and Dearborn on Monday, March 10: "The unique thing about this club is that it must never meet in the same place twice...next meeting will be held at the dungeon of the president." In the words of the reporter, the club was like England in that it had no written constitution.

The record of this club is a superb expression of the spirit of fun so characteristic of American colleges in the twenties. Although there may have existed such an organization, it is far more likely that reportage on Bob Co. was a reporter's or editor's commentary upon the entire matter of college organizations, a subsequent issue of the *Coyote* crying that the campus was over-organized. It was also an engaging way of filling white space, a compositor's nightmare. The April 2 issue informs us that "The Bob Co. Club held its next meeting, March 24 in the president's dungeon...at the zero hour." The speaker for the club says, "We are...sorry to state that because of the fact that membership is limited to the present members, we have no public initiations to announce at this time and probably will have none in the future."

The penultimate meeting was reported on April 16 in a story that corrected the spelling: it is the Bobco Club, whose "minutes are passed down orally from one generation of members to another." The next meeting, the story continues, will probably be in Nampa. Sure enough, the last meeting of this organization was reportedly held in Nampa at "Crescent Hall Retreat," the site of what was then called the State Sanitarium, an appropriate dissolution, perhaps, for an organization whose motto was "I came. I saw. I conquered."

Three interesting items of campus news appeared in the April 16 *Coyote*. The first of these informs the reader that for the first time since the Great War, baseball returned to the campus. Return it did, and with a vengeance. Although football was campus king throughout the twenties and thirties, baseball was at least a prince, and its royal heritage had been declared as early as 1914, when the Coyotes won the Southern Idaho Conference championship. The second item referred to yet another Beale blockbuster, his production of "The Chocolate Soldier," by Oscar Straus. This show received rave notices in both the collegiate and the commercial press. Beale's groups shared the billing at the local American Theater as follows: "The Eleventh Hour," with Buck Jones;

May 12-13, "The Cheat," with Pola Negri; May 15-16, "The Chocolate Soldier," with C of I Glee Clubs!

The third item noted that the intellectual side of the College was recognized that year by the local B.P.O.E. Club, which donated the Elks Honor Tablet to be placed in Sterry Hall. Each year, two students, a man and a woman, were to be selected on the basis of scholarship, leadership, character, activities, and self-help. Recognition started with Brenice Weymouth and Frank Hartkopf of the Class of 1923. This tablet of honor and public recognition disappeared sometime in the late sixties or early seventies, and its absence was regrettably unmourned.

In a trivia item in the May 10 *Coyote*, we read that the Senate—not an organ of student government but a group of men interested in politics and debate—was organized in 1916, that its membership was limited to sixteen and that its annual competition centered around the possession of "the historical gavel made in 1908 by Lawrence Henry Gipson from the first apple tree planted in Caldwell."

Equally trivial was the big controversy of 1924: bobbed hair. Surveyed by a *Coyote* reporter, the following College of Idaho folks responded to the question of what they thought about this bobbed hair:

The Chocolate Soldier, American Theater, Beale's 1924 production.

Dr. Springer: "It's up to the girl."

Ivah Holt, Housemother of Finney Hall: "It makes the small ones look babyish and the large ones overgrown."

Ed Hoshaw, student: "It's according to who it's on."

Charles Robinson, student body president: "In general, I am not keen about it."

Dr. Boone: "I think it's fine."

Prof. Murphy: "Well, it has a bad reputation since it started amongst a bunch of silly girls. But I like it fairly well."

Doc Salomon: "My objections to bobbed hair will hardly bear publication."

Stub Bryant, student: "I like the stuff."

The *Coyote* assessed the statistics of the matter and determined that 96 girls wore truncated tresses and 104 retained their original locks but that the larger number was dwindling daily. The story concluded with a quotation from Lydig Hoyt ("noted woman writer"): "Woman is ruining herself, for what man...wants to nestle up to a cockle burr."

In this preserve called higher education where students are protected for a brief time from the urgencies of the world, it is not surprising that these volatile creatures can flip-flop from the maudlin to the comic, from the consequential to the trivial, from the sublime to the ridiculous in the twinkling of an eye. When these students flaunt their most exasperatingly childish behavior, they can disarm criticism by conducting a drive to help the victims of earthquakes or other natural disasters. Thus the topic of the twenty-third annual Lowell-Columbian debate was a serious one that made reference to the Oriental Exclusion Act: "Resolved: That Japanese immigrants should be allowed to enter the U.S. on the same terms as Europeans." Yet spinning tops was the "in" activity at Stanford at the same time.

For many years, indeed from April 14, 1910, until fairly recent times, Founders Day was the most important holiday on the school calendar—in fact, the only formal college holiday. An opportunity to remind all college constituencies of the abiding indebtedness to those who dug the wells from which we now drink, Founders Day evolved into a day-long celebration through pageantry, floats, skits, musical events, debates, declamations, tennis matches, and

84

a picnic. At first a local celebration, Founders Day came to include high school visitation (226 seniors came in 1924) encouraged by the College's sponsorship of a major, often the district, track meet or an important high school baseball game. In 1924, Founders Day featured the winding of a Maypole, as recounted in the *Coyote* of May 23—an issue in which Eugene Chaffee, who would become president of Boise's junior college, wrote up the news of the Voorheesians.

The final issue of the *Coyote* for the academic year 1923-24 appeared on May 23, and the *Coyote* for this year was crisp in its reporting, clean with respect to grammar, and fairly bristling with College news. It was a good year for college journalism, and to read the *Coyote* is to sense the vitality of this small school in the dusty West. In an editorial alluded to earlier, the editor claims under the headline "Clubbed to Death" that the campus suffers from overorganization. Here we are, the editor says, with a student body of about 360 with more than twenty organizations which, "like bobbed hair...are increasing rapidly." More than that, the literary societies are degenerating. "All we ask is to find some way so that the average C of I student can find time to read a good book occasionally and come to class with...lessons really prepared." If reforms of this sort can be instituted, it might be possible "to save the poor incoming frosh from the nightmare of being clubbed to death."

For those College of Idaho students who felt tuition, fees, and board and room were high, the *Coyote* cited information from one of its exchange newspapers showing what an education cost a medieval Oxonian for a term: lectures, $1.80; rent of room, $2.00; food for 38 weeks, $8.00; servant, $.40. Those who relish tradition and continuity will rejoice to find that the faculty at Oxford were not overpaid, receiving only four and a half times more than the servant.

The Fall Semester—college publications are

From the College's Permanent Art Collection: one of several Clifford K. Berryman political cartoons from the Washington, D.C. Evening Star *featuring Idaho Senator William E. Borah.*

consistent in capitalizing semester and sessions—opened with an appearance by Senator William E. Borah, who addressed the student body on September 30. Football and technology collaborated on October 31, 1924, when C of I students journeyed to Boise to broadcast a "peppy, inspiring team rally" to the football squad in Salem, Oregon, over KFAU, the Boise High School station. The writer in the November 6 *Coyote* asserts that this was the first attempt as far as is known for any college or university to do such a thing. Not only was it a pep rally over the air, but a fund-raising opportunity could not be overlooked, so included in the broadcast was a plea to the public for money: $140,000 for buildings for science and athletics and $11,000 to complete the $50,000 challenge pledge from the Rockefeller Education Board. The College defeated Willamette 14-13.

Embedded in this *Coyote* is a small item behind which one sees the remarkable mind of Orma J. Smith. This academic year Philo Tech would concentrate upon original research in botany, biology, or geology and all the club's programs would develop from the student-originated studies. It is another of those benchmarks or watersheds in the life of the institution: for unlike the fuss over bobbed hair, this matter of student-originated research has helped in the education of countless men and women in the healing arts as well as those taking graduate degrees in the sciences. That record of significant accomplishment started by O. J. Smith in the '20s continues to be a vital component in the preparation of those students who spend a good deal of time in Boone Hall. Not incidentally, Philo Tech is still alive.

In spite of Professor Paul Murphy's urging at a meeting in Portland, ran a story in the December 18 *Coyote*, no new athletic conference would be forthcoming for perhaps two years. However, a temporary organization with chairman and secretary had been set up, and when the plan of the new conference had been ratified by the faculties of the three small colleges (Willamette, Pacific, and Whitman) who were members of the North West Conference, then that nucleus would invite to membership the College of Puget Sound, The College of Idaho, and Linfield, who "can make application after the manner of the present...Conference." Represented at the discussion in Portland were Whitman, Pacific, College of Puget Sound, The C of I, Willamette, Linfield, and Reed.

No chronicle of the College would be complete without mentioning the dates when certain organizations were established. The *Coyote* began in 1910 in the form of a monthly magazine. In 1916 it assumed its present newspaper form, appearing every two weeks until 1925 when it became a weekly paper of four pages. Football as a collegiate institution predates the school newspaper by five years (1905). The Parthenian Forum, later shortened to "Forum," dates from 1917. The school "annual" or yearbook, the *Trail*, evolved from the *Renaissance* and appeared first in 1916. The Bachelor's Club, which evolved into the Beta Chi fraternity, was founded during the winter of 1921. Incidentally, anyone researching the early life of the College will discover what appears to be an anomaly in the dating of the *Trail*, from which these founding dates derive. The publication of the *Trail* was the obligation of the junior class; since the year of graduation is the year by which a class is identified, the class which had junior status in the academic year 1924-25, for example, would be the class of 1926. Since the yearbook was the obligation of the class to be graduated the next year, this class designated the annual as its production; so for a time the year represented might appear to be a year off. The 1926 *Trail* was for the 1924-25 academic year.

But to continue with the founding or chartering dates given in the *Trail* for 1925, both the Ring and Myra Tella sororities were chartered in 1922. Sigma Epsilon, chartered in 1923; P.E.P., a club whose purpose was "to further the study of seven arts, and also to sponsor social activities on the college campus," was chartered in 1924 as was the Orion Club. The local chapter of the National Debate Club, Phi Sigma Rho, was established in 1925, as was the Honor League, a group to which any one could belong by virtue of pledging "neither to give nor receive help in examinations and to promote honor and the spirit of honesty." The Christian Truth Seekers group was launched this year, and a chapter of the first national professional organization to be represented on the campus was established. The Theta Alpha Chapter of Sigma Tau Delta English honorary, one of thirty chapters throughout the United States, conferred a certain distinction upon the College and gave national recognition to Dr. Salomon, who became a member of the national advisory cabinet, along with members from Wesleyan University, the University of Utah, and the University of Illinois.

Although the school might have been overorganized, it is nevertheless true that these social and scholastic clubs supplied certain needs and were of material benefit to the College itself in connection with the familiar appeal for funds made in the first issue of the *Coyote* for 1925 (January 15). By the second issue (January 29), the mildly incredible had occurred: Ring, YWCA, Myra Tella, P.E.P., as well as Finney Hall had made a commitment to contribute to the endowment. Additionally, the senior class pledged $2,500 toward the $25,000 Boone Endowment fund, becoming the tenth of the eleven groups or individuals to do so. The list is instructive; they are the helpers who from time to time have fanned the spark of hope and life in the institution: Robert E.

Strahorn, Spokane; Montie B. Gwinn, Boise; Colin McCleod, Caldwell; Mrs. Mary Kirkpatrick, Parma; Adam Blackstock, Givens Hot Springs; Carrie M. Steunenberg, Boise; Ellen Lyman, Boise; Oakes Brothers, Caldwell; T. C. Catlin, Eagle; Mabel Caldwell, Caldwell; and the Senior Class of 1925.

The name Robert R. McCormick surfaces again and again in connection with fundraising. The man was absolutely tireless in his pursuit of philanthropic assistance and as fearless as he was tireless calling on the Carnegie and Rockefeller foundations, Simon Guggenheim, Beardsley Ruml, Averell Harriman, Harry Sinclair, Frederick E. Weyerhaeuser, W. W. Norton, Mrs. Cyrus McCormick and her son Cyrus Jr., Andrew Mellon: the list goes on. The following letter is one hint of evidence of his good work.

January 21, 1925.

Mr. Robert Rockwood McCormick,
New York City.

Dear Sir:

Referring to your request for a contribution to the Endowment Fund of the College of Idaho, I beg to advise you that acting on your suggestion, I got into communication with Governor C.C. Moore, of Idaho, and he has been kind enough to send me a message to the effect that he heartily commends the work of the College of Idaho. In view of this, it affords me great pleasure to let you have my check for $500. as a donation to the above mentioned fund.

Wishing you every success in your undertaking, I am

Very truly yours,

S. P. Guggenheim

The campaign was a success, as described by the *Coyote* of February 10. By February 1, "the last chapter in the first big endowment drive of The College of Idaho" was completed, after an unsuccessful attempt in 1923. Robert McCormick directed the campaign, which was "but the opener for a broad and extensive financing project for the College."

But there always seems to be an interdiction, a warning, for those who must depend upon helpers. Remember the Fairy Godmother's admonition to Cinderella. The *Coyote* reporter quoted above continued immediately: "However, the College is obligated to raise $18,000 before June 1, 1925, to meet current expenses" and end the year in the black. Moreover, $5,000 was needed to complete the $11,000 Barton Memorial Fund and an additional $7,500 to bring the Boone Endowment up to $25,000. As a recent trustee remarked upon hearing a similar listing of obligations following a major deficit liquidation, "But it [financial insecurity] just goes on and on!" The remainder of 1925 was not uneventful. The debate team defeated Gooding and Intermountain Union College, the wrestlers defeated conference rival Idaho Tech of Pocatello and narrowly lost to non-conference Utah State. The football and basketball teams had won their conference championships; another wrestling victory over the Pocatello school earned the Coyotes their third conference title.

When Boise and the Union Pacific Railroad were finally able to connect the capital with the transcontinental tracks, the Honorable Carl R. Gray, UP president, along with twenty-five other officials and businessmen attended chapel services at the Caldwell college. Boise's celebration was a major event, and to assist in making the Main Line Celebration a success The College of Idaho encouraged her faculty and students to accept the formal invitation from Boise to participate. Miss Eleanor French, who had been elected "Queen of the West" by the student body, led the C of I delegation.

In the March 10 *Coyote* under a headline dealing with school loyalty, an editorial chided students for failing to attend assembly to hear two fine speakers. President Boone was paraphrased as saying that low attendance proves to supporters and potential donors that the College is small and doesn't really need what it says it needs—an assembly hall, a gymnasium, an increased endowment. We must, he suggested, show our visitors that we don't have enough room. The newspaper further criticized students who wear out the grass by taking short cuts, an ever-during problem.

There was pleasant news in the form of a $5,000 gift from the Rockefeller General Education Board for current expenses, something rarely provided by that foundation. However, no editor is satisfied for very long with good news, and an editorial in the April 21 *Coyote* lamented the lack of interest shown by the literary societies:

> Put them [Columbian-Lowell] on their old basis, leave out the latest dancing skit.... Try an experiment. See if students can stand more than one serious number on the program and make the meeting worth attending.

The school year ended with a pronounced upbeat, for in the June 9 *Coyote* Carrie Blatchley announced that the College would receive her gift of four lots on the corner of Ash and Ohio on which a YWCA building would be constructed. Also in June came the news of Robert Strahorn's gift of $50,000 for a library to be built as a memorial to Carrie Adell Strahorn. And back east, Roscoe Bernard Turner, Academy and C of I baseball, football, and basketball player and star debater, class of 1916, was appointed Professor of Law at Yale. News of this sort proved—and still proves—a powerful incentive to the faculty, to students debating whether to return or transfer to another college, and to high school seniors trying to decide where to go to college. In the fall when school opened in September, 407 students were enrolled, the largest number thus far.

That autumn, sandwiched between football triumphs and the graceful social amenities practiced in that earlier, gentler time, was more good news. Headed "College Plans New Buildings," a story in the October 14 *Coyote* announced that because enrollment was up, "A definite campus plan was adopted by the Board of Trustees...which makes Cleveland Boulevard, Ash, and Twentieth the boundaries of the grounds." Strahorn Library, the YWCA building, a gymnasium, a science hall, an auditorium, music conservatories, and a central heating plant were to be constructed. Some of these had been talked about before, but now it appeared that the Trustees were willing to move forward. From 1925 to 1928 the campus increased from thirty-five to seventy-five acres, making the firm boundaries identified above quite temporary (*Bulletin*, 1941).

The 1925 football team was excellent. Capitalizing on the considerable talents of three sets of gifted brothers, Coach Anson Cornell developed a team that lost only two games (non-conference) one of those by 16-14 to the University of Idaho. (The other loss was to Gonzaga, a Pacific Coast power, still basking in the legacy of Coach Gus Dorais, Knute Rockne's teammate at Notre Dame). The brothers were Douglas and Edwin "Josh" Lowell, Joe and Phil Albertson, all of Caldwell, and Fred and Charles Robinson of Middleton. Completing the team were George Stovel, Bud Brown, Bruce Woods, Dave Richardson, Orval Hostettler, Harold "Hap" Logue, Arthur Swim, Selby "Chub" Whittier, Edgar Dille, Felix Dicus, Will Gillam, Everett "Hump" Campbell, Francis McCormick, Harold Teach, George Crookham, and Forrest Strickling.

In the Idaho Tech game, the sports writer noted that Joe Albertson was on the receiving end of Ed "Josh" Lowell's passes in a 27-0 victory (*Coyote*, November 25, 1925). Linfield went down 75-0.

As for the social life in those glorious twenties, the Associated Women Students presented the organization's by-laws to the Board of Trustees, and the AWS became an identity of record, as noted in the above-mentioned *Coyote*. That the school newspaper carried accounts like the following is an indication of what made up the social life for those students and an indication of the kind of material the *Coyote* carried as important, characteristic, or revelatory. It was an item of interest that on a Wednesday evening Kathryn McCurry and

90

Ernestine Brass were dinner guests at the SE house (*Coyote*, October 14), that Doris Baker was a guest of Nell Tobias for Monday evening for dinner, and that Eula Reed, Mary Alice Pierce, and Helen Hull were hostesses to seven of their friends to whom they served rolls, olives, cake, and cookies (*Coyote*, December 9).

The service F. F. Beale gave to the College and to the community was not without cost. He suffered a "nervous collapse," his second since the production of "The Red Mill," according to the *Coyote* of April 28, 1926. "The Red Mill," with student-designed scenery and special effects, the *Coyote* found "the best ever" and declared the heroine's escape from a balcony by means of descent on the revolving sails of the mill "worthy of special mention."

By the end of the academic year 1925-26, *The College Coyote* would boast of many triumphs and accomplishments: Professors Salomon and Bell had served their second annual breakfast of pancakes and bacon for the Myra Tella girls; the baseball, tennis, and track teams had excellent success; and the College had gained its third national honorary fraternity—Alpha Psi Omega, a national dramatic society for which Scarlet Masque would be denominated the Eta chapter.

The library cornerstone ceremony, 1926: Robert E. Strahorn, with Dr. Boone at left.

College doors opened almost a week before the Carrie Adell Strahorn Memorial Library was ready for use in the fall of 1926. The cornerstone had been laid and the building formally dedicated on June 3, when Mr. Strahorn had spoken briefly. In most respects the school year of 1926-27 was off to a good start, the loss to Washington State in football to the contrary. Professor E. C. Preston decided it was time for the Department of History to recognize achievement in that department by giving an annual award for the best talk on a subject from history. And music, both vocal and instrumental, was impressive: Beale, Smith, Johnson, and others attracted talented students. The Hat was rebuilt, courtesy Class of '26. But still the compelling concern of the College was finances. Realizing that capital was in the East, the Board of Trustees drafted a resolution requesting that the Board of Education of the Presbyterian Church begin a campaign for funds specifically for the College. To that end, Dr. Thomas J. Graham, field secretary for the Presbyterian Board, was invited to visit the College and help with the plans. The *Coyote* editors suspected that $10,000 for a stadium might be generated locally.

One of the College's most loyal helpers, Robert Strahorn, opened the student portion of the new campaign by donating $2,000 toward a new stadium provided that the students and faculty raise $8,000 within a week. Strahorn's appearance was unexpected, according to the November 24 *Coyote*, unexpected perhaps, but not unlikely, for he once said that although some of his investments had been good ones and that some had caused him regret he never regretted any of the money he had invested in The College of Idaho. The same *Coyote* carried further news about the campaign, indicating that $50,000 had been set as Caldwell's quota which more than one hundred people would be on the streets soliciting.

As a matter of fact, the *Coyotes* of November 24 and December 1 had a difficult time deciding which of two contending news stories deserved the bigger headlines and the more ink—the campaigns for "A Greater College of Idaho" or the equally inspiriting prospects of a game between Montana State and the C of I. The game was scheduled for Public School Field in Boise for Thanksgiving Day. The Bozeman club, which had accumulated 52 points to 9 for its opponents, was tied with Utah State and the University of Utah for the lead of the Rocky Mountain Conference. The Bobcats had beaten Colorado, Colorado Teachers, Brigham Young University, and Wyoming. They had lost to the University of Montana and had been tied by Idaho. The Coyotes' fine team had steadily improved and had won the new conference title. It must have been one of the College's finer athletic moments as they defeated the larger school 7-0. When the history of athletics at the College is written, the reader can savor the details of the accomplishments of this team and the success of Coach Cornell. But surely among the great athletes of the College's history all the Lowell brothers deserve a place. Josh was named captain of the All-Star team and of him Mike Moran, a conference referee, was quoted by the *Coyote* (December 15) as follows:

> For left halfback one man looms above all others in the conference. This is Lowell, the brilliant star of The College of Idaho. His passing, punting, and ball-carrying were the spark of his team's offensive throughout the season. All critics are agreed that he is by far the outstanding player of the conference. Due to his phenomenal record he is also named captain of the mythical eleven.

It is not surprising that Mr. Strahorn's challenge was met, indeed, exceeded (by $52); such a team deserved a new stadium. However, the Caldwell community fell $30,000 below the targeted amount, and by January 12, 1927, according to the *Coyote* of that date, a total of only $55,000 had been raised in the campaign for a Greater College of Idaho.

It is gratifying, in retrospect, that football in 1926 cost $7,972.69, of which all but $324.58 came from gate receipts or sources other than student body funds: "The cost...per student per game [was] 20.1 cents," according to the *Coyote* of February 9, 1927.

While athletics and athletes were gaining considerable attention and respect from local and regional media (the 1926 Coyote track and field men had won the Northwest Conference championship, and that distinction was sufficient for the team to gain an invitation to participate in the Pacific Coast championship meet to be held at USC in June of 1927), academic accomplishments were by no means slighted. Indeed, one of the most interesting aspects of The College of Idaho has been the fact that no dichotomy exists between students and athletes, that from the time of James Boone and Roscoe Turner it was expected that the athlete should be first of all a student. No one demonstrated this truism more forcefully than Philip Albertson, who, after a fine athletic and student-leader career, was elected by his peers to give the Founders Day Address, a signal honor. His acceptance into the graduate program in history at the University of Wisconsin came as no surprise.

This same *Coyote* (February 9, 1927) reported on a letter to Dr. Boone from the Johns Hopkins University which said the University would be pleased to enroll other College of Idaho graduates of the caliber of Manley Shaw '25, who had just taken his medical-school entrance examinations. The reporter also noted that Roscoe Turner, '16, was teaching law at Yale; that Corwin Hinshaw,

'23, was teaching in the University of California and had attracted considerable attention by his medical research in pyorrhea; that Elliot Smith, '23, had become an assistant professor of economics at Columbia; and that Raymond Griswold, '25, was excelling in graduate work in Spanish at the same institution.

For the first time since 1917, Chapel would no longer be required, even though attendance would continue to be taken, according to the February 16 *Coyote*. Dr. Boone noted that even though catalogs from that earlier time warned that students might jeopardize their degrees by failing to attend chapel, the penalty was never exacted. In an editorial, the same *Coyote* noted the reformation in chapel arrangements, suggested that it was all for the best, then asked "While the faculty row is being occupied by the students—*where is the faculty* [italics in original]?" Honor was a serious matter in 1927.

Another serious matter was grade inflation, not a recent phenomenon. Professor Joe Rankin, who had just completed a study of grades at the C of I for 1924, 1925, and 1926, said that "students [here] must either be an exceptional group...or else the teachers must be issuing the grade [of] 90 percent more often than is deserved since 90 percent was found to be the most frequent score. From 90 to 100 is...exceptional, and about 85 is considered the average standard of the average college student" (*Coyote*, February 23, 1927).

The issue of cheating refused to go away as some students chided the *Coyote* for publishing an editorial wondering about prevalence of dishonesty. Others praised the *Coyote* for its courage and frankness. The student body went on record "as opposed to the opinion that there is wholesale cheating...and as opposed to all cheating" (*Coyote*, February 23, 1927). The *Coyote* editorial on the subject is a model of clarity and reasonableness as it defends its policy of the pursuit of truth.

All of this self-examination indicates an increasing awareness of the need to maintain academic integrity, to be an institution of authentic higher education. It is not surprising to find the administration's Promotion Department seeking answers to questions about College of Idaho students. In a carefully designed questionnaire that required students to give their names (in order to get responses from all students—names were not to be made public), information was sought on such matters as expenses for the school year, appropriately broken down into such categories as transportation, tuition, board, and room; amount and what kind of self-support; extra-curricular activities; why the student chose the C of I; and professional goals. The results were tabulated and reported in the *Coyote* of March 23, with 328 students responding. Such matters as these are of continuing importance in the life of any college, and apropos of this institution is an indication of a growing concern with standards. It is more than likely that the demand for self-analysis was in part stimulated by the Northwest Association.

The years preceding the crash of the stockmarket in October of 1929 were of a design that encouraged the emergence of individuals. Single, separate students were instructed by strong individual faculty who, probably to an extent undeserved by school and community, were often virtuoso teachers. It was very difficult for a student to be a nonentity because the energy of the campus always worked to change the ordinary into the extraordinary.

The athletic program, the musical opportunities, and the academic program were improving. The baseball team defeated Whitman, the University of Idaho, lost to Washington State, defeated Montana State twice, and won the Northwest Conference title; the debate team defeated their counterparts from Whitman; Beale's production of "The Geisha" was another "best ever"; the track team placed fourth in the conference meet; the tennis team won the Southern Idaho Conference title, the College in the awkward though not unique position of belonging to *two* conferences; and graduates went on to teaching fellowships in chemistry, to theological school, to nurses' training, and to school teaching. The College's financial campaign for a greater College of Idaho had expanded from Caldwell to southwestern Idaho, gathering $8,214 in pledges. The school year 1926-27 ended with the expectation that the campaign would be successful and that the endowment would satisfy the Northwest Association.

The new school year opened with high expectations, as indeed every school year should. Over a hundred freshman appeared (actually 132); the College was invited to join Pi Kappa Delta, a national forensic honorary; and three sororities, coyly referred to as "women's social clubs" by the *Coyote* (September 28) found themselves in new homes: The Ring was at 1720 Dearborn, the S.E. at 1701 Everett, and the P.E.P. in the former Ring house at Maple and Ohio. Myra Tella remained at 2102 Indiana. The first segment of the endowment campaign for southern Idaho had ended July 15 with $47,000 pledged. And F. F. Beale decided not to present an opera. The football team, minus a Lowell on the roster for the first time in nearly a decade, dropped its opening (non-conference) game but never looked back.

While this chronology does not presume to be a history of athletics at The College of Idaho, athletes get a goodly amount of publicity, and some might assume that newspaper ink by the column inch is the measure of a college. And it is true that 1927 was memorable for several reasons. In the first place, the Coyotes were undefeated in conference play, winning the second (and their second) Northwest Conference football championship. In the second place, through some kind of magic I have not been able to understand, The College of Idaho and Pacific University were scheduled to play in Multnomah Stadium in Portland, Oregon, for that city's game of the week. The College *Coyote* ran an effective advance story, highlighting the record of the competition between the two schools, provided more than adequate coverage of the game itself, and included some follow-up information on the game in an advance story on the Willamette game. These can be found in the October 5, 13, and 21 numbers of the College paper. In the coverage of the game, the *Coyote* indicates that the dopesters had predicted a Pacific victory. They were wrong: C of I 13, Pacific 6. In recognition of twelve years of outstanding accomplishments, the Board of Trustees named Anson B. Cornell Director of Athletics and coach of three sports—adding basketball to his customary fall and spring assignments. In his spare time Cornell was assistant cashier of the Caldwell State Bank.

While King Football was helping publicize The College of Idaho around the Northwest, at home the endowment fund grew slowly, and Blatchley Hall underwent remodeling and expansion in order to meet the needs of the YWCA. According to the *Coyote* of October 28, 1927, two fund-raising projects had been concluded, one each in 1925 and 1926; now the third and final project was to raise money for furnishings. The remodeling was expected to be concluded in the spring. The second major campus improvement was the completion in the spring of the track portion of the new stadium under the direction of Professor Hayman.

Coach Anson B. Cornell

Another sad time for the College came in March with the death of L. S. Dille, who had served as a trustee since 1893 and as secretary-treasurer of the College since 1901. He was another link with the old College downtown. Although he was sixty-eight and had been in failing health for some time, his death caused the *Coyote* executives to use wide black column lines on the front page of the March 23 paper. His accomplishments and an obituary accompanied a photograph of Mr. Dille, and on the editorial page a long eulogy was printed. The first paragraph reads:

Student bodies are prone to consider themselves the motivating force of an institution. Each year's group feels that it carries the whole weight of the college activities. A few fellowships convince us that classes would be impossible without us; a few publications that we furnish all its publicity; a few stadiums that we're building the campus; and a few Founders' days that we're dictating its activities. However, the shadow of mourning that has passed this week gives us pause to consider. This life we build passes with each class, like some gaseous substance; disappears from sight, leaving only a drop or so of moisture to show that it was ever present; the foundation that remains has been built by trustees, officers, teachers, and friends of our school; such men as our late secretary-treasurer, our president, and a score of others.

The tribute is an eloquent testimony to student awareness of indebtedness to the past.

A final note for the academic year 1927-28 in the *Coyote* of May 18 informs the reader that the AWS (Associated Women Students), which had been organized to insure that women and women's activities received their fair share of student fees, had disbanded and would be replaced by a new organization, the Women's Athletic Association, as soon as a constitution could be prepared.

Finally, sixty-two seniors were recommended to the Board of Trustees for the baccalaureate degree, the largest class of graduating seniors in the history of the College. Of these, seventeen graduated in English; eleven in history; five each in economics and biology; four in education; three each in mathematics, Latin, chemistry, philosophy, and home economics; two in music; and one each in modern languages, political science and French. Nine students chose the bachelor of science degree.

The next school year, 1928-29, witnessed the addition of four familiar names to the faculty—S. S. Walsh in education, L. A. Waterman, in education; H.P. House, in chemistry; and Doys Shorb, in biology. The honorary organization Abbots was established. Originally a way of honoring the scholarship, character, citizenship, and effective participation in C of I activities of a few men, the organization was liberated in 1972 when Susan Fleenor was named along with Alfred "Tom" Sawyer as Abbot (Abbot notebook).

That bête noire of the College, the endowment, grew by $43,000 for the 1927-28 year, the *Coyote* reported in the October 18 issue, with Oregon and California to be canvassed in the present year.

An entree into Oregon philanthropy was natural for the College, which once again played in Portland's huge Multnomah Stadium and defeated Linfield 12-0. It was another fine year for C of I football, as the Coyotes dropped a close contest to BYU (9-6) and the College of Puget Sound (6-0), were smashed by Washington State (51-0), defeated University of Idaho Southern Branch (39-7), and downed Pacific (28-7) and Willamette (44-6) before losing to Whitman (19-12). The record left the Coyotes tied for second in the conference. In wrestling the Coyotes defeated Utah State 18-8.

Other traditions were maintained. Professor Beale was back in the business of producing operettas (*Iolanthe* this year), and the traditional post-examination silly edition of the *Coyote* lived up to expectations: in two inch banner headlines **W A R   R A G E S!** By February 7, the *Coyote* could report that 408 students had enrolled; the *Coyote* of a week later reported that Willamette's enrollment was 502, and that Willamette had just received a $100,000 legacy. The last *Coyote* of the year noted that once again, English was the most popular major for the graduating seniors (18) with economics the next most popular (9).

One cannot but wonder, looking ahead to October, what would have happened had the English majors been in charge of the stock market. But when school opened in September, there was no indication of incipient weakness in the economy. Students came to the College from Illinois, Missouri, Kansas, Nebraska, North Dakota, Washington, and Jarbidge, Nevada.

News of the campaign to increase the endowment appeared in the *Coyote* of October 17. Dr. Frederick E. Hockwell, Director of the Board of Education of the Presbyterian Church, visited the campus. He praised the College to the skies and reported that Dr. Thomas W. Synott of Philadelphia had offered $50,000 to the endowment if the College could raise an additional $100,000. The College had on hand $19,000 that was unencumbered and could count toward the $100,000, leaving $81,000 to be raised in order to get the $50,000 gift. About $450,000 was already in the endowment. The story concludes: "Just what method will be used in carrying on the campaign for endowment funds had not been announced by officials of the College, but an intensive drive will be instituted to raise the required amount in order to receive the conditional pledge."

It is interesting, perhaps even strange, that Dr. Boone's diary makes no reference to this latest opportunity to buck the line yet once more in pursuit of the evanescent challenge gift. Entries apropos of this visit by Dr. Stockwell were made on October 11 and 12 as follows:

> Freeze. Roses done for. Set out from Pocatello [Synod had met in Idaho Falls] at 5 a.m. Rev. E.N. Murphy and Wm Crosby Ross. Fine, drive up home at 1:30. Dr. Stockwell here. Meeting of Trustees at 4. Quorum, we do business. We eat at Finney, Blatchley, Lowells, Dr. Stockwell.... Cold again tonight. Chicago Cubs win at Philadelphia 3 to 1. Athletics won 2, Cubs 1.

And:

Calm clear day.... Dr. Stockwell hit for Intermountain Union College, Montana....

The next *Coyote* to drop a remark about the $100,000 endowment drive to meet Mr. Synott's challenge was the issue of December 12, which said that the Alumni Fund Committee was working on a plan toward that end, although its strategy was still not perfected. The story further indicated that preliminary response to the unfinished plan was positive. In January, refinement of the endowment drive called for the involvement of churches extending out from the Caldwell area through southwestern Idaho, then southern and southeastern Idaho, and into California. The drive was not restricted to Presbyterians; in a truly ecumenical spirit, the official organizing the campaign insisted that all denominations be permitted to contribute. The deadline by which the money had to be in hand was October 1, 1930, that is, the following academic year.

The school year 1929-30 reflected very little impact of the stock market collapse, a perhaps not unexpected indifference since capital was largely centered in the East, and the heavy early losers were there. The Depression was yet to come.

Four items quite unrelated to national matters but pertinent to this history demand attention.

First, an entry in the *Coyote* of March 20, 1930, refers to the improvements on College land "which is just opposite the campus and extends between Cleveland Blvd. and the O.S.L. railroad from 22nd St. to about two blocks east of the intersection of Indiana and Cleveland." Although this land was not part of the campus, which was south of

College benefactor Dr. Thomas W. Synott of Philadelphia.

Cleveland, it did belong to the College.

Also noteworthy is the fact that during this academic year (reported in the *Coyote* of November 1, 1929) two of the most respected, most venerable of the College's institutions died. The Lowell and Columbian literary societies had not managed to survive whatever competed with them for the time and energies of the students. Growing old and feeble and for the last four or five years of their lives taking on the characteristics of delicate lace and the faint bouquet of lavender, the two had served the College well. Considering the ephemeral nature of college organizations generally, theirs was a long life indeed.

Limits of space have kept me from treating the reader to a recital of names of school leaders. Such lists are anathema to real historians; names must be connected to events or to dates or to something. For an institution where individuals matter, the listing of names is perhaps a feeble way of affirming that yes, these separate persons were here and should be noted. The chronicler can occasionally hold up an individual for review as characteristic of or as a symbol for the class to which the person belongs. In that sense the record refers to Bill and Barbara Gillam. Bill Gillam had been an all-star athlete, musician, student leader, and was later to conduct courses in education to a bunch of ex-G.I. students in Commons 14, after W.W. II.

Boone's diary for October 12 is eloquent in its spare treatment. After some details about the weather, about ordering some coal, about Dr. Stockwell heading for Montana, he writes:

> Bill Gillam and Hugh Caldwell came up to tell me that Barbara Grewell Gillam, Bill's wife, is dead, Died this day [Saturday], funeral is Monday.

Then on Monday, he says:

> Day very fine, ideal. Normal school. School dismissed at 2:10 go to funeral services of Barbara Grewell-Gillam at Presb. Church. [Professor] Springer conducts service, I assist. House filled. Body will be shipped to Loveland, Colorado, for burial. The last of little Barbara. She sang sweetly and worked hard.

The *Coyote* for October 17 gives a brief obituary and concludes: "Pallbearers were members of the Beta Chi club of which Mr. Gillam is a member, and ushers were Ring members of which club Mrs. Gillam was a member."

Dr. Boone, Prof. Springer, and Dr. Salomon had attended the Gillam-Grewell wedding, representing the faculty. Who could have imagined that two of them would so soon be called upon to perform that sad final task?

A community develops its sense of communion partly in response to its shared experiences; I don't mean just in what happens to it, but how it develops strategies by which it accommodates those events. Beyond athletics, important though they are perceived to be; aside from intellectual and academic attainment, the very core of a college; indeed, transcending the whole range of college experiences is the necessity to cope with sorrow and loss through death. This sad time with the death of Barbara Gillam showed the presence of community which grieved for a loss and helped a survivor through a dark time.

But it is also true, and perhaps just as bromidic, to observe that a community develops and reveals itself partly in its response to happy occasions. Both sadness and gladness find expression in and through community.

Another event (this time happy) that catches the eye of anyone reading Boone's diary, or at least the eye of anyone for whom New Year's Eve and Day have special meaning, is the subject of the entry for January 1, 1930, a Wednesday:

> We cook the big turkey in the old Round Oak range in the laundry. All folks [guests and callers] gone by 6. I set out for W. E. McCurry's, mile N. of Cole school. Marry Kathryn McCurry to Joseph A. Albertson. 52 present, very fine and very pretty. Home at 10 p.m.

The *Coyote* of January 9, ever aggressive in publishing news of College folk, devoted a nine-inch column to the wedding.

Some social and cultural historians have described this decade as the roaring twenties, and in some respects the description is accurate. Recovery from the Great War, the world safe for democracy, a generally flourishing economy (if one did not take note of the agricultural problems, and difficulties in a few other segments of the American economy): it all produced an optimism that knew no bounds. The campus of a small, and, yes, struggling, western college held activity, witnessed growth, saw unprecedented athletic and academic enterprise and accomplishment. No wonder the Coyote was rampant.

But if history teaches anything, surely one of its great lessons is the unpredictability of the future. If the present held sadness and joy for members of the College family, what of the decade yet to come?

On a spring botany field trip, an aging Dr. Boone stands among lupines, camas, and sage.

CHAPTER SEVEN

C. latrans Couchant

Heraldic iconography again expresses the campus tone of the 1930s when the Depression ate away at the core of the region's oldest institution of higher learning. The cut that hurt more than all others was the death in 1936 of her first and to that time only president. The decade was a time for the Coyote to rest and to regain lost vitality.

The school year 1930-31 got off to a lively start. Collegiate optimism and confidence found a symbol in the increased dimensions of the Coyote, which featured a new format of seven columns, 21.5 x 15.5 inches. The first page of the year's first issue (volume XXI, No. 1) was loaded with news: freshmen were initiated (green beanies and sox), the Trail staff identified (the theme a well-guarded mystery), Foothills (the school's literary magazine) scheduled for a November release, advertising manager, and yell leaders elected. Yells were important then. That covers only four front-page stories; there were thirteen more.

Other stories dealt with the election of class officers, with additions to the curriculum (oratory, General Art, journalism again,), rushing by fraternities and sororities. Delta Kappa Phi pledged nine men, including John Monasterio (d. October 11, 1979), one of the first Basques to graduate from The College of Idaho; Beta Chi pledged nine; the Orions landed nineteen. The sororities conducted a longer rush and had not finished the pledging process.

An overly optimistic story reminded the reader that the Coyotes and Vandals would have another go on Public School Field. The Coyotes had scored twelve points against Washington State while holding the Cougars to forty-seven in an earlier game.

A play entitled "Blackbirds" by senior Lawrence Frazier was "highly commended" by Hinckley, editor of Drama Magazine and teacher of playwriting at Northwestern University, who thought the play would be published.

Three new teachers were added to the staff. One, Harold M. Tucker, '23, became one of the College's legended faculty, a man who knew the region's flora as well as anyone. Professor Tucker was another of the College's devoted teachers to die in the harness (of cancer) in 1959, after a career of twenty-nine years. His appointment, after eight years of teaching biology at Caldwell High School, must have been a pleasant one for Dr. Boone, whose botany classes typically numbered ninety or more.

A final item that catches the eye of anyone looking at this October 2, 1930, issue matched for length the advance story on the Coyote-Vandal football game. It was a glowing treatment of the College's new football stadium, featuring

Biologists Harold M. Tucker, Lyle M. Stanford, and Robert E. Bratz, with William J. Hilty, '51, second from right, posed for this picture some time after 1953.

electric lights for night games. It was Idaho's first lighted stadium. Pre-game publicity for the Vandal contest included an evening broadcast by the pep band over KIDO and a tour of towns on the interurban loop. The official dedication was scheduled for the evening of October 17 when the Coyotes would tangle with Willamette's Bearcats.

One other item must be mentioned. Marion Hine, an alumnus who had been teaching in Greece, died in Paris, France. Dr. Boone's journal for September 29, records:

> Word by the Statesman that Marion Hine died yesterday in Paris. Was unexpected, probably trichinosis. Fine fellow, teacher at Salonica, Greece. The college there. Youngest of Rev. T.W. Hine's family. Grad. B.A. here in 1928.

An affecting part of the *Coyote's* story and the detail that is richly C of I is in the list of survivors - "three sisters, all of whom are graduates of The College of Idaho." The College has enjoyed this sibling connection time after time, from the Cupp family to a great many of today's students who are here in part because of a brother or sister who came earlier.

In the October 16 *Coyote* appeared a shadow forecasting events deeply concerned with and growing out of the Depression. Headed "College Time Is Extended," the story began:

> An extension of time has been given The College of Idaho to complete the endowment fund which was started almost a year ago when Dr. Thomas D. Synnott of Philadelphia signified his willingness to give...$50,000 providing [The College] would raise $100,000 in one year....
>
> The College has $80,000...and is sure of the remaining $20,000. Dr. Synnott's endowment is being managed by the Board of Christian Education at Philadelphia.
>
> "This has been a rather bad year to raise money for such a purpose, but we are confident that we shall achieve our goal," said J. H. Lowell.

This understated commentary on economic conditions to the contrary notwithstanding, the general mood on and about the campus of The College of Idaho continued bullish. It was impossible not to be enthusiastic. Indeed, the prospect for the whole community was bright: an addition to the local cavalry barn; a Southwestern Idaho Dairy show there with cattle from Idaho, California, Arizona, Washington, Oregon, and Utah; local business contributing $3,100 toward Dr. Hayman's stadium (excavated with horse power and fresno and slip scrapers) through ticket sales for the Willamette game. The Caldwell community and its college were thriving. Although it is difficult to date a photograph after the fact, a print from about this time (using automobiles and styles of dress as artifacts) shows a city block with no parking space available, people lining the sidewalks, and all stores occupied. Strahorn's dream for his favorite town and his favorite charity as the cultural center of a vibrant region was being realized.

In this same *Coyote* (October 16), Dr. Hayman commented as follows on the College's corn production (the crop, not professorial humor):

> The corn crop raised...on...C of I property across Cleveland Boulevard...was a great deal better than was expected....

> Although only one block of the forty acres was planted to corn this year, the heavy yield...shows what can be raised on the alkali ground after it has been reclaimed.

Night football was an exciting new wrinkle for this community, indeed for the entire state. It provided several column inches of material for the *Coyote* staff— how the lighted stadium was once swamp land owned by Montie Gwinn and only six years ago (1924) grew "cat-tails projecting gracefully above the dark green swamp foliage"; how much power the stadium used (66,000 watts, enough to illuminate the Nampa-Caldwell highway with lights placed 200 feet apart, rendering headlights unnecessary); how the entire stadium project, seating 4,000 but able to accommodate 6,000, cost $13,985.

The contagiousness of undergraduate silliness is remarkable. Seemingly immune to the claims of mortality and sequestered from the cares and toils of the world in the arms of a sustaining mother on a green and blightless campus, students think, why ought not these precious moments be spent in the nonsense of the latest fads—swallowing goldfish, affecting ear studs, earrings, cultured hairdos of any or all sorts, clothing fashionably low style? So it was that "a world record was set for standing on one foot when the Misses Gladys McManimie and Nettie Theodore stood on one foot for 39 minutes and 4 seconds." The same story (October 16, 1930) also noted that

> a checker and cat contest was held the same evening. In the finals, E. Ewer won two games and Cazer won one. Interest ran high as the crowds cheered the winner on to victory.

> Though this is probably the first cat tournament to be held on the campus, it was found that there was no lack of contestants as much practice has been put in on the game at education classes.

The children of the two faculty families contracted infantile paralysis during a serious outbreak of the disease in 1930. Both recovered. Schools were closed and public places generally were off-limits to those under eighteen. The *Coyote* of October 23 noted that fifteen girls from Finney and eleven from the sorority houses went home because of the outbreak.

Two additional items catch the eye. The forty acres extending from Cleveland Boulevard to the railroad tracks, bounded by 22nd street to approximately two blocks east of Indiana and Cleveland, were to be made more attractive by the planting of a lawn along the Cleveland front and extending back toward the tracks, to a depth of about two blocks. The second refers to an item respecting the naming—"in all likelihood"—of a newly discovered species of snail in honor of the discoverer: Polygra tuckeri, after Professor Harold Tucker. He knew fauna, too, and geology and local history.

The *Coyote* for November 20, 1930, in the biggest, blackest headlines available, announced "New Frat on Campus" and in two related stories discussed the absorption by the national Theta Kappa Nu of the Beta Chi local social club, the old Bachelors' Club. At a banquet at the I.O.O.F Hall, Walter Lybarger, the national secretary from Cleveland, Ohio, assisted by a delegation from Oregon State College, presided.

In football, a so-so season ended with the Coyotes tieing Brigham Young University, 13-13. The *Coyote* of December 18 observed that the College's competitor for a Rhodes Scholarship, Malcolm Brown, lost out to Harvard senior Grenville Holden, of Idaho Falls. Finally, it was fortunate for Professor of French J. D. Bell that the Buckley Amendment sanctifying the privacy of student grades had not been passed: Professor Bell posted on the bulletin board of his room all the names and grades of students in the beginning French class, from 0 to 99, thinking that the strategy might inspire the lackadaisical to Spartan efforts. The *Coyote* was forced by fiscal necessity to revert to its old six column, eighteen inch size. Enrollment for the spring semester held at 414, about the same as that of the fall semester A quaint squib filling a column on the first page called attention to a wedding in Iowa City, Iowa, whose principals' surnames challenged the writer of the headline: "Wedding Culminates Smoke-Ash Romance." The bride was Margaret Adel Smoke, and the groom, David Fuller Ash.

The remainder of the winter saw activities fairly central, now, to the life of the College—basketball (it is surprising that the team won any games since there was nothing like a real gymnasium on campus); preparations for baseball and track; debates; a new musical fraternity, Lambda Mu; and the contest for most popular C of I students won by Miss Amy Gipson and Mr. George Judd.

The YWCA continued to fill a niche in the lives of students, presenting musical programs, one-act plays, 'and afternoon teas.

The expected and probably ignored editorials in the *Coyote* pled for school spirit, admonished students about campus appearance, begged pedestrians not to ruin the lawn by cutting corners, and worried about the social life. No one complained about an inadequate library, and, so far as I have been able to determine, few students wrote in or underlined library books. Indeed, the physical presence of the College was a bright one until sometime in the late 1960's or early 1970's. Caldwell and the student body of the C of I were proud of the green and spacious lawns, the shining buildings, and the sense of order that characterized the public life of The College of Idaho. It is likely that the private, unobserved aspects of the institution have remained fairly constant over the years, for human nature does not change. Many students and their families undertook considerable self-denial if not downright sacrifice to secure an education. That education and the respect for the institution that conferred it seemed to go hand in hand. The campus was not littered, the dormitory rooms were not physically damaged. Coffee was not spilled in the classroom buildings because coffee was not consumed in class. There was more serious business to attend to.

In both bound volumes of the *Coyote* for 1929-1935, publication suddenly and without explanation ended with the March 12, 1931, number. It is easy to supply probable cause—a worsening national economy was having local consequences. An entry in Boone's diary for December 9, 1931, is pertinent:

> The College is on the rocks financially, first time in many years. Mr. Lowell, the financial manager, put the case to the trustees. Present were Judge J. C. Rice, H. D. Blatchley, H. D. Baldridge, E. H. Plowhead, Dr. E. N. Murphy, Walter Kerrick, C. E. Norquest, and J. H. Lowell. Others—Thurlow Bryant, Frank Mumford, and O. J. Smith.

Not until October 5, 1932, did the College *Coyote*, with a new format and masthead, reappear in its larger-format glory.

A story on page one of that issue noted that it was the first in a year and a half. It reiterated the paper's philosophy of communicating "to the students of the College what its members do, feel, and think," and of interpreting "the immediate news of the school and the more general occurrences of the world...of pertinent interest to students of today." But the lead story detailed an enrollment decline—376 students, down from the 414 who had registered for Spring Semester in 1931, although the figure for Fall Semester of 1931 was up by twenty-two students over the previous fall. Still, the Depression was beginning to be felt. A story datelined New York, in the October 26 issue discussed the Depression and reported that colleges in the Midwest seemed to be having the greatest problem with declining enrollments; and whereas Amherst, Fordham, Harvard, and Vassar showed slight increases, Columbia reported a decline of more than 1,000 students.

Meanwhile, Depression or no Depression, life must go on, and so it was that Lyle Stanford and Wendell Smith were chosen to represent the College in the Rhodes Scholarship competition, and the Ecclesia Philathea hung on...but just barely, its customary twenty members dwindling to five, three of whom were officers. The Coyote Rhodes competitors were unsuccessful.

The *Coyote* reported some of the more bizarre campus practices. For some time, Professor O. J. Smith's classes in comparative anatomy found and prepared their own cats. The embalming process was an instructive one and at the same time kept expenses down. In the *Coyote* of December 15, 1932, a brief unsigned feature discussed with delightful whimsy the cats that sacrificed their all in the interests of medicine. When this practice was finally abandoned and commercially prepared felines were procured for students in "Comp. Anat." (this must have happened in the 1970s), one could almost predict that in a few more years anatomy undergraduates would be working with human cadavers. And it came to pass. The distance between the eighth grade and graduate school continues to close.

Dr. Boone's diary records periodic faculty meetings, and the entries would please the reader trained in Laconian rhetoric:

> October 13, Monday [1930]. [After serious entries regarding weather, Harold Tucker's daughter and infantile paralysis, the following:] Faculty as usual.

> October 20 [1930] Had the usual faculty meet.

> October 27 [1930] Faculty meet at 4 p.m.

> November 3 [1930] Usual faculty meet.

Even when the faculty meetings saw the generation of both heat and light, the laconic style prevails:

> January 19, Monday [1931] Faculty meet rather strenuous one. Students run bills. Coyote in debt $500. Drs. Springer and Salomon committee to see what can be done.

> February 9, Monday [1931].... Faculty meet as usual. We fired some 15 students; 8 for bad conduct, the others for failing to make more than 8 credits during last semester. Sure a tuff [sic], lazy lot of students; yet seem all right. But will drink and girls out by fire escape at midnight. It is sure disheartening to be compelled to clean out so many.

One cannot get a clear picture of the structure of the academic administration from Boone's diary although one can infer something like the following from a careful reading of the diary, the *Trail*, and the *Coyote*. By the 1920s the faculty were meeting once a week, Monday at 4 p.m. the usual time—presumably with Boone presiding, although minutes of those early faculty meetings have not been uncovered. When we remember that Boone traveled extensively, figuratively holding out his hat on Wall Street and Riverside Drive, someone must have had the responsibility for the conduct of faculty and college business. It is clear that he had much confidence in the judgment of the little biologist from Ohio, and in the Catalog for 1931-32 (with announcements for 1932-33), O. J. Smith is identified as dean.

So the president could call upon the dean for assistance in conducting faculty meetings, or he could turn the meetings over to the dean when the president was out of town, but still it was Boone's faculty and the conducting of its meetings was his responsibility. There was no academic council or faculty senate: matters appropriate to the faculty were the business of the entire faculty.

Ever the soul of brevity, Dr. Boone made the following entry for March 8, 1932:

> Spring day. Morning fine, but an East wind blows late. Usual school. Mr. Lowell...busy on finances. We are up against it [impoverished]. Committee of faculty, Dean Smith, J. M. Rankin, Paul Murphy; Trustees, J. H. Lowell, Gov. H. C. Baldridge and Walter Kerrick work late.

On March 22, 1932, Boone wrote:

> Spring day; but late looks like rain. Usual school. Trustees meet at 3 o'clock and finish budget scheme for 1932-33. A slash of 15% in salaries.

Nineteen thirty-three saw the Hat re-built yet again, surely one of the few bright spots in the Depression year. The *Coyote* for January 16 noted that Oliver Hardy and Mickey Mouse were favorites of the pledges of Scarlet Masque, that the *Trail* editor was desperate for students to get their class pictures taken, and that two candidates each were running for the student body presidency, vice president, and corresponding secretary. That there was only one candidate for the post of financial secretary might well be a commentary on the bilious cast of mind for everything connected with economic matters in this depressing time. There was no *Coyote* for March, but the April 12 issue provided a synopsis of events between the two issues. Founders Day, which had not been held for the last two years, seemed on the point of re-birth; the 1933 Summer Session looked encouraging, with a faculty of nine—Mary C. Anderson, Anna S. Eyck, H. H. Hayman, Margaret F. Nichol, Knute Ovregaard (a faculty member since 1929), J. H. Roblyer, O. J. Smith, and Stephen L. Walsh.[*]

In this same *Coyote* (April 12, 1933) appeared a story detailing a student recruiting trip by Dr. James Millar and Thurlow Bryant, the latter having worked diligently in setting up a news bureau through which home-town newspapers would be supplied with news of local students attending the College. A final item from this issue concerned the Hat: it had been demolished again and the *Coyote* lamented that the re-building process seemed to be on indefinite hold. The re-built structure had been knocked down by a motor bus which had "caught a pillar," according to Boone's diary.

Raising the Hat, the hard way.

---

[*]   In this story appeared an object lesson in pied type and copy editing: "Miss Judith Mahan serving as visiting faculty member will direct the course inpubic school ect the course proved very popular last summer and large enrollment is expected." The course was one in public school music, and etc. was meant. Error-free copy is rare.

The remainder of 1933 went for The College of Idaho community as for the rest of America, with alternating hope and despair as politicians and economists pondered unemployment and all that went with it. Even the hope was not unqualified, for although the endowment had reached $513,000 in 1931-32 and remained as a hoped-for bulwark against institutional dissolution, it appeared to be stuck at that figure, generating in livestock terms $55 per head for the 413 students. That amount, combined with tuition income and with gifts for the annual budget, was grossly inadequate. An annual deficit was just over the horizon, if indeed dissolution could be forestalled.

There was another disquieting development: Anse Cornell, one of the College's most successful coaches and a Coyote institution for seventeen years, resigned to take a position with Pacific University. From the present vantage point the causes impelling the separation seem inconsequential—three poor football seasons (fans seem to forget that the coach wants to win just as badly as the most rabid fan), the College's failure to construct a basketball facility and the attendant embarrassment of having to negotiate playing and floor space with nearby high schools, and declining enrollments. But in 1933 these were matters of grave concern. Cornell was replaced by the successful and popular Boise High School coach, Loren Basler, who would win his share of victories.

The Depression refused to budge. On Monday, March 13, 1933, at "Usual School, usual faculty meet," President Boone shared with the faculty "the payroll for the 1933-34 year Some real roarbacks because it implies another

How to neck →

ry entry of that date. The entry is a bit enigmatic: porting the first salary slash? Was it 20 percent ad earlier recorded. Or did he mean this was yet cept 20 percent?

ege students, Depression or no. A story of eight ch headline on page two of the May 12, 1933, lege sheik how to neck. The verb was relatively irly old; the sensations...well, let the writer tell

Lean lightly forward with your head, take good aim (this is the most important thing; many a good kiss has been spoiled by aim.) The lips meet, the eyes close, the heart opens, the soul rides the storm and weathers the blast. (Don't be in a hurry.) Heaven opens before you. The world shoots from under your feet as a meteor flies across the evening skies. Don't jab down on a beautiful mouth as if you were spearing frogs. Don't grab and yank the lady as if she were a struggling colt. The main thing is to be brave and firm but don't hurry.

And that was the last *Coyote* for 1933. What appeared as the campus news organ instead, was a one-page typewritten and mimeographed publication entitled "The College Coyote Pup." After fifteen issues, the Pup disappeared, replaced by an authentic four-page six column printed *Coyote*, on September 27, 1937.

Circumstances permitted a grand Homecoming on the weekend of November 18, featuring a football game with Whitman College on Saturday afternoon and a covered dish dinner for alumni in Blatchley Hall, with a special program under the direction of Reby Feuling. The game ended in a tie, but all proved a satisfactory diversion from unemployment, unbalanced budgets, and soup kitchens. Veteran Coyote watchers wondered how Basler's team would fare against Anse Cornell's Pacific U. Badgers in Boise on Thanksgiving. The Coyotes lost and the ever fair-minded Boone recorded in his diary, November 30, 1933,

> We seemed to outplay the Pacific U. boys, but they got the breaks, so the score was 10-6 in visitors' favor. Anyhow, I am really glad for Mr. and Mrs. Anse Cornell; the victory will put Anse strong with Pacific.

Another Basque, Louis Bideganeta, perhaps another of the first of that group to finish college, played for the Coyotes.

Gerald Wallace competed in the Rhodes Scholarship competition for Idaho, along with a candidate from the University; neither was successful. However, he and Erwin Schwiebert won the annual Walters' Debate, a contest with a cash award sponsored by a former Caldwell attorney and Assistant Secretary of the Interior. As further evidence of the continuing importance of forensics to the campus, the College sent three men to the national Phi Kappa Delta tournament in Lexington, Kentucky, in the spring of 1934.

The year 1934, was a vintage one for the C of I Pep Band. Under the direction of J. J. Smith and the leadership of student Arthur Smith, who, was also a superb track man, the Pep Band took a memorable recruiting trip through what is now called Magic Valley, visiting eighteen high schools in three days.The ever-reliable Thurlow Bryant conducted the tour, a challenging job considering the creative energy of Art Smith, Dick Karr, Harold Hultz, Ralph Cheesebrough, Bob Reed, Bob Stubblefield, Gordon Seal, George Shurtleff, Glenn Barton, Vilas Brandt, Bob Brinkley, Jim Johnston, Jim Gibson, Larry Baird, Loyal Bradley, Jim Tewell, Buddy Peery, Earl Tunison, Howard Hartman, Arthur Postlethwaite, Royal Huey, and Bob Clark. The personnel require identification because, as Bill Rankin observed earlier, these were superbly trained musicians who began instrumental public school music in the Boise Valley. The C of I Pep

Band set a standard for excellence that persisted well into the 1950s, with a tradition of playing "The Star Spangled Banner" in a unique and musically satisfying style that still lingers here and there in the Valley. You may hear it when the trumpet abandons the melody line and streaks for the stars on a high note, when the verse reaches "free," in the line "O'er the land of the free."

Although teacher training was more vocational than a liberal-arts philosophy might accommodate (a noted educator, himself the president of a liberal arts college, once reminded the audience at a C of I commencement that a liberal arts education is and ought to be "good for nothing," that is, non-vocational), such training at the Caldwell college had been almost forced upon it —not without debate—from early times simply because developing communities and their public schools needed trained faculties. The College's graduates provided the surest supply for this swelling demand.

Basque names have appeared earlier; it is appropriate here to mention representatives of another minority group at the College during these early years of the thirties. Japanese-Americans were solid members of both the College community and the regional community. Among the first, if not the first, of a long line to enroll were Henry Suyehira, Roy Hashitani, Bill Nishioka, and Martha Uyematsu. Henry, Roy, and Bill played shortstop, left field, and third base, respectively, for the Coyote baseball team. The spring of 1934 was a busy one, with drama productions, forensic competition, baseball, track, and tennis games and meets, needling by the *Coyote* editors, musical recitals, and productions far better than one might expect from a small school. The Women's Athletic Association was inspirited through participation in the tennis and archery tournaments. All in all, campus life as reflected in the *Coyote* seemed unrepressed by the Depression.

For Dr. Boone, however, this academic year might

Women's Athletic Association archers.

well have been the nadir of his presidency. Sam Cupp, a friend of many years, died in May of spotted fever, and Boone noted in his journal (May 2, 1934) the irony of a man who "had faced death many a time from man and beast" dying from the bite of a tick. By late May glaucoma had severely impaired the sight in Boone's left eye. The Blatchleys were not well; Carrie suffered a mild stroke May 27. Continuing trouble with teeth and "a flu or cold" left Boone "a bit out of order" (June 3, 1934). But Commencement on June 4, 1934, went off very well with beautiful weather "a goodly crowd.... a good ovation.... 47 grads, 4 Magna Cums, 5 Cum Laudes."

So with a temporary lift in his spirits, on June 5, 1934, Dr. Boone caught the train east to Wooster to receive an LL.D.; to Pennsylvania, for a reunion with friends and family; to New York to see daughter Sarah and her husband Oren Carter and their family, and to hear what Robert McCormick, Field Secretary, had to report; and to travel, visit, and even preach in the Upland South, Ohio, and Illinois. He arrived back in Caldwell on July 20. One must look elsewhere than in Boone's journal to find strong evidence of his depressed spirits; McCormick wrote of his talk with President Boone in Manhattan.

> A most difficult remark to unravel was made for me in Central Park in New York in the summer of 1934. Dr. Boone had said "goodbye" to the alumni of the region in a meeting of the American Museum of Natural History; he had parted for the last time, as it turned out, with his daughter Sarah and her husband, John Oren Carter of Emmett, Idaho, now a successful New York realtor. It was several hours before Dr. Boone's train would leave. We wandered into Central Park [and]...found a bench in the shade.

> For five years after the 1929 crash I had had subscriptions cancelled, or legacies dropped.... I am sure I could not hide my uneasiness about the work in the East while conditions in Idaho had grown steadily more difficult.

> It startled me and left me wondering when Dr. Boone quietly said, "My life has not meant much to me."

> Dr. Boone had reached a low point in his career when we had that conversation. His statement continued to seem enigmatic because all of us on his staff considered him highly successful....

> Only much later did I find evidence of a crushing blow to Dr. Boone's feelings when I found the payroll schedule for the year 1933-34. I had not seen the payroll...reduced by 20% all down the line....

> This record must have saddened Dr. Boone more than anything else (169-170).

Although I have been unable to find a copy of the 1933-34 payroll, one from 1932-33 is now before me. Salaries of folk employed in the public sector are and ought to be a matter of public record; taxpayers have a right to know. The other side of the coin is that salaries of folk in the private sector are, as the popular song of the 1930s had it, "nobody's doggone business but my own." Efforts to know what salaries are paid by non-public moneys ought to be resisted, for that matter of privilege is one of the differences between the public and private sectors. For these reasons I hesitate to quote the salaries of 1932-33, but few on the roster are now living.

I assume that salaries had not improved significantly from 1932-33 to 1933-34. Do with them what you will by way of upward adjustment, but then reduce them by at least 35 percent!

PAYROLL of THE COLLEGE OF IDAHO
School Year 1932-33

Administration:

Wm. J. Boone, President	$ 500.00
J. H. Lowell, Secretary & Financial Director	2,400.00
F. D. Mumford, Treasurer	1,920.00
Bess Steunenberg, Registrar	1,200.00
Ivah L. Holt, Dean of Women	1,440.00
Paul Murphy, Librarian	1,000.00
Olive T. Bess, Assistant Librarian	100.00
Rutheda Johnson, Assistant Librarian	100.00
O. J. Smith, Dean of the College	400.00
	$9,060.00

Instruction:

Wm. J. Boone, Botany	500.00
Paul Murphy, Classical Languages	1,000.00
O. J. Smith, Zoology	2,000.00
H. H. Hayman, Economics	2,000.00
F. E. Springer, Dean of Education	2,000.00
Margaret F. Nichol, Home Economics	1,200.00
J. M. Rankin, Mathematics	2,000.00
Carl E. Salomon, Dean of English	2,000.00
Sara Rankin, Spanish	800.00
Ancil K. Steunenberg, Physics	2,000.00
John D. Bell, French	1,600.00

J. H. Roblyer, Chemistry	2,000.00
J. H. Barton, Religious Education	2,000.00
E. C. Preston, History	1,600.00
Louise Blackwell, Expression	1,200.00
Anna S. Eick, [later spelled Eyck] English	1,600.00
H. P. House, Assistant Chemistry	1,600.00
S. S. Walsh, Education	1,600.00
L. A. Waterman, Sociology	1,440.00
Mary C. Allison, Assistant French	1,200.00
F. F. Beale, Glee Clubs	800.00
J. J. Smith, Orchestra, Band	640.00
A. B. Cornell, Men's Athletics & Coach	1,440.00
George R. Stovel, Intra Mural Athletics and Assistant Coach	600.00
Florence Rudger, Women's Athletics & Coach	1,200.00
Knute Ovregaard, German	1,600.00
Tom Steunenberg,Harmony,Appreciation of Music	800.00
Hazel Barnes, Assistant Classical Languages	880.00
Harold M. Tucker, Biology	1,440.00
Frances Westfall, Art, Drawing	160.00
James Millar, Dean of Religious Education	2,500.00
Elsie B. Trueblood, Assistant Home Econ.	100.00
Helen Norton, Assistant English	204.00
Daisy Linn, Assistant, Women's Athletics	204.00
	$41,828.00

Promotion:

Thurlow Bryant, Western Field Secretary	1,680.00
	$1,680.00

Grand Total	$52,568.00

When school opened in the fall, registration was down; 341 signed Dr. Boone's register, of whom 131 were freshmen; 100, sophomores; 50, juniors; and 41, seniors; with seven unclassified and six special students, this information from the *Coyote* of September 26, 1934.

From the *Directory*, which is printed two columns per page, about 6¾ inches per column with each full column containing about fifty names, it is clear that fewer matriculating students were completing their education at The College of Idaho during the Depression years. For example, in 1932 the list of graduates required some 9½ inches, the non-graduates required about 14 inches; in 1933, graduates required 7¼ inches, non-graduates 19¾ inches. The next year was nearly identical with graduates' names requiring 7¼ inches, and non-graduates requiring 19¼ inches.

But in spite of the supercooling effect of the Depression on enrollment, those students who showed up for school came with their wonted high spirits. The *Coyote* for September 26, 1934, paid judicious attention to the College's (and its President's) past with stories on Dr. Boone's return to Wooster for the fiftieth anniversary of his Class of 1884, and on the Little Theater addition of 1928 to Blatchley Hall. Other stories dealt with the decline in enrollment, with the I club's intentions to enforce the green caps rule for freshmen and nine other rules, including no smoking by students on the campus, and with the activities of the faculty over summer vacation. Coach Basler's football team, with the coach as M. C., explained football plays and fundamentals to all who wanted to take in the Wednesday evening show.

In the next issue, October 17, 1934, appeared similar stories, with added information appropriate to the intensification of school activities; Voorheesians—yes, they were so called in the twenties and thirties—had the law laid down by George Stovel, Dormitory Director: "(1) Don't bring liquor into the Dorm. (2) Try to be gentlemen at all times. (3) Keep quiet after 8:00 p.m." Finney Hall news was reported, as was the news that ninety girls were

Dr. Boone's Ford, a surprise gift from the student body.

118

recognized as members of the YWCA. The social clubs announced the pledging of thirty-nine girls and thirty-six men. (The substantives are those used by the reporter, who had not anticipated the present concern with sexist language.) The football team defeated "the highly touted College of Puget Sound," thanks to the drop-kicking skill of Mark Maxwell, and thumped Eastern Oregon.

The October 31 issue announced the organization of the College chapter of Intercollegiate Knights, an honorary service club doing what it still does today. The "Alumni News" column called attention to the large number of recent graduates who were teaching school, and the football team defeated the Twigs—The University of Idaho, Southern Branch at Pocatello,—19-14. O. J. Smith's museum, situated on the top floor of Sterry in what used to be the school's gymnasium, accessioned material from New Guinea which included two sorts of boomerangs, a "man-catcher" (you must read the description in the *Coyote*), three human skulls, a "five-pronged instrument of incantation used to dispatch victims...and vanity bags (carried by men)." The reader should be cautioned that this issue—volume XXV, No. 4, carries the date 1924 on the front page, an error corrected on subsequent pages. An editorial showing that the College was alert to national impulses and fads referred to the growing member of student protests against "R.O.T.C. units and the like."

Those who followed the College's athletic fortunes took great satisfaction in the football season; the Coyotes defeated Albion 24-0, College of Puget Sound 3-0, Eastern Oregon Normal 20-0, Albany College 20-6, U of I Southern Branch 19-14, losing to U of I (Moscow) 12-0, but defeating Whitman 26-0, and Oregon Normal (Monmouth) 31-6—the last game played before 4,500 people at Public School Field in Boise. Basler fielded a surprisingly strong team; in fact, the Coyotes looked so good that Caldwell High School star Jimmy Johnson was reported by a Coyote staffer to be considering matriculating at the C of I. However, the College's loss was a gain for the U. of Washington and, later, professional football.

In conversation with me on the occasion of honorary degrees awarded to him and his wife, Paul Tate x'26, (married Eleanor French '26) referred to the College in the terms his classmates good-naturedly employed: "Doc Boone's Marriage Mill." It is a fairly accurate description, for it is in no sense surprising that young people of courting age had a remarkable opportunity for that natural and wholesome activity. Many are the marriages between College of Idaho students; and although those contracts may not have been foreseen by the school's founders, what better place was there for the discovery of the person with whom to launch into the life after graduation, with whom, indeed, to commence the life of responsible adulthood? The stage manager in *Our*

Town, that greatest American drama, says in Act II that he is interested in how Emily and George's decision to spend a lifetime together came about:

> concerns like these are endearing ones for all who believe in family. How is it that two people, impelled to unite in marriage, find themselves facing their fiftieth wedding anniversary when the marriage seemed only yesterday?

How do such things begin?

Some of those things began under the benevolent supervision of Doc Boone and his dedicated faculty on the campus of a small but not undistinguished college, in a thriving Western American town.

With this note of seriousness, for love and marriage are serious but heaven forfend! not maudlin matters, a moment of reflection is appropriate. This chronology is now in the Academic year 1934-35. The next is, ineluctably, 1935-36, and that will be Dr. Boone's last year. I do not know how many funerals and weddings Dr. Boone conducted, although I suspect the figures exist somewhere. He will have another year and a half during which he will perform those chores. The principals in many of those marriages have within the last few years celebrated their golden wedding anniversaries; indeed, if they married at twenty-two (projecting the ordinary 18-22 college age), they would now be somewhere around seventy-six years of age, if they were members of the Class of 1935. The following lines from *Spoon River Anthology* seem appropriate to this approaching *kairos* moment for Dr. Boone, to the fullness of time which will not be denied, as we lose from sight the people whose weddings he performed.

> There is something about Death
> Like love itself!
> If with some one with whom you have known passion,
> And the glow of youthful love,
> You also, after years of life
> Together, feel the sinking of the fire,
> And thus fade away together,
> Gradually, faintly, delicately,
> As it were in each other's arms,
> Passing from the familiar room—
> That is a power of unison between souls
> Like love itself.

In spite of the emotional ebb in Central Park, Dr. Boone returned to Caldwell, worried over budgets, fished, ate good food (his zest for life is reflected in the numberless references to food, its procurement, preservation, preparation, and consumption...all described with laconic delight). Sororities and fraternities carried on in their wonted ways. Students serenaded before Christmas, as they still do. Debaters debated, editors editorialized, the latter bemoaning the apparent passing of cords—corduroy trousers—from collegiate clothes closets. (And the editor was quite wrong; cords, the dirtier the better up to a point, were a mainstay during the forties. They were sturdy until their first washing, and they could be restored to an approximation of their pressed condition by an overnight under a mattress with something between them and the bed springs.) Voorhees and Finney halls were confirmed in their pre-eminence as the oldest living quarters. So the institution that the Wood River Presbytery had established, with Boone as its first president, was moving under its own momentum. It was a college.

Over against all this, Boone continued to write in his diary, and the entries for those last months show a heightened sensitivity to the beauty of Idaho weather. It was with great relief that he returned to the aridity and cool nights of Idaho after that last sojourn in the East and South. It is possible, of course, that I attribute an awareness to him, a prescience that he did not have. And I'm sure someone will remind me that Boone was the weatherman for Caldwell and would surely be alert to weather conditions. Perhaps, but the Latin epigram from Virgil that serves as an epigraph for *My Antonia* cannot be ignored: *Optima dies...prima fugit.* The best days are the first to flee. Perhaps Boone sensed that in some respects the growing time of the institution may have coincided with his youthful vigor and zest for life, and time had diminished both.

His entry for January 31, 1935, reminds us of the world opening for us back in those years as radios brought word of the activities of the planet into our homes. From Calgary, Canada, station CFCN broadcast the old time music of Si Hawkins—"all the old hornpipes, reels, waltzes, square dances..., all too late, runs to midnight," Boone wrote. He also entered every visit of Jim and Mary Boone and their family, every visit of Babe (daughter Margaret), each visit of Margaret Sinclair. A comment on the excited conversations of these young women when they got together, or an observation on the optimism of Margaret Sinclair, was nearly always made.

Dr. Boone's energies waned—as they must for people in their seventies, as Dr. Hayman points out in his sensitive final chapter of *That Man Boone* entitled "Consummation"—at a time when the entire national system seemed to be running down. It became increasingly difficult to find money for the endowment, raise funds for operating expenses, and attract students, in spite of hard and devoted work by McCormick and Bryant and others. Entropy was setting in. Since 1933, in spite of "two successive salary cuts of twenty per cent each," the College had suffered an annual operating debt, amounting to $30,000 by the summer of 1939 (Hall, *The Small College Talks Back*, 74). (By Dr. Boone's diary the figure is thirty-five per cent, in either case a serious reduction.)

An entry in Boone's diary for January 6, 1936, is instructive. It reads, in part,

> Trustees meet in Strahorn at 2 p.m., have a goodly number. Finances the big problem. Some talk about the merger with Gooding [College], nothing definite.

Gooding College, founded with the blessing of the Methodist Church, did not survive, and the proposed merger came to naught. Indeed, the Depression was having its baneful effects.

On February 28, Boone recorded the following:

> Trustees meet at 2 p.m. First, a special committee meeting.... Then 2 p.m. a 4½ hour meeting, same place with near a full board of trustees.... The toughest meet since 1909 and 1910. School low ebb, especially in finances. Not much show for any money or real stability. If the M.E's come in may possibly become stabilized. Locked horns on athletics and Bible.

Carrie Blatchley

The life of the College seemed tenuous, and old timers identified with the College's founding were dying off: Dr. Joseph Barton died on February 2, 1936, and Julia Finney, retired and in California, died February 20. Sara Rankin, who died August 18, 1990, at 103, remembered Julia Finney as a power on campus, one to whom you listened (tape II 00058 "RAN" Caldwell Public Library

Oral History Interviews). A "dumpy" little "woman," ordinarily quiet Miss Finney nevertheless had a quick wit and a soft chuckle. "She was an encyclopedia," Professor Rankin recalled. "And she was a good businesswoman." It is interesting for the historian to hear Professor Rankin describe Professor Finney as "one of the old timers," but it is true that she was of the original college faculty, predating Professor Rankin by thirteen years or so.

Montie Gwinn had died November 16, 1935, and the will that directed certain funds to go to the College and to Carrie Blatchley, his sister, was vigorously contested by his widow with the result costing the College considerably. The old college community was suffering some serious losses.

Still, the students came to the College, albeit in smaller numbers, and they were actively determined to be collegiate. The *Coyote* of November 6, 1938, listed thirty-three separate student organizations, complete with the roster of officers: 106 of them, with some duplication. Students could not know the despair that wrung the hearts of the trustees and the faculty as the academic year 1935-36 came to a close with the future of the College in grave doubt. Forty-two seniors received their degrees at Commencement on June 8, 1936, according to the last *Coyote* of the year.

One month later, Dr. Boone died, and an epoch if not an era ended.

I have said before that it is not my present task to write a biography of Boone, but in writing the history of this school I have watched that life become so enmeshed in the College that it is nearly impossible to dissociate the institution from the lengthened shadow cast by this man.

A story that appeared in The New York Times for Saturday, July 1, 1936, reads as follow:

> Dr. William Judson Boone, oldest college president in point of service in the United States, who founded the College of Idaho and had just completed forty-five college years of service at that institution died of heart failure at the college town of Caldwell, Idaho, on Wednesday, it was learned here yesterday. He was 75 years old.

> Dr. Boone, whose life as a pioneer, preacher, educator and natural scientist has become almost legendary, was an important figure in the life of the "intermountain" valley. He was taken ill on the campus of the college he founded.

> A descendant of Daniel Boone, the divinity student and college president was born in Canonsburg, Washington County, Pa. He attended Elder's Ridge Academy and was graduated from Wooster College. Following family tradition, he studied at Western Theological Seminary and was ordained in the Presbyterian ministry in 1887. The

same year he married Annie E. Jamison of Pittsburgh, and under the presbyterian Home Missions auspices they left for the West, settling at Caldwell, where they founded the First Presbyterian Church, for many years a practically interdenominational seat of the community's religious and civic interest.

Assiduously preoccupied with the duties of his [college] administration, he found time to increase his influence in many related fields of interest, particularly in botany and paleobotany. He went into the same field for his hobby, the culture of roses, his own garden claiming some 225 varieties, including one which horticulturists named the "Doctor Boone rose."

He returned to Wooster for Master's and Doctor of Divinity degrees and the fiftieth reunion of his class there brought him an honorary LL.D. in 1934.

In 1931, on the occasion of his fortieth anniversary as the college's president, a resolution of the Presbyterian General Assembly noted that he had "declined high political and educational preferment at the hands of the State in order to devote his life to the building of a Christian College. Under his prayerful and sacrificial leadership the institution has grown from a feeble school in the sagebrush to a Class A, fully accredited college, and an incalculable blessing to the young people of the far Northwest."

In 1914 Dr. Hayman's championship debate team included, left to right, William Runciman, Roscoe Steffan Turner, and Haven Goodrich.

> Dr. Boone was a Mason, a Kiwanian and a member of the American Geographical Society, the American Forestry Association and the Botanical Society of America.

His institution grew into an authentic college as he nourished those three sources of energy without which no independent institution of higher learning can survive. He recruited; the student body numbered at peak enrollment more than 400, a figure reached through the efforts of many, but he was behind those efforts. But since student tuition and fees never pay the cost, Boone was always there to hold out his hat and to encourage the efforts of Robert McCormick, Thurlow Bryant, and others in the unending task of annual solicitation for current operating expenses. And his work on the third source of energy so necessary to the health of a private school, the endowment, led to an accumulation of slightly more than $500,000.

And what had the school produced? Josh Lowell '27 and Jim Lyke '28 went into professional baseball; Elmo Smith '33 and Bob Smylie '38 into governors' mansions; Roscoe Turner (or Steffen: he used both names) and Ralph King into distinguished careers in the teaching and practice of law. The list could be extended to include medicine, scientific research, teaching, and public service. Dr. Hayman summarized to Boone's educational philosophy thus, and it is cited here as a tribute to the man:

> Boone's thought of education was the value that an education would give the one who was in possession of it, not so much in helping you get a job nor in having a high salary but in the pure satisfaction of knowledge and understanding and appreciation of...truth. Such understanding...one carries with him at all times. (207)

Thus for Boone how one earned a **living** was not the primary task with which a college education was concerned; rather it was how one **lived** a life.

The gap left by this man's death created a void, and the problem of filling that void exceeded the worst imaginings of the college community.

Main Street, Caldwell, and the Springer Residence (17th and Cleveland), about 1930.

Part II

The Smith–Leach–Smith Interregnum   1936-1939

*The original
Finney Parlor.*

CHAPTER EIGHT

C. latrans Dormant

The campus, the community, and the region were devastated by the death of the only president the College had ever known. Even the Eastern press noted the passing of this singular man. It is an effort to find a shorthand expression for Boone's forty-five year presidency, but the word that comes most readily to mind is "integrity." He had it by the ton or the erg or joule, however integrity may be measured, and his individual probity was infused into the College and institutionalized.

Beyond that, Boone loved the region—not just southwestern Idaho but eastern Oregon as well, for his out-of-doors knew no state boundaries. This love led to field trips, forays striking a responsive chord in Orma J. Smith and later in J.H. Roblyer. Together they created a tradition of using the region as a laboratory that completely captivated Harold Tucker, Lyle Stanford, and a host of other students (not all of them in the sciences). This tradition bore most of the responsibility for the institutionalization of regional matters under the aegis of the College's Regional Studies Center in 1971.

What was it that Boone had invested his life in?

At the time of his death, the faculty numbered thirty-one: Boone himself; Paul Murphy, Greek, Latin; O. J. Smith, Biology; H. H. Hayman, Economics; Francis E. Springer, Education; Margaret Nichol, Home Economics; Joseph M. Rankin, Mathematics; Frederick F. Beale, Piano, Organ, Harmony; Carl Salomon, English (the lone Ph.D.); Sara Rankin, Spanish; Frances O. Westfall, Art; Ancil K. Steunenberg, Physics; John D. Bell, French; J. J. Smith, Orchestra and Band; J. H. Roblyer, Chemistry; Anna S. Eyck, English; Elford Chilcote Preston, History; Mary Louise Blackwell, Expression; Mary Clara Allison, French; H. P. House, Chemistry; Stephen S. Walsh, Education; Lloyd

Waterman, Education, Sociology; Knute Ovregaard, German; Harold Tucker, Botany, Zoology; Thomas B. Steunenberg, Music; George R. Stovel, Physical Education; Loren Basler, Dean of Men, Coach; Olive T. Bess, English, Librarian.

Listed in the Catalog of 1935-1936 (Announcements 1936-37, Vol. 45, No. 1) were the following "Officers of Administration and Promotion": William Judson Boone, President; Herbert H. Hayman, Syndic of the Campus; Robert R. McCormick, Field Secretary and Vice President; Paul Murphy, Custodian of the Library; Orma J. Smith, Dean, Curator of the Museum; Bess Steunenberg, Registrar; Ivah L. Holt, Dean of Women; J. H. Lowell, General Financial Director and Secretary to the Board of Trustees; Frank D. Mumford, Treasurer; Carrie S. Blatchley, Custodian of Blatchley Hall; Thurlow Bryant, Field Representative. To go about the work of the campus, these were divided into nine standing committees, a listing of which would seem strange to contemporary academics but which met the needs of the school in 1936.

The Board of Trustees consisted of seventeen individuals, most of whom were local and many of whom had enjoyed a long-standing connection with the College. It would have been difficult to find a cadre of trustees more loyal to the College, and indeed that quality as much as any other may well have been prerequisite to candidacy for membership on the board. It is quite true, too, that some of them were people of affairs—former governor Baldridge, C. C. Anderson, Judge John C. Rice, Robert E. Strahorn, and John F. MacLane of New York City. But most of them were local people: William E. Welsh, Boise; Rev. William Crosby, Caldwell; J. M. Thompson, Caldwell; Mary E. Kirkpatrick, Parma; Montie B. Gwinn, Boise; James L. Boone, Boise; Walter E. Kerrick, Parma; and John P. Congdon, Boise. It was a concerned board but a board with limited financial clout, at least as that quality is measured today. Consequently, the fiscal weakness of the College was beyond its collective power to remedy.

As to the curriculum of the College, it was strikingly close to that under which the institution had been first accredited. Four groups of subjects had been declared as the areas of study from which work must be taken in order that a student might be liberally—broadly—educated and within which a major must be declared, in order that the student might be certified as possessing special and detailed learning in a particular discipline. This quadrivium consisted of the Literature and Language group, the Philosophical and Social Science group, the Science and Mathematics group, and the Additional Subjects group.

Requirements for graduation from the College were tied to admission requirements. For example, to be graduated from the College, students were required to have a minimum of sixteen semester hours of one language. Those who had taken two years of a language in high school could meet this requirement by taking one more year of that language in college. Additional general graduation requirements included English composition, science and mathematics (also articulated with high school credits), history, and Bible. Finally, after meeting the requirements for a major and a minor field of study, the student had to present a college career of regular and prompt attendance at classes, of good behavior, and of acceptable academic standing (GPA).

Majors could be taken in fifteen academic disciplines: Biology-Botany, Biology-Zoology, Chemistry, Economics, Education, English, French, History, Latin, Mathematics, Music, Philosophy, Physics, Political Science, and Religious Education.

A brief look at admissions requirements will help complete the outline of the College that Boone had headed for nearly half a century. The following appears on pages twelve and thirteen of the Catalog cited earlier:

> Applicants for admission to the College are expected to present fifteen units of secondary school work from an accredited four-year high school, or twelve units from an accredited three-year senior high school. A unit represents credit for a subject pursued for at least forty-five minutes five times per week for a year of not less than thirty-six weeks, or an equivalent amount of work.
>
> When fifteen units are presented, eleven of these must be selected from the following subjects: English, history, mathematics, foreign language, and natural science with laboratory. (Laboratory science must be chosen from the following: biology, botany, zoology, chemistry, physics.)
>
> When twelve units from a senior high school are presented, nine must be selected from the academic subjects mentioned. If less than eleven in the one instance or less than nine in the other be presented, the deficiency must be made up without college credit in the ratio of four semester hours (college) for each unit of deficiency.
>
> It is desired that the units be distributed as follows:
>
> | | Units |
> | ------- | ----- |
> | English | 3 |
> | History | 2 |
> | Algebra | 1 |

Geometry	1
Foreign Language	2
Natural Science (biology, botany, zoology, chemistry, physics)	2
	11
Electives: Subjects exclusive of physical education accepted by an accredited high school toward graduation	4
TOTAL	15

In case fewer units in history, foreign language or natural science be presented, then additional work in these subjects must be taken in college during the Freshman or Sophomore year, for which college credit will be given, provided the full entrance requirements pertaining to the number of units previously mentioned have been met. Deficiencies in English, algebra, and geometry must be made up without credit.

CREDENTIALS

FRESHMAN STANDING

Applicants for admittance to the Freshman class must present at the Registrar's office an official statement from the secondary school, showing the units of work completed. The Idaho state uniform Principal's Certificate of Recommendation must be used for this purpose. This statement should be in the office of the Registrar on or before September 1 for first semester registration, and on or before January 1 for second semester registrations. No Freshman may register before such statement is received by the Registrar.

To this information should be added Boone's personal philosophy of college admissions, a principle that to a degree still operates in our admissions strategies. Dr. Hayman quotes Professor Murphy on this point:

Toward the individual student his [Boone's] attitude was one of the utmost consideration. None should be rejected, provided he showed the ability to learn and willingness to work (162).

This was a philosophy of inclusion, not exclusiveness. Let the students come, he seemed to say, and we'll see what they can do. It is a precept that has paid off in countless instances that cannot be documented, but former Admissions Director Bob Post has cited a specific instance that is arresting. A certain student had applied for admission and presented a spotty high school record and generally indifferent admissions credentials. However, the Admissions Committee took a letter of recommendation seriously and decided to admit the lad: "Let him come and we'll see what he can do." He became a Rhodes Scholar.

This, then, was the College and this a tiny scrap of the educational philosophy of a man who liked cats, who had four at different times that he named Mogul (I,II,III,IV), who knew the nephew of Jane Welsh Carlyle (a stockman-farmer named Thomas Welsh in the Big Bend Country west of Roswell; Boone presided at the wedding of Mary Welsh and Charles W. Powell in that Eastern Oregon setting). A man completely without pretension, Boone left shoes difficult to fill.

Nineteen thirty-six had dealt harshly with the College. Boone was gone. Henry Blatchley a trustee, benefactor, and librarian, died in September. J. J. Smith, much respected musician and music teacher, died in November after a year's illness, succumbing to multiple sclerosis. Reluctant to act, unsure of any future for the College, and generally dispirited, the Trustees decided not to hire a new president but to place the management of the institution in the hands of a devoted and excellent teacher, Orma J. Smith, the closest to an alter-president available. If the College survived, the Trustees would have a year, at least, to seek a replacement for Dr. Boone.

O.J. Smith: biologist by choice, acting president by necessity.

Many graduates of the College whose careers overlapped the brief administration of President Raymond Leach have said that no one could have replaced Dr. Boone, and certainly not Leach. From the distance time has provided, it is easy to agree. His administration was quite without integrity. But an epigraph supplied by Robert McCormick is cautionary: it is from George Santayana, who advised, "Respect the past...knowing that it was once all that was humanly possible."

Let casuists argue whether Leach's tenure was the best that could have been at that moment.

Dean Smith was identified by a reporter for the *Coyote* (September 18, 1936) as the "head of the institution, in fact if not in name." By this the reader is to understand that John C. Rice, Chairman of the Board of Trustees, became acting head of the institution but that the real chief executive was O. J. Smith.

The year began, in stock market parlance, mixed. Enrollment was low (340 students); the Beta Chi Fraternity sought its old identity and petitioned Theta Kappa Nu to suspend the charter; Peter Kim, Caldwell swimming instructor and assistant Caldwell High School coach, returned to Hawaii to teach; Pat Page, distinguished University of Chicago athlete and assistant coach under Alonzo Stagg, replaced Loren Basler as the Director of Athletics and coach; and new faculty members were hired. In addition to Page, Conan E. Mathews, art; Viola Springer, music; and a little Scot named John L. Anderson, religion, were hired. Mathews stayed only three years; Springer and Anderson stayed over ten years and distinguished themselves. Page's bright record sustained him two years. Lorn Christensen replaced Tom Steunenberg in the music program, Steunenberg having served since 1930. Perhaps one word that summarizes the **zeitgeist** on the campus is **change**.

Surely one of the highlights of the Fall Semester was the Peace Conference on the campus in October, featuring Senators James Pope and William Borah and Justice Givens of the Idaho Supreme Court. Recollections of visits of Charles Alexander Eastman and Vachel Lindsay connect with the visits of the foregoing distinguished citizens and serve to point out that the College has, from time to time, basked in the glory reflected by authentic luminaries.

If change seemed the order of the day, there was also continuity. The "old" faculty, the heart of the College, stayed intact. Their names need not be mentioned here. One of the senior members of the College community, however, did not survive the year of her husband's death. Anna Jamison Boone, widow of Dr. Boone, died on January 30, 1937, as a result of a fall in a New York subway station, according to the *Coyote* of February 12. She died at

74, having lived in Caldwell since November 9, 1887, and having been a supporter of the Presbyterian Church, The College of Idaho, and numerous civic, cultural, and social groups.

Continuity was apparent, too, in the customary activities of debate, music programs, school elections—all those collegiate matters that had evolved as the institution claimed its place in the world of higher education. Change, however, was noted when a story in the February 26, 1937, *Coyote* discussed the National Youth Administration and its program of federal financial assistance for college students. This was the first time that College of Idaho students were beneficiaries of tax money, and this measure by the New Deal was of material benefit to both student and college. Although the *Coyote* does not specify when NYA assistance arrived on campus, I infer from a publication entitled *An Evaluation of the NYA College Work Program* (Federal Security Agency, National Youth Administration for Idaho, 1941), prepared under the leadership of William W. Gartin and published in 1941, that the program had been operating since 1936 (6).

Mrs. Anna Jamison Boone, bottom row, center, in a photograph of the Caldwell Art Study Group. Information on the back of the photo is as follows: "Organized and led by Mrs. H. D. Blatchley, about 1900. A sort of forerunner of the Chautauqua Circle. From left, back row: Mrs. Roop, Mrs. Hay, Mrs. Egleston, Mrs. Dille. Center row, Mrs. Pinney, Mrs. Foote, Mrs. Morrison, Mrs. Olmstead. Front row, Mrs. A. K. Steunenberg, Mrs. Boone, Mrs. Blatchley."

A furor in a teacup erupted in the spring of 1937 when Coach Page won his pout with a special committee appointed by the Board of Trustees. It agreed to try to finance athletics at a higher level than had been done heretofore, after Page left town for California, dissatisfied with the status quo. In addition to trying to finance the athletic program in a manner more acceptable to Page, the Trustees, alumni, and local businessmen named alumnus George Stovel as Graduate Athletic Manager (all this in the *Coyote* for March 12 and 26).

The ever-active Pep Band announced a second frolic, a show featuring C of I talent, highlighted by the performance of an eighteen-piece dance orchestra playing, according to director Earl Tunison, "the latest...hits from *On the Avenue* and *Stowaway*." About seventy-five students were involved in the production (*Coyote*, March 12, 1937). News of another kind of show appeared in the *Coyote* of March 26 in the form of an account of Miss Harriett Holverson, Ring Sorority, who would compete for the Miss Idaho title and the right to represent the Gem State in the Miss Western America contest (*Coyote*, March 26, 1937).

But the big news came in an extra of the *Coyote* on April 9: Raymond M. Leach of New York City was chosen by the Trustees to serve as the second president of The College of Idaho. Identified as a "graduate of Oberlin with a broad background of educational and administrative experience...with graduate work at Stanford, Columbia, and at New York University where he is now completing his Ph.D. degree," Leach was reported to have served two years as president of Trinity University (Texas). (This big news muted a story of a different sort that called attention to the major fire at Caxton's Printers, Ltd., on March 17 that set back the publication date of the *Trail*.) More ink was spread for President Leach in the April 16 *Coyote*, byline Washington, D.C. If the story is authentic and not a delayed April Fool's gag nor the product of Leach's own public relations campaign, Senators Pope and Borah, of Idaho; Copeland, of New York; and McCarran of Nevada rhapsodized about him. Other political figures and functionaries were also reported to have approved of the appointment in language intemperately encomiastic.

The real accomplishments on the campus that year were not presidential but political (Bob Smylie and Bill Young appeared as comets), musical (the Pep Band show was a remarkable endeavor, and Beale's *Fatima* has already been identified as a winner), and social (Myra Tella, Sigma Epsilon, Ring, Finney and Voorhees—all were vibrating with activity).

Among the 171 freshmen who registered in September of 1937 were some true exotics: Betty Reed, New York City; Franklin Dog Eagle, a Sioux from McLaughlin, South Dakota, who came "to play football on the Coyote squad";

Douglas Anderson, Valparaiso, Indiana (by way of the CCC and the baseball diamond); Franz Hertrich and John Ellington, Pomona, California; Fabian Joyal, Nevada City, California; Alice Davis, Olympia, Washington; and Louise Hefner, from Ohio (The *Coyote* of September 24, 1937, doesn't say what town in the Buckeye state. It was Lafayette.) Thirty-six freshman students came from Caldwell, thirty from Nampa, and fifteen from Boise. Other regional towns well represented were Meridian, Parma, Shoshone, Payette, Wilder, Jerome, Middleton, New Plymouth, Cambridge, New Meadows, Weiser, Twin Falls, Wendell, Eagle, Ontario, Buhl, Homedale, Mountain Home, Council, Nyssa, Ustick, Collister, Prairie City (Oregon), Preston, Montpelier, Huston, Idaho Falls, and Jordan Valley—83 men, 88 women.

Meriting a banner headline on the front page of the *Coyote* of October 1, 1937, was the Myra Tella alumnae gift of $1,000 to be applied toward the purchase of a pipe organ for the William Judson Boone Memorial Chapel "to be built on the campus [behind] Voorhees Hall, at a similar angle from Sterry Hall as is Strahorn Library.... Plans were begun last spring to construct the chapel and have progressed rapidly."

Gossip columns in the *Coyote* were filled with who was dating whom, who had been cut out by whom, contemporary scenes and events introduced by topical gags such as "Knock! Knock!" jokes, and jokes borrowed from the humor columns of exchange newspapers. Some of these are marvelously witty and humorous, by any standard.

On page three of the *Coyote* (October 1, 1937) in a short three inch story appeared news of the visit of yet another dignitary. One can only speculate about the planning that got Franklin D. Roosevelt to stop on the C of I campus on a trip whose destination was Owyhee Dam, a regional showplace. The tour also took the President to Wilder, where the Peckham onion crop had been harvested in such a way that the onion crop still in rows looked twice as plentiful as it really was. A folklorist might call attention here to the old settler-city slicker tale type, in which the settler pulls the wool over the city slicker's eyes in the form of a practical joke, although the joke is only marginally successful because the slicker never knows that he has been tricked. At least it is doubtful that F.D.R. ever knew the truth about the Peckham onion crop.

Faculty committees were relatively few: the Committee on Curriculum, Courses, Schedules, and Credits; the Athletic Committee; the Committee on Religious Life; the Committee on Literary and Forensic Activities; the Committee on Student Publications; the Social Committee; the Scholastic Accreditation Committee; the Buildings Committee; the Attendance Committee; the

Placement Committee; the Counseling Committee; the Student Affairs Committee; and the Inauguration Committee. Of these thirteen committees, one was obviously an *ad hoc* group, for the inauguration of a new president is a sometime thing. Twelve committees, then, were adequate for the needs of The College of Idaho, all filled by appointment by the chief executive.

The *Coyote* of October 29, 1937, was enhanced by the publication of a letter to Carolee Purton, the editor, from a distinguished and long standing supporter and trustee, Robert E. Strahorn. The first paragraph read:

> I cannot resist rejoicing with you and expressing my appreciation of your enterprise in announcing the several important voluntary additions to College of Idaho equipment and adornments. Surely your interesting news features should revive and enthuse the spirit of contribution in others along the many lines the College could so well absorb.

He continued his extensive remarks by praising the Myra Tella organ gift and the gift of a pulpit by the 1937 graduating class, a gift also intended for the memorial chapel to be built in honor of Dr. Boone. It is quite true that the College held a special place in the affections of this man until he too passed on.

November and December were difficult months for the College family. District Judge John C. Rice, chairman of the College's Board of Trustees, died in November. He had served on the first faculty of the College, was one of the incorporators in 1893, and had continued to serve as a trustee. And in December, Carrie Gwinn Blatchley (Mrs. Henry) died. An Idaho pioneer, she moved from Iowa to Idaho in 1870, settling in Caldwell in 1885. She was one of the College's first teachers and one of its fondest benefactors. She and Henry had given the College the original twenty acres of the second (present) campus, the wooded triangle (where sparking couples were wont to park after automobiles became portable courting parlors), and, of course, Blatchley Hall and the Blatchley house just east of the Hall.

Leach's inauguration was given a significant amount of space, as college dignitaries, domestic and exotic, spoke, welcomed, received, invoked, addressed, installed, prayed, and banqueted. The last named activity cost seventy-five cents a plate, and the committee in charge was under the efficient chairmanship of alumnus Robert Troxell, class of 1930.

Radio Station KIDO proved interested in the College and in quality broadcasts and so arranged to feature The College of Idaho Men's Quartet in a series of the broadcasts. The quartet consisted of some of the finest voices in the region: Ronald Street, tenor; Robert Biggs, tenor; Harold Schwiebert, baritone; Leland Goodell, bass.

Many C of I students from the '30s and '40s will remember Sunday evening vespers under the stimulating leadership of John L. Anderson. This weekly opportunity to reflect and to refect in the gloaming of a Sunday was a popular activity, and many pre-ministerial students and aspiring church musicians had opportunities to perfect their marketable skills in the friendly environment of Blatchley Hall. It was, moreover, like the camp meeting that the King and Huck "worked"—an opportunity for young folks to court on the sly.

J. H. Lowell, who for thirty years had served as a trustee, asked to be relieved of his duties as Financial Director of the College, although he agreed to continue as trustee and secretary, according to the *Coyote* of January 14, 1938. Vacating the Director's post left an opening that no one could fill in quite the same way, for he was one of the truly knowledgeable individuals in all matters respecting regional economics.

Some of the popular songs of the time seem particularly apposite to the unsteady nature of the Leach administration—"Once in a While," "There's a Lull in My Life," "You're Out in the Cold Again," "Dark on Observatory Hill," "Smoke Dreams," and perhaps "The Merry-Go-Round Broke Down." But his departure is still four months away, and the College was behaving pretty much the way a college should at the tail end of the Depression. Norval Heath was elected student body president, Reed Sower directed another delightful Pep

John Rice

J. H. Lowell

Band show; the Pep Band itself chartered a Union Pacific stage (bus) and offered consistently excellent musicianship to the region. Though J. J. Smith had died, his legacy continued to sustain the Pep Band for a number of years.

Although it is tempting to publish the entire program of the Pep Band Show for 1938, that artifact must be pushed aside so that another element can be summoned to suggest the **zeitgeist** of that happy time. I refer to the 1938 *Trail.*

Under the editorship of Harold Schwiebert and business management of Robert Smylie, the *Trail* was an uptown book. This annual publication had ceased to be an obligation of the junior class; since it had become a student body publication, the year of its appearance was also the year of the graduation of the senior class. The 1938 *Trail* celebrated the graduating senior class of 1938.

Replete with photos of the campus, Betty Co-eds and Joe Colleges (this language from the *Trail*) walking, sitting, posing, appearing candidly, the yearbook projects a campus that would look familiar to a graduate of the Class of 1988. Students dressed neatly if not nattily, with short hair for men and women, ties or open-necked sport shirts for men and skirts and sweaters a popular garb for women.

After about a dozen pages of synopsized history, dedication, foreword, and memorial message, the *Trail* features a photograph of a handsome film star autographed with "Best wishes to the Staff, The Trail 1938" by the star himself, Tyrone Power. A letter to Robert Smylie dated February 17, 1938, and signed by Mr. Power graciously and gracefully put into context his reluctance to serve as judge for the beauty contest that would pick from six lovely coeds the one to be honored as sweetheart of The College of Idaho. But serve he did, however unwilling a Paris he might have been, and Elizabeth Hawkes, "lovely, charming, intelligent," was named over Helen Hoskins, Dorothy Lawson, Elouise Mackey, and Lona Jean Stewart. Elizabeth was the only one of the roster to finish her degree, graduating in the Class of 1940 with a major in French.

Indeed, the students in the 1938 annual matched the campus for attractiveness, and a visitor from a small planet looking at the photographic evidence of both must surely have concluded, "This, indeed, is veritably a neat place with handsome denizens." A list would be unfair, for omissions are odious but when shall we see the likes of Norval Heath, Reed Sower, Bob Haddock, Ace Coulter, Buck Selders, Jim Tewell, Leland Goodell, Art Van Slyke, Everett Van Slyke,...or the entire I club...or Shield...or YWCA again? The question is not rhetorical; the answer is "Next year in the 1939 *Trail!*"

This was also the year the trustees did the right thing by naming the athletic field for its creator: "**Be it resolved** that the Board of Trustees of The College of Idaho hereby name and designate the athletic field of the College 'Hayman Field' in honor of Dr. H. H. Hayman," (*Coyote*, March 18, 1938).

The Caldwell *News-Tribune* carried news of great national and international significance during the 1937-38 school year, and news of significance to the College as well. Western Oregonians threatened to break up the Northwest Conference because of "discrepancy" [disparity] of size among the members—Whitman formerly 400 now 800; Albany College, 150 now 200; Willamette, 350 now 800, Puget Sound 250 now 750, Pacific University 220 now 280, C of I 300 now 450, Linfield (now out of the league) 150 now 585—according to Coach Folgate of Pacific University as he compared growth from 1926 to 1937. Other stories featured the accomplishments of a good C of I basketball team—Ace Coulter, Doug Anderson, Bob Haddock, Franklin Dog Eagle, Walt Long, John De Geus, and Delbert Burkhalter. Pleasant news dealt with the wedding of former student Martha Uyematsu and George Nishitani, performed by H. H. Hayman with Dr. Carl Salomon as vocalist and Thomas Nishitani serving as best man.

And 1938 saw the resignations of Coach Page and of Dr. Springer, who had served the College for thirty-two years. Indeed, it was a tough year on many colleges: Gooding College closed in the spring. However, the story carried in the June 25 News-Tribune was more than a bit shocking. Former governor H. C. Baldridge, Chairman of the Board of Trustees was surprised by the resignation of President Leach:

> Leach's resignation was unexpected by me. His resignation is entirely voluntary, and I regret to have him leave us.... I have been reliably informed that he will go to New York soon to continue his educational work.

The causes impelling the separation are difficult to discern at this distance but the following seem not unlikely.

The first two causes appeared in an undated missive from Marian Munro Frahm, 1938, an English major, titled "The Presidents of The College of Idaho."

> Dr. Raymond Hotchkiss Leach became president our senior year.

> Dr. Leach went on our senior sneak—I don't know who invited him—in an open farm truck to Lowman. Not only did he keep us waiting a half hour to start our trip, he came dressed in a business suit, (complete

with hat and tie). Then he made the truck stop at every little town between Eagle and Gardena to solicit money for The College of Idaho.

Not long after that Dr. Hayman started our economics class talking about gutter references, a rather out of order subject, but knowing our professor we listened because there was always a punch line to follow. It seems that the Board had not verified "Dr." Leach's references before

Raymond Hotchkiss Leach, second president of The College of Idaho.

142

they hired him and they were all false. Dr. Leach would not attend our graduation because he had been escorted to the train the night before.

Leach, then, appeared socially maladroit, offending students by practicing mendicancy on what should have been a joyous occasion. Further, he appeared to be guilty of mendacity in respect to unsubstantiated references, perhaps the product of his own personal news bureau. Finally, I suspect the chore of raising money for the projected (as per Caldwell *News-Tribune*, February 28, 1938 and *Coyote*, March 4, 1938) William Judson Boone Memorial Science Hall—a lordly sum of $100,000 (*Tribune*) or $150,000 (*Coyote*) may have been more of a task than President Leach felt he could manage. The record of his administration concludes abruptly with the effective date of his resignation, June 30.

Whether institutions can breathe collective sighs of relief is arguable. Something close to that must have been sent heaven-ward when the running of the College was returned to Orma J. Smith for the academic year 1938-1939. The rise in spirits at the College was matched by the slow retreat of the Depression. Though not over yet, it nevertheless had lost its severity. One piece of evidence adduced to support that assertion was the improvement in enrollment. The *Coyote* of September 23, 1938, announced the largest enrollment ever—488 students, a fine number indeed. Moreover, three new faculty members were hired—one of them, Coach Clem Parberry, to establish himself as one of the successful coaches in the Northwest Conference. Finally, progress was apparent in reconstituting the Board of Trustees of the College with the naming of Hugh Caldwell, prominent Caldwell attorney; D. L. McBane, Nampa; Edgar L. Oakes, Caldwell; and Dr. C. E. Palmer, Ontario, Oregon. These facts comprise the first bracket around the academic year 1938-39; the closing bracket is the appointment of the College's third president, Dr. W. W. Hall, Jr., an authentic administrator whose presidency advanced the College toward the maturity it finally achieved under Tom E. Shearer.

Coeds with culotte, c. 1930-35

Interclub Council, 1939-40: Front, left to right, Norma Farmer, Anna Stein, Maxine Souer, Elizabeth Hawks, Barbara Graham; middle, Angus McDonald, Don Colver, Reed Souer, Delbert Burkhalter, Gordon Barrett; back, Eloise Heath, Lee Nackleby, Marjorie Mabbott, Irene Estes.

Part III

William Webster Hall, Jr., 1939-1947

B.A. (Princeton), B.D. (Union Theological Seminary),

Ph.D. (Yale)

The third College president, Dr. William Webster Hall, photograph from the early 1960s.

CHAPTER NINE

C. latrans Redux

The condition of the institution improved under the capable administration of a genial Easterner who was pointed toward the College by Dr. C. C. McCracken of the Department of Colleges of the Presbyterian Board of Christian Education. But the matter is not so simple as that. The school revived, nearly (oh so very nearly!) died, but rebounded again. It was an exciting period in the continuing story of The College of Idaho.

The comets had disappeared into the outer darkness of law school (they would return), the Depression edged away slightly, and the way seemed clear for a new president to show what he could do.

A student who had matriculated in the fall of 1938 or 1939 might look somewhat like the following. You might know someone like this from Jordan Valley or Midvale or Weiser. Irrespective of gender, the student would have come from a family that knew what hard work was and was suffering from the Depression. The student had grown up having to work and contributing substantially to the maintenance of the family. The student would have had considerable anxiety about the wisdom of the undertaking, of being out of what little job market there was for two years (many who wanted to teach could do so with two years of college) or for the terribly remote four-year degree. If the student thought of graduate or professional school, the dark tunnel must have seemed endless with no terminal illumination.

But the student was resolute, though daunted, and fully prepared to work for self-support and tuition money through college. Faced with the following costs per semester, the student must have felt sorely tried:

double room $30.00
room deposit 1.00

table board	72.00
registration fee	6.25
student body fee	6.25
tuition (10-17 hrs.)	50.00
final examination fee.	.50
change of course after 1st week	1.00
a variety of fees	7.50
	$174.50

To meet these costs, which did not include books, transportation, and such miscellaneous expenses as health care and recreation, the student might find a campus job (and such jobs have not changed remarkably over the years) or undertake work in the community, with the full realization that academic success might well be compromised by the sacrifice of time and energy to the job.

One young man hitchhiked to Caldwell from his home, saving the expense of commercial travel for the seventy or so miles. He did not own a car; it would have been awkward to travel horseback. He got a job at Robb's Toggery for after school and Saturdays, and such other times as he could manage. He persuaded the proprietor to permit him to sleep on a cot in the backroom, saving the expense of a dormitory room. As he developed a regimen for work and study, he discovered, over the course of time, that the bus depot could use custodial services, so he arranged with Josh Lowell to clean and mop between 4 a.m. and his 8 o'clock class. I might add that included in his course of study—not the first and second years—were comparative anatomy and embryology. He was also a leader in student government.

It is always deceiving—now and in any era—to draw comparisons between our predecessors and our descendants, for it is tempting to attribute self-conscious fortitude to the former and self-indulgent sybaritic behavior to the latter. The truth might well be that formerly society required fortitude, and latterly society accommodates indulgence. The personal will, perhaps, has little to do with the matter, and this study is not calculated to solve that problem but rather to show the state of things and the kinds of students here when W. W. Hall, Jr. arrived.

There is no question that Dr. Hall was an authentic college president. The truth of that statement is borne out in many ways, but I shall detail five: his success in fund raising, without which no president can make the grade; his success in improving faculty salaries and bringing a retirement plan to the faculty; his great success, or perhaps great good fortune, in making quality faculty appointments; and in reaffirming the will of the College to be an

148

authentic institution of higher learning. However, his signal success lay in keeping the school alive during World War II. The student body numbered 419 by the October shakedown date, having dropped from the initial and premature figures which the *Coyote* of September 24, 1939, declared "the record high" in the College's 49 years. Dr. Hall was deeply gratified by that figure and explained that it represented "not so much...the increment of new students as...a proportional gain in returning former students...." Attrition seemed to be allayed, an indication that the Depression was beginning to wane. So the enrollment figures bolstered the new (and young, he was only 35) president. He was further encouraged and advised by O. J. Smith, of the College faculty, and C. J. Strike, of Idaho Power. Though not the only sources of help, certainly, these two stood out in Hall's mind, and he dedicated his delightful *The Small College Talks Back* (1951) to their memory. To this book, the present chapter owes a great deal, and the citations refer to it as *College*. It should be read by all who are curious about Hall's background.

With characteristic wit and a gracefulness of style surely caught rather than taught, Dr. Hall declared that the ideal person to tell the story of the small, independent but church-related College was the man from Mars: "Someone from New York City and points east [might] qualify as a second choice." And he must have felt that he was an outsider much if not most of his successful administration. Nothing in his formal training had prepared him for the American West; that he came to love the region and to discern its great promise is therefore a tribute to a resilient character and genomic makeup that would have been understood by John Winthrop and other sturdy colonial divines. In one respect, however, he remained obdurate, yielding nary a whit to regional dialect: he remained committed to the highest standard, the most formal level of American English usage. For him English was the irreducible gold standard of all academic accomplishment.

Dr. Hall arrived in Caldwell in the summer of 1939. He would have two and a half ordinary years in which to exercise his considerable abilities before Pearl Harbor threw everything out of kilter. His college and his students would barely have caught a breath after the Depression before another trial of severe proportions. The Panic of 1893, World War I, the Depression, and now this, the worst of all.

But those two and a half years were glorious ones. In 1939-40 music matters, Beale had not lost his commanding presence; student wit and energy found expression in countless ways with the Pep Band thriving under leadership provided by students Reed Sower, Bill Rankin, and Bill Rodenbaugh; Professor Louise Blackwell directed the school's dramatics societies in a stunning performance of *Our Town* at the high school's auditorium; and Ralph "Rabbit" Bennett and Leslie "Buck" Selders established themselves as anybody's Hall of Famers in football. In basketball, Doug Anderson, Ace Coulter, and Curt Jarvis made the sports columns regularly while the baseball team, one of the College's best, was the first Coyote team to win the Eastern Division of the Northwest Conference in thirteen years. Two familiar names were those of Bennett and Selders, with Ralph Rogers, Jerry Camman, George Blankley, Earl Howe, and Dick Birdsall earning considerable respect. When the new semester came, the February 9, 1940, *Coyote* could boast in banner headlines "Enrollment Breaks Former High," with a subhead "This Semester's 442 Mark Tops 1933-34 High of 435." The next year's *Trail* would carry the first mention of the *Scarab* honorary, from which I infer it came into existence in 1940-41.

It was a time of local and national resurgence with America and her institutions poised for greatness. If I had to pick only one popular manifestation of American drive and energy and the coming together of the best of our traditions of individualism and the cooperative barn-raising spirit of rural America, I would pick the Big Bands.

Theirs was the music to which C of I collegians danced, to which they did homework (or attempted to do so), to which they paid court to their lovely girl

Campus guest Col. Theodore Roosevelt, son of the nation's 26th president, posed for pictures with Dr. Hall and students.

friends or were courted by their handsome boys. And surely to their eyes all cottages were enchanted, a perhaps esoteric allusion that breaks chronology and looks ahead to a popular post-World War II movie with Robert Young and Dorothy McGuire that demonstrates touchingly the truth to the canard that beauty is in the eye of the beholder.

Just think for a moment of the sheer energy and optimism expressed in Tommy Dorsey's band playing "Marie" and "The Song of India," with Jack Leonard vocalizing in the former and the remarkable Bunny Berigan playing trumpet soli in both. Add to this enormous currency the slightly earlier success of Benny Goodman and the slightly later popularity of the greatest of them all—Glenn Miller—and it is clear that as cultural icons these men were saying something about pre-World War II America. Granted the debts of all three to earlier—and even contemporary—black musicians, and recognizing the vital work of arrangers (to say nothing of composers), still these were the Tinckers to Evers to Chance of popular swing. Who can listen to the dynamics of "In the Mood," the lilt and lift of "Little Brown Jug," the hopeful and lyrical serenades—"Sunrise" and "Moonlight"—and the irresistible "Moonlight Cocktail" and escape the conviction that our popular music in the form of swing was remarkably congruent with our deepest feelings about our national identity. In the numbers of instrumentalists in each section, in the quality of musicianship of each single instrumentalist, and in the quality, the spirit of the ensemble—the very Miller sound—the parallel with our national dreams can be drawn. Comparing "Tuxedo Junction" and the "Horst Wessel" song, even a visitor from a distant planet would anticipate the triumph of controlled freedom over militaristic fascism. These were the tunes and the musicians (I almost wrote "magicians") that inspired American youth and, central to our concerns, the C of I Pep Band. Controlled energy, lyrical sweetness, resourcefulness—these and more provide entries for our examination of The College of Idaho in those brief years before the war and our endurance and victory in it.

To swing back to the new president, if Hall's signal success lay in keeping the College alive during W.W. II, is there a key to it?

Forty-two graduates in the Class of 1942; thirty-two in the Class of 1943; sixteen in 1944; five in 1945! Not since the first decade in the life of the College had there been so few. A wartime economy that directed spare and philanthropic coins into war bonds and stamps compromised the annual fund-raising. And a small endowment's interest-generating capacity continued to decline, delivering what would have been the third strike, under standard conditions of temperature and pressure.

But they were anything but standard, and Hall was not a run-of-the-line president. He did what Boone could not do: He was convinced the College had matured to the point that it could enter the competition for providing education for the military. It was quite likely (writers of histories are sometimes humble) that the College survived because of the 311th College Training Detachment (Aircrew). The presence of that Detachment deserves a close look.

Hall waged his own Battle of the Potomac, as he termed it, laying siege to various and sundry Washington officials until "in the early days of 1943 it was announced that The College of Idaho had been selected among the first eighty colleges for an Army Air Forces College Training Program" (*College* 67). In a publication titled *Bulletin of the Association of American Colleges* for December 1944 appeared Hall's account of the entire experience under the title "Education, Army Style." It is a clever articulation of the change from liberal arts and culture to "a citadel of war," a transformation which would endure for sixteen months, or from March of 1943 until June of 1944. Hall concluded his essay thus:

> The main thing is that the job was done. It was education by short-cut, education by remote control, education by contract, but it accomplished its purpose. The professors are proud that they have done the Army's job. But they are more than ever aware that the Army's job is not their job (73).

Be that as it may, the infusion of capital and the presence of males on a predominantly female campus restored the appearance of a college.

First Lieutenant William G. Phelps prepared a 110 page account of the 311th College Training Detachment on The College of Idaho campus, and the historical officer's typescript deserves a look. Consisting of a preface, nine substantive chapters, a summary, biographical sketches, a bibliography, eleven appendices, and a map of the campus, the undated history begins militarily with a statement of the authority under which it was written. The chapter titled "Survey and Selection of Caldwell" calls attention to what the College had already done to justify its claim that it was ready to go to war and highlights the enlisted reserve program (enrolling 58 students in reserve officer procurement for the Army, Navy and Marines) and the presence of a Civilian Pilot Training (later Civil Air Patrol) program. A visit to the campus by three military officers resulted in their enthusiastic endorsement of the College as an institution prepared to receive 250 Army Air Force Trainees. This chapter concludes with standard printed information from College publications, calling attention to a 75-acre campus of which 40 "are beautifully landscaped." By this time the

Covell Chemistry building and Kirkpatrick Gymnasium have been built, a tribute to the generosity of friends of the College from Wendell and Parma and of its own students, and also a tribute to the efforts of Dr. Hall and Thurlow Bryant, among others.

On Monday, February 1, 1943, the College was informed of its selection as a participant in the Army Air Forces College Training Program. The first contingent of 125 men arrived on March 3; the second, of 123 men, about April 1. Expenditures were limited to no more than $10,000 for "instruction and training of trainees; for furnishing quarters and subsistence for trainees and...personnel; for providing emergency medical and dental service and maintaining...medical records" (3).

The contract that was finally agreed upon, to be supplemented by at least three subsequent agreements, entitled the College to $39,072.34 for equipment and such remodeling as was necessary to meet military requirements and $1,172.17 for overhead and administrative costs. These amounts were spelled out in Article 1 of the contract (4). On July 19, 1943, supplemental agreement No. 1 became contractual, providing a standard for payment of dining-hall workers and the costs of raw food. (4) The second supplemental agreement concerned the use of Caldwell's municipal swimming pool; the third supplemental agreement called for a review of the complete contract with changes scheduled to go into effect January 1, 1944 (5).

The old saw has it that there are three ways of doing something: the right way, the wrong way, and the army (military) way. So it was with education. Under the leadership of Dean "Johnny" L. Anderson, the College began training

Army Air Forces Cadets on campus, 1944.

153

the aircrews in February of 1943 (34). There were problems: with text books (too simple—too difficult), with professors (too lax—too demanding), with style.

The last is too serious to be parenthesized. In a college like The College of Idaho, the individual is all-important. In matters of fact, there is little dispute, although whether something is indeed a fact or standardized error may be debated. But many matters culturally based are matters of interpretation and taste. Informal opinion must be expressed coherently, argued logically, and supported by evidence drawn from and pertinent to the case at hand or to analogs to it. However, the military looked at the matter with different eyes:

> A communication...dated 5 April [1943] focused the most serious problem in academic training at the 311th CTD...that of converting types of highly individualistic, informal instruction which had produced some considerable success with students of liberal learning, to that type which was to prove most effective for Aircrew Training. [That] these men were under military discipline and, of necessity, were expected to continue uniform practices in all classes under all conditions was easy to comprehend, but difficult to put into practice. (36)

There were faculty arguments that "military conduct and discipline" had no bearing on learning. It was a further source of professional discomfiture that men had to stand in order to ask a question, and the issue of whether written lesson plans would restrict instructors' abilities to modify and improvise on the basis of class responses to questions and discussions based on comprehension of assigned material bothered most of the faculty (36). Two sentences in the *History of* [the] *311th College Training Detachment* (Aircrew) underscore the difference between liberal education and training army style:

> Time pointed out the wisdom of uniform, attentive classroom procedure, the necessity of careful planning in terms of minutes per item of a lesson unit and so on. The point is that, for example, [since] the new physics plan was vastly different from the old wherein a few eager students of physics, with a mind for research spent long leisure hours in probing the mysteries of physical theory and practice, conversion took some time (36).

A final sore point with the faculty was the military practice of "classroom visitation and observation" (37).

A change for the worse occurred with a replacement of the commanding officer; the new CO "inaugurated an immediate policy of direct action to obtain strict adherence to all 'regulations' involving academic procedures" (37). The noticeable decline in faculty morale caused the army "to improve the academic instruction" by (1) improving the morale of instructors; (2) using daily lesson

154

plans uniformly; (3) using outside study assignments; and (4) using such "classroom techniques as had been previously outlined to all instructors" (37-38).

This was the army talking, and the College listened. It was not the way **education** might take place, but it was a uniform means to **training**. Remaining tensions were finally relieved through a series of conferences held on October 23, 1943. If minutes were kept of these conferences, I have not been able to find them.

What was the curriculum that an aircrewman had to face for his five months here, training that was to prepare him for further training as a pilot, navigator, or bombardier? It consisted of mathematics, physics (The *History* notes that "Contrary to the practice at some institutions, at The College of Idaho, physics experiments are actually performed by the student whenever possible."), history, geography, English, medical aid, civil air regulations, and physical training (*Coyote*, March 5, 1943). These were taught by the College. Military training and flight training were undertaken directly by the army and by contract with Caldwell Flying Service and Jack W. Medlin (March 25, 1943 to June 30, 1944) (68). The curriculum required of the College was not a college curriculum but a sort of "para"-collegiate offering.

Indeed, there were two co-existing, separate but not quite equal educational establishments: the aircrew—often called the "cadet"—program, and the traditional college program. It is appropriate to consider how these two establishments co-existed. In a chapter titled "Services," army historian Phelps offers the following insights, attesting to the autonomy of each.

With respect to medical care, the detachment initially had its own physician, a Captain Goldstein, who actually stayed longer than his original orders provided because of the arrival of measles, mumps, and scarlet fever with the first batch of aviation students. (74) He was later replaced by a local physician through a contract with the College. (74) (These medical expenses are not included in the budget offered later.)

Special Services provided the usual sorts of recreational opportunities—pool tables, radio, phonographs, newspapers, magazines, a post service store, Friday night movies, and a glee club. Arrangements with local organizations resulted in club space at the Elks' Temple with a juke box, piano, magazines, and writing paraphernalia, where on weekends light refreshments were served. On alternate Saturday nights, a dance was held at the I.O.O.F. Hall. Special rates to a local theater were granted, greens fees were waived by the golf course, and special rates and times at the swimming pool were offered. Robert Troxell, a local attorney, offered free legal advice to the cadets (78). Indeed, town and military appear to have got on famously.

As to the precise manner in which the two almost gender-specific elements co-existed on the campus, the record is not so clear. There was, in the first place, limited opportunity for the cadets and the mostly female college student body to mingle. Even though the cadets occupied most of the College housing (Finney, Voorhees and nearly half—45 percent—of Kirkpatrick were used as living and mess facilities), they were preparing to fight a war. Courtship was a secondary trial by arms. In the second place, there were not many women on the campus. The College was miniscule. It is difficult to get an accurate count of the student body those years because nothing was normal. The *Coyote* cut back on publication for 1943-44 and 1944-45. The *Trails* are not helpful, for a senior in October might be drafted before his picture could be taken in March for the senior page. Thus, in 1945 although Fern Stevens and Mary Reynolds are identified as the lone seniors, Glen Cloyd Krebs, Adrianna Lanting, and Robert Waud are listed by Bess Steunenberg as graduates of the Class of 1945. The 1945 *Trail* further identifies, with photographs and captions, sixteen juniors, three of whom are males; twenty sophomores, one a male; seventy-five freshmen, twelve of whom are male. A photograph in that yearbook of a weekly student body meeting yields a count of 44. Six juniors, ten sophomores, and forty-seven freshmen are identified as "not pictured." That gives a total student body of 179, but the actual number of legitimate students at any one time was undoubtedly less than that. And the ratio of men to women was small indeed. However, for the time the cadets were on campus, there was at least the appearance of a college environment—shady lawns, brick and ivy, co-eds, and men...in uniform. That was the discordant note.

There were dances, and there were a few opportunities for dating, under generally supervised conditions. If all of this seems medieval to recent students, their grandparents can remind them that coeds in an earlier time had to be back in their dormitories by reasonably early hours on weeknights, with later hours and special hours for Friday and Saturday nights. An editorial in the *Coyote* of October 15, 1943, urged female students not to bother the cadets on class days, for "they are not to speak to civilians." If a cadet was seen talking to a girl any time other than on a weekend, he was penalized by having to undertake extra duty.

The military program concluded in the late spring of 1944. A story in the *Coyote* of April 25 noted, "With the evacuation of the Army Air Force Training Detachment from the College, arrangements are being make to take back many of the advantages of the pre-war era." A story of May 6 observed that "the last large group...of the College Training detachment left April 21." By June, the military establishment was gone.

What had this presence meant in the life of the College? The real answer must lie with someone more profound than I, but here are some comments that may be helpful to that ideal historian. In the first place, their being here meant something to the cadets, an opportunity to gain some time by being back in the classroom; a time to get to know some girls and to connect the values of home and country with idealized feminine qualities of grace and gentleness and perhaps even love or hoped for love; a time when war however real and imminent was held off, suspended for a moment. Their presence here also exposed the cadets to some superb teaching, teaching so satisfactory that some of these Army Air Force men returned after the war to undertake or finish college work. A sense of what I am implying appeared in the annual *First Call*, a yearbook legacy of the 311th College Training Detachment, 1943, under the editorship of Phil Ritchie, Bill Sharon, and Tom Taylor:

> We meant "First Call" to be a memorable record of the first stage in our flying career. Something on which we can look back ten months or ten years from now and recall such little incidents as the Open Post we spent in an all-night bull session in the Dewey Palace, the time we were gripped by a touch of homesickness...and that unforgettable evening we first went star-gazing with a Caldwell girl.

As for the College, there is little question that the income from the military presence meant survival, or so it appears as I study the record. Appendix B of Lieutenant Phelps' *History* shows $40,244.51 estimated for the Commissary Expense, for the cost of supplies, equipment, and remodeling in order for the work of training the Detachment to be done, including a 3 percent general administrative expense. Additionally, $5,084.46 was required for operating expenses associated with maintaining the living quarters (Appendix C). Instructional expenses, subsistence, living quarters' maintenance and Instructional Plant and Classroom Operation came to $16,030.26 (Appendix E). Facilities Use amounted to $4,945.43 (Appendix F). The annual salary for the 17 1/3 person instructional staff came to $44,604.48; salaries for administrators and supervisors and a fee for the library came to $14,133.34 (Appendix G). An infusion of $125,042.48—not all profit, of course—was significant; the presence of students was essential. The next question was survival in the short term (1944-45, 1945-46) until the war ended and the veterans returned. It would be touch and go, but Hall and his loyal faculty and trustees would keep the place open.

A look at Hall's success as a fundraiser is instructive—he was successful. Two buildings were constructed during his administration—the Alice Heron Covell Chemistry Laboratory and Kirkpatrick Gymnasium, the former built in 1941 with funds from the Charles H. Covell estate of Wendell, Idaho. This estate had been nurtured over the years, the work of Dr. Boone, Bob McCormick, Thurlow Bryant, and Dr. Hall. Kirkpatrick resulted from continuing support from the Kirkpatrick family of Parma, Idaho, from student pledges of financial support, and from community help. Robert McCormick said that G. M. Kirkpatrick, the father-in-law of Mary Kirkpatrick, helped make the gymnasium a reality (177). But surely one of Dr. Hall's most notable successes lay in establishing the friendship between the College and Jack Simplot, a connection that has proved invaluable over the years.

A further indication of Hall's capabilities as a fundraiser and as an administrator who recognized and appreciated the fund-raising abilities of staff members like Bryant and Erwin Schwiebert was his advocacy of the "living endowment" plan. This plan was the brainchild of J. H. Lowell, seconded and supported by one of the gifted chief executives of Idaho Power, C. J. Strike. There was no magic to it; it was simply an appealing name for continuing a carefully planned and well executed program of annual giving (*College* 171) and it worked. Executed by Schwiebert, the program met with a success probably unanticipated. Dr. Hall offered the following analysis:

> The year before the program was launched, [1940] the College received $6,000 in gifts for operations. The first year of "living endowment" netted in the neighborhood of $11,000, the second year $13,000, the third year $19,000, the fourth year $30,000, the fifth and sixth years were provided for by the $75,000 allocated from the development fund, and the seventh year $45,000. This was in addition to the $5,000 annual appropriation from the Presbyterian Board of Christian Education. The subscription list grew to include almost 500 individuals and organizations...in amounts ranging from $1 to $1,500 (171).

Robert McCormick put a slightly different construction on the matter:

> Dr. Hall had decided to use the term "Living Endowment" for an account in the Treasurer's books from which current expenses would be met. The concept was that gifts for current operation expenses came from **Living Donors** who [comprised] the College's **Living Endowment**. On the other hand gifts specifically designated to the **Permanent Endowment** were to be held in **Trust** and only the **Interest Income** was to be used each year in meeting college expenses (214).

McCormick further commented that it was Schwiebert's hope that many of the living contributors would have both the inclination and the wherewithal to establish trust funds providing in the future an amount equal to their current gifts. That is, it was hoped that what had been given under the terms of living endowment would continue to be available as permanent endowment (215).

Hall's efforts in improving faculty salaries and in implementing a retirement plan must be given high marks—not only for Dr. Hall but for his father as well. The story runs something like this.

Hall had been president for a short time when his father visited the school, observed what was going on, and approached his son with the prospect of "what amounted, in those days, to a substantial contribution. What did I want the sum used for?" (170) As Hall considered the matter, the lack of any kind of retirement income for "superannuated instructors" coupled with the corresponding absence of any kind of specific retirement policy seemed of transcendent consequence. Faculty who perhaps ought to retire could hardly afford to do so. Hall was convinced that if some kind of plan could be generated it could be sustained; "the difficulty lay in taking the icy plunge." Dr. Hall's father financed the College's initial contribution to the Teachers Insurance and Annuity Association, including a group term life insurance feature, for the first three years (170). In today's climate of private, public, institutional, corporate, IRA—the list goes on—retirement plans, the College's bold step in seeking to reassure a living standard during the employees' waning years seems less than bold. But like other cultural phenomena, it must be viewed in context. McCormick observed that at Dr. Boone's last board meeting, the subject of a retirement plan had come up but had not been acted upon (215).

Another contribution which must be laid at the feet of Dr. Hall

G. M. Kirkpatrick

was his extremely fine success in getting good faculty. Without benefit of faculty search committees, without bringing candidates for positions to the campus and putting them through an inquisition that includes a formal presentation to all and sundry who might wish to hear—without, in short, the instrumentality through which hiring is done today, Dr. Hall was able to hire many fine teachers who stayed to invest their lives in the College and the community. There were some failures, but Hall's sense of what a college and a colleague should be combined with his Ivy League network to supply him with a cadre of remarkable folk. Space will permit the mention of some of them. As a debate coach and fund raiser, Erwin Schwiebert was an excellent appointment. Profiting from his training and experience under Dr. Hayman, Schwiebert was able to put together forensic squads of national standing, debaters like Les MontgomeryI, Harley Barnhart, Bake Young, Morgan Beck, Gordon Barrett, Grace Shocky, and Rachel Woody.

Another appointment was also to affect generations of students, who, in the course of time and the nature of things, often became alumni/ae. Dr. Hall somewhat coyly avoided naming the individuals: "We had our eyes on one of the College's most brilliant and promising graduate as successor to the strongest man on the faculty" (45). The two were Lyle M. Stanford '33 and Professor O. J. Smith. Dr. Hall's instincts were sound in respect to both.

Two other appointments, although of shorter duration, were nevertheless of unimpeachable merit—Dr. George Burch, Philosophy, and Dr. Betty Burch (Mrs. George) as Dean of Women. The Burches returned to the East Coast to develop triumphant careers at Tufts University, and, later, for Dr. Betty Burch, at Radcliffe and Harvard.

To continue the College's education program, Dr. Hall hired a public school administrator of much experience, alumnus Ledru Williams, Class of 1918. Some will remember him as an administrator in the Caldwell public schools, some will remember him for his detailed knowledge of Idaho school law, and others will never forget his ringing bass voice. Dr. Edith Atwood Davis was engaged to teach psychology and served well until 1957.

Erwin Schwiebert

Yale University supplied two targets for Dr. Hall's net—James L. Martin and David Gelzer, both for the Department of Religion and Philosophy, although Gelzer also taught German. They were both instrumental in raising the standards by which college success is measured and saving the College from the general insouciance that had pervaded the campus during the later war years. Ian Morton, Music, replaced Professor Beale as head of the Music Department. Dr. George V. Wolfe, of Vienna, Austria, was also in this group of capable, devoted, and demanding professors. Dr. Wolfe stayed to invest his life in the institution. Also coming for the fall of 1946 was Margaret "Babe" Boone, English professor and Dean of Women.

For the fall of 1947, Dr. Hall was able to present additional new faculty, twelve according to *The College of Idaho Bulletin* of September 1947: David Fuller Ash, English; Ned Bowler, Drama; Leslie V. Brock, History; Theodore Hanum, Sociology; William Gillam, Education; Bernard Bettman, Chemistry; W. LaMar Bollinger, Economics; Helen Nahas, French; Richard Skyrm, Music; Sam Hungerford, Music (a returning faculty member); Florence Keve, Art; and Shirley Kroeger, Physical Education. Margaret Sinclair came this year to serve as alumni secretary (and news bureau), becoming a member of the Department of English in 1950.

Much could be said of many of these folk. Shirley Kroeger, like Wolfe, Skyrm, Stanford, and Williams, stayed with the College, as did Leslie Brock. Hanum, as a sociology teacher, was a rather good portrait painter. He did not stay long. Dr. Bettman was a fine chemist, a nearly virtuoso pianist, and an alcoholic. His tenure was brief. Bill Gillam was a big affable, educator whose eyes—and only his eyes—occasionally betrayed a profound sadness. He stayed two years. The reader may recall the death of the young wife in that youthful marriage of Chapter 6. Helen Nahas was a fine and demanding instructor who left the College to finish graduate work and take up her life's work elsewhere. Dick Skyrm will have to be cited in a subsequent chapter, for his remarkably productive life ended during Dr. DeRosier's presidency. Sam Hungerford taught violin until 1950. Professor Keve was a short-term bird of passage. Ned Bowler, my track coach, teacher of freshman composition, and drama coach, left the C of I in 1951 to complete a doctorate in speech pathology and launch a long and successful career as teacher and speech pathologist at the University of Colorado.

The reader will recall the humorous squib borrowed from a midwestern paper and used to fill space in The *Coyote* of January 8, 1931; in a frightfully humorous headline it referred to the wedding of a man named Ash and a woman named Smoke. They came to Caldwell in 1947, both with Ph.D.'s in

English, he to head the College's English department. They returned to Iowa in 1949.

Thus the appointment and retention of excellent teachers served Hall's further purpose of reaffirming the will of the College to be an authentic institution of higher learning. Some of that will had been eroded during World War II when national resolution was quite specifically directed toward absolutely critical ends, the winning of wars on two fronts.

In reaffirming the institutional will to be an authentic college, so readily apparent in the Catalog published at the time of accreditation, Dr. Hall profited from the advice and good will of President Donald Cowling of Carleton College. Dr. Hall put it this way:

> We decided that our task was two-fold: to make The College of Idaho **look** like a college and to make it **function** like a college. No priority was assigned to the one objective over the other. We set out to accomplish the two simultaneously (*College* 102).

Some might argue that in the fall of 1939 the College indeed looked like a college, with three large brick buildings, a large sandstone library, a neoclassical mansion, a lighted football field, the brightness of the acres of clipped green grass broken into pleasing shapes by maturing elms. This is not the way a campus should look? Forebear, Dr. Hall!

But he was absolutely correct. One dormitory for women and one for men, one multi-purpose classroom-gymnasium-auditorium-administrative building-*johannes factotum*, one library: these did meet the needs of a growing college. Dr. Hall's account of his visit with President Cowling is interesting:

> We compared notes.... Dr. Cowling informed me that when he had first come to Carleton as president some thirty years before, Carleton, although it was a long-established institution, possessed approximately the same amount of material resources in plant and endowment as The College of Idaho possessed at the time of our discussion. After a year at the job, he had been ready to quit. He felt that the time had come for Carleton to do likewise, but he decided to give it one more try (102).

Cowling then "sought and obtained the support [financing]...to accomplish two fundamental objectives: first, an improved faculty, and second...extensive...dormitory expansion" (102). That Carleton is one of our nation's fine liberal arts colleges today (and the *alma mater* of the holder of the Bernie McCain Chair in the Humanities at The College of Idaho) is eloquent testimony

162

to Dr. Cowling's success. To Dr. Hall, the Cowling cure seemed appropriate for the College's problems.

The function issue has been detailed: a good faculty and provision for it respecting salary and retirement. The appearance issue in respect to "a liberal arts college in the American tradition" was the inadequacy of student housing. Kirkpatrick and Covell took care of two crushing needs. J.R. Simplot's gift of another dormitory for women was an important step toward resolving the inadequacy matter.

But Dr. Hall resigned and left the College in the fall of 1947 to become president of Westminster College, Fulton, Missouri. Simplot Hall was finished in the administration of Acting President Ledru Williams.

As a coda to this chapter on the Hall years, I offer a few matters that deserve to be remembered. In the first place, the College continued to try to bring to the campus those persons who had gained distinction in the world, those whose presence would confer dignity upon a campus host. Thus Alexander Kerensky was brought to Caldwell in March of 1945, the same Kerensky who for five months was President of the Provisional Government of Russia and commander-in-chief of its army, overthrown by Lenin. Almost exactly five years earlier, Thomas E. Dewey visited the campus. In the summer of 1943, Lord Halifax visited the campus and was honored with a degree; at that time, he was a British ambassador and the Chancellor of Oxford University (*College* 129).

Campus guest Alexander Kerensky, on the right, March 1945.

Another item: in 1941 the YMCA and YWCA merged to form the Boone Christian Association, an organization that endured until the summer of 1957. The merger had its origins in the Student Christian Movement: the plan was championed by YMCA president Frank Chalfant, who was encouraged by suggestions from Dr. John Nelson of the Presbyterian Board of Education, according to The *Coyote* of October 17, 1941.

Also in 1941 the College celebrated its fiftieth anniversary. That event must be noted.

Twenty-five years earlier, a quarter-century birthday had been observed. In 1941 the school was old, a half-century old, and in the new American West—that is, the West that had developed along EuroAmerican lines—fifty years equated with antiquity. To direct the College's anniversary, a committee was formed, a campus queen (Patsy Cochrane) named, and appropriate activities organized by homecoming chairs Maxine Sower and Jim Attebery. As the reader might imagine, it was a busy and happy time with far more going on than can be discussed here. The *Coyote* of November 7, 1941, treated the subject quite adequately, and both the Caldwell and the Boise media—KFXD had radio studios in Boise, Nampa, and Caldwell—recognized the event as significant to the life of the region. The Committee on the Fiftieth Anniversary began to call itself the Semi-Centennial Celebration Committee, a name that is attractive because of the implication of a centennial celebration only fifty years away. Thus the continuation of institutional life and the celebrations of milestones along the way (Folder, "Boone—'That Man Boone'").

The publication of a book or books was suggested as a fitting way to memorialize Dr. Boone and his college. Ruth Gipson Plowhead offered some sensitive and intelligent insights as to what such a book or books might discuss. A letter from James L. Boone advanced both general and specific reservations about such a book, not as impediments but cautionary and well-founded.

Out of all of this came the formal dedication of Covell and Kirkpatrick, an anniversary anthem by Professors Eyck and Beale, and, ultimately, *That Man Boone* by H. H. Hayman.

A final comment is partially demographic. When the war ended, the G.I. Bill, one of the noblest scholarship programs ever devised, brought veterans in increasing numbers to the campus. The *Coyote* of October 23, 1946, offered interesting statistics: 477 students were enrolled, of whom 273 were freshmen; the total count consisted of 315 men and 162 women. Veterans made up about half of the student body—239, of whom 109 were women.

Under Dr. Hall, the College revived as the Depression waned, survived World War II by the slenderest of margins, improved its physical plant, added significantly to its faculty, improved salaries, and introduced a respectable retirement system. The old Commons building, added during Hall's administration but procured largely through the efforts of Thurlow Bryant, was an important but ugly facility, one of those "T" buildings (T = temporary but eternal!) that sprouted on college campuses across the country as military structures were declared surplus. The acquisition consisted of two buildings parallel to one another and joined by a hall creating a U-shaped facility, one wing serving as a dining hall, the other as classrooms and offices.

Hall indeed left the College stronger than he had found it. Many of the core of the old faculty were approaching retirement, but they were by no means in their dotage. To show that there was still a glow in those fading lights, so brilliant over the years, I offer to the reader the program for the senior recital of an unnamed senior piano student of Professor Beale. It added up to a brilliant performance by one of the last students of a man who had been considered for the post at UCLA finally given to Arnold Schönberg.

26 May 1947

I

Nocturne Pastorale—John Field
Sonata Op.53 (Waldstein)
     Allegro con brio—Beethoven
Nocturne (Nachtstueck)—Schumann
The Prophet Bird (Vogel als Prophet), Schumann

II

Sonnett—Tsidor Achron
In the Chinese City—Walter Niemann
Etude in D flat major—Liszt
Polonaise in A flat major, Op.53—Chopin

III

Capriccio Brilliante, Op.22—Mendelssohn
     Professor F. F. Beale at the second piano

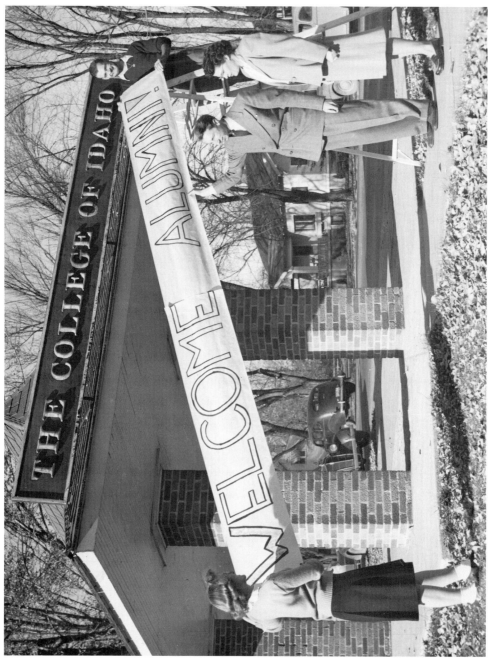

Promoting a Homecoming in the late '40s: student co-chairs Erma Neiwirth and Gene Odle, alumni co-chairs Earl Tunison and Louise Mitchell Talcott.

Part IV

The Interim of Ledru Williams (1947-1950)

and the

Presidency of Paul Marsh Pitman 1950-1954

Pep Band musicians,
c. 1950.

CHAPTER TEN

C. latrans ?

The question mark in the title might well address the motives for Dr. Hall's move. Why would he leave an institution, where he had enjoyed considerable success, to go east, first to Missouri and finally to Franklin and Marshall in Pennsylvania?

A clue may lie in the fourteenth chapter of Hall's book. I quote the second paragraph:

> Very politely I asked a trustee for his photograph to use along with the photographs of about twenty other community leaders in a leaflet devoted to financial promotion. "I won't give you my picture, but I'll tell you what I will give," he replied. Pausing for effect, and noting perhaps the expression of happy anticipation on my face, he concluded: "my resignation" (194).

Later in this chapter, Dr. Hall remarked that "the trustee [element] was and remains a blur of inconsistencies, contradictions, and paradoxes" (195).

Romanticizing and myopic vision (characteristic of alumni/ae trustees), lack of a sense of belonging and anti-sentimental notions (characteristic of non-alumni/ae trustees): these different attitudes could have been mutually corrective, producing creative tension, Dr. Hall believed. But he failed to find them so (205).

In his analysis of trustees and their responsibilities, Dr. Hall devotes three pages to two trustees meriting special consideration: Robert E. Strahorn (who lived until 1943) and Jack Simplot (206). Had they been asked to contribute photographs to a fund-raising leaflet, they would have assented and probably offered to pay the printing costs. How different from the tendered resignation.

169

Such reluctance on the part of some trustees to be identified with the absolute necessity for their participation in fund-raising might well have contributed to Dr. Hall's decision to leave.

Ledru Williams was a devoted administrator. He had much on the credit side to start with: a good and improving faculty, expanding enrollment, a collection of superb athletes, students who would have been outstanding on any campus, a strengthening alumni group. And the comets had returned from the outer darkness of World War II and law school. They would prove to be forces in Idaho and national politics and in the life of their alma mater, as will be shown later.

The faculty were good indeed. To those members previously identified, bright additions for 1948 included Arthur A. Hart, Art; Howard J. "Nick" Weddle, Physical Education; and Gilbert J. Hunt, Chemistry.

The College *Bulletin* for November 1955 (Vol. 65, No. 4) listed enrollment figures for the decade 1945-46 through 1955-56 as follows:

YEAR	MEN	WOMEN	TOTAL
1945-46	89	145	234
1946-47	311	143	454
1947-48	342	163	505
1948-49	333	141	474
1949-50	344	131	475
1950-51	237	125	362
1951-52	274	140	414
1952-53	277	165	442
1953-54	259	169	428
1954-55	267	147	414
1955-56	339	209	548

Although there were fluctuations—1950-51 is anomalous because the Korean conflict ate into the pool of young men from whom enrollment might have been expected—the figures were encouraging.

Not only were there wholesome numbers of students, there were also students of high caliber, genuine intellectuals from east and west. The former included people like John Abram Quackenbush Davis, Edmon B. Lee, Diane Slonim, Ovide Desmarais (yes, Ovid Demaris, the writer of investigative best sellers); among the latter were people like Henry Hopkins, Gene Odle, LeRoy Ehlers, Dan Knipe, Vance Peckham.... The list could go on.

170

With respect to athletes, the College finally shook off the athletic doldrums of World War II. When Coach Clem Parberry returned in 1945 the Coyotes once again became a respectable member of one of America's fine small-college athletic organizations, the Northwest Conference. Although higher education is not about athletics, when this activity is well managed and carefully integrated into campus life, it can be a source of wholesome entertainment for its community, a source of pride for its various constituencies, and a means by which impecunious young men and women can be encouraged to proceed with their education. In the nature of things, athletics can also be a source of abuses (of almost unbelievable proportions) of human and institutional resources. But as Mark Twain might observe, you can say the same thing about Congress. It is sad but quite true that athletic accomplishment will receive far more column inches in a local newspaper than will, say, a student who gets an 830 on the Graduate Record Examination, a score that is surely All-American if not All-World. A liberal arts education is about ideas, about clarity of thought and responsible assessments of the human condition. It has to do with the examination of self. It does not necessarily prepare the student to earn a living, but it must prepare the graduate to live, to have life and have it abundantly. Athletics and higher education are not mutually exclusive categories.

Among student-athletes earning distinction at the C of I in the Williams-Pitman years, the following merit more than a mention. Richard Gardner performed well in football, basketball, and baseball. Bob Jensen was an outstanding guard on the basketball team and a fine tennis player. Both went on to earn M.D. degrees. Bob Williams and Reid Faylor played on the same basketball team, Williams also lettering in football and track and Faylor in baseball. Both became dentists. Bob Bourland, a returning veteran, excelled in basketball and track and became an insurance executive. Two athletes merit special attention because they would surely be named to everybody's Hall of Fame: Tom Winbigler and Steuben Thomas.

Clem Parberry had two durable starting tackles in Denny Whitman and Steuben Thomas. Both had skills that carried over into the other sports of boxing and track and field. Denny looked the way an American athlete should, thick of chest with massive shoulders but narrow of waist and legs. He was, moreover, a serious and handsome-featured student. After graduation he put his economics major into practice and became an entrepreneur of modest scale. He was ever the good citizen, parent, and husband. After a series of health problems, Denny succumbed to a heart attack on March 30, 1990.

At the other tackle spot was a much heavier athlete—indeed, one who looked fat. Appearances are deceiving. Although he may have weighed 220 or 225 pounds, the weight was compressed onto a frame perhaps six feet tall. Round-faced and given to hearty laughter, Steuben in white whiskers would have made a good Kris Kringle. But the jolly appearance and the Celtic wit concealed an athlete of fearsome capabilities. He was a vicious and skillful boxer (and fighter), a speedy low hurdler (and effective in the shot put and discus). On the football field all of these capacities were unleashed, making him a tackle who enjoyed matching his skills with those of anybody across the line of scrimmage. He was All-Conference for two years, then left the College without taking a degree and disappeared from its annals.

From Weiser, Idaho, long a supplier of students to the College, came Tom Winbigler, our first Little All-American although not the first to deserve that distinction. Named to the All-Northwest second team his first year at the College (1946), Winbigler thereafter was a unanimous All-Northwest conference halfback. Upon graduation in 1950, Winbigler was invited to try out with the Los Angeles Rams as the understudy to Army's All-American Glenn Davis. Valley football fans were not surprised, for Winbigler brought to the game a clear intelligence and almost unlimited physical capabilities. At six feet and 190 pounds, he had the speed of a sprinter (he ran the 100 and 220, pole vaulted and broad jumped for the Coyotes) and the nimbleness of foot essential to negotiate a broken field. His weight gave him the mass necessary to break tackles, and his uncompromising spirit of competitiveness provided the courage to hit the line again and again. With Steuben or Denny or Warren Barry or Joe Caldwell working in front of him, Tom rarely failed to make yardage; with his remarkable speed, he frequently burst through the opposing line and defensive backfield for impressive yardage and often a touchdown. He was always a threat to score when the kickoff came his way.

But only Tom knew the pain of his bad ankles, and it was probably this condition that cut short what appeared to be a promising professional career. He became a successful coach and educator in the Oregon public school system.

The quality of student attracted to the College has always been a source of pride, and some bright students who were also athletes have been identified in this chapter. A further look is in order.

The pre-medical program continued its excellent record of placing students in professional health care programs, picking up where it left off with the declining enrollment of the war years. Hal Reynolds, '48, entered the University of Washington Medical School, Gurny Caddy headed for the University of Oregon Medical School. Dean Benedict was accepted by the Medical School of the University of Utah; Evelyn Shirck accepted a teaching assistantship in the biology program at the University of Oregon which enabled her to work on her first graduate degree. Edmon Lee and Weldon Thomas also went on to medical school. Among others concluding successful graduate professional programs were Bertha Newman, Howard Bavender, Robert Bowles, Barbara Bowman, Don Emmel, Shirley Epperson, Elwin Ovist, Pat Packard, Vance Peckham, Bill Vandermeer, Jim Wolcott; these and many other distinguished themselves and reflected brightly upon their alma mater. It was students like these, to say nothing of that largest freshman class—the Class of 1950—which enabled the College to produce more than its share of entrepreneurs, professional people, and educated citizens. All of these accomplishments contribute to that statistic so important to secondary students trying to decide where to attend college: between 45 percent and 55 percent of our alumni/ae over the years have progressed to graduate or professional school.

To cite others who left the College in refulgent splendor might prove tedious to the reader who is not so passionately partisan as I, but I must mention the continuing acclaim won by the Pep Band for its superb shows. Under the direction or inspiration or spell of leaders and arrangers like Paul Murphy (of

Wayne Chatterton and Leslie Brock performing one of Ralph Berringer's infamous Black Masque *skits.*

Dr. Hall's era), Vance Peckham, and Don Roblyer, the then traditional Pep Band shows performed for enthusiastic audiences that filled the auditorium of old Caldwell High School.

Boone Christian Association continued to play a significant role in the spiritual life of the College, and the young-ish and ambitious faculty geared itself up to stimulate the institutional intellectual life. Among such endeavors, the establishment of a "club" for English majors—and others not yet saved—was a shining light. Overworked professors gave time they did not have to curious and intellectually aggressive and grateful students. Professor Boone talked on Chaucer, Professor Bowler shared his respect for G. B. Shaw, and Professor Newbry enlightened his audience with a presentation on W. B. Yeats. Professor Chatterton demonstrated how Dickens might have read "The Death of Little Nell." Even upper-division students were invited to present their findings to the club.

Some of the above names require more than a word or two. Wayne Chatterton, a gifted writer, came to the College in 1949 with a master's degree and remained a vital and contributing member of the College community for a score of years, earning a Ph.D. in English before leaving the institution. Burton Newbry was graduated from the College in 1947, earned a master's degree from the University of Montana, and returned to his alma mater to teach English. He left the College to take a doctorate in education and worked through the State Department with various foreign governments, establishing modern educational systems. I shall return to him in a different context a bit later.

Nineteen-fifty was an interesting year in the life of the College for in that year was graduated the largest class in the school's history: 107. Its members included many veterans, men and women, who were serious about their work and about their future. Children of the Depression, they appreciated the material resources provided for them by the College—a legacy from the many folks who had husbanded their resources and had made gifts of appreciation to Dr. Boone's college. This freshman class was to become a first in the College's history, for with it the taking of the Graduate Record Examination became a requirement. That signal event requires elucidation.

The College *Coyote* of May 29, 1947, in a front page story informed the reader that beginning the next academic year—1947-48—sophomores and seniors would be "required to take a series of tests called the Graduate Record Examination...designed to show the nature and extent of the student's knowledge and understanding in comparison with that of other college students." In addition to taking a generalized test covering a wide range of specific disciplines and vocabulary, seniors would be required to take an advanced test in their major field of study.

Dr. Hall had expressed concern for the cultural literacy of C of I students and agonized over the question of whether they had been prepared to compete on equal terms with the graduates of other colleges. This concern he shared with me when he returned to the campus to fill a vacancy in the history department in 1961-62. It is echoed in his book:

> I was thoroughly conditioned...against the loose and sloppy colloquialisms prevalent among Idaho students...and many college instructors.... I was firmly on the side of the...English department in their...efforts to lift high the banners of literacy and to stand, thereby, on the side of the angels. When one of the science instructors for whose opinions I had great respect...observed that he considered it preferable to say "acrosst the street" because that was the local accepted usage, the remark was met with a stern glance of disapproval and dissent (20).

How shall a college be measured? By what yardstick is quality determined? These are enduring problems, and that the College under the care of Acting President Williams and Dean Anderson was concerned with what amounted to "quality control" (an ugly expression) was to its credit. Certainly one way of arriving at judgments about a school's products is to compile and study the record made by those products. This is not terribly difficult in some respects, for there is a record created by those who are accepted into graduate and professional schools and who complete the work there. It is also possible to arrive at some approximation of the success of graduates who become public school teachers.

Another way of measuring the quality of an educational program is through the use of such institutional instruments as senior comprehensive examinations and the senior thesis. For many years, the College required both oral and written "comps" of every graduating senior, the former a public examination. For the musicians and art students there are the senior recital and the senior exhibit. Finally, there is the accreditation process. A good institutional research program is essential to collect, organize, and interpret the data these provide.

But Williams and Anderson, among others, realized that the foregoing lacked a certain kind of statistical **national** integrity. How do we measure up when we are placed in the national currency? Williams' comments in the school newspaper of February 24, 1950, vindicated Dr. Hall's concern: "Our seniors made the poorest record in the Verbal Factor of the test—that is the section dealing with vocabulary...."

The story continued that western students rank lowest annually on this section of the test. Eastern students generally, and students in New England colleges specifically, excel in this portion of the test.[*]

Other events in the College's life introduced a note of sorrow—appropriate, for with the midpoint of the twentieth century came the end of an era for the College.

Dr. Lyle Stanford, who had been groomed by his mentor O. J. Smith as Smith's replacement, sickened during the middle of August in 1947 and entered the lists of those stricken with polio. Physiotherapy under the watchful eyes of the staff at the Elks Convalescent Home in Boise helped Dr. Stanford in his long convalescence, but he remained a paraplegic the rest of his life. The loss of most of the use of both legs did not diminish his effective teaching, however, and until his death he was a superb teacher. But Lyle's illness forced O. J. Smith out of retirement and back into a heavy teaching load.

On the morning of December 22, 1947, Mary Elizabeth Meyer Beale, wife of F. F. Beale, died. She had been associated with the College from the time of

Lyle Stanford and students at a Bruneau Canyon overlook.

---

[*] The showing by C of I seniors vindicated Dr. Cowley's assessment of the College's programs: "In the sciences you shine, but in most other departments you lack staff and continuity and therefore strength" (15). Cowley is cited later in this chapter.

the Beale School of Music back in 1911, teaching piano. Almost exactly two months later, on February 20, 1948, Beale himself, Idaho's most gifted piano-organ teacher and composer, died. The niche he left vacant would never be filled, for men of that stature are not replaced. Instead, new great ones come along and create their own places in the pantheon of greatness. Such a one was Richard Skyrm.

Less than a month later, on March 11, 1948, Professor Orma J. Smith died of a cerebral hemorrhage, again leaving his niche forever unoccupied, a tribute to his greatness. And once again, a new place would be created for a new one, the brilliant Lyle Stanford.

It was also in 1948 that Dean Johnny Anderson left The College of Idaho for Lewis and Clark College in Portland. Anderson, an excellent teacher and administrator, had served the College well. He filled the role formerly taken by Boone, Hayman, and Springer as the presiding minister for campus weddings. Recent graduates of the College will recall Dr. William Chalker in this role.

May the reader forgive this personal reference; I make it to show how lives become intertwined as a result of growing up on the campus of this College of Idaho. People gradually learn to put away most of their adolescent silliness and selfishness and mature into adults for whom ideas become more important than the top fifty, the library and laboratory more significant than the tavern, and a good book more challenging than frisbee golf. Professor Beale had arranged to play for Barbara's and my wedding on December 31, 1947. He was too ill to meet the commitment, to his profound regret, for she had been one of his shining lights as a piano and organ student.

Barbara and I had made arrangements to move into the upstairs apartment at 1822 Dearborn, the home of Dean and Mrs. Smith, when the apartment was vacated by Mr. and Mrs. Bob (now Dr.) Williams. Dean Smith, his voice tenuously sustained by the thin column of air to which his asthma rationed him, asked did we smoke. He reminded me that smoking made it even more difficult for him to breathe. The Williamses were nice tenants because they did not use tobacco. So we passed muster and were living in that apartment when our daughter was born. On a campus like this lives do get connected, and often one finds the way home by tracing and re-tracing those connections.

If 1950 was an interesting year because of the size of the senior class, it was also interesting as the year the College named its fourth president, Paul Marsh Pitman, who gave the commencement address for our class even though he would not assume office until July. The search process was a careful one. J. R.

Simplot commissioned a study that resulted in the "Report to the Committee Seeking a President for The College of Idaho," by W. H. Cowley of Stanford University, presented October 8, 1949.

Dr. Cowley carefully established the College's record as "in point of operations you are the oldest college in Idaho" and called attention to the legislature's failure to appropriate funds for the state university at Moscow until 1892 (4). Then he raised the question of whether our venerability serves any useful purpose. As if that were not enough to set our teeth on edge, he reminded us that many people think of us as a state-controlled college or confuse us with the universities at Moscow or Pocatello. (It is even more confusing today with a community college at Twin Falls: the College of **Southern** Idaho.) Accordingly, he suggested that at the appropriate time the matter of changing the name should be explored, as he reminded his readers of some of the famous colleges of the country that underwent name changes to honor donors (405).

Dr. Cowley sounded a warning: "[It is nearly certain] that the state of Idaho will directly or through the junior college at Boise...move into your territory and offer you stiff if not destructive competition" (5-6). The warning was prophetic for when Boise's junior college dropped the "junior," so dropped the number of students matriculating at the College for their upper- division work.

Another assessment concerned the affiliation with the Presbyterian Church: while in 1949 that connection brought in $5,000 annual dollars, created friends, and helped generate student enrollment, the connection also caused confusion on the part of the public both as to the extent of church control and as to the amount of funds derived from the church. Indeed, Cowley suggested, some support could be withheld on the false assumption that the College is sectarian, and it might be necessary to clarify that connection and to remain in the Christian rather than the narrowly Presbyterian tradition (6-7).

Although the strength of the science division did not escape the attention of this percipient investigator, he characterized our general program of liberal education as "firm and orthodox but not generally distinguished" (9).

Other areas of the College's life and welfare calling forth warnings include the inadequate endowment—$550,000!—the defects in the physical plant (too few classrooms, no auditorium), a failure to "exploit the potentials of smallness," and a failure to develop "snob appeal" (17,19,21,25).

Two final comments from Cowley, and we can turn to another perspective: the faculty, he noted, were woefully underpaid. To keep them happy it would only be necessary "to increase their salaries." The second observation was that "good college presidents who are popular with their faculties are as rare as southpaw shortstops" (35).

From another perspective comes additional light on this matter of presidential unpopularity. In a fascinating little monograph titled "The Evolving Role of the President's Wife at the University of Michigan," edited by Kathleen Koehler, (Michigan Historical Collections Bulletin No. 37, July 1989), three wives of university presidents discuss their lives and times under the microscope. Anne Hatcher, the wife of former president Harlan Hatcher, forthrightly set the stage:

> My family has always lived a university life. My father was a professor, and my grandfather; my brother was a professor, my sister married a professor, I married a professor.... I have always loved university life....

> However, I did grow up with the typical faculty mistrust of the administration on whatever level. This is especially true as my father, after having spent almost 20 years of his early academic career as a law dean on three different campuses, decided to go back to teaching and research and never ceased to tell us what a wise decision it was.

Her husband accepted the presidency of Michigan "over my protest, even tears" (2).

Whether such faculty distrust of administrators is genetic (a difficult position to sustain; but if territoriality is indeed programmed into most species, then faculty may have an almost subrational impulse to defend their territory, that is, their prerogatives) or whether it is acquired (learned as a result of observing administrative maladroitness), it is a very real consideration. I find no evidence that this pariahdom was extended to Boone. He stands as a shining exception to the general rule. In nearly all other cases, presidents are vulnerable to the admurmuration of the grumbling hive. The best palliative for this inclination might be to make every faculty member president for a year, or, failing that, academic vice president.

At the commencement exercises for the Class of 1950 (a class I have hesitated to celebrate extensively, for it was my class and it was a group of serious, goal-oriented, mature people, numbering many professional and graduate school candidates), we listened to Pitman's golden oratory. He spoke with great force and great conviction and, in orotund phrases, told us that a new president must satisfy the various constituencies of the College but reminded us that "no alumni are ever satisfied." At least, that is the way I remember the talk. But that is all I can remember of it.

Dr. Pitman appeared to be well-credentialed, although he held not the Ph.D. degree but a doctorate in education instead. A Presbyterian of many years, he also held a B.D. degree from the San Francisco Theological Seminary and had been ordained. Moreover he was energetic, and this characteristic he shared with his wife. Indeed, Paul and Martha Pitman seemed to be everywhere and involved in everything.

In spite of this energy, in spite of his oratorical ability, and in spite of his unquestionably good intentions and ministerial inclinations, the Pitman years were at best uneasy and at their worst fraught with faculty-administration distrust.

Blatchley Hall, the College's multi-purpose building.

CHAPTER ELEVEN

"Four Years as

College President"

The title of this chapter is the title of the twenty-nine page document Paul Pitman wrote in mid-1954, after he had resigned. Latinate mottos have been abandoned appropriately, perhaps, in view of the elimination of a foreign language graduation requirement that occurred in Pitman's first year in office (1950-51). The dropping of this humanizing requirement helps establish the tone of his presidency. The tone is further established by the minutes of the Administrative Cabinet: from the sixth meeting on, the Cabinet began its deliberations with prayer.

To argue the matter from hindsight, it seems clear that Pitman urged change in the curriculum and a critical analysis of the College mystique: how the school was perceived by those who—for whatever reason—had formed perceptions of it. It seems clear also that his pathway to change was of sufficient difficulty to invoke the assistance of the Almighty.

The record, though, is difficult to reconstruct.

To begin with, Pitman found a faculty organized simply as a faculty accustomed to weekly meetings. To do its work, the faculty was divided into committees, the pattern inherited from Dr. Boone and unchanged by Dr. Hall.

One of Pitman's first acts was to establish the Administrative Cabinet "to serve [according to the first minutes of that group, August 15, 1950] in an advisory capacity considering broad questions of administrative policy." In ten substantive paragraphs, the minutes show that the problems considered were broad indeed, ranging from freshman orientation to the serving of cafeteria-style meals during orientation to a health program and military training program. Student petitions were to be directed to the Cabinet.

By the fourth meeting, September 26, 1950, the workload of the Cabinet had become so heavy that President Pitman sought relief through the formation of another committee, the Dean's Committee, to consider "matters which should not occupy the time of the entire Cabinet." The reader of these minutes cannot but wonder who made up the entire cabinet. No clues appear in the minutes as to the composition of this body.

Also by the time of this meeting, the president had decided upon nine faculty committees—Buildings and Grounds, College Life (Extra-curricular Activities, Athletics, Social Functions, Publications, Student Government); Concerts, Speakers, Convocation; Curriculum; Loans, Scholarships, Grants-in-Aid; Placement (Student and Graduate Employment); Post-graduate Study; Religious Life; Teacher Training.

Dr. Paul Pitman, fourth president of The College of Idaho.

In a memorandum dated September 29, 1950, the president informed the faculty that the Board of Trustees had "refurnished and redecorated [part of Blatchley Hall] for the dual purpose of providing an attractive 'home' for the Faculty and a facility of sufficient dignity to be used by the Trustees and the College Administration in the entertaining of guests." The memorandum referred to the facility as the Faculty Club and affirmed that "in the absence of a functioning Faculty Association the Cabinet has prepared an application blank and has requested the President to set down instructions which must be followed by all users of the facility, meaning the hall, parlor, dining room, and kitchenette." In turn, this classical revival structure had been a private dwelling, the presidential manse, a classroom building; and at one point the basement had served as a student headquarters, a primitive student union. And now, excepting The Little Theater, a Faculty Club.

By September of 1951 the Faculty Association had been formed at the behest of President Pitman as the instrument of the faculty concerned with the bread-and-butter issues of salary and benefits. In its function as the professorate, the entire teaching cadre was identified simply as the Faculty and would continue to be thus identified until a report by a faculty-administration group designated the Organization Committee could be implemented.

The Organization Committee met on December 17, 1953, "to study and examine faculty and Administration relationships and bring in a concrete proposal as to how the group [Faculty] might best be organized" (Faculty Assembly Minutes, February 6, 1954). President Pitman called for a meeting on February 9 to consider the proposal. The membership of the Organization Committee was as follows: Ralph W. Berringer, J. William Ladd, Dean Dwight Rugh, Lyle M. Stanford, Vice-President Brinton H. Stone, George V. Wolfe, Dean Ledru Williams.

The report carefully called attention to the imprecise definitions of responsibilities and powers respecting the operations of "the General Faculty and the Academic Council." Until such time as a Faculty Code could be developed, the Committee recommended "that the meeting of the Faculty be redesignated 'The Faculty Assembly.'" The functions of Faculty Assembly, as well as its composition, were outlined; the same process was then applied to Academic Council.

At the fifth meeting of the Faculty, February 23, 1954, the report and its recommendations were debated, with President Pitman the presiding officer. At this meeting, an Amended Report of the Committee on Organization was distributed, debated, modified slightly, and passed. The salient features are as follows:

1. The meeting of the Faculty shall be redesignated "the Faculty Assembly."

    a. The Faculty Assembly shall be given full legislative powers to initiate, to debate, and to recommend action to the President on [curricular matters].

    b. The Faculty Assembly shall be given full legislative powers to debate and recommend action to the President on all other matters which he may delegate to the body.

    c. Whenever a recommendation is tendered to the President under either a or b above, he shall submit to the Faculty Assembly as soon as possible a written response to that recommendation which shall include the reasons for his decision.

    d. The Faculty Assembly, for purpose of debate, shall be composed, as at present, of:

        1. Officers of Administration and Officers of Instruction.

    e. Voting privileges, however, shall be held only by:

        1. Officers of Administration on an employment basis of at least half-time.

        2. Officers of Instruction on an employment basis of at least six semester units taught in regular session.

2. Academic Council shall function as a steering committee for problems of academic import. It will receive questions and suggestions as well as initiate its own inquiries.

    a. It will investigate every such problem, prior to consideration by the Faculty Assembly, either through its own members or through the appointment of committees drawn from the Faculty Assembly, which the Academic Council shall be empowered to select.

    b. The Academic Council, after due investigation and consideration, shall, within a reasonable time, present its findings, together with its recommendations, to the Faculty Assembly.

    c. To permit such augmentation of its present activities, and to permit greater Faculty participation at the planning level, the Academic Council shall have the following membership:

1. The Chairmen of Divisions

2. Two members of the Administrative Staff, appointed by the President

3. The President and Vice-President of the College, ex-officio

4. Two members-at-large elected by the Faculty Assembly from voting members of the teaching faculty, as defined

   a. In order that as many faculty members as possible may gain the experience of serving in this capacity, the elected members-at-large shall serve for a single academic year and shall become ineligible to succeed themselves in the year immediately following.

The above represents the substance of the proposals and is essentially in the language of the Committee.

The record now turns to the first meeting of the Faculty Assembly. Paul Pitman had already resigned, and the presiding officer was Acting President Margaret Boone, who opened the proceedings with prayer and then reported that

1) contracts would, it was hoped, be out by March 15

2) a committee had been formed by the Board to find a new president

3) the commencement speaker had been chosen already

4) the Board had approved the formation of a committee to work with the Acting President—Miller, Stanford, Williams, and Wolfe, and

5) the Board, working on plans and budgets for next year, "feel heavily their responsibilities to the College."

After these announcements, the first ever Faculty Assembly elected two members-at-large from the teaching faculty to serve on the newly organized Academic Council. The modern era with respect to the structure through which curricular matters were attended to begins here.

It was an irony of Pitman's administration that organizing the faculty into an **assembly** respecting the curricular responsibilities and the maintenance of student discipline (the two enduring charges to the faculty by the Board of Trustees) and an **association** respecting the bread and butter issues of salaries and benefits was a sound and effective strategy but a strategy that served his own tenure at the school very poorly. His administrative style, as will be shown, was abrasive, authoritarian, and arrogant.

I cannot resist quoting further from the minutes of Faculty Assembly, for Leslie Brock was elected secretary and Brockian humor is apparent in certain entries—in this one, for instance, from the minutes of April 13, 1954:

> Miss Boone announced that Founders' Day would be observed on April 30, 1954. As customary, the Students requested that classes be dismissed for the day; but, as customary, it was resolved to dismiss classes on Founders' Day beginning with the 11:35 class.

There was much work for Faculty Assembly and its right arm, Academic Council, by way of economizing on classes, eliminating pointless programs, and generally concentrating on the force and effectiveness of the entire curriculum. To that end, the first order of business was to eliminate the Child Development Center as an autonomous entity and place it within the Division of Education. The Child Development Center had been an interesting experiment in the education of children, the product of the fertile if misdirected imagination of Martha Pitman. The Center had its own building, the one "monument of unaging intellect" attributable to Mr. Pitman; and among its interesting features was a panel of one way glass that enabled children to be observed without their knowing it. Those who know the campus identify this as the present Art Center; the building was finished and dedicated on October 18, 1952. The *Coyote* of Friday, October 31, 1952, reported that the

Ralph Berringer and Leslie Brock.

total cost including furnishings was approximately $50,000.

The second order of business was the elimination of the Department of Family Life at the end of Spring Semester 1954. With Pitman gone, the Faculty was once again in control of the curriculum.

The story must return to one of President Pitman's earliest attempts to improve The College of Idaho. At the fifth meeting of the Administrative Cabinet (October 2, 1950), after routine matters of announcing the name of the Commencement speaker (Willard E. Givens, Executive Secretary of the National Education Association), moving the awarding of an appropriate honorary degree to the speaker, and attending to other equally unexceptional chores, the President dropped, if not a bomb then a rather large grenade: What about a name change for The College of Idaho? Should it not become Boone College of Idaho?

President Pitman was probably aware of the printed appeal in the early college catalogs that said, in effect, whoever will contribute $10,000 may name the College. He certainly had read the Cowley Report, which called attention to the confusing name. A personal reference may be forgiven in this connection.

When I was introduced to the thirty-five member Department of English of East High School in Denver, my chair spoke as follows: "Another teacher new to the Department is" and giving my name, he blithely identified the origin of my B.A. degree as "The College of Idaho State at Pocatello." Our name can confuse even people who are highly literate. The College of Idaho State, indeed!

When all had been said and the canvassing of constituencies done (students voted on the matter twice; faculty and graduates voted once) the only element to oppose a name change was the students. The vote, of course, was advisory only; the Trustees hold the power to change the name at any time. (At the same time, the students approved a proposition which would have established an ROTC program.) In the *Coyote* of December 12, 1950, the tabulation of alumni/ae voting on the issue was given: 406 favored the change to Boone College of Idaho, 45 were in favor 'with reservations,' and 24 opposed the name change. In view of the conservative student opinion, the Trustees decided against a name change by a vote of eight to seven.

The Catalog of 1950 (with announcements and course offerings for 1950-51) identified five "groups" or divisions from which a major would be selected and selections from which general graduation requirements would be met, thus giving assurance that products of this liberal arts college would indeed be liberally educated through the general graduation requirements and reasonably well prepared in a narrower specialization. Those divisions were as follows: Literature and Fine Arts (Languages, Literature, Music, Art, Dramatics, Public Speaking); Natural Sciences (Biology, Chemistry, Geology, Mathematics, Physics); Philosophical Sciences (Psychology, Philosophy, Religion); Social Sciences (Economics, Education, History, Political Science, Sociology); Health and Physical Education. Graduation requirements specified certain numbers of courses or hours of credit from the first four divisions; each department required certain courses and number of hours for its majors to be certified as mastering the specialty offered therein. A reading proficiency in one foreign language was required of all graduates.

The Catalog for the next year featured the following six divisions: Humanities (English, Foreign Language, Philosophy, Religion, Speech); Natural Science (Biological Sciences, Mathematics, Physical Sciences); Social Science (Economics, History, Political Science, Psychology, Sociology); Fine Arts (Art, Music, Theater Arts); Education (Education, Health and Physical Education); and, in the largest type in the Catalog the Division of Applied and Vocational Arts (Business Administration, Merchandising, Secretarial Science, Family Life Education, Medical Technology, Nursing Education). To say that the new division was ambitious is an understatement. The College could not begin to sustain such a program. Reflecting upon the earlier discomfort caused by the introduction of education courses—too vocational!—one wonders at this gambit of President Pitman. However, justification is not difficult to find: the College needed tuition income, and Pitman was not the last president to strain the College's credibility as a liberal arts institution by exploring alternative sources of tuition income. Whenever it has appeared, vocationalism has consistently posed a threat to the institutional mission.

The manner in which President Pitman eliminated the foreign-language graduation requirement is indicative of his style of leadership. This insight comes from conversation with Arthur Hart and from James L. Martin's unpublished autobiography. At a meeting of the Division of Humanities, President Pitman asked members to express their opinions respecting the foreign-language graduation requirement. At the conclusion of several impassioned speeches in support of the requirement, the president thanked the advocates and affirmed that the meeting was adjourned, in spite of such queries as that of Professor Ian Morton: "Aren't we going to vote?" No vote was taken. "Asserting that he possessed emergency powers by virtue of the Korean War and [the resultant] conscription of man-power out of student populations, [Pitman] terminated the...foreign language requirement effective immediately" (Bollinger, "The Development of Business and Economics Programs at The College of Idaho, 1910-1982," p.3, unpublished typescript).

If a graduation requirement could be so summarily disposed of, revising the curriculum through adding a vocational division was no obstacle. And so it was done, at least on the books. The sixth division was never fully operable, as a review of the college Catalogs or Bulletins from 1951 through 1954 makes clear. Nursing Education, for example, is listed in the 1952 Catalog (or Bulletin) with announcements for 1952-53, as a department, yet no such courses were offered. "Nursing Education" appears in the index referring to page 38. Nowhere on that page do the words appear. Ambition exceeded capability.

Professor Bollinger's typescript surveys the matter coolly:

> During the Korean War, no military cadet corps was stationed on campus to soften the blow of declining enrollment. Dr. Pitman was eager to access nontraditional markets with particular focus upon women who were exempt from the draft. A major in Secretarial Studies was introduced to prepare women to become executive secretaries and to add another option for secondary education teachers in...business education.

> A new Department of Business Education appeared for the first time in 1952-53. A program in merchandising was created, utilizing adjunct faculty from the business community, and second-and third-year accounting majors added one full-year course in accounting to their work assignments. Courses previously offered in economics were allocated between economics or business, according to the nature of the course. The program in merchandizing included salesmanship, advertising, and retail store management (3).

President Pitman further attempted to modify tradition by eliminating written comprehensive examinations as a graduation requirement, thus depriving departments of an in-house means of assessing themselves. (*Coyote*, December 12, 1950. A subsequent issue of the *Coyote* affirmed that written comprehensives were not eliminated but stated that they **might be**). Other fiddlings with academic matters tended to be minor and short-lived, such as the somewhat silly use of red and green cards to indicate students' academic standing. Intended primarily for athletes, the red card earned for a student one point if his work was unsatisfactory but passing, two points if slightly below passing, and three points if seriously below passing, the score to be multiplied by the number of units carried by each course for which a red card was issued. A green card meant the athlete was in satisfactory status. If the student accumulated fifteen of these red card points in a semester, he was to be examined by the Deans' Committee (Cabinet Minutes, October 22, 1952). A subsequent Cabinet meeting modified this ruling as follows: "The Deans' Committee will also review the eligibility of any student who received three or more Red Cards at any mid-term period regardless of point value" (Minutes of November 12, 1952).

Although President Pitman's administration can hardly be accounted one of the College's sparkling presidencies still there were some accomplishments and some fine teachers were attracted to the College, a fact that offsets somewhat the loss from the College community of people of the caliber of Thurlow Bryant, Art Hart, Ian Morton, Burt Newbry, Ned Bowler, and Nick Weddle, to mention a few.

Cheerleaders in 1948 included, left to right, June Sherman, Helen Crofton, and Carole Mueller.

Some of those bright and promising oases of accomplishments include, surely, the drama program under the capable and demanding Asher Wilson. Working (as all drama coaches have had to do) with precious few students for whom acting was an academic major, Wilson, in play after play, brought hidden histrionic talent out of history, mathematics, physics, chemistry, English, and other assorted majors. His success was such that he took shows on the road, the cast debouching from an unreliable bus to present Shakespeare of a surprisingly high order to high schools throughout the valley. I was in the audience as a Nyssa High School teacher in the 1952-53 academic year when the group presented a matinee to an appreciative audience, and I can still recall with some degree of surprise the performance of a mathematics major in a Shakespearean role he obviously relished. His name, I seem to recall, was LaVerne Ruby.

Music, traditionally one of the College's **fortes**, continued to set high standards. Ian and Jean Morton were excellent musicians; though Jean was not a faculty member, she gave instruction in organ and occasionally performed in recital at the piano, showing skills of an extremely high order. Dick Skyrm continued to show his skills as a pianist and his growing administrative capacities as well as his competence as a classroom teacher of theory and music history. Charlie Ross, who taught voice to students and faculty for decades, came to the College in 1950. His presence was surely a bright spot in the institution's history, as was the presence of Gene Wisler and Carol Meyer. Walter Cerveny added his considerable musicianship to the music program in 1952.

Many others should be named—Don Parmelee comes to mind—but any one wishing to know of the faculty and administration during the Pitman years may consult a college catalog. Two, however, must be mentioned. The gentle and gracious Olive Bess continued to serve as librarian, having joined the faculty in 1933. And Clem Parberry left the College for the last time. In response to a recall from the navy, one of the College's most successful coaches made the break cleanly, for upon his second discharge from the service he cast his lot with the University of Idaho. In today's age of specialization, one wonders at people like Cornell and Parberry who coached **all** the major sports, except track.

If the C of I faculty contained many gifted individuals, what is the evidence? The record shows a continued high acceptance rate of pre-health care students by professional schools. Music majors could be relied upon to thrill the audiences at their senior recitals. LaVerne Ruby received a National Science Foundation graduate fellowship, not in Shakespeare but in mathematics. The products spoke well for the education received here, and (according to a story in the *Coyote* of February 22, 1952), *Good Housekeeping* identified The College of Idaho as one of the top independent liberal arts colleges in the region, along with Pacific, Willamette, Whitman, and Reed. But there is another indication of a faculty of a high order, an item that might easily get buried in the detritus of accolades falling upon a maturing institution. I refer to a couple of teachers who collaborated in the writing of a radio drama, received a national award for it, and saw the play produced (the rest of us, if we were fortunate, heard it), and received a cash reward for their efforts. They were Professors Burton Newbry and Asher Wilson. The play was "The Storm," presented by CBS on January 9, 1952. The award was the Dr. Christian Award. Radio, one remembers, was a major medium in those pre-TV years.

If further evidence be required to demonstrate that in spite of major administrative problems the pulse of the College was strong and steady, one need only refer to the successful competition of Rhodes Scholar aspirant Erling

The C of I's first Rhodes Scholar, Erling Skorpen, at left, posed with his family on the steps of Voorhees Hall in 1954.

Skorpen, '54. That Skorpen was a philosophy major, one of James Martin's students, is an indication that departments outside the science division were getting stronger.

One of the most interesting propositions debated at the College during the Pitman Era was a projected interdepartmental program, quite consistent with the liberal arts philosophy, through which "technical assistance to under-developed areas" could be rendered. In a carefully constructed six-page document dated December 23, 1952, six faculty members outlined the need for such a program and set forth in remarkable detail how such a program would work. The document was signed by Margaret Boone, Professor of English; Yin T'ang, Visiting Professor of Geography; Milton Charles, Assistant Professor of Sociology and Anthropology; Dwight Rugh, Professor of Education; Lyle Stanford, Professor of Biology; and George Wolfe, Professor of Political Science. Unable to sign because they were away at vacation time but participants in the deliberations were Robert Farley, Assistant Professor of Psychology, and Shirley C. Kroeger, Assistant Professor of Physical Education.

Two aspects of this proposed program for educating college students to assist in the areas of the world most needful of help are clear. First, the claim is often (justly) made that faculty in liberal arts colleges talk to one another across the borders of disciplines. Here is evidence. Sacrosanct barriers are the problem of multiversities, not of liberal arts colleges. The second aspect, though, is perhaps more interesting: here was a blueprint not very different in its projected results for what the world would later receive as the Peace Corps.

R.C. Owens, '59.

Until the Student Union Building was built in the early '60s, the Den was located in the basement of Finney Hall.

Another bit of evidence that good things were happening at the C of I was provided by two faculty members who won prestigious Ford Foundation Fellowships (Fund for the Advancement of Education). Dr. Stanford chose to study at Harvard; Dr. Martin selected the university at the other Cambridge, the one across the Atlantic Ocean.

Evidence of intellectual acuity among students at the College can be adduced by studying the school's newspapers. Editors, business managers, and feature and column writers consistently provided a vigorous record of school life. It is not an exaggeration to say that a school newspaper rightly conducted is the best single biography of an institution. Blaine Jolley, Carlton Tappan, Richard Rice, Clyde Swisher, Bob Purcell, Ray Vinson, and Roger Sayre produced papers loaded with news. But it was under the editorial leadership of Erling Skorpen and the managerial skills of Darrell Perkins that the *Coyote* became not just a source of information about college events but a source of ideas. And ideas, after all, are why a college exists.

Mention must also be made of athletics, before the record of the Pitman years concludes. Eddie Cole inherited a good football team from Clem Parberry, recalled to active duty in the navy during the summer of 1951, and Nick Weddle was replaced by Sam Vokes, to whom Nick passed along a basketball team of fine talent. When the story of C of I athletics is written—and the present institutional story is not that—the Pitman years will be connected with exceptional football and basketball powers, featuring the names of R.C. Owens, Bob Morford, Boyd Crawford, and a modest and rather small halfback from Fruitland, Idaho, named Ted Martin. In the words of a famous old music hall-college song, "There were heroes a-plenty and well known to fame." The 1953 team enjoyed an undefeated season.

President Pitman summarized his mistakes (pp. 6,7) and accomplishments (pp. 8-29) in "Four Years as a College President." His self-scrutiny is informative.

The first mistake was "I aimed too high. I did not realize that excellence is irritating to many people, and that greatness is frightening." The second was "I worked too hard. I did not take enough time for relaxation, for fun, for getting acquainted, for opening channels of communication." In the third place "I moved too fast. I doubt that a slower pace could have saved the College, but certainly the tempo of change was hard on everyone." The fourth mistake was that "I was not tough enough. Many people misinterpreted my patience for softness and my kindness for cowardice." Fifth, President Pitman declared, "I tried to do too much. I kept trying to delegate responsibility, only to find that the staff I had inherited wasn't up to it." He continued: "I felt compelled...to perform...many functions which would normally have been carried by such officers as the dean of the faculty, business manager, dean of students, director of athletics, chaplain, director of publications, and dean of the school of education. Sixth in his list of mistakes:

> I misjudged the trustees. Too late I discovered that they did not know **how** to organize themselves for work. Too late I discovered that I was moving too fast for them, too. Too late I saw that I should have told them the blunt truth about the condition of the College and made them face up to the decision as to whether or not we could afford to build an institution which could compete with the growing power of public institutions....

The matter of the name change was error number seven: "Alarmed by student opinion, the Board ignored the alumni and the faculty and voted eight to seven to postpone the decision," resulting in a failure to capitalize upon the institution's 60th Anniversary. And finally, the eighth mistake required only a seven word statement: "I recommended the wrong man as vice-president."

Readers may decide on their own the merit of this analysis, for there is forthrightness, there is self-exculpation, there is error, and there is percipience in the bill of particulars. If it is true that everything occurs at just the right moment and that everyone performs that special role created for the actor and that actor only, then it is a bit pointless to dwell on such a list as that offered by President Pitman.

It is, however, quite clear that Pitman's Administration offered some genuine accomplishments. These seem consequential.

The College gained re-accreditation, or, rather, its accredited status was re-confirmed, a condition absolutely essential to the life of any educational institution. Not only was it re-accredited but it was re-evaluated in accordance with new standards advocated by the National Commission on Accrediting (Pitman 23).

The College produced a Rhodes Scholar, important in and of itself but since the winner was a philosophy major important also for demonstrating academic strength in the humanities. (As an aside, a charming bit of campus tradition has it that Erling Skorpen was a free and wide-ranging thinker, not given to the accepting or promulgating of dogma. His reply to classmates who persisted in asking, "Are you saved?" was a puzzled, "From what?") Two College of Idaho faculty members earned Ford Foundation Fellowships. Surely that fact says something about the quality of the faculty—surely about the quality of Lyle Stanford and Jim Martin—and about the College that had the good sense to hire them (without the mixed blessing of a faculty search committee). "No other small [under 500 enrollment] college in the West and only two in the United States were awarded two of these coveted fellowships" (Pitman 22).

Major figures continued to consent to speak to faculty, students, and community. Henry R. Luce—*Time* and *Life* publisher, for younger readers of this—and Elton Trueblood, noted theologian and preacher, graced the campus with their presence.

Another significant accomplishment was the establishment of a dual-degree program in engineering with Stanford University, establishing a precedent that would ultimately involve at least three major universities.

Loretta Warner, Class of 1953, was the first woman to be admitted to the Harvard Law School from the State of Idaho. Ms. Warner is one of many minds honed by Dr. George V. Wolfe and pointed toward either law school or a career in political science. Another teacher hired (by Dr. Hall) without the assistance of a faculty search committee, Dr. Wolfe earned a reputation as a demanding and knowledgeable teacher almost at once, for one of his first students here was Howard Bavender, who had been a second lieutenant and Post Adjutant for the College's cadet program (Phelps 13). Bavender returned after the war and proved a first rate student, becoming a professor of political science in the course of time.

Surely another step forward for the College resulted from Pitman's urging that salaries be increased and that the College be brought within the federal program of Social Security (Minutes of the Cabinet, October 31, 1950). Additionally, a policy of leaves of absence, tenure, retirement, illness, and death benefits was established (Pitman 10).

The increase in the annual appropriation for the library from $2,000 to $7,000 was noteworthy, appropriate, and timely (Pitman 10). These figures seem pitifully small, even when allowance is made for a shrinking dollar. But a threefold and a half improvement is consequential.

Finally, it should be noted that another benchmark in the life of the College was established with the approval by the Idaho State Board of Education in January of 1954 of the Graduate Program launched by the College (Pitman 24). The Northwest Association had included a recommendation for its accreditation in the Report to the Higher Commission in November of 1953 (Pitman 13). Based partly on data accumulated by Ward Tucker and included in his dissertation, the graduate program seemed to fill an educational lacuna in the region since no graduate degree-granting institution existed.

But a distressing statistic emerges as the penultimate observation, a statistic that would compromise the administration of nearly every succeeding president irrespective of all other redeeming graces he might possess: the operating deficit. Just as it is fatal in the management of personal affairs, so it is fatal to the last degree of fatality in the management of the fiscal affairs of a private school. The May 31, 1950, audit showed a deficit of $24,931.30; that of May 31, 1954, showed a deficit of $85,963.90 (Pitman 20). Even with the shift in accounting procedures and other qualifications offered by the president, the deficit was there (Pitman 20).

President Pitman's resignation was accepted on March 3, 1954. In The *Coyote* of March 16, an editorial appeared that is a masterpiece of diplomatic yet sensitive asseveration:

> Whatever it was about Dr. Pitman's dreams for The College of Idaho and his ways of making them real that could not find a home here, there are few of us who will forget his unrestrained devotion to them and his tenacity of purpose. Whether he was right or wrong we may well borrow some of his zeal of the job set out before us. In many respects, Dr. Pitman leaves an example that will tax his successor to duplicate.

That successor was not to be Margaret Boone, nominated for the post by The *Coyote* of April 21, 1954, and by others, but a tall nearly bald Iowan, whose first five years were to point the College toward a destiny almost undreamed of and whose last five years created grave problems, both personal and institutional. His name was Tom E. Shearer.

Tom E. Shearer, fifth president of the College, with trustee Jack Simplot and Professor Shirley Kroeger.

Part V

Tom E. Shearer 1954-64

Strahorn Library reading rocm.

CHAPTER TWELVE

Uncle Tom's Campus

The title of this chapter was supplied by one of the entertainments written by Professor Ralph Berringer, skits presented annually to the student body before Christmas breaks. Lighthearted and witty, clever to the nth degree, they were calculated to send students home chuckling over the antics of their teachers—who had proved they could act the fool as well as the tyrant. Other titles included "Malice in Blunderland," "The Littlest Freshman," and "Raising the Dickens."

The "Tom," of course, was Tom E. Shearer, who came from Parsons College to become the fifth president of The College of Idaho.

President Pitman's resignation left the College in the capable hands of acting president Margaret Boone, daughter of the first president. The quest for a new president was launched, and by the time Fall Semester had begun, Tom E. Shearer was the new chief executive. He was destined to serve from 1954 to 1964.

What kind of college had he inherited and what manner of man was he? Neither question is easily answered. It is clear that the College was still a small residential church-related liberal arts institution. Each of those adjectives requires a bit of clarification. The *Coyote* of October 11, 1954, reported that 460 students were enrolled, 325 of them from Idaho, 33 from Oregon, 9 from California, 8 from Illinois, with a thin scattering from nine other states and one student from Korea. Respecting denominational preference, 94 were listed as Presbyterian, 93 as Methodist, 44 as Baptist, 43 as Roman Catholic, 34 as Christian, 24 as L.D.S., 15 as Lutheran, with smaller numbers from nine other Christian denominations and one Buddhist. Forty-four students gave no preference. Most of the students were Christian, and the college preserved its association with the Presbyterian church through the Articles of Incorporation governing the composition of the Board of Trustees.

It is appropriate to look at those articles now, for it is from them that the College proceeds as an institution independent of legislative control and they have been amended from time to time. Finally, it is appropriate to spend a bit of time in this legal framework because in the 1950s profound shifts were taking place deep within the bedrock of American higher education, shifts that had a lasting effect upon how the College's trustees saw their role.

The Articles of Incorporation, dated April 1, 1893, signed by Boone, Maxey, Blatchley, Greenland, and Rice, in the presence of Notary Public Morrison, establish the name of the institution as The College of Idaho, owned and controlled by a Board of Trustees, of whom there were twelve besides President Boone, member *ex officio*, "two-thirds of whose members shall always be members of the Presbyterian church in the United States of America." This document was filed April 12, 1898, with the Secretary of State.

On December 10, 1929, the Trustees filed a certificate with the Secretary of State, amending the Articles of Incorporation to accommodate an increase in the number of trustees from twelve to eighteen. It was signed by Boone, Lowell, Rice, Blatchley, Plowhead, Murphy, Baldridge, Thompson and Anderson.

The next change, that of June 24, 1943, boosted the number of trustees to twenty-four. This Certificate of Amendment was signed by Mary E. Kirkpatrick, Walter S. Kerrick, William E. Welsh, Edson H. Deal, H. C. Baldridge, Edgar L. Oakes, William Crosby Ross, J. H. Lowell, William W. Hall, Jr., D. L. McBane, J. F. Congdon, and C. C. Anderson. This increase was made possible by a change in the Idaho Code which provided that the number of directors or trustees of institutions like The College of Idaho be not less than five nor more than twenty-four.

On October 27, 1949, in response to another change in the Idaho Code, allowing thirty directors, the Trustees filed a third Certificate of Amendment of Articles of Incorporation increasing their number to thirty. Trustees signing the document were William E. Welsh, Walter E. Kerrick, G. L. Stanton, Edson H. Deal, Frank A. Rhea, Charles E. Palmer, Bernard Mainwaring, M. B. Shaw, Marcus E. Lindsay, Robert I. Troxell, P. G. Batt, Ezra B. Hinshaw, Jessie Little Naylor, Mrs. G. L. Crookham, Jr., and J. R. Simplot.

Up to this point, changes in the Articles of Incorporation had been confined to enlarging the Board in response to state legislation. However, the fourth Certificate of Amendment was of a different order. By changing the heretofore ironclad and untouchable requirement that "two-thirds of [the Board of Trustees] shall always be members of the Presbyterian Church," a fundamental re-orientation in the church relationship was accomplished; the amendment said simply that "a majority of the Board of Trustees shall always be members of the Presbyterian Church." The instrument was signed on June 2, 1962, by Trustees Warren Barry, Margaret Boone, Mrs. George L. Crookham, Jr., Edson H. Deal, Mrs. Glen L. Evans, G. F. Jewett, Jr., C. J. Kniefel, William D. Millen, Mrs. Robert M. Naylor, Charles E. Palmer, A. M. Popma, Gilbert L. Stanton, Darwin Symms, N. L. Terteling, Mrs. Lyman D. Wilbur, and A. C. Garber.

This fourth amendment was one of Tom Shearer's signal accomplishments, and it paved the way for the fifth and, at this writing, the last amendment. It was filed during the administration of Shearer's successor. The fifth Certificate of Amendment changed Articles Two and Four. Article Two provided that the members of the Board of Trustees "evidence a continuing desire to relate The College of Idaho to the United Presbyterian Church in the United States of America or the latter's successor." Article Four anticipated various legislative fiddling with what the State's wisdom from time to time decreed the appropriate number of members of such a board as that governing the College: "the number of Trustees shall not be more than the maximum number of members now provided by the laws of the State of Idaho and as the same may hereafter be amended." The Trustees who signed this Certificate of Amendment will be identified subsequently.

It is clear that the College was moving away from real or perceived church control. It is clear that such a move was an honest and forthright strategy by which the College's independent character could be made clear and public while still cherishing and maintaining a special relatedness to the church which founded it. And it is clear to all who have the shallowest knowledge of the history of higher education in America that the College was doing what had been done at Harvard, Yale, and innumerable other—indeed, most other—private institutions of higher learning. The College of Idaho is not a church college. Its connection with a Christian denomination is not that of being owned by the denomination but is instead historical, emotional, traditional, and sympathetic. All of that was made clear by the strategy promulgated by President Shearer and approved by the Board of Trustees.

The residential nature of the College was quite real, and the presence of Simplot Hall enhanced the institution's capacity to house its students. Thus was met one of Dr. Hall's abiding concerns, and the College "was on its way to becoming a predominantly residential college," being transformed "—let us not

203

overdraw the picture—" into something like "Carleton, Swarthmore, Wooster, and Oberlin" (*College* 113).

The liberal arts part of the series of adjectives can be understood by referring to such publications as the Catalog. In the 1954-1955 Bulletin (or Catalog: the terms are most often interchangeable), with announcements for 1955-56, the faculty include several short-timers but also some stalwarts whose lives and careers are almost inseparable from their institution: Robert D. Bratz, identified as the holder of the J. R. Simplot Chair of Biological Sciences, appointed in 1953; Fern Nolte Davidson, pianist and teacher of piano teachers throughout the region, appointed in 1953; Elizabeth B. Jensen, instructor in Secretarial Science; Eldon R. Marsh, instructor in Business Administration, appointed in 1952; Robert M. Peter, Professor of Art, appointed in 1953: L. S. "Sam" Vokes, physical education and coach, appointed in 1952; Douglas D. Tiffany, Lecturer in Religion, appointed in 1954; and Harold N. Nye, Lecturer in Religion, appointed in 1949. Alvin Allen, 1949; David Blackaller, 1954; M. R. Charles, 1950; R. E. Farley, 1951; Arthur E. Huff, 1953; and Donald Mammen, 1954, were among those who served the College for varying lengths of time. To these should be added Pauline Crooke, 1950; John Ford Sollers, 1955; Eddie Troxell, 1955; and William Wallace, 1955. Pauline Crooke replaced Margaret Sinclair as news director and alumni secretary, Margaret becoming Professor Sinclair of the Department of English.

The philosophy that animated the institution and to which these folk subscribed—that is, the nature of the liberal arts education of this college—was admirably set forth on page 15 of that Catalog:

> The plan of education at The College of Idaho is founded upon four assumptions: first, that [human beings] live in an intelligible and purposeful universe and that therefore, human life has meaning and value; second, that each individual is important; third, that each person yearns for, and is capable of, a real measure of creative achievement; fourth, that personality comes to fruition only in a social matrix through a process of awakened sensibilities, appropriated meanings, discriminating choice and self-discipline, and heightened loyalties.

> It follows that education at The College of Idaho does not consist of a sequence of academic courses, no matter how venerable such courses may be. Rather, the life of The College of Idaho is deliberately designed to assist young men and women to achieve wholeness, to develop themselves as persons, to translate their physical, intellectual, emotional, and spiritual potentialities into actualities.

The College is residential so that students may be graduated from the protective guidance of home into the larger freedom and wider experience of living in a selected community.

The College is small so as to give students that personal attention and those experiences in leadership which are less easily provided on a large campus.

The College is co-educational because it believes that democratic homes and a democratic society can be built only upon the foundation of mutual understanding, mutual respect, shared responsibility, and shared power.

The College is independent because it believes that society is an organization rather than an organism, and it intends so to conduct every aspect of its life as to foster in each student a wholesome spirit of independence, initiative, and resourcefulness. The College is concerned about vocational fitness. While it would not substitute vocational skills for scholarship, it recognizes that men and women can neither enjoy nor invest the fruits of scholarship unless and until they are able to provide for themselves and their dependents. Consequently, the College seeks to bring each student to the point of intelligent vocational choice, to develop...skill in leadership, and insofar as possible, consonant with its basic objectives, to equip [the student] with that knowledge and those skills which will enable [the graduate] to maintain self and...family through some useful and creative work. For some students, such as candidates in teacher education, The College of Idaho can meet the full need. For other students a broad program of cooperative education leading to two degrees has been developed with the University of Idaho and with major colleges and universities across the United States.

Finally and supremely, The College of Idaho is a Christian college because it recognizes in real religion the only relationship which can make men and societies whole.

Earlier I suggested that some profound shifts were taking place in the bedrock of American higher education. Those must be touched upon before we turn to the examination of President Shearer and take a brief look at life and times in his Coyoteville.

The first change, the one on whose coattails a host of other changes rode in, was cited in a study by the title *Values, Liberal Education, and National Destiny,* (McGrath, 1975, p. 54). As late as 1950, about half of students enrolled in college were taking this work at private, that is to say, independent, colleges. After the middle '50s, things began to change from this happy equity. At least, to enjoy half the market would appear an equitable arrangement. Why, we might ask, did that shift to public tax-supported education occur? I should like to propose some tentative answers.

(1) Inflation. You have met this parasite before. Inflation increased the costs of everything, and when everything costs more, personal economies have to be practiced. The tightening up of the philanthropical urge is always a convenient way to economize. So, large and well-endowed independent colleges and universities took up the slack by spending their capital (their endowments) and raising tuition. Small and under-endowed institutions had to abandon projects for increasing their endowments, turning instead to raising funds for current expenses...and to increasing tuition.

So the ravages of inflation were at work, and in consequence of increased tuition some students turned to the cheaper tax-supported institutions. But other things added to the already tough competition for students and funds faced by the independent college. The second one of these let me call (2) Extra-Territoriality.

It occurred when tax-supported institutions increased their assault on those private sectors traditionally the sources of funds for independent colleges. No private college has ever been able to pay its way on tuition alone. The tax-supported institutions hired development officers, mounted slick and effective campaigns, courted wealthy citizens, and interestingly enough, laid siege to corporations and foundations, diverting who knows how much wealth away from the private and independent branch of higher education to the tax-supported public institution. The playing-field became less and less level, for while private institutions receive no tax support, tax-supported institutions have unlimited access to private philanthropy. I do not question the alumna who makes a bequest to her *alma mater*, be it public or private. That is a fine and generous thing to do. My concern is with the assault, well-mounted and fraught with great hazard to the independent college.

The third condition I shall call (3) Exploding Altruism. I refer to the increase in the number of those benefit activities that siphon money away from traditional recipients. I refer not so much to such charities as CARE, Foster Parents, The Christian Children's Fund, and the occasional and local charities and benevolences that arise from time to time (although all these may divert funds away from such traditional recipients as independent colleges) but to the encroachment by government upon private financing to meet obligations that are statutory. When legislators tolerate the decay of the infrastructure in order that they may run on such campaign slogans as "we promise not to raise taxes this year" or "another year with 'no new taxes,'" the only alternative is the cheap and shoddy appeal to public charity, the sort of thing one sees in campaigns to get the population to "support a road" or "adopt a bridge" and contribute to a fund for those purposes. Such tactics can only mean a gross ignorance respecting both the promotion of the general welfare and the diversion of philanthropy away from its traditional concerns in order to help prevent the collapse of infrastructures that are the statutory obligation of tax money.

These various and sundry matters impinged upon the administration of this Iowan, whose first six years or so were remarkably successful. Because a small college almost necessarily takes on or projects the character of its chief executive, it is appropriate to offer at least a profile of Tom Shearer.

Another without the Ph.D. degree, Shearer came to the College as its fifth president from a successful tenure as fourteenth president of Parsons College, whose accreditation he helped regain after the North Central Association had denied that most important seal of acceptability in 1948.

One of his admirable traits was his ability to size up a person, to judge character. A result of this capacity was the enhancement of the faculty at The College of Idaho. Ralph Sayre had been Acting Dean of Parsons College, and Shearer and he had worked well together there. When Shearer asked him in 1956 to come help at the C of I, Sayre writes, "I could hardly believe my luck"(*The Fairfield Ledger*, Parsons Reunion Edition, June 22, 1989). In this reminiscence, Sayre, who was associated with The College of Idaho through the administrations of four presidents (Shearer through DeRosier), describes his first meeting with Shearer upon Sayre's arrival at Parsons to teach history:

> My new boss didn't match my image of a college president. He was a loose-boned man of medium size, with a lined and scarred face, a receding hairline, and tobacco-stained teeth. He was dressed in rumpled army chinos and scuffed brown shoes imperfectly tied. But the impression of somewhat dismayed curiosity lasted only for a flash. His handshake was firm and confident, and he took command of the meeting immediately. His hands, by the way, were his best physical attribute. Large and strong, impeccably manicured, they figured to great effect in ordinary conversation as well as in public speeches.

Sayre continues:

> From that time on, until he left in the spring of 1954, my admiration and respect grew. When he asked me to follow him to Idaho in 1956, I could hardly believe my luck. For the next nine years, working more closely with him than I had in Fairfield, my respect and regard multiplied, punctuated by short periods of apprehension bordering on

panic, when his human weaknesses bubbled to the surface like ugly patches of crude oil on calm waters.

.   .   .   .

If I may play the totally uninformed amateur psychologist, I strongly suspect that many of Shearer's strengths grew out of his perceived weaknesses. His deep compassion and sympathy for others, his great admiration for people whose strengths he did not find in himself, his ability to make his admiration known might well, I think, have come from this. But he was anything but the self-pitying, down-trodden self-effacer. He valued his strengths—his basic intelligence, his quick analysis of situations, his way with words, and above all, his independent spirit.

Everybody who knew him will understand that his story is not complete without the darker side. He was ridden by some powerful demons. The first, as none of us will forget, was alcohol.

.   .   .   .

President Shearer and students observe progress on the construction of Jewett Chapel-Auditorium.

> I think that another even more powerful [demon] was that indepen-
> dence of mind and spirit that was his genius. That...demon bred a set
> of standards that no human being—at least this human being—could
> bear...without a friend. Alcohol was a bad friend.

That is a keen assessment of a remarkable man. Shearer and Sayre added considerably to the substance of the faculty, for the following were appointed by them: Boyd Henry, Edward R. Allen, C. Larry Hagen, J. A. "Babe" Brown, and Lester McCrery. Additional Shearer-Sayre appointments through 1960 included Frank Specht, Patricia Packard, Roger Higdem, John Willmorth, Dick Winder and Bob Post (Admissions), Joseph Dadabay, Jeanne DeLurme (Regis-trar), R. Curtis Westfall (Development), Richard Elliott (Librarian), Ralph O. Marshall, Elmer Thomas, William Chalker, Ruth Grob, and William W. Nish.

More evidence of the effectiveness of President Shearer is supplied by the record of building that took place during his tenure. In the first six years of his administration Simplot Dining Hall was enlarged to accommodate 350 persons (contract let in August 1956, according to the 1957 *Trail*), Anderson Hall was begun and completed in 1957 (according to this source), the Student Union building was completed in 1958 and remodeled in 1964 ("Walking Tour," p.4), and Jewett Chapel-Auditorium was completed in 1962 ("Walking Tour," p.1).

This was a legacy of bricks and mortar of which any leader could be proud. In addition to these new buildings and remodeling, President Shearer under-took the modification of two of the three original crown jewels. Nathaniel Hawthorne observed that the hand that renovates is the hand that destroys (it's in "Mosses from an Old Manse") and the modifications of Finney and Voorhees support Hawthorne's conviction. The alterations destroyed the integrity of the architects' work, for the graceful and appropriate terminal floors were modi-fied so as to increase the occupancy of both. The work on Finney was described in the *Coyote* of May 17, 1957, as follows:

> A colonial style false front will be added. The first floor will include a
> lobby-lounge, dorm director quarters, guest room, and accommodation
> for twelve residents.

> The present roof will be removed and a complete third floor will be
> added. There will be new wiring, plumbing, plaster, and woodwork
> throughout, as well as a study-snack room on each floor.

All of this for $80,000. And for $126,000, according to the *Coyote* of Septem-ber 25, 1959, Voorhees was to receive the blessings from the same hand:

On completion, the building will include 68 student bedrooms, a director's apartment, a guest suite, an office, a recreation room, laundry facilities, and a reception lounge....

Exterior of the brick building is to...be painted a creamy white.

Financing...came through a loan from the Federal Housing and Home Finance Agency.

Subsequently the paint began to peel and it was up to another administration either to restore the painted surface on the now characterless rectangles or to sandblast the paint and in so doing erode some of the baked surface of the bricks, making them vulnerable to the process of weathering. The latter was done in 1978.

But students were knocking at the doors, and they had to be accommodated, further evidence that Shearer and his team—Margaret Boone remained as Dean of the College until Ralph Sayre arrived—were doing many things right. The *Coyote* of October 10, 1955, announced in a banner headline "C of I REGISTRATION RECORDS SMASHED." The total was 573, a 17 percent increase over the 1954 total and a 4 percent increase over the previous all-time high of 525. Those numbers translated into wholesome statistics at the other end as well, the end that really matters. "Largest Senior Class in History to Get Diplomas in June 1, Ceremony," declared the *Coyote* of May 17, 1957. The story said that "a total of 126 students will receive bachelor's degrees" at Commencement.

Indeed, so many things were going right at the College that the chronicler must exercise great care in selecting from among the many elements contending for inclusion.

The Sun Valley summer session of 1956 for instance, under the directorship of Dr. Donald Mammen, was a bold attempt to extend the reputation of the College, to secure always needed tuition dollars (it lost money), and to provide summer income for faculty who were not overpaid even then. Dr. James L. Martin was scheduled to offer courses in contemporary philosophy and the world's living religions. Dr. Lyle Stanford offered classes in geology and biology of the Rocky Mountains, including (no surprise to any of his former students) field trips. Professor Robert M. Peter agreed to conduct an open-air studio as part of his course in basic painting and to offer a history of modern art. Ann Southern was one of the better students. Professor William Wallace offered beginning and advanced French. Other offerings, from modern and folk dancing by the Physical Education Department to general psychology and including contemporary drama and various music courses, indicated that this

210

was indeed a venture taken seriously by both The College of Idaho and the Union Pacific Railroad, an old friend of the College and owner of the resort.

The session was repeated for the summer of 1957, although it again incurred a debt and was then abandoned. Regular summer sessions continued to be held on campus.

In the meantime room had to be made for an enlarging student body. The report from admissions director Frank Tucker showed that enrollment for Fall Semester, 1958, stood at 730. Of this group, 350 were identified as new students, broken down not by age and sex, as the wags put it, but by point of origin. Of this group, 30 percent (102) were from outside Idaho, 8 percent (30) from Magic Valley; seventeen students came from North Idaho, and sixteen came from Eastern Idaho. Fifty-four percent (185) were local. Another loan, $175,000, from the Federal Housing and Home Finance Agency made additional expansion of Simplot Hall a reality. The *Coyote* of October 23, 1959, noted that the new addition would increase the capacity from 91 to 147, although that number stabilized at 135 according to the description in a "Walking Tour" leaflet (p.3).

In the nature of things, losses as well as gains must be noted. I find no systematic necrology for faculty, staff, and students and in its absence note the deaths as they are recorded, perhaps in tributes in school publications, perhaps in the local press, sometimes in personnel folders in the Vice President's office or in the Development Office, and in memorial pages in the Catalog for the appropriate year. Who among us remember the death of the popular and talented Roberta Blondell, Class of 1940, taken too soon by the grimmest of reapers? The lovely and gifted Jean Moore is memorialized by a scholarship, but there should be a biography on file so that a recipient of the award carrying her name could learn something of her. And Tim Magnussen...and other names will occur to readers. Professor Emeritus Paul Murphy died in the spring of 1959; he is lamented in an entry in the Minutes of Faculty Assembly for April 3, 1959. So it was with Professor Knute Ovregaard, who died in 1960 and whose wife was sent a letter of condolence by the secretary of the Faculty Association of September 30, 1960.

But these men were retired, and the fullness of time had a fair claim upon them. It was not so with Professor Joseph M. Rankin, who died at age 66 on June 8, 1956, and had not retired even after 44 years of teaching mathematics at The College of Idaho. It was not so with Professor Harold Tucker, a valued and knowledgeable faculty member since 1930, who died, like Professors Hemphill and Boulton and J. J. Smith, and Boone, before retirement. Professor

Tucker died of cancer in 1959. He was honored in the 1958 *Trail*, which was dedicated to him.

And on November 16, 1956, The *Coyote* paid tribute to one of the finest of scholar-athletes to have graced the campus. That issue was dedicated to Ensign Ted Martin, who died in a plane crash in California. He had graduated in 1954 with a GPA of 3.5, had been All-Conference for three years, and was a Little All-American candidate. "Too soon to faithful warriors cometh rest."

But there was still further evidence that this small but growing college was also growing up. On April 5, 1955, after careful study, the faculty approved an Honors Program through which exceptional students could challenge themselves and thus be prepared for the kind of work expected of students in graduate and professional schools. This is another benchmark in the College's continuing story, and although the roster of students graduating with honors is far too extensive to be cited, there is no question that the program served and continues to serve well.

A further important step was taken by the faculty when it called for the dropping of the Secondary Education major effective with the beginning of the 1958-59 academic year, calling instead for the preparation of secondary school

A publicist's inspiration: Simplot Hall coeds in bermuda shorts during a snowstorm, c. 1959

teachers in a recognized academic discipline or field of study (Faculty Assembly Minutes of December 16, 1957).

How foundations and other sources of financial support make decisions about what institutions of higher learning they should assist will probably remain something of a mystery. If, however, such decisions are even partially based on the quality of the institutions' products, then The College of Idaho merits a second and even a third consideration. The College is small, its endowment has been scant, and it is easily misidentified as a tax-supported institution in a state still confused with Iowa and Ohio. The universal law that everything supports what is already strong, cited before, can be adverted to yet again in this connection.

Even so, judged on the basis of its products, such evidence as that contained in a detailed study undertaken by the Public Health Service of the U.S. Department of Health, Education and Welfare and published as Public Health monograph No. 66, *Baccalaureate Origins of 1950 - 1959 Medical Graduates* would reveal that this school deserves a close look by those who serve philanthropic causes. The study is quoted as follows:

1. There were 1,008 colleges where at least one M.D., graduate received his pre-medical training out of the 1,400 four-year colleges and universities in the United States.

2. THE COLLEGE OF IDAHO was one of the 389 such colleges and universities where 25 or more male M.D. graduates had taken their pre-medical training.

3. A separate listing was made of the 100 undergraduate colleges with the highest proportion of male graduates receiving M.D. degrees during 1950-59. THE COLLEGE OF IDAHO was included among the top 100.

   a. Among these top 100 colleges only four (out of 45 such colleges) Presbyterian-related colleges were included. They are THE COLLEGE OF IDAHO, Westminster College (Missouri), Centre College (Kentucky), and The College of Wooster (Ohio).

   b. Only six colleges and universities out of all the colleges and universities (66 of them) in the Northwest and Pacific coast states (California, Idaho, Montana, Nevada, Oregon, Washington, Wyoming) were included. They are THE COLLEGE OF IDAHO, Carroll College (Montana), Walla Walla College (Washington), Reed College

(Oregon), Willamette University (Oregon), and Stanford University (California).

c. Among these 100 colleges, upon the basis of the rate of science doctorates per 1,000 graduates (1946-50), THE COLLEGE OF IDAHO (6.1) ranks number 38, outranking in this group such institutions as Stanford (4.6), Willamette (5.4), and Duke (2.8), and behind Reed (26.0), Carleton (9.9), and Dartmouth (6.4).

As to the quality of life on the campus, it is clear that much was going on. Many familiar organizations contributed to that vitality—Shield, IKs, Scarlet Masque, and others. However, one organization, the Boone Christian Association, died in the summer of 1957.

The *Coyote* of February 17, 1957, called attention in a banner headline to the second annual Miss College of Idaho contest. A 6½ x 8 photograph spilling across four columns on the front page features the six young contestants. The accompanying story includes even their vital statistics, and a brief biographical sketch. They were Phyllis Redfield, Beverly Huffman, Sharon Miller, Sharon Transue, Pat Clark, and Dixie Garfield.

Professor Les McCrery, who joined the faculty in the fall of 1956 and served many years as speech and debate coach, was given an extensive write-up in the *Coyote* of November 16, 1956. The story gives appropriate recognition to his professional distinctions (and there were many) but makes no mention of his special fly, "the McCrery Killer," or his not inconsiderable skills as a fly fisherman.

Occasionally, a student letter to a student editor provides a rough sort of index of student concerns, and it assuredly yields an accurate impression of student intelligence and rhetorical skills. Anyone who questions this judgment should turn to the *Coyote* of May 17, 1957, and read the letter by Ted Wills and Charles Westfall. It is upper division in its organization, its polish, its clarity, and its wit. Space will permit the citation of only one paragraph:

> Your editorials have raised no timely or important issues. Your campaign for a cigarette-machine in the Den has been utterly overplayed and overpublicized. Let us make it clear...that we are not arguing the pro[s] and cons of a cigarette-machine in the Den; we simply feel that the editors could forget their nicotine fits long enough to consider issues of deeper significance (such as campaigning for the Hungarian student fund drive or discussing something besides strictly local matters).

214

On a campus where athletes and athletics were, to say the least, prominent, it is noteworthy that the intellect was not being neglected. One of the brightest of the College's athletes was a transfer from Boise's junior college—indeed, one of several from there dating back even before the fine lineman Dick Nelson. He was Ed Lodge, later a successful and much respected jurist. It is interesting to note that news stories in Boise's *Statesman* about graduates of the junior college who take their bachelors' degrees at the C of I are often written up in such a way as to suggest translation from the junior college directly into law or medicine or graduate school without benefit of the experience here.

Still on the subject of athletes, some of whom were also scholars, if you mention the C of I and the 1950's to almost any knowledgeable outsider, you will strike a spark of recognition and your conversational ally will sputter, "R.C. Owens and...Elgin Baylor!" If your ally is expert in matters athletic, the next observation might well be, "Didn't those two invent the Alley Oop pass to the basket there at your school?"

Not only were these the years of Owens, who finished his degree here and has been a loyal supporter of his alma mater, and Baylor (one year), but they were years when young Chicago-area athletes amazed the community not so much with their duck-tail haircuts and shirts unbuttoned to midriff (anybody could dress that way: hadn't the movies projected such styles?) but with the way in the most extreme cases, they tipped their vowels and changed tongue-point voiceless fricatives into voiceless tongue-point alveolar stops. (He tinks we're from Chicaago.) But the surprise as great as any came from the eventual recognition that these young men could become civilized, respected, and productive, even outstanding members of society. Of course, they had the right elements in them, for no one has yet made a silk purse from inferior material, but the College deserves its fair share of credit for effecting the change.

It would be pleasant if this chapter could conclude on such an upward beat as has been suggested by most of what has preceded this paragraph. But the facts indicate that in spite of all the good he had done, the buildings, the faculty and staff he had helped attract, a Steele-Reese Foundation grant that gave a modest salary rise to the faculty, his ability to work in and with the community, a remarkable planning document—campus plan and the critical self-analysis that had preceded it—in spite of all these there was indeed a dark side to the man, of which excessive drinking was but one manifestation. Another was a thread of coarseness in his makeup. I do not mean simple earthiness, the wholesome odor of an Iowa barnyard on a spring morning. The characteristic was apparent, for instance, in his describing the relationship of a dean to a college president. He affirmed this, *sotto voce*, one day in the hearing of several who, however, heard it imperfectly. When Shearer was asked to repeat it, Dr. Sayre carefully edited the coarse language thus: "He said that as a fire hydrant is to a dog, so is a dean to a college president." Today when the coarsest of expressions can be heard throughout the land, the analogy seems close to Comstockery. But this was in 1961 or 1962. There may be in the use of the expression a kind of repressed contempt, both for the larger world of affairs and for the man Shearer.

All that is speculation. What is clear is that in the last three or four years when drinking and other problems began to control the man, his credibility as a college president declined. The legends speak of meetings where he showed up—if at all—out of control, appointments with powerful philanthropists that were not kept, and similar breaches of conduct and good faith. In spite of the remarkable growth in bricks and mortar, the College failed to increase its endowment, and this failure may be one of the greatest flaws in the Shearer era.

The American economy, especially the agricultural segment, was booming in the fifties and early sixties. It was a time when inspired leadership and hard work could have increased the fragile endowment. Of course buildings were needed as enrollment climbed, and certainly a man's energies have their limits. But a superb opportunity for adding to the endowment was lost, and instead of reaching upwards of five or six million dollars, as of May 27, 1957, the endowment stood at $1,666,204.07, as reported by the Hogle Investment Advisers, Inc. The minutes of the Investment Committee of the Board of Trustees on December 22, 1959, show that beyond first mortgages held on Anderson Hall, Simplot Hall, Voorhees Hall, and the Student Center (SUB) "plus gross revenues derived from the operation of [these] plus full faith and credit of the institution, additional security [for them was] supplied in the form of Debt Service collateral consisting of marketable securities having values of $100,000, $20,000,

Twelfth Night, *Blatchley Little Theater, directed by John F. Sollers, Jr.*

and \$30,000." If my arithmetic is right, the unencumbered portion of the endowment in 1959 stood at about \$1,115,096. But indebtedness stood at \$693,000 (Dormitory Bond of 1956, Student Center Bond of 1958, and Dormitory Bond of 1959). Subtract that from \$1,115,096 and it would appear that the endowment (free and clear) was closer to \$422,096.

To assure that these bonds would continue to be self-liquidating, the College administration projected modest increases in tuition and fees. According to the *Profile of The College of Idaho 1954 to 1974*, submitted on December 7, 1963, the guaranteed tuition rates (a new wrinkle) were as follows:

1965-66—\$1200 per year
1966-67—\$1400 per year
1967-68—\$1600 per year
1969-70—\$1700 per year
1972-73—\$1800 per year. (19)

The same source projected increase in the endowment—"to be increased from gift campaign in 1964-66 by \$2,500,000, by \$1,000,000 in bequests 1967-71, and campaign gifts of \$2,500,000 in 1971-74" (20). Clearly, boosting the endowment by \$6,000,000 of new funds was bold thinking. Additional income essential to the fiscal health of the institution was to come from modest increases in dormitory rental, proposed as follows:

1965-66—\$240 per year
1966-67—\$290 per year
1968-69—\$330 per year
1970-71—\$350 per year
1973-74—\$390 per year. (21)

And, finally, charges for board were to be increased:

1965-66—\$500 per year
1966-67—\$560 pre year
1969-70—\$580 per year
1972-73—\$600 per year. (22)

Former students may compare these figures with the expenses they remember, and present students may repine over what they perceive to be charges more nearly in line with expenses at tax-supported institutions instead of costs of attending a private school.

But while the College was thinking ahead and developing what seemed then somewhat grand plans, President Shearer was encountering difficulties with the financing of the chapel-auditorium. The principal difficulty lay in the execution of the will of former trustee C. C. Anderson. It may well be that in this matter lay Shearer's increasing use of alcohol. The Minutes of the Investment Committee meeting held September 12, 1960, show that the College filed a claim against Mr. Anderson's estate for $150,000, and the Committee asked the president to seek from the executors of Mr. Anderson's estate "written assurance of ultimate favorable action...involving the chapel pledge of Mr. Anderson, so that, when chapel plans are ready, the Board can proceed with financing plans." It was a time of considerable tension and anxiety, for the Anderson pledge had been secured as a sort of challenge amount, and those who had pledged gifts would not unreasonably hesitate to follow through on their pledges unless and until the base amount was a reality.

The Minutes of the Board of Trustees for their annual meeting, held on November 4, 1960, mentioned another disturbing fiscal fact, buried as Item #21 in the "Notes to Estimated Budget 1961-62." An operating deficit of $22,000 had developed, and there was a provision in the Estimated Budget for its elimination. The problem of a deficit and hoping to raise funds to eliminate it would not go away, contributing to the dimming of President Shearer's luster in his later years at the College.

As if trouble with the Anderson estate and the continuing operating deficit weren't enough, old Sterry Hall began to show not only signs of its age but also the consequences of structural tampering. The Minutes of the Board of Trustees for January 17, 1961, called attention to it thus: "The walls are leaning out and the roof may be in danger of falling. Tours by grade school children have been discontinued." Inspection and recommendations were called for in order that the problem could be solved. It was not.

In the meantime, the pros and cons of the advisability of litigation to collect what was due from the Anderson estate were discussed. One of the difficulties in this matter was the claim of Inspiration, Incorporated, "the residuary legatee of the Anderson estate," according to minutes of the Investment Committee of the Board of Trustees for February 9, 1961. In reporting to the full Board at their April 28, 1961, meeting, President Shearer

> pointed out that efforts had not been successful in effecting any settlement with the interested parties including the executors of the estate [Driscoll and Learned], Inspiration, Inc., [represented by Attorney Clemons], and Mr. Simplot. On March 1, 1961, the executors formally rejected the claims which the College had filed with them for payment

of the chapel pledge for $150,000, and for the amount of the deficit in the...account with J. A. Hogle and Co., the deficit...being approximately $600,000.

It was a painful time for all parties, and the question recurred whether a suit should be filed and, if so, for what amount—$150,000 for the pledge on the chapel-auditorium? $600,000 for the deficit in the investment account? $750,000 for all the College believed due? A further question asked whether either plaintiff or defendant ever won in litigation between two non-profit institutions, in this case the College and the Reverend Herbert Richards' Inspiration, Inc. The Board members "agreed that, in an effort to avoid any kind of legal action involving a suit by the executors of the C. C. Anderson estate in regards to any deficit in the...account with J. A. Hogle and Co. [the managers of the College's portfolio], the finance committee should continue its negotiations with the executors and the attorney for Inspiration, Inc., to try to effect a settlement of the whole matter."

However, in regard to the $150,000 claim against the Anderson estate for the chapel-auditorium pledge, one trustee, Robert Pasley, forthrightly moved that the College should proceed with legal action against the estate, should it prove necessary. Al Garber seconded the motion, and it was passed.

Dedication ceremonies for Jewett Chapel-Auditorium: the notables, the choir, the great organ, and more than 900 in the audience.

As if these estate problems were not enough, two blocks of stocks seemed to be rapidly declining in value—Crucible Steel and the Erie Lackawanna Railroad. On these stocks the College lost a considerable amount of money; it had to sell 6,900 shares of the railroad stock for slightly less than $34,000.

Finally an accord was reached with the executors of the Anderson estate, and bids were submitted on one of President Shearer's finest accomplishments, the chapel-auditorium. When the bids were opened, it came as no surprise that they all exceeded funds available, so Jedd Jones of the architecture firm Hummel, Hummel, and Jones, agreed to meet with Ray Luekenga, whose firm was low bidder, to try to reduce the costs while Shearer agreed to try to raise money for furnishings and for other costs, according to the Minutes of Board meetings on May 24 and August 1, 1961. A further meeting on August 14, 1961, revealed that Lyman Wilbur, husband of Trustee Henrietta Wilbur, volunteered to help with the task of raising the additional funds this in addition to his original chore of serving as state chairman for soliciting gifts for the chapel-auditorium from the churches.

The Minutes of the meeting of the Board of Trustees for October 14, 1961, contain several bits of pertinent information. In the first place, a prominent Boise physician, Dr. A. M. Popma, was elected Chairman of the Board, the name presented by Chairman of the Nominating Committee, Darwin Symms. Clarence Kniefel was elected Vice Chairman. Then came a stirring reprise by President Shearer of the planning and the hopes for the new chapel-auditorium, the disappointments and frustrations that always seemed to lie in wait, the harmful effects of inflation, and the decision by the Board to cut the costs and get on with the construction, even though the costs of furnishings and other elements could not be met. Here the Minutes must be quoted:

> Dr. Shearer and Dr. Westfall [Vice President of Development] decided to interview one Trustee who might help in this emergency. They called on Mr. Jewett in Lewiston. After considering the matter for thirty days, Mr. and Mrs. Jewett agreed to provide the necessary funds to complete the building and provide the furnishings, **according to the original plans** [emphasis mine] as a memorial to Mr. Jewett's father. Mr. George F. Jewett was Chairman of the Board of Potlatch Forests, Inc., a leading citizen of Idaho, and a long time friend of the College. Dr. Shearer recommended that the building be named the Jewett Chapel-Auditorium in memory of George Frederick Jewett, and a suitable plaque be placed in the building.

And what a magnificent contribution this building continues to be, serving the College and the wider constituency of the region in countless ways. The reader may recall those earlier comments about the story of the College taking

220

on the structure of a fairy tale. Jewett's assistance at this critical moment qualifies him as one of those helpers who appear to assist the protagonist of the tale. Although it is tempting to sing the praises of the remarkable acoustics (acoustical engineering by the same firm responsible for the acoustics in the Lincoln Center), singer Jan Peerce summed it up by saying that Jewett Chapel-Auditorium tempted all singers to fall in love with their own voices. Indeed, there is no finer acoustical setting than Jewett. Economies had to restrict what could be done with the pipe organ (there are no trumpet pipes, for instance, although the capability is there), and the light system was deemed inadequate for stage presentations. In correcting this latter flaw, additional lights have recently been attached to either side of the walls above the forestage, adding illumination but destroying the graceful planes and causing the spectators to note the technology instead of the dramatic spectacle.

Further faculty changes came in Shearer's time, too. In 1961 Ancil K. "Buck" Steunenberg retired after forty years as Head of the Department of Physics, and Ledru Williams was eligible for retirement but was allowed to continue to teach on a part-time basis for 1961-62. In the fall of 1961 several new faces appeared, attesting both to the College's desire to maintain an appropriate faculty-student ratio in the face of an expanding enrollment (720 students for the fall of 1962) and to the success of the sabbatical leave program that had been approved by the Board of Trustees at its June 1, 1957, meeting. New faculty included alumnus Dick Carrow, basketball and track coach, a successful Fruitland, Caldwell, and Borah High School coach. Bill Roberts, another alumnus, was hired to teach in the Department of Art, and Friedrich P. Alber, of Germany, to teach in the Department of Modern Languages. Having taught in the summer sessions of 1954 and 1955, I returned as a regular member of the Department of English. We were hired upon the recommendation of Dean Sayre; there was no search committee. Finally, Dr. Hall returned to replace Franklin Specht, who had won a Danforth Teacher Study Grant and was on leave of absence from the Department of History.

It may be that the work Mr. Shearer saw looming above the horizon gave him some disquieting moments. In the nature of things, the time comes when (if you will grant the metaphor) the fullback simply cannot buck the line for those necessary yards, just one more time. In any case, President Shearer began to look elsewhere for help with fund raising, and the Cumerford Corporation was engaged to assist with this essential task, according to the Minutes of the Board of Trustees for October 14, 1961. These minutes also show that only $20,000 of the costs of Jewett Chapel-Auditorium had come from the Caldwell community.

And assuredly the intense negotiations in the matter of the Anderson estate, complicated by the presence of residual legatee Inspiration, Inc., were a source of pain. But that was all behind, those claims having been resolved in a manner that provided for payment by the estate of the $150,000 pledge to the chapel-auditorium fund and "payment by the estate of one-half of the indebtedness to J. A. Hogle and Company in exchange for one-half of the securities held in the Improvement Fund (68,675 shares of Erie Lackawanna and 9, 658 shares of Crucible Steel)" (Minutes, June 3, 1961).

Still, President Shearer's resignation on Commencement Day, May 30, 1964, came as a surprise if not a downright shock. John Graham and Company of Seattle had been engaged to prepare the Master Campus Plan, the Cumerford Corporation was making favorable reports on its campaign, and the College had provided twenty-five acres of land north of Cleveland Boulevard for a community stadium-field house-recreational park (becoming the new rodeo grounds)- practice field. On the drawing board, or more accurately on the list of priorities, were a women's dormitory, an addition to the student union, a science building, dining room expansion, an addition to Strahorn Library or the construction of a new library building, remodeling Sterry and Blatchley, a

Biology students in the basement of Kirkpatrick Gymnasium, with a promotion for the 9th Mexico field trip on the bulletin board.

men's dormitory, remodeling Covell, remodeling Kirkpatrick, a classroom building, a fine arts building, and other non-physical plant improvements respecting such matters as salary and benefits. A formidable list.

It is difficult—perhaps impossible—to describe the campus Barbara and I returned to in the fall of 1961. It fairly shone, and even the damaging hand of renovation seemed not to have wrought irreparable harm. The new student union building fairly gleamed, with no unsightly marks, no walls and corners damaged by thoughtless use. It was a facility of which we were all proud. Shearer's competence seemed everywhere in evidence.

But there was handwriting, not on the walls of this campus but on the larger blackboard of American higher education. In reading it and in re-reading the foregoing formidable list, President Shearer may have been wise to resign.

Earlier I adverted to changes deep in the foundation of post-secondary education. This chapter concludes with a look at those bleak shifts. From the *Statistical Abstract of the United States and The Yearbook of American Universities and Colleges* (1988) come the following figures, supplied by Dale Corning:

		Enrollment	Percentage
1930	Private colleges and universities	568,000	51.59%
	Public colleges and universities	533,000	48.41%
1940	Private	698,000	46.69%
	Public	797,000	53.31%
1950	Private	1,304,000	49.04%
	Public	1,355,000	50.96%
1960	Private	1,384,000	43.03%
	Public	1,832,000	56.97%
1970	Private	2,152,753	25.09%
	Public	6,428,134	74.91%
1980	Private	2,639,501	21.82%
	Public	9,457,394	78.12%
1987	Private	2,793,243	21.88%
	Public	9,975,064	78.12%

There are no real surprises here. The balance favoring private education in 1930 was offset by the Depression, which caused the 1940 statistics to favor the cheaper tax-supported institution, but not by much. In 1950 with GI Bill money to assist them, veterans chose private about as frequently as public. In 1960 a gap developed, and it grew wider nearly every decade. Private education began to find itself in even sharper competition, not with sister institutions but with tax-supported and thus comparatively inexpensive schools (Figures for 1970, 1980, 1987 from the *Yearbook of American Universities and Colleges*, 1988).

President Shearer's successor would face a battery of local and national problems. Who would he be?

Library moving day, January, 1967: Carefully boxed books are trucked across campus to waiting shelves in the new Terteling Library (above), and the empty boxes are returned to Strahorn via student "box brigade" (right).

Commencement, 1969: left to right, Warren B. Knox, sixth president of the College, Distinguished Alumni Annie Laurie Bird and Kinsey Robinson, honorary degreee recipients Dr. Lawrence H. Gipson, Richard Armour, and Dr. Harold Viehman.

Part VI

Warren Barr Knox 1964-1973

A detail of the sculpture by Harold Balaz located above the entrance of Terteling Library.

CHAPTER THIRTEEN

The Expectation of Plenty

It was a complex and difficult time. The "Unchained Melody," the Four Freshmen, "The High and the Mighty," and "Cherry Pink and Apple Blossom White" gave way finally, to the grim, humorless, and unyielding anti-establishment years of Viet Nam, protests, and acid rock. But it was also a time of growth and progress: the current calendar of a fall semester, a winter session, and a spring semester dates from this time, as does the College's Regional Studies Center.

After Tom Shearer resigned on May 31, 1964, to become Director of Development for the Center for the Study of Democratic Institutions, the Board of Trustees set about finding a new leader. His name was revealed by Board chairman A. M. Popma at the opening fall faculty meeting luncheon. The announcement came as something of a surprise to the faculty, although I seem to recall that we felt to high-grade the vice president of Whitman, especially the one who, we believed, had garnered a fine Ford Foundation grant for the Palouse school, was a real accomplishment.

Students and new faculty raise the query, "Why was the Mackey Room so named? Who was Relan P. Mackey?" He was a very bright political science major, Class of 1952, a student leader who after graduation entered the Harvard School of Business and earned the MBA degree. Four months after arriving in Hong Kong, where work had taken him, he slipped on a treacherous path and fell 300 feet to his death, according to the *Coyote* of October 25, 1961. His parents, Mr. and Mrs. Edward Mackey, furnished the Mackey Room in the SUB in his memory.

The bookstore in the SUB was named the Barbara Sherman Memorial Bookstore after the death of its manager, the former Barbara Bowman Peckham Sherman, Class of 1949.

As an undergraduate, where did you and your gang hang out, when, that is, you were not in the library or the lab? Frosty's? The College Inn? Todd's? Quasty's (Clyde Schurr made the best hamburgers and milk shakes this side of Stanford's)? the Premier Barbecue and Fountain? the Signal? the Black Anvil? Bowe's Confectionery? Surely someday when the possibilities for research grow narrow and narrower, an enterprising social historian will make a study of the social dynamics of selected collegiate dives.

This chapter has somewhat more serious business to attend to.

Although I have not overlooked the Trustees, the record so far is hardly more than that. Names have been mentioned in some connection or other, but little of substance has been said about them. It is surely true that a good college has at least the following characteristics: a strong endowment, a good administration, a good library and facilities, a good faculty, a body of good students clamoring to learn, and a good board of trustees. Over the years the College has had excellent boards of trustees. And over the years there has been a steady evolution in the kind of trustee agreeing to serve. Initially, trustees were local people who tended to be committed personally to President Boone and to his idea of a college. In addition to the familiar names of the founders, Walter Kerrick should be mentioned, as should Edgar Oakes, a prominent Caldwell businessman who was a classmate of James Boone of the Class of 1913.[*]

Ever so gradually, the trustees began to reflect the world of affairs and power far beyond Canyon County and Idaho. C. C. Anderson was a man of wealth and power. Jack Simplot cannot be categorized. But even the trustees of modest circumstances have worked hard. Because the trustees (even those of modest personal means) cared for the College, its growth was assured. Because they worked in the College's best interests, its quality was constantly reaffirmed. And because they were people of vision, the College drew upon that precious resource and survived in the face of a competition for funds and students so powerful that many independent institutions caved in.

---

[*] It was from Oakes that I learned of Dr. Boone's thrifty practice of helping the Boone children clean up their plates so that food would not be wasted. Oakes remarked that Dr. Boone referred himself as the family swill pail because of this practice.

The list of good schools that have closed their doors since 1960 is appalling. William Allen White's beloved College of Emporia is one; Yankton College, among whose graduates was a superb Denver surgeon, Dr. B. T. Daniels, is another. The name is not gratuitously or casually offered. I had all three children of "Dan" and Helen Daniels in class—Jean and Jim at East High and Jim and John, who chose to cast their lot with the C of I, both graduating from it. And even Parsons College, connected to the C of I through its former president and several faculty who followed him to Caldwell, is another. The demise of these good schools causes the social historian to wonder whether the traditional two-track system of higher education—the public and the private—will become a monorail.

The College's trustees have sought over the years to maintain that essential balance between the public and the private ways to higher education. Their task was and continues to be a formidable one, and their names deserve space. Some must be identified and held up for our admiration. They, too, have filled the role of helper in the märchen-like quality of this institution's life.

Simplot has been identified, and Anderson as well. Others will appear from time to time. But the two whom I mention at this time were second to none in their concern, their labor, and their vision. Dr. George Wolfe used to remind the faculty that it is one thing to donate money to a cause and another to contribute time. The former can be redeemed, but the time—which is to say a portion of one's life—invested in the interest of a cause will never be redeemed. The trustees have characteristically done both.

I mention two at this juncture—Henrietta Wilbur (Mrs. Lyman) and Bernice R. Crookham (Mrs. George L., Jr.)—because there may be students who wonder about their names given to the two pleasant seminar rooms in Terteling Library, whose erection is still in the future as far as this chronology is concerned. Mrs. Wilbur was a devoted trustee who helped plant vineyards whose grapes we now enjoy. She was memorialized by her husband, who is now a trustee, through the furnishings in this pleasant meeting room. Bernice Crookham—the R. stands for Robinson—graduated from the College in 1929. Her brothers had been outstanding athletes for the College, and a sister, Nell, a superb English teacher for many years, concluded her career as a colleague of mine in the Denver Public Schools. Nell did her college work elsewhere. George L. Crookham, Jr., who had attended the College but did not graduate from it, memorialized Mrs. Crookham, who had helped dig the wells from which we now drink, by providing the furnishings for the heretofore unnamed seminar room. Mrs. Wilbur began her lengthy service as trustee in 1951, Mrs. Crookham, in 1945.

The Catalog (1964-65) that contains a page of memorial entries for Ralph Berringer (1953-1963), Anna Smyth Eyck (1924-1949), Margaret Nichol (1912-1939), and Trustee Frank Rhea (1943-57) identifies the Board of Trustees, with officers heading the list: Alfred M. Popma, Chairman; Clarence J. Kniefel, Vice Chairman; Ruth M. Evans (Mrs. Glen L.), Secretary; Eldon Marsh, Treasurer and Assistant Secretary; Robert Alexanderson, General Counsel. Of the trustees, several were alumni (anyone attending the institution) and some were also graduates: Clarence Kniefel, Reece Shaffer, Margaret Boone, Ed Springer, Bernice Crookham, Robert Harvey, Raymond White, Gilbert Stanton, Darwin Symms, Harold Holsinger, Jerome Smith, and Warren Barry. Kniefel was a banker, Shaffer a former football and baseball player of considerable talent on four of Parberry's fine teams of the late 40s. Margaret Boone is the daughter of the College's first president. Ed Springer was an executive with the Idaho Department Stores, the son of long time teacher Dr. Francis Springer and while a student a scatback and baseball player of great talent; Harvey a minister and a trustee by virtue of representing the Synod; Gilbert Stanton a student leader who became an executive with Idaho Power; Darwin Symms, one of several of that name to attend the College and serve on its board, was an entrepreneurial horticulturalist on Sunny Slope. Holsinger, a physician, was likewise one of several of that name to attend the College, two of whom have served as trustees. Jerome C. Smith was the son of the Valley's first great teacher of instrumental music, J. J. Smith; Jerome was an electronics scientist and chairman of the

Members of the Board of Trustees present at the October 12, 1962 Board meeting: seated, left to right, Margaret Boone, T. M. Robertson, Robert L. Wylie, Jr., Jerome Smith, Grant Gordon, Bernice Crookham; standing, N. L. Terteling, Dr. Harold Holsinger, Henrietta Wilbur, Clarence J. Kniefel, Ruth M. Evans, Mrs. Robert Naylor, Dr. Charles E. Palmer, The Reverend Lyman Winkle, A. C. Garber, J. E. King, Edson H. Deal, Gilbert L. Stanton, Dr. A. M. Popma.

Board's committee on investments. Warren Barry had distinguished himself as a starting guard for Parberry's football team and as a student of economics under Professor Bollinger. He became a businessman of considerable prominence in the Magic Valley.

It was a good group of citizens who cared about independent higher education, and perhaps I will be forgiven if I let them stand for all trustees before and since who gave of their talent, their substance, and, most important, their time.

One further diversion and we can return to the story. The traditional way of supplying food to the campus residents had been changed under Shearer. No longer would Mrs. Garland, Miss Cooley, and staff preserve fruit and vegetables during summer and early fall for feeding students during the school year. Instead, the first of several commercial food services—Saga Foods—took over that chore, Mrs. Garland becoming "Executive Housekeeper." As noted elsewhere, the Cumerford Corporation had been engaged to conduct a survey of financial resources that might become available to the College. President Shearer followed up the favorable report the corporation prepared by urging the trustees to engage the John Price Jones organization to conduct a fund raising campaign (Trustees' Executive Committee Minutes, May 11, 1964). Some may still remember the S & H trailer that sat next to Sterry Hall as this campaign was launched.

As to the manner in which the curriculum was organized and by which, in turn, breadth of education could be assured while a major or specialization could be offered: the course of study was divided into the fairly traditional subjects which, in turn, were placed within one of four divisions. These were Education and Physical Education, Humanities and Fine Arts, the Social Sciences, and, finally, the Natural Sciences. Except for the later establishment of the J. A. Albertson School of Business, it was very close to the present scheme.

From time to time, the members of the faculty debate at great length such problems as the essential difference—if there is one—between the lower and the upper division: that is, between the first two years and the junior and senior year. These are not trivial matters, for on more occasions than one the College has been encouraged to offer a two-year "degree," an A.A. "degree." Thus far, the temptation has been resisted. One of the most cogent arguments I have heard in this connection came (not unexpectedly) from Dr. William H. Chalker. To the best of my imperfect memory he characterized the difference as the distinction between the accepting of textbook information and the generally agreed upon truisms (freshman and more particularly the sophomoric model) on the one hand, and challenging the very epistemology upon which such information and truisms rest, on the other.

In the course of his ten-year career here, Ralph W. Berringer responded to the challenge by Dean Sayre to clarify this matter of lower-upper division work in the following missive. It is appropriately mentioned here because the College was about to undergo the periodic spasm of re-accreditation, and part of the institutional self-study always involves the examination of presuppositions supporting an institution's convictions about itself. Here is Dr. Berringer's response to the problem of the difference between lower- and upper-division work, as far as the English curriculum was concerned. His assessment is still valid.

> Subject: Upper-division courses
> To: The Dean
>
> Upper-division work implies a distinction from lower-division both in the material covered and in the approach to that material. Lower-division courses tend to lay open a field of study, to **reveal** its general content and principles. In approach, they remain primarily on the informational level. An upper-division course seeks penetration rather than broad coverage. Its emphasis is critical and philosophical rather than informational. The student is expected to master and apply basic principles, and is often required to show evidence of ability to apply theory in a research paper or other critical exercise.
>
> Thus literature courses at the lower-division level stress **what** was written; at the upper-division level they stress **how** and **why** that writing was accomplished, with considerably increased emphasis upon analysis, interpretation, and critical judgment. Composition courses in the lower division seek to reveal the principles of good writing and encourage their application in student themes; in the upper division, training in composition seeks to make the student aware of how and why such principles have arisen, that he may apply linguistic theory critically both to his own writing and to that of others.
>
> It is perhaps unnecessary to add that these are relative distinctions, both the acquiring of information and the critical interpretation of that information being in some degree present in all college courses. Yet I feel that the increased emphasis upon critical interpretation constitutes a real and valid distinction in upper-division courses in English.
>
> Berringer

Some new faculty arrived about the same time as Warren Barr Knox. John Sullivan came in 1962, and Jim Gabbard arrived in 1963, as a replacement for Elmer Thomas, who was on leave in 1963-64, with an extension granted for the next year. Jim stayed on, imparting his own special magic and inspiring a love for choral music in the many who performed for him.

President Knox was yet another chief executive without what some people think is the prerequisite advanced degree. He had the B.A. and M.A. but no Ph.D. However, as a successful fund-raiser, he met the profile of what the Board's screening committee was seeking. When he and Mrs. Knox were introduced to the homecoming crowd in Simplot Stadium by Professor Margaret Boone on October 10, 1964, Professor Boone, as I recall the occasion, used an expression of her father's, "Young hands on the wheel." The reference was to the necessity to have young eyes and young hands at the control of an automobile when negotiating Idaho's mountain roads. And so it was with the managing of a college, especially during trying times.

Without question a new dormitory was needed, and in September of the semester Mr. Knox became president (but before he was in residence) the Trustees opened the bids for a new dormitory, which would be named Hayman Hall. The successful bidder was the same firm that had built Jewett Chapel-Auditorium, R.W. Luekenga, with a bid of $730,000. This amount was $50,929 over the amount available through a government loan, so Eldon Marsh was authorized to file an application with the Housing and Home Finance Agency to increase the loan for $750,000 to $800,000, for the 180-bed dormitory. At the same meeting of the Trustees' Executive Committee (September 15, 1964) the Walter Opp Construction Company won the bid for alterations and additions

Hayman Hall (New Dorm) under construction, 1965.

235

to the Student Union Building, in the amount of $142,000, again borrowed from the Housing and Home Finance Agency.

At the next meeting of the Executive Committee (October 12, 1964), Knox had not yet moved to Caldwell, but in his absence Curtis Westfall, who had been elevated from Vice President for Development to Administrative Vice President by Executive Committee Action of April 13, 1964, had in tow John McMurdo, representing the John Price Jones Company. The campaign seemed to be progressing.

Knox's first meeting as resident president was at the November 2, 1964, session of the Executive Committee. Among other items of business was placing on the high-priority list improved presidential housing. It was a lengthy meeting, the minutes requiring five ledger-sized pages. His first meeting with the full Board of Trustees was November 21, 1964, requiring eleven and a half pages. A motion was made to clarify ownership of property in Boise which had come to Whitman College and to The College of Idaho in the dissolution of the Intermountain Institute, and action was taken to determine the status of a half section of land in the Covell Estate near El Centro, California, which the College had apparently inherited. The Board of Trustees agreed with all actions recommended or taken by the Executive Committee, including moving the matter of presidential housing "relatively high on the priority list on the campus plan."

In his report to the Board, Dean Sayre reported difficulties with faculty recruitment, observing "that about 50% of the faculty have Doctor's degrees." He also questioned the wisdom of having more majors in Secretarial Science and wondered whether the program should not be relegated to the status of a minor program (rather than offering a major) or changed to a night course as a community service.

The Dean of Students, the capable and long-serving alumnus Gene Odle, who had been on the staff since Pitman times, reported an enrollment of 750 day students, 500 of whom lived on campus. "Dr. Odle," say the Minutes,

> further reported that the campus morale is excellent, that the students have great respect for, and pride in, the College. He says that their greatest concern is for achievement; that if there is a fault, it is that they are too apt to try to please the professors. He believes that on the whole, their values are wholesome.

From time to time money had to be borrowed from the bank to pay the difference between accounts receivable ($130,000) and accounts payable ($200,000)—a margin made worse by $20,000 worth of "Deferred charges." This condition had occurred before, though on a smaller scale. Now, in 1964, the gap required borrowing "$90,000 to handle payment of bills when due.... Housing and Dining System and Student Center Bond collateral requirements" amounted to $240,000. This amount subtracted from the $1,113,921 endowment fund left $873,921 unencumbered, although another figure in the Minutes says: "Indebtedness on the [Physical] Plant totals $1,064,428." I would assume that the $240,000 is included in this amount. Another disquieting item in the Minutes reads as follows:

> Operations during the year will, from time to time, require some borrowings with the possibility of indebtedness by late summer 1965 being near $200,000. We will [this is in the Business manager's Report] request authorization to borrow as necessary to meet payrolls and bills payable, pledging tuition incomes and/or gift incomes as necessary to a limit of $200,000 through September 15, 1965.

Eldon Marsh also included comments about planning for a science facility, for a library facility, and for the president's home.

The grim tone of the meeting was further darkened when President Knox told the Board that the Ford Foundation said the profile the College had submitted was nice but its irrefragable rule was that no grants were made to a college "if there is a resignation of the President and a subsequent change of administration during the processing of a Grant application."

So much for those dreams.

But President Knox was undaunted. Dean Sayre's report at the February 13, 1965, meeting of the Board of Trustees, concerning a change in the calendar as envisioned by Dr. Stanford stimulated Knox to tell the Board the he was applying to the Carnegie Corporation for a grant to explore the possibilities of the short Winter Session, if that was the choice of the faculty and trustees.

At this same meeting, Dr. Odle reported that the head count of students for Spring Semester was 731, the largest spring enrollment in the school's history and the second highest semester ever, second only to the 750 enrollment for fall. These were encouraging statistics, indeed.

Three items in the Minutes of the Executive Committee meeting of the Ides of March, 1965, must be noted. In the first, Vice President Westfall remarked that the Canyon Multi-Purpose Stadium was costing the College $10,000 a year, since some donations to the College were in the form of Multi-Purpose Stadium Debentures that would mature only after a number of years. It would therefore be necessary, he said, to find $75,000 in new money.

In the second item, in one of his most forthright and courageous acts, Knox called for termination of the John Price Jones Company contract. He said, in essence, they've done their work, all they're capable of doing; we've a crew of professionals—Schwiebert, Westfall, and me—as good as, probably better than, the Jones Outfit. This was music to the ears of several faculty, for the message was packed with energy and confidence, and the Trustees concurred.

The third item is illustrative of the kind of person willing to give time to serve as a trustee of the College. N. L. Terteling asked for specific information about the College that would be useful in approaching prospective donors. What, he asked, does the College stand for? What does the College do for people? How does a C of I graduate turn out? Is the College unique? Does the College teach freedom of thought? Self-reliance? Here was a trustee who really wanted to know about this institution. He was not interested in whether being identified as a trustee would confer upon him any merit badges or space in the society pages; he was concerned about how he could come to know the College in order that he might best serve it. The second element—service—is clearly apparent. Unlike the trustee who offered his resignation to Dr. Hall when it became apparent that trustees were expected to participate in the challenge of raising money, Terteling of his own volition took the initiative by asking for information to be used in approaching prospective donors.

This meeting of March 15 concluded with a report from Marsh that the building projects were going well and that planning for the science building was proceeding nicely, all according to the long-range plan of Shearer and the John Graham Company.

Then, on March 31, 1965, Terteling presented the College the following agreement:

> THERE WILL BE DEPOSITED $750,000 worth of securities at market value in the Terteling Foundation in a separate account for The College of Idaho to be invested by the Foundation.
>
> The income and interest from said account will be allocated to The College of Idaho.
>
> The capital gain if any from said separate account will be at the disposal of the Foundation.
>
> It is understood the College will secure a 30 year loan for construction of a library in the amount of the above separate account, and that the Foundation will pay to the College out of the above separate account, a sufficient amount of the income plus a portion of capital if necessary to make the required payments on the above loan.

In a time when so much of the endowment had been collateralized to secure building loans (with the expectation that fees for board and room and perhaps, if necessary, a bit of tuition income, would make the loans self-amortizing), the generous gift—generous under any circumstances—was particularly gratifying. It was another infusion of energy that helped make this first year of President Knox's administration a resounding success.

And the year was not over. There was still the inauguration, which was billed as the first event in the seventy-fifth anniversary year, and there was an honorary degree to be awarded Knox by Whittier College, a ceremony scheduled for June 12, 1965. Those who receive the alumni *Bulletin* may remember a picture on page 4 of Volume 22 (April 1965) showing three people in caps and gowns—Warren Knox flanked by Bob Hope and Richard Nixon. All were involved in the honorary degree ceremony, Nixon assisting in the hooding, and Knox and Hope the recipients of degrees. It was at least a noseworthy ceremony, for Bob Hope was reported to have said as the photo was snapped: "Do you think the world is ready for three noses like these?"

Minutes of the June 5, 1965, meeting of the Board of Trustees point to a cloud on the horizon. In making his financial development report, Vice President Westfall reported a fiscal year end deficit of $144,000, attributable, he said, "to the fact that last year's budget was not realistic." This information should be swallowed and digested along with Business Manager Marsh's request for "authorization to borrow up to $300,000, as needed on short term loans, to be paid off by October 1, 1965." Authorization was granted.

And so was confirmed the not uncommon practice of borrowing (like the farmer identified by the porter in *Macbeth* who hanged himself in the expectation of plenty) against future income. It was a familiar pattern, but the scale was startling.

But clouds are dispelled by sunshine, and so many rays were spilling over the College that no one could waste time over red ink. It was at this meeting that Dr. Holsinger, of the Board's Academic Affairs Committee, recommended that the Board explore the possibility of a retreat for trustees and faculty to become acquainted and discuss problems. Mr. Simplot immediately offered the use of his home on Payette Lake for such meetings any time the Board and faculty desired. It was an appropriate recommendation and a generous offer, a boost, when announced, to the already high faculty morale.

Another ray of sunlight was the calendar reform, a product of the creative mind of Dr. Lyle Stanford. When Dean Sayre sought permission of the Board to continue to study the advisability of a calendar featuring two regular semesters bracketing a session of six weeks, the Board gave its approval.

And the College prepared for this 75th Anniversary. How quickly those twenty-five years intervals seem to have occurred. This was to be a jubilee celebrating seventy-five years of college life and inevitably pointing the way toward the magical centennial. But that jubilee must await its turn in the forthcoming 1965-66 academic year, the year chosen for most of the 75th anniversary celebration. It appears to be a year premature, but remember that the Wood River Presbytery by formal resolution on April 21, 1890, agreed to locate a college in Caldwell, and that as early as September 19, 1889, money had been raised to establish a college in the Territory of Idaho. To recognize the 75th anniversary an academic year early was not, after all, early but late.

The campus was a busy place during President Knox's first year. The College and the community created a Fine Arts series that was a model of town-gown concord. "H.M.S. Pinafore," produced by Tyrone Guthrie; contralto Claramae Turner; and duo-pianists Milton and Peggy Salkind helped launch the third season of use for Jewett Chapel-Auditorium. The multi-purpose recreational facility across Blaine was named Simplot Stadium. Borah High School supplied six top-quality players for the football team. Ed Bonaminio, one of the Chicago recruits in an earlier presidency, was elevated from assistant to head football coach following the retirement and sudden death of one of the deans of Idaho coaches, James Allen "Babe" Brown.

Coach James Allen "Babe" Brown

It was not unexpected on the campus to hear once again those tilted vowels and the exotic tongue-point consonant delivery. But these young men from Chicago and environs seemed in most cases to realize that athletics was a means to an end, that college exists to provide an education and that in ninety-nine cases out of a hundred, team sports conclude with the B.A. degree. It is difficult for many (if not most) players to realize how brief a time interscholastic and intercollegiate competition endures and how much of their lives will be led after their playing days are over. Education lasts a lifetime; athletic garlands last briefer than a bridal bouquet, or nearly so. The Bonaminio teams were good teams, and the players traveled in slacks and blazers, spending bus time on homework or fierce chess competition. They earned their fair share of graduate degrees, and their numbers include CPAs and other professional men. One could hardly wish for a better student, for example, than Ron Sproat (M.D.).

Dr. Berringer's replacement, Dr. Franklin Osborne "Bob" Cooke, launched a series of cultural programs on literary, artistic, political, and topical matters. Through these programs the Department of English sought to provide a forum for student, faculty, and community research and ideas. Dr. John Ford Sollers' string of outstanding stage productions was unbroken as Thornton Wilder's *Such Things Happen Only in Books* and Chekhov's *The Sea Gull* were done to perfection. *Romeo and Juliet* required a thirty-three-member cast. The community had come to expect this kind of competence from Dr. Sollers, who was, after all, the grandson of the Ford of Washington, Baltimore, and various Southern theaters. The ordinary school activities of choir rehearsal, Philo Tech meetings, dances, and appearances by guest speakers continued with a kind of intensity that suggested enrollment was edging ever closer to the desired critical mass, which in the thirties was reckoned to be about 400 but now, in 1990, about 900. Pat Holton was named Miss Wool of Idaho; pitchers Brad Biegert, John Hull, and Gary Gaviola led the baseball team to wins over the University of Idaho, the University of Montana, Linfield, and Whitman, among other schools. The 1965 *Trail*, the source of what of these "factoids" did not come from my own memory, was edited superbly well by Darlene Moulds. The *Coyote* was at first capably run by Dave O'Neil, Pete Sawyer, Lindy Rankin (these latter two were or were to become professional journalists). Alumnus

For his 1965 production of Ibsen's The Sea Gull, *Jack Sollers worked with the cast on character development.*

Clare Conley, in 1965 the Managing Editor of *Field and Stream,* addressed the College and the community.

The decline in quality (rhetorical, grammatical) and newsworthiness of The *Coyote* was just beginning to set in, as the "let it all hang out and I want to do my own thing and like you know, man, where it's at" mode of thoughtless and inarticulate expression caught the febrile imagination of some of America's youth. A column by young Tom Shearer headed "Here I Lie" may well have indicated the continuing alcohol problem of the son of the former president. It is also possible—though who is to say?—that his own suicide of 1979 was prefigured by the headline.[*]

President Knox was inaugurated in an academic convocation on May 1, 1965, a Saturday. Dr. Louis T. Benezet, President of the Claremont Graduate School and former President of The Colorado College, delivered the address, "College Status and College Standards." Thus began the first event of the 75th Anniversary year.

After Governor Nelson Rockefeller of New York gave the keynote address at ceremonies in Jewett Chapel-Auditorium commemorating the College's 75th Anniversary in October, 1965, ASCI officers presented him a memento of the occasion, with Peggy Graves doing the honors. Others visible include Dave O'Neil, Pauli Crooke, Karl Willig, Chuck Winder and Barbara Sall.

---

[*]   Vesper (Mrs. Tom E.) Shearer had taken her own life upon learning that her husband had terminal cancer.

CHAPTER FOURTEEN

The Seventy-Fifth Year

Celebration

and Times Thereafter

Partly or perhaps largely through the friendship of Governor Robert Smylie with Governor Nelson Rockefeller, the chief executive of New York was prevailed upon to deliver an address as the first major public event of the College's seventy-fifth anniversary year, during the 1965-66 academic year.

Earlier I mentioned the comets on the College campus, Smylie and Young (Smylie had gone into the service and Young, a Morrison-Knudsen employee, into a Japanese prison camp). They returned from the outer darkness of law school. Bill Young served in the state legislature and became Speaker of the House and later a state senator. Smylie, when the Republican party swept into power in 1946, was appointed one of two assistant attorneys general by the new attorney general, Robert Ailshie. When Ailshie died in office, Governor C. A. Robins appointed Smylie to that post. In 1950, he won the office in election and served four years. In the election of 1954, the forty-year-old College of Idaho graduate was elected governor, having served with distinction as attorney general and as President Eisenhower's Western Affairs adviser. (All of this can be found in a book by Thomas R. Cox titled *The Park Builders: A History of State Parks in the Pacific Northwest.* It was published by the University of Washington Press. I also interviewed Mr. Smylie on March 22, 1990, on the College campus.) Who was speaker of the House when Smylie took the oath of office? His old college chum, R.H. "Bill" Young. (George Greenfield, Class of '38, was state Democratic party chairman.) Another College of Idaho graduate was governor of Oregon at the same time: Elmo Smith, 1932.

Getting Rockefeller was a coup. Representing reasonable Republicanism, he was a bright prospect for the presidency. He proved to be a most engaging human being, giving two full-scale addresses in Jewett Chapel-Auditorium in connection with homecoming festivities as well as sharing his convictions about higher education with Northwest business and industrial leaders who had expressed interest in private higher education (Alumni *Bulletin* of August (Vol. 72) of 1965.) Some credit for landing Rockefeller should probably go also to Erwin Schwiebert, who, as a moderate Republican, former distinguished state legislator, and a fearless fundraiser, was known to Rockefeller. And it is likely, too, that George Crookham's name appeared in the correspondence respecting the invitation to New York's governor, for Crookham had a sound and growing reputation as an expert on Western water problems and as a fiscally responsible and reasonable Republican.

The planning that went into the year-long celebration was extensive and elaborate. Alumnus, supporter, and former Trustee Walter Kerrick was named chairman. Three major events were planned around traditional observances: Homecoming, October 1965; Religion-in-life Week (sometimes known as Religious Emphasis Week), February 1966; and Founders Day, May 1966. The last occasion had continued to be an on-again-off-again celebration, and Kerrick rightly thought this would be an appropriate year for Founders Day to be "on." In addition a new event was planned for March, an event that would in time become traditional although its name would undergo change. This was an opportunity for women to meet and hear a couple of speakers of national stature comment upon a topic of significance: Ms. Margaret Hickey of New York City and Mrs. David Gaiser of Spokane addressing the conference theme, "Women's Role—A Changing Challenge." Out of this would emerge the Women's Symposium, which would evolve into the Spring Symposium with little reference to gender, although women still comprise the greater portion of the audience. It was by any standard a significant year in the College's continuing history, for the campus was put on display to an enlarging public. Rockefeller gave excellent addresses, was awarded an honorary doctorate, looked, spoke, and acted like a leader; "Happy" Rockefeller charmed all who met her.

As chairman of the Homecoming Sub-Committee of the Seventy-Fifth Anniversary Committee, I had the opportunity to do and say much more than I was comfortable with, including attending some meals with important people. I recall welcoming the full house at Jewett Chapel-Auditorium for Governor Rockefeller's first address, and I have a further recollection of saying something like the year long celebration was off to a fine start and that the Minnesota Twins had even won their game that day, an unveiled allusion to former C of I student Harmon Killebrew.

After Homecoming was history and campus life had returned to normal, I was surprised to receive a letter from Albany, New York. As I read Governor Rockefeller's -expression of thanks for having been asked to participate in the celebration and his expression of hope that he had done an adequate job, I realized that there may have been—not in the letter, but in the context surrounding it—a gentle piece of social instruction. That is, he had written the letter in the absence of my having written him to thank him and to tell him how much his being here meant to the College.

The tempo of the year increased. Senators Frank Church and Len Jordan made time to address students, faculty, and the community in convocation (October 28 and November 12, 1965, respectively). Marilyn Horne sang a concert on October 26, sponsored by the Department of Music and the Fine Arts Series. R. Curtis Westfall resigned in November, his duties falling to Warren H. Page, who had been appointed Assistant Vice President as of October 4 (all of this detailed in the *Coyote*.)

Scarlet Masque presented *Waiting for Godot*, Samuel Beckett's joke on an audience that could be persuaded to endure mostly ennui (not to be confused with the French dramatist of the same sounding name) for upwards of three hours, so confused were people in the '60s about relevance, existentialism, meaningful relationships, absurdist theater, and other catch words. Ground was broken for Terteling Library, and Professor Gabbard prepared his choir for a memorial concert honoring Professor F. F. Beale on December 7, 1965.

The last requires an additional word. According to the *Coyote* of December 3, 1965, the first part of the program was to consist of performances of Beale's own compositions by, in many cases, his own former students, but also by the C of I-Community Symphony and by the Baroque Choir, conducted by Professors Cerveny and Gabbard, respectively. Just before intermission, Professor Beale's library of his own work was to be presented to the College by Professor

Beale's son, F. S. Beale, of Sunnyside, California, and by Mrs. Edgar L. Oakes (Marjorie Beale), of Caldwell, the composer's sister. Additionally, former C of I student and Musical Director of the Disney Studios, Paul Smith, was to be recognized for his gift of a concert grand Steinway piano. Following intermission, Dr. Gabbard was to conduct the concert choir and orchestra in Durufle's *Requiem*, Opus 9, among other numbers on the program. It all came off well.

This was the year the massive concrete marker appeared behind the Hat, advertising our founding in 1891. The football team had great moments playing surprisingly well at the University of Santa Clara for the first half, defeating Whitman and Lewis and Clark, losing to Pacific, Willamette, and Linfield. Ron Boyd, Dick Horyna, Steve Mendoza, Gary Hirai, Elmore Brooks, Cisco Garcia, Ron Washington, Dave Barton, Dennis Richardson, Jim Coverly, Louis Nakroshis, and Ron Sproat played well for the Coyotes.

Dave Barton, Rex Johnson, Dick Powell, George Scott, John Woodbury, Tom Lankford, Jim Graham, Carl Johnson, and Taft Jackson performed well for Coach Dick Carrow's basketball program.

In 1965, Dr. Herbert H. Hayman, a faculty member for more than forty years, died, and it was to be the last year of service for another of the College's fine teachers as Dr. J. H. Roblyer, the then, J. H. announced his retirement coincident with the end of the academic year. The *Coyote* of December 17, 1965, quoted Dean Sayre as follows:

> Dr. Roblyer is one of the most distinguished persons ever to have served on The College of Idaho faculty. It is due, in no small part, to his efforts, that this College ranks in the top 40 colleges in the country in having the highest percentage of students who go on to achieve doctorates in science. Many of his former students have achieved regional and

Football action, 1969: the Coyotes gain yardage as Gary Hirai sweeps right end.

national renown for their scientific careers. Dr. Roblyer exemplifies the type of teacher [that] has made the small private liberal arts colleges such an important part of this nation's system of higher education.

"Roby's" successor was to carry forward the great competence of the Department of Chemistry—Dr. Bruce Stewart Schatz, whose appointment began with the next academic year.

And the Anniversary year moved on. From the high jinks of Homecoming, including a performance by Duke Ellington and his band, and the ground breaking for Hayman Hall and Terteling Library, on to another major event or series of events: the Religion in Life celebration of March 1 and 2, featuring Dr. Eugene Carson Blake, Stated Clerk, United Presbyterian Church in the United States of America and General Secretary-Elect for the World Council of Churches. His first address was titled "This Controversial Ecumenical Movement"; the second, "Is God Really Dead?" The reader may, if sufficiently mature, recall the God Is Dead movement, the brainchild of an Emory University teacher of religion, who had perhaps forgotten that the German philosopher Nietzsche had made the pronouncement much earlier and the American poet Stephen Crane began one of his best lyrics, "God lay dead in heaven." *Le plus ça change*, etc.

Founders Day does, indeed, have a distinguished though not uninterrupted history at the College, as recognition had been paid to some of those faithful servants who "dygged Y welles from whyche wee nowe drynke." On April 30, 1966, J. R. Simplot addressed an academic convocation as the principal event celebrating and paying tribute to the founders of the College. His remarks were titled "The Exciting Future," and many parents who had assembled—Founders Day was held in conjunction with Parents Day—were captivated by the vision and the verve of this trustee. Just to show how temperaments differ, recall the trustee who would resign from the Board before he would permit his picture to appear on a brochure to help raise money for the College and compare his 1940s attitude with the 1960s attitude of Robert V. Hansberger, President, Boise Cascade Corporation; T. E. Roach, President-General Manager, Idaho Power; J. R. Simplot, President, J. R. Simplot Company; N. L. Terteling, President, J. A. Terteling and Sons, Incorporated; and J. L. Scott, President, Albertsons, Incorporated. All of these leaders contributed photographs and messages in brochures used to advertise their support for The College of Idaho.

The anniversary year ended with Commencement 1966, at which Dr. Ernest Hartung, new President of the University of Idaho, gave the principal address.

247

At the meeting of the Board of Trustees for February 26, 1966, the proposed calendar on which the faculty had met, debated, and finally concurred was approved. It was another benchmark in the institution's continuing story. It was also at this meeting that dissatisfaction with plans drawn for the new president's home was expressed, leading the committee to look about for a local architect who might come up with a better plan. The next meeting of the Executive Committee of the Board, April 7, 1966, resulted in Lewis Keys' engagement to design the home. (It was actually designed by Stan Olson.) It was also revealed at this meeting that the College would have a new dean for the next year: Ralph Sayre would be on a sabbatical for the full year, and Dr. William Chalker was appointed Acting Dean. John Sullivan, it was then announced, had resigned for a position at the University of Idaho and would be replaced by Alvin Buzzard.

The next meeting of the Executive Committee, April 30, 1966, contained a recommendation from Warren Page that Halbert Larry Leasure, Associate Director of the University of the Pacific Alumni Association, be considered for the post of Alumni Director for The College of Idaho Alumni Association, if approved by the Executive Committee of the Alumni Association. That approval was forthcoming, and Leasure was confirmed at the meeting of the Board of Trustees on June 4, 1966. That action placed Leasure on the staff of the Development Office. At this same meeting, it was estimated that at the end of the fiscal year, the budget would be in the black by about $935.00. Next year, Mr. Springer, Chairman of the Budget Committee, expected that $220,000 would have to be raised from the living endowment.

> This is a substantial figure. The administration and staff feel confident that this goal can be achieved by proper planning and a full year's program. We are ending one of the best years in The College of Idaho's history. I feel we can look forward to many more....

Part of that forward look depended upon increasing tuition. Adopted in 1962, the Guaranteed Tuition Plan could be modified only for new students, those not enrolled and thus not protected by the guarantee. By action of the Board at this meeting (June 4, 1966), the following rate was approved: for the fall of 1967, from $1,200 to $1,300 per year; for the fall of 1968, from $1,300 to 1,400 per year.

A continuing item of business for the Executive Committee and the full Board was the matter of the president's home. Keys and Smith Associates of Nampa prepared acceptable sketches of plan concepts, "with minor modifications," (Minutes of the Executive Committee, July 11, 1966), Knox having urged that the College "has long needed a suitable facility for the kinds of entertaining and functions necessary to the office—not primarily a residence for a president and his family" (Minutes of the Board of Trustees, June 4, 1966).

Another spot of brightness in the actions of the Executive Committee at its July meeting was the pleasant matter of what to do with Strahorn when Terteling Library was finished. The inclination was to use it for faculty and administrative offices and seminar rooms. Classrooms were later added to the list and administrative offices removed. Further refinements respecting the president's home were to be presented at the next Executive Committee meeting, scheduled for October 10.

At the October meeting, the Executive Committee learned that the latest cost estimate by the John Graham Company for the science building was $1,913,000, including basement excavations. Following discussion it was moved by Trustee Eugene Dorsey and seconded by Trustee Terteling that working drawings be prepared, the fees paid from monies coming to the College from the "100 Million Fund" of the United Presbyterian Church in the U.S.A. in order that a layout might be presented to possible donors in the expectation that bids would be asked for by May 1, 1967. The motion carried. In executive session, it was the Committee's decision to recommend to the full Board that the construction of the president's home be financed to the extent of 60 percent from this same fund, with 40 percent to come from other sources. Already there were three likely contenders for Presbyterian money that was not guaranteed. Would the Board of Trustees follow these recommendations?

At the October 27 meeting of the Board of Trustees, some interesting items were shared. In the first place, full-time student enrollment in the regular day program was up from 767 to 806 although the evening program dropped slightly from 185 to 160. In the second instance, it was decided to "use $150,000 from the Board of Christian Education Capital Funds Program (Fifty Million Fund) for the remodeling of Strahorn Library." The amount of the fund apparently had been halved. A further motion tapped the amount to come to the College, $80,000 to be used to develop drawings for the science building. In executive session it was decided not to follow the recommendation of the Executive Committee in requesting monies from the Capital Needs fund of the Presbyterian Church but to seek financing elsewhere. The old bugaboo of having to borrow in the short run "against the anticipation of plenty" was allowed, up to $300,000, until October 1.

The Academic Year 1966-67 was the first year of the new calendar, an innovation of some consequence although no rival of the Julian and Gregorian calendar reforms. A few words about it are in order.

The need for reform had been perceived by Lyle Stanford, and the time was right for the examination of all institutions, creeds, and values. It was a time very much like an earlier time when a highly intellectualized and reasonable temper of mind began to evolve into—or yield to—the kind of attitude that inclined toward reliance upon the feelings and the intuitions. In EuroAmerican culture it was the evolution of the enlightenment into romanticism, so apparent from the last quarter of the 18th century into the first thirty years of the 19th. Our own Declaration of Independence is a marvelous artifact in which the two—the intellectual and the emotional, the mind and the feelings, the head and the heart—are in accord.

And so it was, in the sixties, and apparently the emotional has become dominant in this latter cultural phenomenon as well, for in the 1990s there is much to suggest that we are still in a time of sensate indulgence with the feelings dominating the reason. The attraction of mind-bending drugs is but one indication. A fine story by Washington Irving titled "The Adventure of the German Student" establishes clearly the quality of mind of that earlier romantic revolt. The new one was much the same.

So the time was right for re-examining the calendar, and colleges throughout the nation did so with great eagerness. Here, we chose to try a fourteen-week first semester, somewhat traditional with sixty-minute classes. Then in a six-week period, with classes lasting an hour and twenty minutes (students taking no more than two) so as to preserve the integrity of the semester unit of credit, we were encouraged to offer classes that were innovative, stimulating, and above all heuristic in their philosophy. That is, students were to be encouraged to find solutions to problems on their own through the careful encouragement by wise mentors and through the use of libraries, laboratories, and other resources. This period was followed by a second rather traditional fourteen-week semester. The period was known as the AbC calendar. There was even a "d" component, as ways were explored by which the summer sessions could be more clearly integrated into the school year to create an AbCd continuum.

It would be possible to write a fairly detailed study just of the Winter Session. Here I must summarize.

The reformed calendar worked well for some departments, adequately for some, and created great distress for others. It was a fine opportunity for field study, whether for biology and geology, sometimes out of the region, or for economics or for dialectology and folklore. It was also a time when foreign language study could be concentrated into "house" environments with nothing but French or German or Spanish spoken in a residence for the entire session. It did not work well and subverted the purpose behind Winter Session when a regular semester course was force-fed to students in six weeks. It was very difficult for the music program, especially applied music.

It was hoped that most courses would be new, not the kind usually taught in the regular school year, so that faculty would have the opportunity to present a special study or prepare a special series on matter that, although interesting and in every sense respectable, could never make it into the rigidly controlled semesters. There were major requirements, graduate and professional school expectations, and general graduation requirements that must be met. The Winter Session was an opportunity to "free up" the curriculum but not sacrifice its integrity.

Another expectation was that writers, political figures, and perhaps former students who had reached some kind of plateau or juncture in their own professional or graduate programs could be invited to return to offer the special insight into their own programs that only they possessed, thus enriching both faculty and students.

Max Peter's 1970 Winter Session Cultural Field Trip to San Francisco included a visit to the studio of noted painter Alexander Nepote.

This expectation the Winter Session has met; Pulitzer Prize novelist A. B. Guthrie, Jr., came for part of Winter Session 1967; Vardis Fisher came in 1968. Governor Smylie has been a sometime and effective teacher for the Department of Political Science; and Dr. Joan Houston Hall, while finishing Ph.D work in dialectology at Emory University, conducted the most detailed survey of regional dialect ever undertaken in connection with a class in that subject.

Most students continue to like the Winter Session; many faculty, particularly those approaching redundancy or superannuation (the English have such nice euphemisms), find the pace extremely taxing.

The Winter Session formerly had its own budget for assisting with field trips and for bringing in speakers, writers, and others who would enliven the campus, people like Kenneth Boulding, secured by Professor Bollinger; Dwight L. Dumond, a guest of Professor Brock; and Thomas Richner, arranged for by Professor Davidson.

The College has properly resisted the temptation to reduce Winter Session to only four weeks. Keeping it at six weeks makes the interim session quite unlike all others, but in addition to uniqueness, the session as now constituted makes it possible for some departments to do field trips of significant scope and depth. The additional cushion of two weeks minimizes the erosion of field study time in getting to and returning from the study site.

At the February 24, 1967, meeting of the Board of Trustees, Robert Smylie, former student leader, football player, attorney general, and governor, was introduced as a new member of the Board. Names under consideration for the new dormitory included "Pioneer," "Hayman," and "Albertson." It was also agreed to proceed with the president's home, cost estimates (excluding the structure itself) for landscaping, carpeting, preparation of public areas, and architects' fees amounting to $91,000. Then at the meeting of the Board of Trustees on June 3, 1967, the name of the dormitory was established as Hayman Hall, thus memorializing one who had helped dig and plant as the College evolved into the institution it now is.

The Trustees recognized by resolution the deaths of two staff members: Dr. Oaks Hoover, College Physician from 1958 until his death on April 29, 1967; and Barbara Bowman Sherman, alumna and Manager of the Bookstore from 1960 until her death on May 21, 1967. The plans for remodeling of Strahorn were approved, the project costing $220,000 to $230,000, fees for architects $22,000, and furnishings $35,000. Support in the amount of $50,000 was to come from the "Fifty Million Fund" and $135,000 from funds administered by the Terteling Investment Agency.

To meet costs until the "Fifty Million Fund" could be tapped and to meet the accumulated deficit of $270,000 (approximate to 5/31/67), Marsh and Knox were authorized to borrow $700,000. New faculty appointments for 1967-68 included Gordon Gochnour, P.E.; Dennis Haley, Mathematics; John Myers, Economics; and Gary Strine, Physics, the only one of the four still with the College.

And Bill Blevins finally made it out of the basement! Pauli Crooke, the aggressive and competent news bureau for the College for ever so long, had managed a coup by getting a full-page free advertisement in *Time Magazine*. Tied to the construction of the new science building, the ad was headed, "Help us get Bill Blevins out of the Basement" and read as follows:

> Bill, one of our finest pre-med students, has already been accepted at three medical schools for next year. But right now he's got troubles. You see, Bill recently received a grant to work on a special biology research project. All the equipment has arrived, but there simply isn't any place to set it up. So Bill is working down in the basement. As if that's not bad enough, the basement is located directly beneath the gymnasium. Can you imagine trying to work with a horde of strapping athletes thundering overhead?

> It's a sad situation. So we're trying to raise enough funds to build a brand new science center. A center conducive to research, with plenty of quiet, and space, and light. One that will be truly worthy of the talents of Bill Blevins and hundreds of students like him. Your contribution will help us get them off the ground.

Although it is difficult to measure the effectiveness of the ad, the combination of a handsome student and attractive copy must have had some impact. (Dr. Blevins was recently recognized for his diagnostic work involving L-Tryptophan.) He was among those approved for graduation with the Bachelor of Science degree (magna cum laude) by action of this Board of Trustees, meeting June 3, 1967.

During the meeting of October 14, 1967, the Trustees approved Dean Chalker's report respecting the dropping of the Secretarial Studies program beginning in the 1968-69 academic year. He also reported that a new organization, the Northwest Association of Private Colleges and Universities, had been incorporated during the late summer and that The College of Idaho was among the seventeen charter members. The Northwest was coming of age.

In testimony to the reality of increasing financial stress upon the College, Business Manager Eldon Marsh presented the administration's request to increase the charges to students as follows:

(a) Annual tuition rate from $1,000 to $1,450

(b) Annual charges for double rooms by $40, single rooms by $30

(c) Annual board charges by $10.

Other increases applied to part-time, night, summer, and graduate students.

The Trustees held a regularly called meeting on March 9, 1968, to consider a particularly heavy agenda. One of the first items of business was the consideration of an invitation by Columbia University School of Engineering and Applied Science for the College to participate in a five year program by which a C of I student, might, by taking a prescribed series of courses, transfer to the New York institution at the end of the third year, continue the approved curriculum at Columbia for two years, and receive the appropriate bachelor's degree from each school. It was recommended by the Trustees that the invitation be accepted.

Other tasks engaged the Trustees—revising the "...relationship of the College" with the Board of Christian Education, worrying over the Development Committee's report that funds were slow in coming in, cutting $42,000 from the amount expected to be raised as "unrestricted gifts" in the budget for 1968-69—but the most serious matter taken up by the Board was a strategy explained by Marsh for financing the proposed science building. Following the explanation and discussion, the following motion was made, seconded, and carried, with one dissenting vote:

A. The college will lease the site for the proposed building to the lessee for a term of 20 years, for the amount of $1.00. This lease would not provide a renewal option.

B. The lessee will construct the building to College specifications on the leased site and in turn lease the building to the College for a term of 20 years, under the following conditions:

    1. Lease would not be renewable.

    2. Lessor would have right to salvage.

    3. Annual rental to be at the rate of 9.3% of the project cost (Capitalized).

    4. Lessor will pay costs of:

        a. Maintenance of structure.

        b. Fire and ECE Insurance.

    c. Property taxes, if any, during the life of the lease.

  5. Lessee ([The] College of Idaho) would provide for and agree to:

    a. Lessor approval for remodeling and/or modification.

    b. Continuous use for purpose agreed upon at execution of lease.

    c. Reasonable and proper care and maintenance.

    d. Public Liability Insurance.

    e. Cost of operation, heat, light, and power, etc.

C. The College will attempt to secure sufficient funds to provide a sinking fund sufficient to cover the rental payment for the 20 year period.

The lease-lease back arrangement got the building project going and bids were called. The Budget and Campus Committee of the Board of Trustees recommended the contract for the building in the amount of $1,807,258 and that G. V. Sweet Company be awarded the contract to supply and install fixed laboratory equipment and casework in the amount of $373,125.50. Finally, after years of hoping and making do, after years of superb teaching of bright students under conditions hardly approaching minimal never mind adequate, the figurative Bill Blevinses of The College of Idaho seemed about to be taken from the basement.

The report of President Knox to the Board of Trustees at the annual commencement meeting of June 1, 1968, was a message of hope and caution, of success offset by only partial success. Enrollment, he said, would stay about where it was [around 896 for the fall of the current academic year]; student problems on campus called for administrative action which he hoped the administration would defend; the administration would exercise strong budget control with detailed quarterly review; the AbC plan was working well; more students had won honors than for several years. (This last comment could well indicate the onset of grade inflation, a common enough occurrence in the '60s and '70s.) Library use, he continued, had increased four-or fivefold. He was absolutely correct when he reported that the faculty took great pleasure in the newly modified Strahorn Hall.

The subject of the enlarging deficit appeared, and he expressed his profound disappointment about it, suggesting that it could be managed and future deficits forestalled. As the Board approved the proposed budget for 1968-69, Business Manager Marsh was requested to prepare a summary of the accumulated deficit from 1960 to the present.

These data, included as attachments to the Minutes of June 1, 1968, contain the information sought and also a summary of enrollments. The latter are not identified as FTE (Full Time Equivalent), and I therefore assume the figures include all students enrolled. The accumulated operations deficits were as follows: 1960—$28,041; 1961—$27,302; 1962—$23,703; 1963—$54,730. The tally continues, but let Marsh's summary suffice: "Since 1960 General fund operations have incurred three (3) deficit years totaling $269,851 and five (5) surplus years totaling $28,082 for a net deficit of $241,769." The budget deficit for 1967-68 was estimated at about $50,000; Trustee Simplot indicated he would contribute $25,000 toward its relief if the balance would be met by the other trustees.

Enrollment from 1960-61 to 1967-68 was summarized thus, fall figures only: 1960-61—728, 1961-62—709, 1962-63—737, 1963-64—690, 1964-65—750, 1965-66—814, 1966-67—836, 1967-68—896.

From time to time properties are received by the College, sometimes from graduates, sometimes from people loyal to the institution or to its presidents, sometimes simply for altruistic reasons. Alumnus Dr. Ed Heath gave fifteen acres of land to the College to be used by the Department of Biology for ecological, geological, and botanical studies, under the direction of Dr. Stanford, a gift from a grateful student. The property was later sacrificed to the College's debts.

Then, too, from time to time I am asked when thus and so happened, the interrogator assuming that I have at my command the entire one-hundred-year chronology. I have attempted to put as much of that in this work as I can, but all historiography is selective. However, I include the date of retirement for Professors Margaret Boone, Leslie V. Brock, Lester L. McCrery, and John F. Sollers. They all retired at the end of the 1968-69 academic year, according to the Minutes of the Meeting of the Board of Trustees for October 12, 1968. At this meeting, it was reported that full-time enrollment was 853, down from 862 the year before.

Three further bits of information conclude this chapter. Earlier I mentioned that the Trustees whose names appear on the amended Articles of Incorporation would be identified simply for the record, their action reflecting the will of the General Board of Education of the United Presbyterian Church. Those trustees were Robert L. Alexanderson, Eugene C. Dorsey, Bernice R. Crookham, Leonard H. Crofoot, Gilbert L. Stanton, Robert E. Smylie, Darwin Symms, Harold F. Holsinger, Jerome C. Smith, Mrs. H. Westerman Whillock, A. C. Garber, E. D. Springer, Warren Barry, Lyman W. Winkle, C. J. Kniefel, Alfred

M. Popma, Margaret Boone, Joseph W. Marshall, N. L. Terteling, and Lloyd L. Nelson. Their action removed any requirement respecting Presbyterian membership on the Board of Trustees.

Surely a bright spot of the 1967-68 Academic Year was the winning of the third Rhodes Scholarship by a C of I student, Thomas G. McFadden, an Idaho native. When one considers the many fine institutions of higher learning which have never had a Rhodes Scholar and then recalls that Tom was our third, one must pause and reflect upon what this small college does so well. That reflection is intensified, prolonged, suppled, and driddled when the College's fourth Rhodes Scholar was named the next year. He was James Milton Roelofs of Caldwell. The likelihood of back-to-back Rhodes Scholars is so rare as to be infinitesimal. But it happened in 1967-68 and 1968-69.

The dreamer might suppose that the halls of the great and powerful would resound with this news, and that emissaries from the Ford Foundation, the Carnegie Foundation, the Mellon Foundation and other such objects of quests by the impoverished would arrive on campus bearing quantities of cash with which to recognize and reward this signal accomplishment. If judged upon the quality of its products—not upon size, not upon publications of faculty, not upon athletic prowess—it would appear that the small Caldwell school *deserved* reward. But that is not the way this universe works, where everything nourishes what is already strong. Somewhere—perhaps in the Book of Psalms, perhaps in Proverbs—it is written that promotion cometh (the language is approximate and I am selective) not from the east or the south. What is becoming clear is that security will have to come through the growth of the endowment, and that growth will have to be generated by local support. There is little alternative. When our fundraisers' requests of Eastern foundations are rejoined by responses like, "We could direct **all** our charity to one or two institutions that are older, bigger, and better than you," it becomes clear that this school's destiny lies west of the one hundredth meridian.

The final bit of information is contained in the Trustees' Minutes of October 11, 1969. It was a commendation from a grateful faculty to President Knox for his five years of service and was "spread upon" the minutes in the form in which the faculty had prepared it. Because it contains a fair summary of the accomplishments of this administration, it may appropriately be paraphrased here. It calls attention to the new library ("both pleasant to use and delightful to behold"), the alteration of Strahorn Library into Strahorn Hall ("a commodious office and classroom building"), construction of a science building ("whose completion must surely augure well for continued pursuit of excellence by the science division"), the summer sabbatical program ("with the expanding professional horizons...it makes possible"), and finally, "the many acts of kindness and generosity, courtesy and praise, fidelity and concern he consistently demonstrates...."

With one exception, these Rhodes victories and this commendation may well have been the crest of the wave of Knox's success. Another achievement lay ahead, but clouds were gathering.

*Instrumental in the successful completion of Terteling Library were, left to right, trustee
N. L. Terteling, Vice-President and Treasurer Eldon R. Marsh, and architect John Graham.*

Protests, causes and demonstrations: Above, students and faculty join others in Boise at a 1914 temperance rally (College of Idaho, Sky Juice For Us); below, the first Earth day, 1970, students march on Indian Creek in Caldwell.

CHAPTER FIFTEEN

What *Can* I Count on,

Mr. Willmorth?

T he note of levity introduced by the title (it is from a Christmas enter-tainment by President Knox) will be sounded again at the appropriate time, for surely this chapter requires some relief from its mordant tone.

A backward glance will discover a great deal of campus unrest. This was a period of protest or, as some would have it, a revolting time. Students were excited about the free speech movement on the Berkeley campus of the University of California, deriving from that reaction considerable concern about their rights. Other campuses protested the war in Viet Nam, some young men burning their draft cards and some moving to Canada or Sweden. Be-tween these two poles of protest—the right to be coprological in speech and the right to object to war—there was an enormous gulf, not apprehended by a great many of the revolutionary cast of mind. About the one issue, nothing more serious than good manners or a respect for the sensibilities of an older generation was involved. It was largely a matter of politeness. About the other issue revolved matters of great significance,—life, death, the obligations of citizens, morality, social ethics. All this and more. The pity was that in the minds of many no distinctions were drawn between the poles.

Some students were fascinated by consciousness-altering drugs, and far too much journalistic attention began to be paid to gurus like Timothy Leary and his advocacy of LSD. They seemed to forget that the altered mind can only generate altered impressions or register altered understanding. Somewhere in Frank Waters' *The Man Who Killed the Deer* is expressed the conviction that only in full consciousness is there valid perception. It is truly the fully and wholly conscious mind that is capable of rational judgment.

But indulgence is one of the characteristics of romanticism, and we entered a neo-romantic world view about this time, anti-establishment and rebellious to a severe degree. Trust no one over thirty, and by all means find "Oh! Calcutta," "Hair," and "I Am Curious, Yellow" attractive. How dated it all seems now.

The College of Idaho was not untouched by all of this, although we were spared most of the extreme behavior. There was, I think, no serious drug problem on campus, although there may have been more than I knew. The Trustees' Minutes carry occasional references to students and drugs; two serious offenders flunked out of school and disappeared.

A shift occurred from hard (judgmental) to soft (non-judgmental) language in describing drug users, generated by pop-psychologists. In the 1930s users were "dope fiends," later they became "drug addicts," then "drug users," "substance abusers," and finally "chemically dependent." "Drunks" became "alcoholics," then "substance abusers." To some people these semantic shifts met the Christian objective of hating the sin—loving the sinner, by diminishing the idea of guilt; to others, the shifts indicated the ascendance of liberalism.

I recall only one student whose performance in class indicated that his gyroscope was badly askew. While giving an oral report, he tried hard, apparently, to express coherent ideas, but his language betrayed him as he moved from one illogicality to another and the sweat stains steadily increased around the underarms of his shirt. It may have been that I so intimidated him—I do that to students—that he became incoherent. I later learned that he was under suspicion as central to drug use on the campus.

Another indication of student problems was the decline in quality of the student newspaper. I mentioned that under the editorship of Dave O'Neil it had an auspicious beginning. That prospect quickly dimmed, and the paper became a repository of coded vulgarity and pointless and irresponsible non-news. In several places in Trustees' Minutes, Mr. Knox felt called to apologize for The *Coyote.* In the Minutes of October 11, 1969, for instance, he "reported the usual trouble" with it. It is in these minutes also that one can find the trustees considering a document from a national student organization bearing the title "Joint Statement on Rights and Freedoms of Students." Trustee Jerome Smith not unreasonably suggested a better title might be "Joint Statement of

Responsibilities, Rights, and Freedoms of Students." The pressures on all presidents of institutions of higher learning were enormous. Added to the pressure was discouragement and anxiety about Mrs. Knox's health (a kidney removed) and the President's bout with bleeding ulcers. These problems made the agitation by the Lambda Zeta fraternity for its own house inconsequential. Some regarded the presence of a national fraternity as a compromise of the College's long-standing tradition of independence from such fraternity-sorority emphasis. More people than one had come to the C of I instead of attending a university because they prized the independent spirit.

But to summon the spirit of levity glanced at in the chapter title, I refer to the Christmas Party of 1969 for the faculty and staff. Knox was host, and for entertainment he presented a program of his own composition. In verse form he recognized each academic and administrative department and each member of the department. As a special tribute, he composed additional "special ballads" and interspersed them throughout his presentation. Space will permit only a few; the influence of Ogden Nash is apparent.

To the staff and the administrention
Who are far too numerous to specifically mention
May your Christmas vacation be full of joy and of holiday flowers
Like a gigantic coffee break that will last for days instead of the usual
couple of hours

Santa says:
Don't be harsh
On Eldon Marsh
He buys the gas
For the College carsh

In our Christmas wish for Physics
We would be grossly remissity
If we didn't hope for more support
For Heat, Light, Mechanics, Magnetism and Electricity

Special Ballad: To the tune of "Gallagher and Sheehan"

Mr. Willmorth, Oh, Mr. Willmorth.
May I be of service, Mr. Strine?
I thought an honorarium should go with my planetarium
Good idea, Mr. Willmorth?
You're dreaming, Mr. Strine.

Mr. Willmorth, Oh, Mr. Willmorth.
Go ahead and lay it on me, Mr. Strine.

A least a calculator, to measure Mars' equator?
What *can* I count on, Mr. Willmorth?
On your fingers, Mr. Strine.

Ode (Owed) to Sterry Hall: To the tune of "Old Smoky"

On top of old Sterry
All covered with slats.
The pigeons are leaving
Along with the rats.

The ivy is dying
And so are the bees.
Who's that softly crying?
The Board of Trustees.

When the walls have all crumbled
And reduced to a mound,
Then Eldon will tell us
That the basement's still sound.

When the staff has deserted
And the safe turned to rust,
There's Eldon still working
Under eight feet of dust.

This, then, is a tribute
To sing up to the starsh;
It's not Sterry's quagmire,
It's just Eldon's marsh.

On January 29, 1970, the Executive Committee met to consider further the financing of the William Judson Boone Science Center. A report by Knox and Marsh announced that plans had been made for a two-year loan of a million dollars by First Security Bank. The College would then assign a like amount from the moneys pledged for the building (a total of about $1,736,000) to the Terteling Foundation, Inc. for a debenture note that would then be assigned to

First Security as collateral on the two-year loan bearing nine and a half percent per year.

At the meeting of the Trustees of February 21, 1970, among other items of business was the approval of the new fiscal year, a change from May 31 to June 30, to take effect the 1969-70 year. Another important item was the naming of Duane Leach to the deanship of the College. Further, the College's Drug Policy Statement, approved by the faculty, the school attorney, the student senate, the Administrative Council and the President's Council, was ready for consideration by the Board of Trustees. If approved, it would become the official policy. It was, and it did, as strange as it may seem that the intellectually gifted (college student) should have to be advised of the harm of drug use and the legal penalties involved. The College reaffirmed its membership in the body politic of town, county, state, and nation, and thus subject to their respective laws regarding illegal substances. Finally, it was announced that Dr. Gene Odle, Dean of Administration (one of the Multi-deans of Mr. Knox's Christmas entertainment) and loyal College of Idaho staff member for seventeen years, going back to the days of President Pitman, had resigned and the office was terminated. Odle moved to Alfred University and earned a reputation as an outstanding administrator, working up to the position of, as I recall, vice-chancellor and sometime acting chancellor. He died in 1990.

At the May 11, 1970, meeting of the Board of Trustees, George V. Wolfe's retirement was announced. What a contribution he had made to the small school in the dusty West. Hired by Dr. Hall, George Victor Wolfe invested his life in this school, and it was largely his efforts, his example, his presence that first of all inspired young people to choose law as a profession and in the second place prepared them for the rigors of law school.

So many traditional materials in the form of legends have been generated about this man that not to include a few would be a dishonor to his memory. In the first place, his driving set fright records for his passengers. Students attending Model U.N. meetings or other political science gatherings devised stratagems for keeping George from behind the wheel. He often failed to stop at stop signs or lights but would stop where he had unrestricted right of way. It was said that when Dr. Wolfe finally quit driving there was great joy in heaven, and the angel whose special charge George had been received awards for extending care above and beyond the call of duty.

Dr. Wolfe enjoyed having students in, and at one of these early "at homes," he set about preparing tea. In those months before Alice was able to join him in

Caldwell, the preparation was his sole responsibility. Preparations made, he asked his guests to sit and filled their cups with hot water, no tea: just hot water.

His handwriting, too, created delightful stories. He returned a student's test once and had found little to say beyond a question mark for a grade and an enigmatic note terminated by a spot the student took to be a period. The student wished to know what he had done right or wrong, took the paper to a classmate in a fruitless effort to decipher the message. Failing to get relief, he took the paper to a faculty member, then another, and another. Dr. Brock gave up and made the reasonable suggestion that the student ought not be intimidated but should go to George for a translation. Summoning his courage, the student did so. George read the comments as follows:

I cannot assign a grade, for I cannot read your writing.

Having linked Dr. Brock and Dr. Wolfe in the same paragraph, I am compelled to write, though ever so briefly, of their animadversion. It is quite true that they were often at odds on academic matters and on many matters about which faculty were expected to take a position. To hear those intellectual titans in debate in Faculty Assembly was somewhat like (I do not want to overstate the case) hearing Webster and Hayne debate an issue in the U.S. Senate, just short of "my worthy opponent from South Carolina" and "the distinguished gentleman from Massachusetts." I once inquired into the causes of this contrariety and was told that Dr. Wolfe had once said, apropos of an opportunity to gauge faculty performance, "I would give us a C." Dr. Brock was deeply and forever offended that anyone had the temerity to thus generalize about faculty competence. Whether this account is the true one, it is the only explanation I have heard.

It was also announced at this meeting of the Trustees (June 6, 1970) that the Hill Family Foundation had approved a

Dr. George V. Wolfe

proposal through which the vast 110,000-square mile Snake River Basin and contiguous areas could be studied. At this meeting Dr. Wolfe's retirement was formalized by a resolution. It was also the meeting at which the Trustees approved President Knox's recommendation that two ex-officio members be added to the Board: the president of Faculty Association and the president of the student body. This was surely another highlight in the administration of Dr. Knox. Indeed, it is close to the mark to say that the remainder of his term was fraught with increasing difficulties until his resignation was accepted three years later.

Much has been written about the Snake River Regional Studies Center, and it is not necessary here to chronicle its twenty year history. However, it is not inappropriate to tell of its purpose and its beginnings, the latter first, as I remember them.

Lyle Stanford, Bob Bratz, LaMar Bollinger, and I were once visiting about the wholeness of knowledge and how that wholeness might be grasped. In a small college folks talk to one another. Someone suggested that one way to approach an understanding of wholeness would be to examine a region. What if we could get a grant to study the Owyhee Region, for instance? Someone else suggested that that might be too small, that totality might better be exampled by a more careful description of an area of larger geographical extent: what if the region consisted of an entire river system? The conversation was exciting and in the course of time, it seemed appropriate to meet with the chief fundraiser, Larry Leasure.

The prospects were sufficiently attractive to him to request that Doc Stanford, Larry, and I take a weekend, put our heads together, and write a proposal for the funding of the means by which a region could be defined and studied. Agreed. We went to Frenchglen, Oregon, where we knew there were no telephones; where we knew that if there were connections between landscape and inspiration, we could sense them; and where we would be constrained by the absence of all else to concentrate upon our task for the entire time.

There were no models of how to do what we thought we wanted to do, but by drawing from the depths of that great Stanford mind we came up with a proposal we thought we could defend, if given a chance.

The next step involved a flight to Portland, Oregon, where Ralph King, the very fine Yale-trained lawyer—a brother-in-law of James Boone—had arranged an appointment with a representative of the Hill Family Foundation. After an exciting landing at PDX, we made our way to King's office and were shown from there to the representative's office on, I believe, the next floor down, for

I seem to remember that King's law firm had an entire floor. Introductions were made, the purpose of our visit was clarified, and we were all taken as King's guests to an elegant luncheon at the Benson Hotel.

When the interview finally ended, we returned to Caldwell to await the decision of the Trustees of the Hill Family Foundation. After a decent interval, word came that the proposal had been well received, and we were given a grant in the amount of slightly over $100,000 with which to establish a Snake River Regional Studies Center, preliminary to the study of the entire region drained by this, one of America's fifteen or so greatest rivers.The selection of one of Caldwell High School's most gifted teachers, Donna Parsons, was a master stroke, and she remained as its only full-time director from 1970 until her retirement in 1988.

A first order of business was the selection of an advisory board, and to meet this objective we invited representatives from commerce and industry, from various local, state, and federal agencies, from livestock and agricultural interests, and from the amorphous general public. John Fery served as the first chairman of the advisory board, and to observe the skillful manner in which he conducted the first meeting of the board was to see an intellect and an imagination of the first order.

The first three major activities of the Center involved economics, biology, and folklore; the coadjutors for the Center believed that ultimately every academic department in the College could find some niche that could be

On January 9, 1975, Masatada Higaki, Japanese Consul- General, from the Portland, Oregon consulate, far left, joined President William Cassell, Idaho Governor John Evans, Dr. Louie Attebery and Marshall Scholar and alumnus Barry Fujishin '72, in opening the Regional Studies Center's Japanese-American Conference.

appropriately connected with regional studies. We also realized that the College is a teaching, not a research institution; that our mission is the dissemination of knowledge and the inculcation of habits of critical, responsible thought and the habits of effective expression, not the generation of new knowledge. Hence the teaching-learning element was ever foremost, while research was always student-centered rather than directed toward enlarging a professor's list of publications.

A valuable function of the Center was to serve as a clearing house, a bibliographical center, in a sense, for work done by agencies and others but perhaps unknown by a wider public. Thus it became important for Director Parsons to have an extensive card index of the titles of all regionally based studies. It was not uncommon to find two or more agencies at work on something in the region but working out of different offices and each unaware of other work being done.

As difficult as it now is to conceive of such totally discrete research, then the oneness of existence was only beginning to be popularly received. **Ecology** was the magic word; in the argot of the long haired and unwashed it was , "Like, you know, man, like it's all one." Indeed, it is. Nothing is ever simple, and you can never do just one thing.

Ours was one of the first, if not the very first, regional studies centers. The Center put on conferences, ranging from the Japanese-American component of regional population to a conference on the livestock industry and a later one on irrigation. Space will not permit extensive citation, but the 1976 Congress on Public Lands was an extremely early and successful attempt to develop colloquy among all the (sometimes contentious) users of the public domain. Under the skilled moderator and Chair of the Advisory Council Al Eiguren, the Congress shed much light into dark corners, and the two field trips to ranches (one the remote Alvord Ranch of Tom Davis) gave participants an unexpected slant on Western problems. I recall that a geographer from the University of New Hampshire remarked on how instructive the Congress and the field trips were for him.

From that time through the 200-page baseline interdisciplinary environmental assessment of Nutmeg Mountain for a mining firm and including a series on sustainable agriculture developed by Acting Director Bollinger featuring Wes Jackson, the Regional Studies Center has served well.

Bits and pieces of anecdotal material follow, in chronological order. At the meeting of the Executive Committee of the Board of Trustees on September 14, 1970, borrowing in the amount of $800,000 was authorized. At the meeting of the Board of Trustees on October 23, 1970, Dr. Gerald Wallace, Erwin

Schwiebert's old debating partner, was accepted as ex-officio representative of the Synod of Idaho on the Board. At the same meeting it was announced that Dr. Stanford would take a class to Australia and Dr. James D. Marshall, a class to Hawaii. Negotiations for student research at the Newberry Library of Chicago, at the University of Oklahoma, at the Argonne Laboratories, and at the East-West Center in Honolulu were looking productive. From the Minutes of the Executive Committee meeting of November 16, 1970, comes information that the "church corporation is withdrawing support," the information deriving from a meeting of a committee of the Presbyterian College Union, causing Mr. Knox to grumble: "Ten years hence [it is likely that] we will be financially connected to the Presbyterian Church by a local gift of $500 or less from the Boone Memorial Church of Caldwell; and that we will be connected to the larger church by a page in our catalog which refers to our...founding...."

The Executive Committee met again on January 18, 1971, and the Minutes record Eldon Marsh's report that Winter Session enrollment dropped substantially to 856 full-time students, compared to Fall Semester's 937 and against a budgeted enrollment of 908, causing tuition receipts to drop by $38,000. The Executive Committee met the following month (February 8, 1971) and continued the development of the theme (in musical terms) of hard times. Borrowing from First Security against pledges for the science building had seemed a good idea on January 20, 1970, but "pledge proceeds were insufficient at February 1, 1971, to make the principal payment." The generous Terteling Foundation agreed to lend the needed $225,000 upon the execution of a note in that amount, forestalling a crisis in the completion of that essential building. In developing the budget for 1971-72, an estimated enrollment of 887 full-time students was used. President Knox had been a passionate and successful advocate of salary increases for the faculty, and upward adjustments were incorporated into the budget of $1,931,000, less $50,000 of contingency funds.

At the next full meeting of the Board of Trustees, February 20, 1971, honorary degrees were approved for U.S. Senators Len B. Jordan and Frank Church. Additionally, the Board approved the promotion of three faculty—Edward Bonaminio to Associate Professor, Roger Higdem to Professor, and Gary Strine to Associate Professor. In his report to the Board, Dean of Students Russ Monahan mentioned that the students were in the process of revising the constitution, a habit with them. I have not kept count of all the times that poor document has been altered, but it has always proved a broad target for rising student politicians.

A new motif in the developing depressing strain was sounded when Dean Leach reported that "the decision had been made to reduce the faculty in the

Department of Biology by three part-time people and by one full-time person in the Department of English." Professor Sinclair had announced her retirement; she would not be replaced in 1971-72. Leach further announced an ongoing study of teaching loads and course offerings with the attendant prospect of a reduction in course offerings. The potential reduction of faculty was implied.

The next meeting of the full Board was on June 5, 1971, and there was little to modulate the increasingly dismal tone of the life of The College of Idaho. President Knox's report pulled no punches:

> Our current budget has taken a terrific beating, even after squeezing $50,000 of projected expenditures out of it in January. Two factors, both of which are completely outside the realm of management, have caused our problem: an atypical drop in enrollment from fall to winter; and a poor atmosphere for fund-raising. These phenomena are nationwide.

In the face of declining numbers of students and difficulties in raising money, President Knox recommended an increase in tuition by $150, from $1,950 to $2,100, effective Fall Semester of 1972 for entering freshman, sophomores, and new students. Continuing students' guaranteed tuition plan would continue at $1,600 for seniors and $1,750 for juniors until the plan was phased out.

Margaret Sinclair's retirement was acknowledged in a grand way through a resolution and a commendation that are part of the permanent record of the Board of Trustees. The resolution identified five attributes that contributed to her greatness as a teacher, and although space works against mentioning them all, her concern for the students, her selflessness, her self-improvement, her sense of humor, and her function as a gadfly or campus conscience are clearly part of her personal legacy to the institution. From her concern for the appearance of the campus, all should draw the moral resolution to pick up the beer cans, the waste paper, and the trashy detritus of trashy people. I can almost see the sparks of indignation if she were to see the litter around the Student Union.

I have said much about the helpers who assist the central figure of traditional tales. In the course of this meeting of June 5, 1971, Jack Simplot announced that he had to leave the meeting and that he understood there would be a deficit for the current year of approximately $200,000. He thought the College was a good institution, worthy of support, he said, and would therefore match gifts up to 50 percent of the anticipated deficit.

A bid to enlarge and remodel Simplot Hall and Dining Room was accepted, according to Minutes of the Executive Committee meeting of September 13, 1971, to be financed through the sale of Series D bonds by arrangement with the Department of Housing and Urban Development. In the meantime, Marsh requested permission to borrow $800,000 until the receipt of money from the Fifty Million Fund and Science Center Campaign Funds. Further, President Knox informed the Board that enrollment as of September 13 was below the number projected. The national wage-price freeze, he said, applied to private schools, and the College would comply.

It was announced at this meeting that Charlie Ross, long-time voice teacher, had resigned and would be replaced by Estyn Goss. One of the most highly respected of musicians, Charles M. Ross brought an incredibly rich background of musical experience to the College. It included vaudeville, baritone operatic leads, solo roles in oratorios, the teaching of Robert Shaw, Hollace Shaw (sister), and teaching innumerable beautiful voices at The College of Idaho. Kenton Allen, writing in The *Coyote* of April 4, 1956, said that Ross's "crowning musical triumph came last December 16 at Blatchley Little Theater when he sang the [starring] role in the Black Masque presentation of 'The Littlest Freshman,' written by the well known literary figures Ralph Berringer and William Wallace."

As a teacher he inspired such confidence and so helped students develop vocal strength that several faculty whose voices were weakened from poor vocal production were significantly helped by studying with him. They will remember the exercise "My Fa-a-a-ather," and the art songs "My Love's an Arbutus" and "Who Is Sylvia?"

But perhaps the most engaging aspect of Charlie was his in-

Music major Olive Fairchild, '69, MA '78, a pupil of Charlie Ross, commuted daily to campus from her home in Midvale, a round trip in excess of 150 miles; in the process of earning her bachelor's degree she literally wore out three sedans.

fectious, hearty, sometimes profane sense of humor. He had a vast reservoir of jokes, anecdotes, and personal experiences to draw upon, and he was a skillful story-teller. He enjoyed telling about helping one singer who had come to Charlie with a "bleat like a sheep." Another had a vibrato "you could drive a truck through." Some other singer was so inept "he couldn't find middle C with a private eye." And a Kansas physic? "You swallow a grasshopper and he kicks the crap out of you." *Orare Carolus.*

Student numbers continued to decline (Minutes of the Meeting of the Board of Trustees, October 23, 1971): 856 enrolled for the fall, as opposed to 937 the year before. In view of this decline and the accumulated deficit of $545,481, President Knox prepared to take draconian measures—reducing the faculty from 58 to 54, eliminating four or five administrative posts, eliminating "several traditional programs, academic and otherwise." Such programs, for instance, as the summer grant program (a program by which faculty were encouraged monetarily to undertake research or otherwise improve their teaching), the plan by which those on sabbatical leave were replaced by temporary appointees, and football were all fair game for elimination.

By this time the internship program, which had come under the umbrella of the Regional Studies Center, was attracting attention. Able seniors interned with attorneys, in various business enterprises, and on the staffs of various media in the valley. This from Dean Leach's report to the Board and from my memory.

At the next to the last meeting of the Executive Committee (November 8, 1971), Knox and Marsh reported on a project they had been considering which involved the creation of a corporation for the benefit of The College of Idaho; if the Trustees approved, it would be called College of Idaho Foundation, Inc. Incorporators were Chairman Alexanderson, President Knox, and Business Manager Marsh. The project was approved. It is not clear how a non-profit foundation within an eleemosynary organization serves a useful purpose, but the incorporators must have imagined a bit of advantage.

Then at the first meeting of the Executive Board, February 23, 1972, not January 17, 1972, as the Minutes of December 13, 1971, had specified as the meeting date, President Knox and Eldon Marsh "presented problems the College is having financing accumulated debt." They were grave problems, casting before them shadows portending a crisis. Only a historian, I suppose, is inured to a recital of noxious news. For the record, then,

> [By] June 30, 1971, the College had incurred operating deficits totaling $460,950....

For several years, cash flow requirements have been financed with the local banks ($800,000 at First Security Bank in 1970-71). In September 1971, following repayment of the previous year's loan and in negotiations for renewal of our line of credit with First Security Bank, we were required to fully collateralize short term loans with that bank. Subsequent conversations have resulted in a limiting of such borrowings to $450,000. Since it will be necessary to finance approximately $350,000 between now and September 1, appropriate actions to provide for the orderly payment of expenses as incurred are necessary....

To resolve the long term financing, it is now recommended that the Board authorize an interest borrowing from the Endowment Fund in the amount of $500,000 at 5% for five years. In addition, it is recommended that $100,000 per year plus interest be authorized as a budget charge to repay this borrowing to the Endowment Fund.

This recommendation would still require an annual borrowing line of credit of approximately $300,000 on an unsecured basis....

At June 30, 1971, the Endowment fund contained $519,975 in unrestricted funds, funds functioning as endowment at the direction of trustees....

After the Board approved changing Mr. Marsh's title from Business Manager to Vice President and Treasurer of the College, it was moved and seconded that the long term financing suggested by Knox and Marsh be approved. The motion carried.

The Minutes of the meeting of the Executive Committee for April 10, 1972, carried no explosive information. Professors Peggy Gledhill, William Hedley, and Gary Strine and Dr. Duane Leach were given tenure, and Larry Leasure, the busy and affable Director of Development resigned. It was Larry Leasure's work with Opal Fisher that resulted in her decision to give her Hagerman property to the College for the uses to which the Regional Studies Center could put it (a decision she later revoked).

Subsequent reports to the Board of Trustees on October 14, 1972, February 17, 1973, and May 19, 1973, were redundant with depressing reports about declining enrollment and mounting deficits. Before the climax of this symphony of despair, a couple of items merit a brief mention.

First, in the Minutes of the Board meeting of February 17, 1973, a meeting loaded with the usual minutiae of terminations (Dr. Spero, Drama and English, was terminated as had been his predecessor, John Perry or, as he came to call himself "Jon Perri"), a resignation (Don Parmelee, Associate Professor of Physical Education and Director of Athletics, a C of I figure since the days of Pitman), sabbatical leaves, leaves of absence, tenure recipients, and promotions, it was also recommended that the honorary degree Doctor of Letters be conferred upon Robert V. Burchfield at Commencement 1974 should he deign to be Commencement speaker. Burchfield, one of the tutors of Rhodes Scholar James M. Roelofs and also editor of the Oxford English Dictionary Supplement, was a figure of considerable international repute.

Finally, an *ad hoc* committee of Robert Alexanderson, LaMar Bollinger, Shirley Kroeger, Edwin Springer, Warren B. Knox, and Eldon Marsh had been formed and charged to develop recommendations respecting the disposition of Cleveland Boulevard property. The Committee separated the property into two parcels, "A," bordered by Cleveland Boulevard, 24th Avenue, Blaine Street, and 22nd Avenue; and "B," bordered by 24th Avenue, Cleveland Boulevard, 26th Avenue, and Blaine Street. It was the Committee's recommendation to the Board of Trustees that Parcel "A" be retained but that Parcel "B" be considered "for revenue producing development."

It was at the meeting of the Board of Trustees on Saturday, May 19, 1973, after Commencement and following the traditional luncheon recess that Dr. Peggy Gledhill, Chair of the Faculty-Staff Association (a change in the name and identity of the former Faculty Association), presented to the Board a letter on behalf of the Association communicating to the Board "deep, continuing, and growing concern about the financial situation."

Added to this was news of the resignations from the Board of Gilbert Stanton, Robert L. Wiley, Jr., and Eugene C. Dorsey. They had all been effective trustees, and both the quality of Dorsey's paper (*The Idaho Statesman*) and its concern for Idaho's oldest college went into decline following his resignation from the Board.

President Knox's letter of resignation was read in Executive Session at 4:15 p.m.

Those nine years had taken their toll. Comfortable playing jazz piano and engaging in witty repartee, ever concerned about faculty compensation, and one who genuinely loved the College—after all, his son had been a speedy halfback and sprinter on the track team—Warren B. Knox had been compromised by the times, manifest, principally, in budget deficits and declining numbers of students. Two specific sources of—in some cases—contention unrelated to the times were the President's house, which the College could not afford, and the time he spent writing *Eye of the Hurricane: Observations on Creative Educational Administration,* published by the Oregon State University

Press, Corvallis, 1973. It was vintage Knox, warm, intimate, engaging, filled with felicitous turns of phrase:

> Any school or college [we read] should be a vital, vibrant entity. It lives and it can give life. It has its moments of failure, of frustration, of crisis; but it also enjoys respect, affection, and good will, as do all humans and human institutions.

His legacy of buildings—Hayman Hall, Terteling Library, the President's House, the William Judson Boone Science Center (delays in construction caused by a steel strike and a high water table added to its cost), an enlarged Simplot Hall and Dining Room—was as great as that of any of his predecessors, and the nub of the matter is that excepting only the President's House, the buildings had been called for by the Long Range Plan the College had accepted. Is it rebarbative to say that he did what he was expected to do? He did, that is, in every matter but the raising of money.

How would his successor fare?

An impromptu soccer match with Terteling Library as a backdrop, autumn, 1973

November, 1967: The Knox Family in the newly completed President's Home. Left to right, John, Warren, Nancy, and Chuck.

Chairman of the Board of Trustees Robert E. Smylie, at left, with the seventh president of the College, William C. Cassell and his wife, Jeanne.

Part VII

The Smylie Interim (1973-74) and

the Cassell Years 1974-1980

Commencement, May, 1974: John T. Lezamiz, Political Science major from Richfield, becomes the 5000th graduate of The College of Idaho.

CHAPTER SIXTEEN

Academic Excellence

Soon after Warren Knox's departure from the College, Danforth Associate and Chairman of the Department of Economics LaMar Bollinger submitted a modest proposal to the Danforth Foundation. It was swiftly approved for that philanthropy saw merit in the humble request for a planning conference-retreat to improve the quality of communication among "students, faculty, administration, trustees, and the region served by the College, involving representatives from each of these components."[*]

With his usual clearsightedness, Professor Bollinger used the 1973 re-accreditation to balance our present effectiveness (as measured by re-accreditation) against an uncertain and surely difficult future. The question uppermost in his mind was, "How can The College of Idaho forge ahead in a region where there is much public apathy toward the small private college?" Hopeful of bringing in an experienced and successful administrator, perhaps from a school like Cornell College, the Associates requested $1,000 from the Foundation.

The retreat went very well indeed. One of the participants, John Corlett of the Boise *Statesman*, made several sound suggestions—among them, "Get yourselves a flack." "But, John," we replied, "the noisiest flack west of the hundredth meridian cannot get news items into a paper whose idea of coverage extends only from Tablerock to Cole School." Then we gave a little; and he

---

[*]   Professor Bollinger was one of the three Danforth Associates on campus, faculty members who, with their wives, had a special charge from the Foundation to get to know and work with students.

observed something about the marketing area served by the paper, which was by nature and by economics the area whose news would likely gain the most attention. "But," he said, "don't give up." From him and from James Bemis, chief executive of the Northwest Association, from Governor Smylie and from Dean Leach—indeed, from all who participated in the retreat—came energy and resolve. We might break, but there was a lot of bend left in us, we thought.

Professor Bollinger had taken most seriously a shift in emphasis by the Danforth Foundation. In its task of selecting Danforth Associates for institutions of higher learning, large tax-supported institutions were being singled out for special consideration whereas the small private colleges were being shorted. Encouraged by the strong favorable sentiment expressed at the Robinson Bar Retreat, Professor Bollinger launched a campaign to involve the state in private higher education, without compromising the independent character of schools like the C of I.

The effort culminated in a presentation to a legislative committee in February of 1974. Some details will be helpful in understanding the group's concern; for this information I have raided my own memory and have relied heavily upon a document titled "A Statement Concerning Public Policies for Higher Education in Idaho," addressed to the Idaho Legislature by the Public Affairs Committee of the Faculty Association comprised of W. LaMar Bollinger, Chairman, and Edward Sawyer, R. Ward Tucker, John H. Willmorth, and me. In truth, most of the research and writing was done by Professor Bollinger.

After calling attention to the historical public and private ways of conducting higher education, the "Statement" described the present imbalance which favored public institutions. In 1973-74, for instance, resident fees and tuition at Idaho's three largest institutions of higher learning ranged from $340 to $356; for The College of Idaho tuition and fees came to $2,100. Not only were the Idaho public institutions priced drastically below the College, they were priced significantly below public institutions in all states bordering Idaho (*Statement* 5). Additionally, "public universities, despite phenomenal increases in state funding, have greatly stepped up their solicitation of gifts from individual and business firms, siphoning off dollars from the principal external source of funds historically available to private institutions and paring down the aggregate amount realized by them from private philanthropy" (*Statement* 9).

The results of this uneven playing field were given for private education, generally, and for The College of Idaho, specifically: "Collectively, the state institutions of higher education are near their 1974 enrollment projections, but all of the private colleges in Idaho are 25 percent or more below their 1974 projections" (*Statement* 9).

And what plan did this committee of anxious College of Idaho faculty propose that would help level the field? The *Statement* said,

> If Idaho were to adopt a proposal by the Carnegie Commission of Higher Education that resident students attending a private college receive a voucher equal to 1/3 of the tax subsidy at public colleges and universities, students would have a wider range of choice and taxpayers would save money in the long run. In the short run, a modest increase in appropriations would be required, but this increase is only a fraction of the cost [that] will be added if private colleges succumb and their present and prospective students matriculate into state institutions (9-10).

The *Statement* continued:

> Time is running out. Forty-five private colleges, many of whom had survived three-quarters of a century or more, closed their doors in 1973. The cost differential between private and public institutions widens every year....

> The reason...private colleges seek understanding of their problems from state legislatures is crystal clear. All formulas for federal programs in support of higher education are based on the principle that public and private institutions are treated alike (10).

The *Statement* included appendices and tables, making the case clear and compelling; indeed, Appendix B cited the relevant Oregon statutes and presented a list of other states that had made provisions along the line called for by the Carnegie Commission: Indiana, Iowa, Kansas, Minnesota, Nebraska, and New Jersey among them. At least twenty-two states provided funds for their students to attend private colleges and universities, if they chose.

In the face of such overwhelming evidence of the need for and reasonableness of the *Statement's* recommendations, the legislative committee heard the presentation, smiled (actually, some grinned), thanked us, and refused to act. We were not surprised, for this was the body consistently seeking reelection on its record of refusing to propose new taxes, regardless of the need.

But it was at least a tiny, faltering step in the right direction. In the absence of other palliatives, the faculty had to try. And this issue is not dead. The University of Denver *News*, Summer 1990 (28:2) carried a story, which deserves citation here:

Years of hard work and advocacy paid off when this May the Colorado legislature passed House Bill 1182, providing more resources to students who attend independent institutions.

The bill changes the way financial aid is calculated for Colorado students increasing state aid available at the University of Denver, Regis College and Colorado College.

DU received $614,000 in additional aid, about doubling state aid funds for the next academic year. The University may receive about $700,000 for the following fiscal year even if the state does not increase total appropriations.

The bill provides that DU, Regis and Colorado College will share future increases to the financial aid pool according to the number of needy state students who are enrolled.

Chancellor Daniel L. Ritchie...said the previous way of calculating aid to students meant increasing discrimination against choosing a private institution. "As state policy has widened the tuition gap," he said, "independent education has been priced out of reach for progressively larger numbers of our students."

Ritchie said the bill presented Colorado an opportunity to restore choice, to preserve educational resources.

"The bill's passage is a ringing endorsement for the philosophy behind the bill," said Carey Downs Gibson, DU legislative coordinator. "It represents a major change in the mindset of the legislature."

The role of Chancellor Ritchie and the University in the passage of the bill indicates a change for the political climate of independent higher education. Under stress from a diminishing number of traditional age students and reduced federal funding to students, private institutions have turned to more ambitious marketing and fund-raising efforts to keep classrooms open. More than half the states now provide aid to students at independent colleges.

Fund raising from the private sector was once the province of the independent institution, while state-funded institutions lobbied legislatures for funds. But the lines have blurred in the waning years of this century, and state universities now sponsor private foundations, while private institutions such as DU have stepped up their efforts to increase aid to students who want the independent option.

In his testimony before the Senate Education Committee, Ritchie pointed out the true cost of educating a student at a state institution is not reflected in in-state tuition and fees. In fact, at one Colorado state university, the true cost is $8,200 per student, while in-state students pay $1,714. In this light, the state receives a greater benefit (through less cost) when the student chooses to attend a private university, even when that student qualifies for a state-funded $2,500 tuition grant.

"We're not talking about a large number of students compared to the state's total enrollment," Ritchie said. "This bill is not going to erase the tuition gap and send droves of students to us. But it will put the programs we offer in reach for those students who want them."

Ritchie said such a bill "is not a blind leap for Colorado into the unknown. Half the states have taken major steps to help their students at independent colleges."

By Monday, July 6, 1973, the presidential search committee had a list of thirty-five names. The College was also authorized to borrow $500,000 against fall enrollment, an increase from $400,000 previously authorized.

Some figures offered to the Executive Committee in September are useful in plotting the downward trajectory of the College:

enrollment	1970	937 students (all-time high)
	1971	856
	1972	833
	1973	807 (estimated; budget-based on this figure)

(These figures contrast with those announced by Admissions Director Dick Winder at the Board of Trustees meeting October 20, 1973. Winder used FTE (Full-time Equivalent) numbers, beginning with 1971: 1971-804; 1972-784; 1973-722.)

Further, "since 1960, operations have increased deficits totaling $647,186, including $18,000 in 1972-73. The annual average for the sixties was $34,643 per year, so far in the seventies $90,887 per year."

On Saturday, October 20, 1973, the Trustees met to address such personnel changes as the retirements of Registrar Doris Jeanne DeLurme and Professor Shirley C. Kroeger at the close of the 1973-74 year; the resignation of Professor Edward Bonaminio; a sabbatical leave for Professor James H. Gabbard; and a leave of absence for Professor Raymond C. Jolly, Dr. J. Leon Greene was appointed to a position in the Department of Health, Physical Education and Recreation.

One of the unhappy items was the announcement of the death of Dr. C. Larry Hagen, a member of the faculty since 1956 and first director of the highly successful Coe Foundation Summer Institute for American Studies. Dr. Hagen was another who died while yet in the harness, an untimely death it seemed to us. The campus was saddened, and those who were aware of the College's history reflected upon the passing of Lawrence Hemphill, Payne Augustin Boulton, J. J. Smith, Dr. Boone, O. J. Smith (who had come out of retirement because his college needed him), and Harold Tucker—all taken while serving The College of Idaho. Dr. Hagen was a faculty member for seventeen years.

The Caldwell-based Whittenberger Foundation continued to support the College, one of two named recipients of the Foundation's earnings receiving the maximum amount allowed annually (20 percent of the available income).

In a six-page report, ledger-sized, Dean Leach presented his understanding of the present situation respecting America's dilemma in higher education, located The College of Idaho in the large national picture, and made certain recommendations for remedial action.

He noted that the College had lost three full-time teachers, one by retirement and two by termination. None was replaced. (Mr. Edward R. Allen, Professor of Business Administration since 1956, had retired and was not replaced by a full-time appointment.) Next, the Dean summarized his understanding of why President Knox had not proceeded with a directive from the Board in February of 1973 to make necessary reductions of five or six people, if enrollment failed to reach a specified number: the President genuinely wanted to maintain the faculty, and he believed the enrollment would recover and grow.

So, suggested the Dean, it was now time to get the house in order, and to that end a committee—the Task Force Advisory Committee—had been set up "to assist in the review of the total college program." This committee finally came to be called "the Axe Committee," as the faculty saw full well the coming elimination of programs and positions.

The Dean continued with his summary, warning that few donors or foundations give money to colleges just because they need it but do so "because they deserve it and know where they are going." The College, he conceded, has a mission and need not abandon it. Then he outlined a strategy that if implemented in every instance, would have returned the College to a vocation-centered path reminiscent of the Pitman years instead of reaffirming the institution in its commitment as a liberal arts institution. He suggested careful consideration of the following:

> (a) an external degree program, intended for adults and others "in non-traditional ways"; (b) new programs designed for women; (c) social service and social work; (d) allied medical health fields;(e) two-year programs; (f) continuing education; (g) regional commitment—helping solve problems affecting the welfare of the state and its people; (h) establishment of a law school; (i) expanded internship program.

These, he said, were but a few of the possible options to be studied. Although some of them looked attractive, most of them would, indeed, have beguiled the College away from its mission. Most were best suited to a public institution serving a much more heterogeneous clientele than the one the College had served over time. Particularly noisome were the suggestions to offer a two-year program, to develop a continuing education program, and to implement an external degree program. Again, it was doubtful that the College could compete for this market and develop ephemeral programs to satisfy it.

However, Dean Leach was concerned with the survival of the institution; it little matters how pure a concept of the liberal arts is held by a college with RIP as the motto on its tombstone.

The next meeting of the Board of Trustees, held February 23, 1974, addressed the recommendations of the Axe Committee. Professors Gary Strine, Physics, and Hans Tiefel, Philosophy and Religion, were to be terminated; last hired, first fired. Three faculty would be allowed to resign and not be replaced: Carson, Political Science; Hunt, Chemistry since 1948; and Raymond Lord, Assistant to the President and Associate Professor of Humanities. Professor Kroeger and Registrar DeLurme had previously announced their retirements, DeLurme's post to be taken by Professor Wallace. These actions meant the dropping of majors in physics and in French, the reaching of a teaching ratio of 16:1, and maintaining a full-time faculty of 48.

It must be entered into the record, for it is probably not generally known, that there was a short-lived and unsuccessful attempt to redeem the two

These alumni roundballers tested the varsity in 1974. (The varsity won.)

287

terminated faculty. The faculty would agree to salary cuts, the savings to go toward a fund that would, it was hoped, make it possible to continue the contracts of Professors Strine and Tiefel if the fund could be augmented from other sources. First, the idea had to be acceptable to each faculty member, a difficult job of selling. Dr. Stanford agreed that the loss of these two faculty in particular would be devastating and that he would cooperate. Professor Specht fulminated about the inequities in the way the universe was conducted but agreed in principle. Dr. Chalker said he would cooperate. Dr. Wolfe supported the idea. When the problem was mentioned to Dr. Sayre, holder of the Chair of History, he declined to support the concept, for it would not work and even if it did, a dangerous precedent would be set.

Dr. Sayre's forthright rejection and his justification for doing so doomed the perhaps ill-considered strategy, and two colleagues went under the axe. To anticipate history a bit, Professor Strine was shortly returned to the faculty, and Professor Tiefel found employment in the South, where he now heads the Department of Religion at The College of William and Mary.

The Search Committee presented its report at a special meeting of the Board on April 2, 1974. William C. Cassell was its choice for seventh president of The College of Idaho. Since he would not likely be able to preside at Commencement, it was moved, seconded, and approved to appoint Mr. Smylie as Acting President to perform that and other appropriate tasks, thus formalizing the role he had been filling as chief executive of the board.

And so the year ended.

The College's problems raise a critical question: "Had academic standards collapsed in the face of declining enrollment, declining morale, and intensifying financial difficulties?" The answer is, strange as it may seem, no. Here are some helpful data. Two-thirds of the entering freshmen continued to be in the upper one-third of their high school graduating classes. That sounds impressive until an inquisitor asks, "But does that really mean anything? It seems to put the graduate of Rimfire High School in the same class with the graduate of Centerfire High School, whose standards are considerably higher." Now comes the usefulness of a national currency for educational statistics: the average ACT composite score for entering freshmen continued to hover at the score of 23. So, yes, it really does mean something when the 2/3:1/3 ratio is placed in a national matrix.

There is more.

Placement of pre-health care students (pre-medical, pre-dental, pre-veterinary), who tend to be biology or chemistry majors, in professional schools continued to be extraordinarily high. One year—I seem to recall that it was 1974—ten of eleven applicants were accepted, with the eleventh person accepted the next year. A final example: a college senior scored 830 on the general portion of the Graduate Record Examination, thirty points above the top of the chart, and 790 on the major field portion. I suggested to Dean of Students Russ Monahan that perhaps the scores should be validated by a phone call, and, if they were accurate, some comment from the ETS people who prepare the GRE might be forthcoming as a news story for the C of I. I remembered John Corlett's admonition to get a flack. Here, it seemed to me, was material a flack might make something of, for I doubted that there was a higher score in the nation—a combined 1620 out of a possible 1600! Dr. Monahan, however, chose not to follow the suggestion. An Ivy League university recognized the student and extended admission into its graduate program and what in football terms would be a "full ride" graduate fellowship.

To show the hidden dimensions of a College of Idaho education, let us follow that student east. Although the fellowship was generous, the student felt the need for ready cash and having sung in Dr. Gabbard's choirs, having had voice lessons from Charlie Ross and Estyn Goss, and—having taken piano lessons from Fern Davidson, though not a music major—the student successfully auditioned for a soloist's position and salary at a Congregational church and also became part of a salaried ensemble and soloist for a synagogue. The Ph.D. was finished with dispatch, and the dissertation became the first book by this

C of I students made the world their classroom in the 1960s and 1970s (shown here, Frank Specht's classical tour in Greece); other places included Mexico, Australia, England, the Holy Lands, Hawaii, Africa, and Europe.

modest graduate of a small and struggling western liberal arts college whose graduates, I would argue, tend to be remarkable, enterprising, and nimble human beings.

The Cassell Era began with the after-lunch meeting of the Board of Trustees on May 25, 1974. The President struck a note that was optimistic—"The situation of the College is not insurmountable"—and solicitous of cooperation— "It is going to take the help of the entire team." A new chief executive, whether of a college or a nation, always seems to bring a buoyancy, a sense of "things will now be better." Was this the masked man who would save the homestead and ride off into the sunset, leaving only a silver bullet as a token that greatness had passed this way? Who was this man Cassell?

In the first place, he did not possess the Ph.D. degree, the search committee agreeing that that evidence of scholarship was not necessary. Second, he was another who had gone "through the chairs" of development, serving as director of that program at the University of Denver until coming to the College. Before directing DU's development program, he had served various institutions. His wife, Jeanne, was a teacher; their three children were young. Third, he had impressed the search committee as he impressed the faculty with his service as a consultant to the Ford Foundation. The College constituency could not shake the idea that salvation must come from the East. Maybe *this* connection with a powerful foundation would pay dividends.

President Cassell did not attend the meeting of the Executive Committee on July 8, 1974; however, at the first meeting of the entire Board on October 19, 1974, he was present and armed with facts and recommendations for paring $258,150 from the budget. A look at his report to the Board is instructive.

He began with a reprise of the accumulated deficit:

Year	Deficit	Cumulative Deficit
1966-67	$82,321	$219,776
1967-68	18,593	238,361
1968-69	11,361	249,730
1969-70	124,794	374,524
1970-71	86,426	460,950
1971-72	51.511	512,461
1972-73	180,661	647,186
1973-74	289,937	937,123
1974-75	257,974	1,195,097

The figures were grimly eloquent. To balance the budget for 1974-75, he recommended reductions in staff, benefits, salaries, athletics, maintenance;

increases in indirect costs from contract work and outside courses and increases in tuition; tighter budget controls; and increase in the endowment. These steps would realize $258,150, he said.

Such a sum was significant. When placed in the context of anxiety expressed in a letter of October 7, 1974, from the First Security Bank of Idaho, such a savings seemed absolutely essential. That letter, from Senior Vice President James E. Phelps, stipulated that the Bank

> will continue to hold collateral...of various stocks with a market value approximating $108,000, the "common fund" investment...of $190,000, and a deed of trust on real estate...in Caldwell...at an approximate value of $300,000.

> You will pay us on or about October 15, 1974, the interest due on current loan plus a principal payment of $195,000, thereby reducing the loan to a balance of $350,000.

> In keeping with the cash flow projection schedule, which you assure us is correct to the very best of your knowledge, we will loan an additional $125,000 in November, 1974. You are to repay $200,000 in February, 1975; and, your having done this, we will be prepared to again advance credit in March, 1975, this time in the amount of $100,000.

> These advances having been made and these payments having been received, the balance outstanding and due the bank on maturity of April 30, 1975, will be $375,000 plus interest. If you have been unable to solve the College's finances by that time to the point that you can present us with an acceptable and bankable program for continued credit, we will have no choice but to call the loan and exercise our rights to the collateral in order to liquidate the remaining balance.

It was not a cheerful Board of Trustees that approved Cassell's recommended increase in tuition by $250 and board and room by $100 and his cost reduction program. The Board did, however, pledge its continuing support for measures that, though harsh, promised some relief. At the same time, it was necessary for the Board to approve borrowing $650,000 for operating expenses.

The regular meetings of the Executive Committee continued. On January 27, 1975, the President reported need for $1,100,000 line of credit for 1975-76 and also noted that the Japanese American Heritage Series, sponsored by the Regional Studies Center and the Boise Valley Japanese American Citizens League, and funded by the Association for the Humanities in Idaho was generating favorable comments. The series reminded some of the valley residents of long standing of the refuge from invidious discrimination provided to citizens of Japanese ancestry by the College during World War II.

Minutes of the meeting of the Board of Trustees of February 22, 1975, noted the resignations (for 1975-76) of Professor Raymond C. Jolly and Professor William K. Roberts; the retirement of Franklin O. Cooke; and the appointment of D. Jerry White as Assistant Professor of English, replacing Professor Cooke. Professors Frank Blood, William Hedley, Boyd Henry, Edward Sawyer, and Richard Skyrm were given sabbatical leaves for varying periods of time. Because the financial crisis tends to overwhelm all other aspects of the life of the College in this retrospective view, it is refreshing to both writer and reader to note this sort of academic activity and to be reminded that Professors Orville Cope, Bruce Schatz, William Hedley, and Estyn Goss earned promotions.

One of the most pertinent pieces of information shared by President Cassell at this meeting was the fact that

> the College assets in Endowment as of Wednesday, February 19, totaled $639,184.33. Of these...$269,000 is pledged as collateral on dormitory loans to the Federal Government. This would leave a total of approximately $320,000 free in the Endowment Fund. The free amount in the Endowment Fund and a portion of the property located between Cleveland and Blaine valued between $300,000 and $400,000 has [sic] been pledged as collateral to secure loans at the First Security Bank.

The integrity of Endowment was gone. On top of that, a payment of $250,000 was due on the Science Building March 1, and President Cassell requested permission to borrow that amount.

Even with all this, he reported to the Board "we are now beginning to get a momentum going." College presidents have to believe that things will get better. If they are not born meliorists, they must become such, for there is no future in nihilism. Æsop offers an illustration: when the kitchen helper thought to eliminate an offending frog by tossing it into a crock of milk, the frog swam so vigorously that it churned a pat of butter on which it could sit and rest. You have to make the best of what you have; otherwise, you will only make things worse.

The arrangement for two new ex-officio on the Board was apparently working well, although the Board—indeed, the entire college community—was brought up short when the student body's chief executive was arrested on narcotics charges. The charges were sustained; and that such problems were pervasive throughout academe did not make President Cassell's task of raising money any easier.

292

At the end of Cassell's first year Dick Winder resigned as Admissions Director—a job he had held since 1959 and carried out in a highly professional manner.

During discussion of a resolution by which the College agreed to do all the bank required in order that financing might be forthcoming, Cassell said he would come to the Board's next spring meeting with a balanced budget. One of the helpers in the long standing folkloric sense replied that if that were done, he (Jack Simplot) would assume payment of the interest on the debt for the year of 1975-76 in addition to his regular giving. The Minutes record that "President Cassell and Mr. Simplot shook hands."

The president would have to dogpaddle furiously.

A (perhaps symbolic) problem confronted the campus during these hard times. Dutch elm disease hit the College's old and stately elms, those graceful trees that had looked like sticks when planted by Dr. Boone and Dr. Hayman so many years ago. On August 25, 1975, the Executive Committee of the Board of Trustees was informed that twenty-two elms had succumbed to the disease.

Further unpleasantness ventilated at this meeting was the College's first affirmative action suit, filed by Dr. Jan Widmayer, who charged discrimination when Professor D. Jerry White had been hired over her as a specialist in Medieval and Renaissance Drama who would conduct the drama program. The action was ultimately resolved in the College's favor.

Among other applicants appointed to positions, Murray Satterfield, Health, Physical Education, and Recreation and basketball coach, and Donald Weatherman, Political Science, were named as full-time permanent faculty.

Problems over the multi-purpose stadium had been brewing for some time, and at the Executive Committee meeting of October 15, 1975, President Cassell reported on a proposal by the Stadium Board to seek $150,000 from the Hospital Board* to pay off a Bank of Idaho loan and to make repairs at the rodeo grounds. He noted further that action was being considered "to declare Multi-Purpose Stadium debentures which bear no interest and have no maturity date valueless." The Stadium Board intended to transfer the entire complex to Caldwell to be used as a recreation facility. Caldwell School District #132 was identified as the current lessee, paying $14,000; the College would be expected to pay $16,000 for using the facility.

---

*   A discussion of this organization appears in Chapter 17.

At the Winter meeting of the Board of Trustees, March 20, 1976, it was announced that Roger G. "Rod" Sears, football coach since 1971, had resigned. Sears had been a problematic figure. To Sears' credit, he introduced rugby to the valley and created a legacy of players and skill that even today identifies Snake River Rugby with some of the best teams in the Northwest.

At this meeting it was also announced that Dr. Lyle Stanford expected to retire at the end of the 1975-76 academic year. But before he could retire to the life of creative leisure he so richly deserved, brightening the world with his matchless water colors, sharing his store of wisdom with all who might profit from it, Lyle Stanford died. Those who knew him as a teacher before polio struck, and those who had the pleasure of his company and the weight of his mind as a colleague despair ever looking upon his like again. And one should not expect to do so. Such people as he, O. J. Smith, and George Wolfe...do not come again, nor do Anna Eyck, Sara Rankin, J. H. Roblyer, J. J. Smith, F. F. Beale, Payne Boulton, Dick Skyrm, Lawrence Hemphill, Jim Gabbard, Paul Murphy, and Doc Hayman. Others come who create their own niches, and when they, too, are called to rest, new niches are created and occupied by different ones of the innumerable caravan. Mention will be made later of attempts to create a chair honoring two of this distinguished company.

Dr. Richard D. Skyrm hosting his weekly musical broadcast on radio KCID.

Certain problems would not go away; financing required Cassell to recommend increasing tuition and fees from $2,400 to $2,650 and board and room charges from $1,190 to $1,275 for double rooms and $1,240 to $1,375 for single rooms. The budget included $100,000 for faculty and staff salary increases of about 9 percent. Sue Weitz resigned as Dean of Students as of the end of the year.

At the Spring meeting of the Board of Trustees, coincident

with Commencement on May 29, 1976, several pieces of information were shared. Christian Eismann was named dean of the College; Lee Lenuson was introduced as the president's secretary, replacing Norma Allen, who had retired; Richard G. Elliott and Ralph O. Marshall were promoted to full professors. The major financial concern facing the College was the need to resolve the financial obligations of the Boone Science Center:

> To date, payments have been made from a prepaid lease payment account with J. A. Terteling and Sons, Inc., which was later transferred to Terteling Acceptance Corporation, Ltd. Until now the rental deposit has been sufficient to make payments, but beginning October 1976 and in future years there will not be sufficient funds to make the payments.

In response to inquiry by Safeway Stores, Inc., the chairman of the Board and the president were authorized "to enter into an agreement with Safeway Stores...at a price no lower than $225,000." The land sold was Parcel #2 between 24th and 26th streets, where Doc Hayman had once grown corn.

Further negotiations in the rococo arrangements with the Canyon County Multi-Purpose Stadium were reported upon.

From August 29 to September 1, the faculty and administration held a foundation-sponsored retreat to take "a hard look toward the future of the institution." The retreat was held at Mackay Bar, with great exhilaration from the scenery tempered by a pervasive sense of the loss of Dr. Stanford. The retreat accomplished little. An added stress on the College community was Professor Frank Blood's death the weekend before classes started. Blood's suicide came as a shock to all members of the community, for he was both respected and well-liked.

Trustees' minutes record a $50,000 Northwest Area Foundation grant through which retention problems were to be studied. Enrollment was down by 70 students.

As cultural artifacts, college yearbooks can be interpreted so as to reveal something about the times although many of the illustrative materials indicate a kind of indulgence in romantic ego-tripping. Compared to the campus of the '30s and '40s, the C of I campus of the '60s and '70s was seemingly inhabited by untidy folk who were most frequently photographed holding or indulging in beer. That is not surprising in view of the policy of 1971-72 which allowed liquor on the campus.

Trail photograph of the Orions, about 1970.

Those who defended the policy pointed to two considerations. They claimed, in the first place, that social drinking was a sign of the times; not to allow alcohol in the rooms or at "functions" was to create an atmosphere far more restrictive than the home life out of which our students came. Perhaps. But the intellectual life of the campus, it may be supposed, is also more confining and more closely monitored than the life at home. It is the hope of most English Departments I know of that students will develop better habits of expression than those the freshman brought from home, or at least will be confirmed in those good habits gained at home with an intellectual grasp of why they are good habits of expression. The second argument for permitting liquor on campus has, at first glance, a kind of superficial attractiveness: if students are going to drink—never mind questioning the truth of the conditional clause—better that they should drink on campus than get into a car and become a statistic enroute from a bash somewhere. Three accidents that occurred after this "freeing up" of campus behavior (two with fatalities) were alcohol-related.

At the Fall, 1976, meeting of the Board of Trustees, a further drop in enrollment was noted—offset, perhaps, by President Cassell's report that for the first time in ten years the fiscal year (1975-76) ended in the black. Cassell claimed "that this would have been achieved on cash flow alone, without the gift of the Lewiston and Cheyenne shopping centers [from Joe and Kay Albertson]." The President observed "that the College had made fantastic progress in the past two years, especially in the area of financial improvement." President Cassell was granted authority to raise tuition and room and board charges at his discretion **if necessary for purpose of filing financial aid reports.** I have underlined the conditional element, because its meaning is not clear. The authority to raise tuition and other charges is a powerful authority.

At this meeting Professor Margaret Boone's resignation from the Board of Trustees was announced.

One of the constants at The College of Idaho is the quality of student seeking an education here. Some statistical reminders are valuable. From exhibit A, supplied as part of the Admissions Office Report included with the Minutes of the Annual Meeting of the Board of Trustees for October 30, 1976, come these data for the Class of 1980 that is, those who were admitted as the freshman class of 1976-77:

Women	85	mean GPA		3.35
Men	132	(secondary school)		3.20
	217			3.26

Secondary school rank:

92% in the upper 50% of their high school class
74% in the upper 33% of their high school class
56% in the upper 25% of their high school class
34% in the upper 10% of their high school class

Mean ACT composite 23.14

Geographic distribution—		
	Idaho	111
	California	34
	Other states	51
	Trust territories	19
	Foreign	2
		217

Admissions Director Bob Post also supplied an updated table of fall enrollment from 1962-63 through 1976-77:

1962-63	739
1963-64	690
1964-65	751
1965-66	812
1966-67	842
1967-68	896
1968-69	890
1969-70	915
1970-71	937
1971-72	856
1972-73	833
1973-74	760
1974-75	715
1975-76	717
1976-77	652

The discouraging figures indicated a trend in the face of which a meliorist position was very difficult—but not impossible.

Safeway had chosen to exercise its option and buy Parcel #2 between Blaine and Cleveland, 24th and 26th streets, with Safeway and another prospective buyer both interested in the adjacent parcel. Although the seventy-five acres of which the College once boasted had shrunk by this action and by the gift to the community of the land the Stadium Board was now concerned about (excepting the acreage deeded back to the College), the money generated by the sale was a welcome contribution to the budgetary black hole.

The Minutes of the Executive Committee also indicated that things were going well musically at the College, with an extended visit by the Spokane Symphony and an invitation to the choir to perform at the Los Angeles International Folk Festival and for the Northwest Music Educators, whose Conference was in Seattle (January 11, 1977). Opportunities for field trips provided by the Winter Session continued to multiply as Professor Specht conducted his third expedition and Professor Packard led a group to Central America. The graduate program was flourishing, enrolling from 198 to 210 students according to Professor Ward Tucker.

A problematic note was sounded in the March meeting of the Trustees. For a combination of reasons, not the least of which was the possibility that Jan Widmayer might receive automatic tenure if her case dragged on (it had not been resolved yet although the reader has been granted a look ahead to its resolution), the Board agreed to place a freeze on faculty promotions and tenure in order to study the entire issue, the study to be concluded within eighteen months. At the same time, the resignations of Ralph O. Marshall, John Stoner, and John Willmorth were announced.

By the time the Board of Trustees convened for its annual spring meeting on May 28, 1977, President Cassell could report the sale of the second parcel of land, the two parcels netting almost a half-million dollars. In making the report, Mr. Cassell said that criticism of the sale resulted from students, who thought they had lost an athletic field, and from townspeople, who would have preferred greenbelt or parking area; however, "short of total closure of the College, there was really no alternative." Additional information shared at this meeting included the return of Dick Carrow to full-time teaching and the appointment of football coach Ed Knecht to replace Carrow as Athletic Director.

President Cassell was to have three more years at the helm; the theme and variations of his regime would not radically change. Let summary replace chronology for the remainder of this administration, with some attention to accomplishments or benchmarks as a way of mitigating otherwise nearly unrelieved fiscal gloom. In respect to academic matters it remained quite true that faculty taught and students learned, that graduates continued to be accepted into graduate and professional schools in a manner that caused more observers than one to note the similarity of the College to that aerodynamic failure, the bumblebee. Neither had any right to succeed, yet there they were, not just barely existing but soaring and educating.

Continuing problems with the financing of William Judson Boone Science Center and making sense of the elaborate and convoluted arrangements with the Terteling organizations were almost more than this administration could resolve. Payments on the HUD dormitory loans had been sidetracked and arrearage had developed. Loan funds from the federal government that were intended for students drifted into the general budget. The total of full-time equivalent students continued to decline, many folks forgetting that the college had been a fine school with a student body of 400.

In response to the first series of problems—Boone Science Center—an unsolicited pledge of $1,000,000 from Joe Albertson finally helped put that problem to rest. The other bright spot in the Cassell administration was the reassessment of the entire athletic program and the necessary but painful dropping of football and baseball, retaining intercollegiate basketball, tennis, and skiing for men and women, and volleyball for women.

Many valley residents had enjoyed football and baseball and had rejoiced in the College's long and generally successful participation in both, remembering the Lowell brothers and the fine Parberry teams—Houston Garman, Glen Ward,

The spirit of a 1970's Bogus Basin Ski Night reflected by Dr. William Chalker and registrar D. Jeanne DeLurme.

Bill Cudd, and a fine and graceful natural athlete in all forms of athletic endeavor, Ron Dunn. These fans hated to see these team sports dropped. But from the perspective of what Gene Odle used to call "the reality factor," the College could not continue to subsidize these increasingly expensive entertainments. The gate receipts could hardly support one football player, so expensive had equipment, travel, and board and room become. For 1976-77, the football gate amounted to $1,686.66 (committee report, Athletic Expenditures 1976-77). Wisely, it was decided to retain skiing: the College won the first of its many national laurels in 1979, taking the Intercollegiate National Ski Team Championship in national competition in Michigan by defeating a great many "bigger, better, and older" schools!

Evidence of a weakening of executive resolve may be found in an entry in the April 4, 1979, meeting of the Executive Committee of the Board: "President Cassell explained that he had made efforts to have two [fund-raising firms] at this meeting" but only a Mr. Nagle of the Brakely Company of Los Angeles was able to come. The Brakely Company was authorized to conduct a feasibility study.

An interesting entry appears in the Executive Committee Minutes for April 4, 1979: newly-elected Trustees include Klara Hansberger, James E. Bruce, Dr. Don Price, and Robert L. Hendren, Jr. Although Mr. Cassell's administration would not terminate until 1980, winds of change were blowing, and it is time to look ahead to a new and reinvigorated Board of Trustees who would find a new president.

One of the significant events in the life of the College took place on September 22, 1979, at Boise Cascade Corporation Headquarters in Boise. At a special meeting of the Board of Trustees, called to consider whether there was a future for the College, after Board Chairman Smylie welcomed the company and announced the receipt of a gift of about $151,000 from the Margaret Cobb Ailshie Trust he turned the meeting over to Robert Hendren, Co-Chair of the Fund Planning and Priorities Committee which had requested the meeting. The two special guests and speakers were John William Pocock and Robert T. H. Davidson. Pocock was Chairman of the Board of Trustees of The College of Wooster and officer or former officer of several organizations significant in the history of American higher education. The College whose trustees he headed was the *alma mater* of William Judson Boone and also of H. H. Hayman. It was as if history had somehow realized a shadow that had been cast a hundred years before. Was some kind of circle about to be closed?

Of all that Pocock said, the following are memorable: the faculty have subsidized the College for years by working at below professional salaries, and the College must develop an endowment!

Davidson, a New York attorney and a trustee of several foundations, including the Steele-Reese Foundation helpful to the College in the '50s and '60s, also reminded the trustees of their duties and of earlier abdications of responsibility.

Instead of turning away from the College in despair, the Trustees took a firm grasp on hope and with renewed dedication turned to difficult tasks that lay ahead: "Let all who must despair; let all who will begin again." The Trustees began again.

At least, most of them. There was a note of discord here and there: the Trustee who wondered whether the College ought to amalgamate with Northwest Nazarene College, the Trustee who thought Idaho's oldest college ought somehow to be melded into the tax-supported system.

Then, too, there was the allure of foreign capital as a few officials discovered a yen for an Oriental leveraged buy-out. The Minutes of the Executive Committee meeting of February 13, 1980, in the Gold Room of the Owyhee Plaza Hotel, catch the essence of the situation:

> The Executive Committee met with Dr. Taro Tanioka, President of Osaka University of Commerce; his daughter Niki Tanioka; his attorney Yoshio Katayama; and Mr. Murray Howard and his staff of Los Angeles. They presented to the Executive Committee their interest in giving The College of Idaho $2,000,000 cash with the provision that they have majority control of the Board.... The Committee asked for more information.

This proposition was reported to the Board of Trustees at its regular Winter meeting on February 23, 1980. After the usual routine items of approving the minutes, approving candidates for degrees, and similar matters, came the report of the Executive Committee respecting the Tanioka proposal. No action was taken. Then came the information that "President Cassell related the mechanics of the interview process by which he had been hired at Heidelberg College...." Cassell was leaving, taking with him a recently awarded Ford Foundation grant for a study of "The Future of Private Colleges: the Human Aspects." "This" the Trustees were informed, "is normal procedure and no loss to The College of Idaho since it was serving merely as the fiscal agent."

Before Cassell left, there was the matter of settling up with him. The negotiations between the College and its soon-to-be ex-president were difficult, and the final settlement was conducted as an uneasy anticlimax to a difficult administration.

Things could only get better.

302

Part VIII

Arthur H. DeRosier 1980-87

Dr. Arthur H. DeRosier, the eighth College president, joins team members celebrating a championship victory.

CHAPTER SEVENTEEN

Eighth in Succession

A convenient though inaccurate yardstick for measuring the effective-ness of a new president is to assess what he was able to accomplish that his predecessor could not. Cassell's successor faced some unfinished tasks: (1) responding to the serious concerns of the Northwest Association as to whether the College deserved to have its accreditation sustained (fiscal prob-lems); (2) responding to the long-standing matter of a possible default on the HUD loans (fiscal problems of student numbers going back to the Shearer years); (3) indebtedness to local and valley businesses who were carrying more than $500,000 in College debts on their books (fiscal); and (4) restoring National Defense Student Loan funds that had somehow been siphoned into general budget accounts (fiscal).

What would you do if you became the president of an institution thus encumbered? What if, instead of finding yourself up to your ears in milk, you were treading water with no prevenient pat of batter? This new president took the bull by the tail and met the issue squarely in the face. There is some truth in the fractured cliche.

There is, however, an unidentified ingredient. Call it resolve or spirit or the finding of grace under pressure. It was apparent in the trustees newly ap-pointed—Hendren, Price, Hansberger, Symms, Bruce—and they quickly ener-gized the carry-over members. Thus a Board always highly capable but now energized was operating at the time an authentic college president was about to take the reins. The work of Arthur DeRosier, Jr. and the work of the Board of Trustees meshed in a way probably unexampled theretofore.

Townspeople have a way of asking disarming questions. A favorite query is, "How is the new president?" When this was asked about Cassell, meliorists responded, "He's a most industrious, hard working president. He's in his office by 7 a.m., and he stays late." When this same question was raised of President DeRosier, a common response was, "It's rare in the life of a college when an authentic president is matched by a capable and concerned board. This is superb harmony."

Dr. Arthur H. DeRosier, Jr., did, indeed, come to Caldwell with the Ph.D. degree, only the second in our history. The story of his coming and of the events resulting in the energizing of the Board merit a brief narration.

It began with the class of trustees of which Robert L. Hendren, Jr., was a member, for it was this class that was introduced to the responsibilities of trusteeship by Davidson and Pocock. Hendren first became interested in the College when his wife, Merlyn, agreed to help put together the Spring Symposium. A successful Boise businessman and an experienced trustee and former board chairman for the Boise Independent School District, Hendren saw very little compelling reason for him to accept an invitation to serve on the board of a private college in Caldwell. But he did accept, he opposed the sale to the Japanese buyer with such success that he and the proxies he had managed to obtain prevailed, and he became strangely attracted to the idea that it is not wrong for students to pay a significant share of the costs of their education. After hearing Pocock and Davidson, he became one of the College's staunchest advocates.

When it became apparent that Cassell was leaving, Hendren undertook the task of serving on the search committee to find a replacement, and he discovered that DeRosier was not opposed to leaving the university he headed in order to try his fortune in the private sphere. It seems clear in retrospect that the phenomenal successes of DeRosier's administration, particularly of the first few years, resulted from the energy and great capability of the president who worked in tandem so effectively with his board. That the credit must go to both is a commentary on the effectiveness of both.

DeRosier was a president who always said not only the right thing but the graceful thing, just as in public events as widely different as receptions and commencements he never seemed to do anything that was gauche or maladroit. He looked and acted like a college president.

And he immediately faced the old problem of money. HUD was getting more and more uneasy;* other problems cited earlier continued. What was the

---

* The Trustees must have wondered whether Mr. Cassell's forthrightness in describing

306

answer? PROJECT 90! The Minutes of the Executive Committee meeting of June 4, 1980, carry the germ of this highly successful strategy. Honorary Chairmen were Joe Albertson, J. R. Simplot, and N. L. Terteling. Providentially, perhaps, the recently deposed CEO of Continental Life and Accident, L. Warren Isom, agreed to serve as General Chairman of the project at no salary. Robert Hendren was elected to chair the Executive Committee and hence the Board of Trustees.

The ambitions of the project were appropriate to the quality of its leadership; never mind the "honorary" label. Those ambitions? Nothing less than to raise $3,000,000. That amount would erase all indebtedness; and although it would do nothing to level the playing field, it would help restore the integrity of the College—that priceless legacy from Dr. Boone and Dr. Hall—and would enable the new president and the trustees to set about rebuilding the endowment.

The campaign was meticulously conceived and efficiently executed. From Ron Pisaneschi's arresting brochure of white letters and numbers with blue shadows vibrating under them until the shadows disappeared into the predominant black background (another view would suggest hope emerging from the blackness of despair), through the formation and work of the various committees, and including the generosity of all who believed that private education has a place in America, the campaign was a triumph. Trustees were among the vanguard of contributors, redirecting personal household budgets and managing personal economies in such a way as to make substantial gifts. One trustee whose personal plans had included the building of a long hoped-for new house contributed the cost of that dwelling to Project 90.

Eight committees developed under Isom's leadership, each reflecting an important constituency, from alumni-students-parents through Trustees and valley friends. These committees were assisted by the College administrative staff of President Arthur H. DeRosier, Jr.; Director of Development Arthur S. Eichlin; Director of Alumni Relations Randall E. Marshall; Director of Public Relations Ronald L. Pisaneschi; and Consultant in Planned Giving, Erwin Schwiebert.

---

fiscal matters was not open to question, for the Minutes of the Executive Committee of June 4, 1980, state that "a letter from the area manager of the Department of Housing and Urban Development...countered several points made in a memo by President Cassell to Trustees dated May 29."

The College for whose benefit Project 90 was conducted was a lively institution. For the Academic year 1980-81, the curriculum was organized through sixteen departments collected into four divisions: Education, Health, and Physical Education; Humanities and Fine Arts; Social Science; and Natural Science—chaired respectively, by Professors Nadine Maggard, Robert Max Peter, Orville Cope, and Gary Strine. The curriculum was under the control of the faculty, still organized as Faculty Assembly with Academic Council as its steering committee. What had been Faculty Association had recently become Faculty-Staff Association, the organization concerned with social and bread-and-butter matters. Membership was extended to all employees not reporting directly to the President, but voting privileges were limited to those who paid dues. Annual parties, gifts to retirees, flowers for the sick, and recognition of bereavement required the collection of dues, as did the annual award of scholarship assistance to meritorious students. Much of this had not changed since Pitman's time.

It is often said that the U.S. Senate does its work in committee. The faculty, however, does its work in the classroom, in the laboratory, in offices, and in the library. Even so, it also does various tasks through a committee arrangement. These committees vary from administration to administration, ranging from the Library Committee through the Honorary Degree Committee and the Buildings and Grounds Committee.

The members of the faculty, I like to think, lectured brilliantly, presented stunning papers at professional meetings, published modestly, and participated with greater or lesser avidity in local and regional affairs. The local school board frequently had a C of I personality; Boyd Henry, Ralph Marshall, and Garth Cates all served at various times. Others served on the local library board, on the planning and zoning commission, on various church boards, and on the state-based arts and humanities councils and associations.

As to the quality of our graduates, that was an absolute function of the kind of freshman or transfer student attracted to the school, which continued to attract excellent young men and women. Granted that their speech was sometimes hampered by the linguistic and social rebellion against propriety of the sixties; nevertheless they were nearly always of college caliber, and they could learn effective expression. The statistic of between 45 and 55 percent of our graduates going on to graduate or professional training was a constant. Their dwindling number was a more serious problem than their speech, for between 1970 and 1979 enrollment fell from 937 to 482 (*Bulletin-Annual Report*-1981).

Dropping football and baseball and other readjustments in the athletic program seemed not to harm the institution. Granted that a few ex-athletes wrote that football or baseball had meant a lot to them and that the College could no longer count on their support, the move was unavoidable. Indeed, the College was establishing a genuine national reputation for its considerably less expensive (and considerably more successful) ski teams. In 1979 and 1980, C of I men won the four-event championships in the National Collegiate Ski Association competition, competing against teams from BYU, University of Minnesota, Washington State University, and other institutions of great size. And this was only the beginning.

Under Coach Dick Carrow, the basketball team seemed in a fair way to becoming a league contender in NAIA competition, membership in the old Northwest Conference having lapsed because of dropping two major team sports. The team finished the 1979-1980 season with a 15-13 record.

Despite the decline in numbers of students who might turn out for choir, Dr. Gabbard still presented choral music of a high quality, and keyboard masters Skyrm and Davidson had their share of excellent performers on piano and organ. The political internship started by Dr. Wolfe in 1960 was still flourishing; field trips and special guests were the order of the day. The life of a student at The College of Idaho could be busy and rewarding.

When it was finally completed, Project 90 brought in $3.1 million. It was the success of Project 90—so named because the College was ninety years old—that made it possible for the institution to observe its one hundredth birthday, which this chronicle celebrates.

Three items emerge from the Minutes of the Summer 1980 meeting of the Board of Trustees that indicate sources of continuing problems and promises. Respecting the latter, it was with considerable joy that the Board received the nomination of Lyman D. Wilbur for membership. Wilbur served with distinction as Chairman of the Investment Committee. His uncle had earned a sound reputation as President of Stanford University and had served as Secretary of the Interior under President Herbert Hoover. Wilbur himself had been interested in the College for many years; after retiring from executive responsibilities with Morrison-Knudsen Company he could devote time and energy to serve The College of Idaho, whose first curriculum had been sanctioned by Stanford.

As to problems, the IRS was concerned over an amount of money put by the College into "the Cassell children's educational fund."* On August 7, President

---

*   This entry in the Trustees' Minutes suggests that there was some sort of contractual arrangement through which College money had been paid into a fund for the education

DeRosier had met with an IRS agent who finally "recommended that the tax exempt status not be revoked." The second problem dealt with the Nursing Program, another desperate attempt to find additional sources of income for the College despite the departure from its historical mission, its institutional philosophy, and its long life as a liberal arts college that the operation of such a program as a school of nursing would represent. The woman who had been hired as Dean of the Nursing Program resigned. The ill-advised program was soon on its way into oblivion along with PES ("Professional and Educational Services") and other money-grubbing strategies too dismal to recite. So the problem with the Nursing Program resolved itself.

High on the agenda of the new president was reorganizing and revitalizing alumni/ae organizations. Randy Marshall was chosen to assist in this process. DeRosier was committed to the maintenance of strong alumni chapters, sensitive as he was to the common charge by alumni that "We hear from you people only when you need money." There is some truth to the complaint, although if it were absolutely true there would have been a constant flow of communication since the College **always** needs money. But alumni help in other important ways, and those ways were especially important to this new president. They included the recruiting of students and the dissemination of information about the College. That problem seemed well on the way to solution.

Between October 14 and November 18 of President DeRosier's maiden year, a change took place in the academic leadership of the College: Ralph M. Sayre was named Acting Dean of Academic Affairs and Provost, replacing Edward L. Angus, who had resigned November 3. The appointment was another virtuoso stroke by DeRosier, for Sayre had been dean in other dispensations, knew the territory well, and, equally significant, was a continuing member of the Northwest Association of Schools and Colleges (and a member of the Commission on Colleges). The accrediting organization was making loud noises about whether accreditation should be continued. Indeed, the College was required to prove that accreditation should not be withdrawn. It was a job—"an onerous task" was the way he frequently put it—that Sayre had earned the right not to have to do. How it was that he was persuaded to vacate the comfortable John Philip Weyerhaeuser, Jr., Chair of History to resume the straightbacked and

---

of the Cassell children. I have not attempted to review contracts for this chronicle.

uneasy chair in the dean's office this history cannot make clear; he probably simply agreed to do a job that had to be done.

President DeRosier announced at the Fall meeting of the Board of Trustees that James Bemis, Executive Director of the Northwest Association, had been in communication about a 1980 visitation and also about a 1982 reevaluation. The principal concern was not academic but fiscal, and the College proceeded with the required self-study.

Buried in the Trustees' Minutes of the Winter meeting of February 17, 1981, is an item that would have far reaching consequences. President DeRosier's report to the Board noted that he found himself "acting as Athletic Director at present and [was] happy to report that the winning ski team [was] going to Lake Placid for competition...as defending champions (1979, 1980)...." Further, he noted that a replacement was being sought for Dick Carrow, long-time faculty member-athletic director-basketball coach, who had resigned. "Three on-campus interviews for his replacement are being conducted—one assistant coach from a Division 1A school, one head coach from Oregon Tech, and the assistant coach from Idaho State University" named Martin Holly. Another report, this one of a considerably different nature, was made by Dr. DeRosier at the April meeting of the Executive Committee: another of the College's best had died before retirement. On April 20, 1981, Dr. Richard D. Skyrm, Professor of Music since 1947, died of cancer. His passing left a department, a division, and a college impoverished.

Two further items: from Dean Sayre came an announcement that a document on tenure, promotion, and evaluation had been prepared; he stated his conviction that such a document was much needed. The second report concerned the rehabilitation of Sterry Hall. The Trustees had earlier expressed concern for this venerable building, which for a number of years was The College of Idaho. Only now, however, were steps being taken to arrest its deterioration.

The Spring meeting of the board, held, as is customary on Commencement Day—this year on May 30, 1981—saw the continuation of important business. The self-study would be in draft form by summer. The *Faculty Handbook* had undergone its first revision since 1967. Trustee Tom Wright reported on the progress of an *ad hoc* committee investigating the possibility of the founding of a school of business at the College. One of the recurring themes in the discussion of this report was the need for American businessmen to be liberally educated. And the following had been done on the Sterry Hall project: the roof was lifted twelve inches; the walls were pulled in from six to ten inches and secured again by rejoining the cables with rods and turnbuckles whose severing had permitted the walls to lean. The building was on the National Register of Historic Places and, as a historic structure, generated matching funds that made the cost of restoration a bit less painful.

Project 90 was steaming ahead, and at the Executive Committee meeting of July 15, 1981, Chairman Isom was recognized and thanked on behalf of the Board for his efforts—as was Trustee Paul Corddry for his and Ore-Ida's contributions. Even a casual reader would be struck by the meticulous and detailed reports of Lyman Wilbur, whose careful attention was already beginning to pay dividends in the form of the re-emergence of an endowment. That precious fund showed $814,597, of which $414,917 was pledged to HUD. The net of $399,680 was a modest beginning of a rehabilitation project of the first magnitude. While the value of the physical plant had grown enormously since Dr. Boone's time, the endowment had been so compromised that its net worth was still less than it had been in 1936—even without comparing 1980s dollars against those of 1936.

At the August 19, 1981, meeting of the Executive Committee, James K. Kelly, Dean of the Idaho State University School of Business, was identified as consultant for 1981-82 to assist in the organization of the College's school of

September, 1982: Rededication of Covell Hall as the J. A. Albertson School of Business. Joe and Katherine Albertson, with trustees including Jack Simplot, Robert L. Hendren, Jr., and members of the Advisory Board for the new enterprise, applaud (off camera) President Arthur H. DeRosier and new Dean James Kelly.

business. That the College was to establish a school of business generated a great deal of excitement and not a little anxiety. Its story is worth telling.

When the possibility of a business school was first discussed, several matters had to be considered. Was a school of business on the campus of a liberal arts college an anomaly? Was it not another venture into vocational training, that same siren that held the allure of dollars but would create more problems than it would solve? Would the present student interest in business, statistically well documented, continue? Can a college have a school within it? As these problems were weighed, another series of problems appeared. Could a newly founded school of business attract the kind of faculty essential to its success? Part of that problem, of course, was the matter of salary; and salary considerations brought to light the realization that if a business school were established, the College would have two salary schedules, one for the school of business and another for everyone else. One other question appeared: should the new school of business work toward accreditation by the professional accrediting organization established by American schools of business, the American Assembly of Collegiate Schools of Business (AACSB)?

The debate was extensive and intense but never acrimonious. Admitting to only provisional wisdom, the faculty agreed that a liberal arts college could indeed contain a school within its campus, its mission, and its philosophy...never a college of business but surely a school of business. Thus it could occupy a position somewhat more prominent than but analogous to a division in the College's structure, headed by a dean instead of a division chair. Other colleges had successfully developed schools: The College of William and Mary, for instance, if one did not insist on absolute correspondence. As to whether this was another of those allurements created by desperately needed dollars, sending the College on the road to vocationalism, no one could be sure. However, the quality of leadership from the world of business represented on the Board of Trustees suggested that there was nothing inherent in a school of business that opposed a liberal arts philosophy, provided the curriculum for business students included enough philosophy, ethics, literature, foreign language, science, history, and so on. The spokesmen for business were as insistent on these points as the faculty. And it appeared, from all demographic and vocational data available, that prospects for continued interest in business as an academic major were good.

The next problem, that of a two-tiered salary schedule, was discussed with a remarkable forbearance and a minimum of heat. It was, as I recall the arguments, a debate in which the faculty had to admit that "those are the realities of the marketplace." Some college teachers still have the old-fashioned belief that their work is a **calling**, a vocation in that sense; and although they would like to command the income associated with a **profession**, the likelihood of so doing is small. It was something of a shock to the spirit to have to agree that the world is willing to pay a lot more for some teachers, than it is for others. Even so, the faculty seemed to say, this new program may be good for the whole college, and we are willing to adjust to the marketplace if such an adjustment will result in a net good for an institution we care about.

The last problem, however, was a formidable one. Once the faculty began discussing the merits of the arguments favoring and opposing accreditation for the business school, an entire agenda of accreditation appeared. The matter of accreditation for the business school was tied to the desirability of accreditation for teacher education programs, for music programs, and for the chemistry program, for all had their national accrediting processes and seals of approval. All of these operate quite independently of the Northwest Association—the organization to which the College had belonged for many, many years and the only organization whose evaluative processes and mechanisms could assess an entire institution from the ground up, including taking a critical look at the philosophy, the mission, the fiscal soundness, the quality of teaching, and the competence of the products of the teaching of an institution. In this matter of evaluation and accreditation, it is **institutional** integrity—wholeness, soundness—that is, or ought to be, the central concern. It is only this quest for institutional excellence that puts the ultimate seal of quality on the product of the institution.

It soon became apparent that the school of business could not hope to have the seal of approval by AACSB, for the faculty was unwilling to recommend for graduation students who were not educated—trained, perhaps, in fine points of business, but not educated. The curriculum recommended by the AACSB was, the faculty believed, deficient. In any case, it was pointed out that the entire College was accredited, and its economics and business graduates were regularly admitted to Harvard, Stanford, Wharton, and other prestigious postgraduate programs.

After this close examination, the faculty approved the program.

The task force headed by Robert K. Pedersen had done its work well, and the school of business his committee had recommended was approved by the Board of Trustees to begin with the Academic Year 1982-83. Thus what had been an academic program—Business Administration and Economics—evolved into the J. A. Albertson School of Business. From 1947 to 1982, a period of thirty-five years, Professor W. LaMar Bollinger had either directed or helped supervise the "Bus. Ad.—Econ" component of The College of Idaho; he retired just prior to the establishment of the new school.

Meanwhile, the newly found vitality in the leadership of the College expressed itself in many ways—good attendance at various meetings of committees of the Board and at meetings of the Board itself, carefully prepared and detailed reports from committees (I have mentioned those of Lyman Wilbur; Klara Hansberger's Budget and Audit Committee should be cited as well), and more and more pages of minutes of the Trustees' meetings. There was much to be done, and much of it was overdue. For instance, at the May 30, 1981, meeting of the Board of Trustees Eugene Thomas moved adoption of a recommendation by President DeRosier that a new organization (referred to as the Board of Visitors until a better name could be found) be established. The motion carried unanimously.

Such a group was formed, had energetic meetings, but went into a state of suspended animation following the next change in administration. However, according to a memorandum dated September 28, 1988 (Fitzgerald to Hendren), which includes a letter to Eugene Dorsey of the Gannett Foundation, the Board of Visitors was reinstated May 28, 1988. Included with the memorandum was a list of sixty-one members. Article III of the Bylaws of The College of Idaho (revised July 31, 1990) devotes an entire paragraph of some fourteen

In 1984 the Coyote women's ski team and Coach Ernie Meissner brought a national championship to Idaho, which secured for them formal recognition from the Legislature and Governor John Evans.

lines to this organization and its responsibilities, so the Board of Visitors bids fair to enjoy a continuing life of contribution to the school.

Of considerably greater moment at the Board meeting of May 30, 1981, however, were the actions of Trustees Jack Simplot and Velma Morrison, each contributing $100,000 in appreciation of the excellent work of the Chairman of the Board and the President of the College. Simplot offered an additional $25,000 to cover the Simplot Matching Scholarships.

Meanwhile, the HUD debt was slowly but surely dwindling, but $323,000 was still needed to redeem securities held by the trustee bank so that they could be restored as endowment. On August 19, 1981, the Investment Committee reported that following instructions given at the May 30, 1981, meeting of the Board, it had engaged the services of John C. Hunt and Associates, Boise, as investment counselor for the College. Although this was not the first time the College had utilized professional assistance in the handling of its portfolio, such assistance had not been available recently. The wisdom of this action became clear shortly, for the Minutes of the Fall meeting of the Board of Trustees included a report from Lyman Wilbur that the investment counselor "had probably saved the College up to $35,000" by turning over stock. Wilbur also noted that endowment funds totaled $814,597 with earnings judged to be $74,600 compared to $40,000 the previous year. It was also reported at this September meeting that Anderson Hall had been closed because there were too few students to need it. And in recognition of her early interest in the College the President's Dining Room in Simplot was re-named the Merlyn Hendren Room.

A further validation of Trustee Wilbur's request for good investment counseling came at the October 14, 1981, Executive Committee meeting, when he told the group that certain metals stock had been "erroneously valued by the auditors at $102,000." Its true worth was $1, for the only value was royalty rights, and they would lapse in four years. A counselor would have avoided accepting such a gift.

One other item from this October meeting is interesting. President DeRosier reminded the Executive Committee that Ralph Sayre wished to retire after the 1981-82 Academic Year. To avoid having two new deans—an academic dean and a business school dean—the president wondered about appointing a veteran faculty member to the academic deanship. He was soliciting comments from the faculty on the matter.

A month later the Executive Committee heard a report from officers of the American Institute for Foreign Study, introduced by Brett Harrell, C of I

316

Director of External Affairs. This program was a means of enculturating college-bound foreign students—that is, students who wished an education at an institution in an English-speaking country. Although the College would simply be renting space and selling board and room, the instruction being in the hands of AIFS personnel, 50 to 60 percent of those eligible might eventually matriculate at the College. This was another attempt to generate income for the school, but since it did not divert the College away from its mission nor subvert its philosophy, the attempt was justified.

A problem familiar to every property-owning organization of limited financial resources is "deferred maintenance." Nowhere is the consequences of this survival technique more apparent than with institutions of higher learning, public and private. When niggardly state legislatures endanger the soundness of the buildings and grounds it is their obligation to maintain, they serve their constituents very poorly indeed.

A private institution faces similar problems. The Minutes of the Board of Trustees for its meeting on December 9, 1981, contain a report by the Chairman of the Buildings and Grounds Committee, Gus Schade, to the effect that roofs were leaking on Kirkpatrick Gymnasium, Jewett Chapel-Auditorium, and the William Judson Boone Science Center. The cost to repair them: $17,844, $22,564, and $73,819, respectively. Under the constraints of limited income, an unbudgeted expense of $114,227 was a shock; still, the deterioration of the physical resources represented the poorest kind of economy. The old dilemma of short-run survival versus long run institutional integrity, had not disappeared. Is a college really a college when the faculty have been reduced, programs cut, buildings allowed to deteriorate, and no new books added to the library? Dean Sayre remarked that the accreditation team would not be indifferent to these problems.

One way of helping to pay the costs of running an institution is to increase the price of its services to those whom it serves. Unwilling to let the College deteriorate in any way (faculty, buildings and grounds, library), the Trustees on February 12, 1982, accepted the Budget and Audit Committee's recommendation and ordered that tuition be increased 15 percent (with the stipulation that the increase would not exceed 5 percent annually for any student continuously enrolled for the next three years) and that charges for single rooms be increased 14.7 percent, for double rooms by 20.3 percent. This rise would also allow an 11 percent salary increase for faculty, 8 percent for administration, and 5 percent for support staff salaries.

To increase profits, merchants sometimes cut prices, assuming that increases in sales will more than offset the lower price; yet a college can never lower its tuition and other costs in the hope that it will attract more students whose numbers would offset the reduction. Mathematics professor Boyd Henry once undertook a study for an earlier administration based on certain assumptions similar to those outlined, and if all the "givens" were accurate, the study declared, the College would realize increase in income. But could a school dare to try such a strategy? The answer was no, unless a foundation could be found to guarantee whatever losses might accrue for a long enough time to give the experiment a fighting chance. That foundation has not yet been found.

But there was good news spread upon the Minutes of this February meeting of the Board in the form of the announcement of a major gift, the adoption of a resolution recognizing and supporting the good work of the Regional Studies Center, and a citation to be presented to N. L. Terteling on the occasion of the fifteenth anniversary of the Library's opening. The Board also approved the naming of the College archives the Robert E. Smylie Archives, in recognition of the services of this distinguished alumnus to his school, his state, and his nation. Since Dr. Sayre would be vacating the John Philip Weyerhaeuser, Jr., Chair of History upon his retirement, the Board chose to confer this distinction upon another prominent American historian, President DeRosier—an unusual step, since chairs usually go to tenured faculty and presidents are untenured.

The major gift mentioned above requires closer and continuing scrutiny. Area residents of sufficient maturity will remember when Caldwell replaced with a modern facility the antebellum-style private home that had served as a hospital. The new Caldwell Memorial Hospital was built by subscribers and by fund drives. In the course of time, the building was sold to the Hospital Corporation of America and the proceeds placed in the Caldwell Memorial Hospital Foundation. Thanks to the work of many people and the constant oversight and encouragement by Dr. Donald Price, trustee and alumnus, it appeared that the foundation was willing to contribute a large share of its assets to The College of Idaho. When this willingness was translated into action, a grateful Board prepared a resolution through which it could thank the Foundation. Resolutions appear frequently in the Minutes of Trustees' meetings, and I have thus far spared the reader their archaic rhetoric. However, this resolution is an important one, and I quote from it since it is directly related to another matter that deserves commentary, the proposed Smith-Stanford Chair of Biology.

> WHEREAS,...the Caldwell Memorial Hospital Foundation, in its wisdom, sought to cease existence only after a first-class hospital replaced its predecessor, the Caldwell Memorial Hospital; and

WHEREAS, the Foundation voted to contribute a large proportion of its assets—in excess of $350,000—to The College of Idaho's Endowment fund for the enhancement of its various academic programs, especially by establishing an academic chair; and

WHEREAS, this magnificent testimony to the partnership of community and college will enhance even further The College of Idaho's pre-medical academic excellence;

NOW, THEREFORE, BE IT RESOLVED, that the members of The College of Idaho Board of Trustees, faculty, administrative staff, and students thank the Caldwell Memorial Hospital foundation for its generous gift—a testimonial to the pursuit of excellence—and acknowledged the terms of the gift, the hopes it supports, and the confidence it offers by maintaining that a shared partnership benefits all who contribute to it. The Chair that this gift allows, the Orma J. Smith—Lyle M. Stanford Chair of Biology, will forever memorialize this Foundation and the city—Caldwell—it represents.

Adopted this seventeenth day of February, 1982.

Further emphasis was made that the $50,000-$75,000 raised in 1973 and already earmarked for the Biology Chair be included in that endowment fund. It was noted that any balance of earnings not used for the Chair must be used for the Biology Department.

The last word has not been said respecting the attempt to honor the two premier biology professors, Orma J. Smith and his student Lyle M. Stanford, by establishing a chair in their memory.

At its meeting on April 29, 1982, the Executive Committee was informed that Dean and Provost Ralph Sayre had undergone successful quadruple bypass heart surgery on April 21. His retirement, scheduled for June 16, was thereby effected, and his temporary replacement, Dr. Roger Higdem, was able to assume the post early. The continuity was important: the leaders of the team of visitors from the Northwest Association were introduced to the Executive Committee. The on-site aspect of the accrediting process had begun.

Lest the accomplishments of students—the primary justification for the College's existence—be overlooked it should be mentioned that two C of I students had earned considerable recognition in 1981-82. Varina Van Veldhuizen received a Truman Scholarship and Zoe Rayborn won the College's first Rotary International Scholarship, this one for graduate work in Chile. In hope of learning how the College could attract more students like them and how they had been retained by the College, Paul Corddry, Chairman of the Planning Committee, noted the market research under way by an independent group underwritten by Ore-Ida Foods, Inc., to gather information by interviewing 150 present students, 100 high school counselors, and 150 faculty and alumni.

At the Spring 1982 meeting of the Board of Trustees, various matters contended for the attention of the group. Lyman Wilbur reported that the endowment was worth slightly over $1,248,000, further testimony to much hard work by the Investment and Budget and Audit committees. Wilbur, ever anxious to maintain the integrity of the endowment and enhance its value, moved "that the annual spending from endowment sources be limited to five percent of the market value of endowed assets...[to] take effect with the fiscal year ending in 1983." The motion was seconded and passed unanimously. Finally at this meeting, the position of Academic Dean and Provost was changed to Academic Vice President and Provost so that there would be no question of the ascendancy of the Vice President concerning all academic matters.

A plan by which Anderson Hall could have the boards removed from its windows and its interior occupied was presented at the July 12, 1982, meeting of the Executive Committee. That plan involved the leasing of the dormitory's first floor to the Magic Valley Alcoholic Recovery Center (Port of Hope) and negotiating lease of the second and third floors to the American Institute for Foreign Study—English Language Center to house up to 100 Japanese high school students. Additionally, it was proposed that Omega House (the Jensen home across the alley from the third or possibly fourth home of William Judson Boone) be leased to the Center for the Study of Market Alternatives, a privately financed and independent free enterprise study group. These were all approved.

At the Summer meeting of the Board of Trustees, the Trustees named the library the "N. L. Terteling Library," and Dr. Patricia Packard was named the first holder of the Orma J. Smith-Lyle M. Stanford Chair in Biology. Accreditation had been reaffirmed by the Northwest Association of Schools and Colleges.

The long, slow process of repairing roofs was under way, and the Minutes of the Executive Committee for September 22, 1982, praised Trustee Nancy Symms for raising the funds to repair the roof of Jewett. Quest, "a new, low-cost, non-credit, non-traditional program" would offer twenty-one courses, beginning in the Fall. Fees were set at $15 per course: It was another ephemeral ploy to produce income. At the next meeting, that of October 13, 1982, Auditor Mike Clements of Touche Ross sprinkled some cold water on the Executive Committee when he said, "Operations at the College are still not covering what is needed to be funded." Many things seemed to be going well, but two of the stool's three legs were not supporting their share of the fiscal weight: the endowment was inadequate, and there were too few students. Annual fund-raising seemed to be doing more than its share. Part of the success in that venture may be attributable to the success of the "phonathon," an ugly word for a wholesome and effective strategy by which students volunteer to call alumni, graduates, and other potential donors, making sure that the same folk are not called twice and confining calls to those who usually contributed $500 or less. (It brought in $22,560.)

With a full agenda for the fall 1982 meeting of the Trustees, following extensive and detailed Finance and Audit Committee meeting, Thomas remembered the Touche Ross audit admonition "about the still critical state of the College's financial condition and that long-range negative numbers still need be addressed such as reserves." Thomas

> asked if the Finance and Audit committee agreed with those observations and was informed by [Chairman] Smelek it did. Mr. Thomas then expressed his wonderment at the newspaper story recently which gave such a bright outlook on the financial situation of [the] C of I. He thought perhaps more care should be taken in telling the "bittersweet" story of the turnaround so that it doesn't sound better than it is since the College's needs are still great and too much cheerfulness might undermine still needed financial support.

> The argument for casting an optimistic tone to attract and reassure students was presented by Mr. Smylie.

Following the completion of Boone Hall and the Morrison Quadrangle in the early 70's, the campus would remain essentially unchanged for about 20 years.

Both perspectives deserve serious attention, for they complement, rather than oppose, one another. (Some who remember the Cassell years recall feeling that he wrote his own press releases, calling attention to the College's wretched position, its imminent closure, and finally, his saving it. They seemed the sort of puffery a "flack" would write.) The Board of Trustees must know exactly where fiscal matters stand. I recall attending a meeting of the Board, perhaps as Acting Academic Vice President or perhaps as Chairman of Faculty Association, and hearing Jack Simplot say after a forthright presentation of the precise fiscal condition, something like "That's the kind of information I've been trying to get for thirty years!" At a meeting of the faculty very late in President Shearer's administration, Mr. Shearer replied, in response to a plea for more information about why the coming year had to be another lean year of the tightened belt, something like: "Do you really want to know about all these matters? Wouldn't you rather do what you do best—teach—and let Curtis and me worry about the finances?"

Shearer had a point. Smylie's contention was absolutely on target as far as the public was concerned; Thomas' point was just as well-centered for the Administration and the Trustees.

It was also at this meeting that steps were taken to assure that appropriate celebrations would be planned and executed during the Academic year 1991-92, the 100th Anniversary year. Smylie was appointed Chairman of the *ad hoc* committee to prepare a centennial celebration plan. Good news included the gift by Lon and Mary Davis of Eagle of a Baldwin Concert Grand piano. This was the second concert grand, and the many pianists prepared by Professor Beale, Dr. Skyrm, and Dr. Davidson over the years could now team up and perform two piano music of the highest order.

In the interim between the November meeting of the Board and the December 8 meeting of the Executive Committee, the U.S. Department of Education made ugly noises about the HUD loans. Minutes of the December 8, 1982, meeting show that the laboriously worked out and carefully followed schedule of repayments had been rejected as a result of a review. Some collateral would have to be liquidated within sixty days. This did not sit well with the Trustees, and further study was ordered. At the January 9, 1983, meeting of the Executive Committee, opposition to the rejection by the Department of Education was recorded, and it was noted that Senator James McClure's office had been contacted.

The disposal of part of a campus is always a significant move. The sale to the City of 4.6 acres of land adjacent to the multi-purpose complex and the railroad right-of-way, land that had been returned to the College by the Multi-purpose Stadium Board, brought in $40,000. Consummation of the sale and a directive for the application of interest from the funds generated by the sale to maintaining the recreation-athletic areas south of Fillmore were approved at the Winter meeting of the Board of Trustees on February 9, 1983. At this same meeting the Trustees accepted the recommendation from the Investment Committee that assets from the Caldwell Memorial Hospital Foundation be kept as a separate account, with earnings to go to the Biology Department, as stipulated by the agreement and resolution previously approved.

Occasionally the Board will recognize the continuing good work of one of its members. On this occasion Lyman Wilbur was thanked by Chairman Hendren, and the Board responded (say the Minutes) with an ovation.

And finally, at this session, it was announced by the President that Professor Eric Yensen, who had just been granted tenure, was selected to edit the *Murrelet*, "the leading regional journal of ornithology and mammalogy."

Meanwhile, the endowment, the vital center of any private college, continued to inch ever so slowly upward. Wilbur reported at the March 16, 1983, meeting of the Executive Committee that it stood at $1,872,000. At this same meeting, Brett Harrell, Dean of Admissions, discussed the problem of name recognition, always referring to The College of Idaho in **Caldwell** "since many minds credit Twin Falls with the C of I."* Sandwiched between reports on the College's recent offer for satisfying indebtedness on the HUD bonds and an ambitious plan for rehabilitating the old Hayman Field south of Fillmore was the information that for the first time in College history a woman was elected president of the student body, Nancy Letney.

The end result of rehabilitating Hayman Field is the pleasant to behold and delightful to use Symms Athletic Field. Its story is brief but important; this is the area of the campus pertinent to Smylie's motion respecting the use of interest from the $40,000 in the endowment that resulted from the sale of 4.6 acres of campus to the city.

Utilizing plans drawn by Ron Thurber and Associates, President DeRosier described a soccer-rugby-softball playing field and a jogging-walking path with exercise stations, including landscaping and fencing.

---

*   A recent (June 1990) manifestation of this same old and recurring problem appeared at the wedding of the daughter of a C of I faculty member. "What does her father do?" one guest was overheard to ask. "He teaches at the College of Southern Idaho," was the reply.

Community, service club, and citizen interest has been piqued...and President DeRosier says somewhere between $24,000 and $28,000 is in hand now and several "in-kind" gifts are being donated.... The city's recently retired engineer [Melvin G. Lewis, whose brother Arnold had played football for the College] is working at half-salary as strawboss, and others have made greatly discounted offers toward the project (supplies and work). All this raised questions from Trustees about how these gifts will impact...fund raising for current operating expenses...security and scheduling. President DeRosier said it had already been made clear that it would always be a "College first" use but that the summer months are free most...for community use. Legalities such as "title clouding" of college property eventually needed as a site for a building were discussed since the Caldwell Softball Association will have invested heavily in developing a field on college land....

A discussion point was that all agreements must be well documented to avoid issues between the College and community at a later date; the College should not be giving anything away and there must be safeguards toward that end.

These concerns were well founded, for the anxieties that attended the gift to the community of the multi-purpose stadium had not been forgotten.

At the Spring 1983 meeting of the Board of Trustees, the earlier report from the Executive Committee referring to the worth of the endowment was

The generosity of the Symms family in the early 1980s resulted in the conversion of the old football field to a multi-purpose recreation facility suporting soccer, softball, jogging and walking. Volunteers from Mountain Bell supplied the labor to install the surrounding fence.

corrected: not $1,872,000 but $1,761,000 with an estimated annual income of about $101,000. This downward correction made news of Simplot's gift of $125,000 just handed to the President, "no strings attached," doubly welcome, and the Board responded with applause.

Another important piece of business had to do with the ongoing work of Paul Corddry and his Planning Committee. Martin Thomas of Ore-Ida foods, reporting for Corddry, presented a report on the state of the efforts to project a long-range plan for the institution. The format identified the following: "I. Strategy; II. Specific goals and the action to produce them; III. Implementation; and IV. Timing." To accomplish these, the Planning Committee had collected pertinent data about the student body from faculty, alumni, high school counselors, and the students themselves; had developed "wishes" by reviewing institutional strengths and weaknesses; and had projected three categories (Administration, Facilities, and Alumni) within which to develop strategic objectives for the realization of the most important wishes. A more detailed report would be ready by the time of the September meeting of the Board.

The President supplied an update on the sports and recreation field, including the information that "legal ramifications have been tended with Counselor Scott Pasley '72 working closely to safeguard College interests." In connection with Phase I, the recreational complex itself, Dr. DeRosier said he had visited with Doyle and Darwin Symms, who agreed to contribute $25,000 to complete Phase I financing. Trustee Tom Wright moved "that the President be authorized to commence...construction...and to confer with the Symms family in choosing a suitable name...."

Six additional items from this Spring (Commencement) meeting of the Trustees merit mention. The first is Trustee Barry Fujishin's report for the Development Committee. Fujishin, an alumnus and a former Marshall Scholar (the second C of I graduate to win this highly competitive graduate scholarship to attend a British university), reported that the goal for annual giving had been met to the tune of 135 percent subscription—$1,414,074.17. He also noted another source of encouragement in John Matthew's assistance in re-articulating the College-church tie, a check in the amount of $47,309 forthcoming from the Major Mission campaign of the Synod. In the second place, the resignation of Trustee Eugene Dorsey, who had moved to New York, prompted the Board to suspend its moratorium on new members and elect Bayless Manning to the Board, a decision that would ultimately result in some national attention to the college in the years ahead. A third item was the disquieting news that the American Institute for Foreign Study had not produced the income that had been expected of it—a drop from $132,100 to

$50,000, but the latter figure was quite realistic.* The fourth item concerned the success of former Trustee Robert Pedersen in his efforts to get a Board of Visitors organized. The potential for this organization was as great as Pedersen foresaw. Fifth, as Acting Academic Vice President Higdem prepared the Board for his return to the classroom next year, he told the Trustees that in his opinion the College needed more computers, especially personal computers, and the faculty needed higher salaries. He also observed that while Covell had been remodelled to make it an excellent site for the School of Business, it would soon be too small.

The sixth item might easily be overlooked because it takes the form of a resolution, and resolutions are only slightly less fun to read than they are to write. But it was of great consequence. Robert Smylie formulated and moved approval of the following:

> RESOLVED by the Trustees of The College of Idaho that the Chairman appoint a College of Idaho Centennial Fund Committee consisting of members of the Board, and others, for the purpose of planning and executing a campaign to raise a Centennial fund of $25,000,000 of new money and property between the dates of January 1, 1983, and June 1, 1992, and that such Committee be empowered to employ consultants and others in furtherance of the campaign to raise the Centennial Fund; and be it FURTHER RESOLVED that the Committee prepare a listing of giving alternatives...but that the Committee place special emphasis on the accumulation of an endowment of consequence to support the general operation of the College in its next century.

> The motion to approve the resolution was seconded by Mr. Simplot and carried unanimously.

As significant as this record is, life on campus is hardly glimpsed through the Trustees' Minutes. What else was going on? What speakers came to campus? How did the ski and basketball teams fare? A quick search through some other resources will supply partial answers to these questions.

---

* Those who observed Dr. DeRosier closely knew that he was fully capable of rhetorical overkill, that in his perfervid and Southern Baptist-like expression the truth was sometimes embellished. He reported to the Executive Committee on January 19, 1983, for instance, that a student from a neighboring state "entered with the highest SAT scores ever seen at the College." Indeed he had good scores, though other scores were better. Nevertheless it was refreshing and upbeat to find an institutional champion in the President, hyperbolic though he might be on occasion.

The College of Idaho *Bulletin* for Winter 1981 (90,2) answers some questions about the ski team. Even though there was a good women's team that earned either first or second place in every meet in which it competed, the NCSA conducted no national competition for women. The men continued strong. In 1979 they took the national championship, repeated in 1980, and took third in 1981—no mean accomplishment against schools like Colorado State University, the University of Oregon, Boston College, and the University of Minnesota. First and of greatest importance, the C of I skiers were excellent students—pre-engineering, pre-medicine, and biology. From those beginnings of serious intercollegiate competition (some will recall an earlier coach and ski program director named John Zapp; and real old-timers will remember Sam Winn, who as a student generated considerable interest in the sport) to the present, C of I skiers have done well. From Dave Hahn, Sports Information Director, comes the following information:

> Through the years, C of I ski teams have captured 13 national NCSA Championships. The Coyote women's alpine teams posted three consecutive alpine-combined titles from 1983 to 1985 and added another in 1987. The women then teamed with the nordic squads to take the four-event championship in 1984, 1985, and again last year. C of I men posted four event wins in 1979, 1980, 1985 and 1986 with alpine-combined titles in 1980 and 1986 (*Coyote Athletics* 1989-90).

So it was too with C of I basketball, which has also come to stand for intercollegiate athletic excellence in the country. From 1981-82 through 1989-90, the College won five NAIA district championships and progressed from "first out" to the top eight in NAIA finals in Kansas City.

High-quality musical performances thrilled the community. The choir toured and performed well, concluding its Winter Session travels with the traditional home concert. The Caldwell Fine Arts Series continued to delight town and gown, an annual validation of all the expectations President Shearer had for it. An increment that Shearer may not have anticipated, although Dick Skyrm surely did, was the participation of the visiting artists in the musical training of College of Idaho students. These superb musicians gave master classes, conducted (so to speak) tutorials, gave lectures, and even joined the students in public concerts. The Utah Symphony, for instance, after its concert on January 13, 1981, made such a request of The C of I-Community Symphony Orchestra. Harpist Mildred Dilling thrilled her audience and delighted the students of Irene Bevington, whom she worked with.

Two examples suggest the sorts of things that give new life to a campus in the need of a transfusion. Dr. DeRosier demonstrated his sense of timing and his ability to capitalize upon dormant resources in asking Emeritus Professor Dr. George V. Wolfe to accept the task of chairing a new committee—with the graceless name Rhodes, Marshall, Truman Scholarship Committee but with the extremely important task of helping to select the candidates best suited to compete for those prestigious awards. Dr. Wolfe had retired in 1970, and until then he had served as advisor to students who entered the competitions. Further evidence of DeRosier's sense of appositeness can be found in his luring Erwin Schwiebert out of retirement to assist in various fund-raising chores on a part-time basis. Theirs was a considerably more felicitous working arrangement than Schwiebert had experienced with Cassell.

Since 1973 the College had offered Sawtooth Week. Another product of the mind of Lyle Stanford, Sawtooth Week involves from seventy to ninety freshmen, fifteen or so upperclass students, and fifteen to twenty-five faculty and staff who spend from three to five days in Camp Sawtooth and in the Sawtooth Wilderness just before classes start in the fall. A part of freshman orientation, the Sawtooth experience helps students become acquainted with one another, with the ineffable glory of the Sawtooth Wilderness, and with some of the faculty. In the camp and in the wilderness, on the trails and in canoes, students who have not had the opportunity to do so learn about native plants, geology, wildlife photography, natural history; something about the College and something about the nature of a liberal arts education.

Sawtooth Orientation 1984: Dr. James H. Gabbard leading freshmen and faculty in songs around the campfire.

To select one bright year of the time of Arthur DeRosier and let it stand in testimony to the other successful years of his administration, we might look at 1983-84 and begin with Fall Convocation. Convocations at the College are traditional and ceremonial, the faculty and administration gowned, a speaker well prepared to share worthwhile ideas, and a small delegation of students, attending, probably, because of a real interest in their school. Townspeople come because they, too, have an interest in the school.

The speaker at this year's first convocation was Robert L. Hendren, Jr., Chairman of the College's Board of Trustees. In his address, Hendren developed the theme of the integrity of a liberal arts education and argued that the kind of wholeness it represents prepares the man or woman

> for life-long learning...and deals with the long run, more with the mind than with skills, and embraces the very power of life.... [A liberal arts education] is an awareness of science and how it works. It is the knowledge of the social sciences and how people feel and understand. It is the pursuit of mysteries...a concern for justice...an embrace of duty and honor...a sense of place and history (*Bulletin* Fall 1983).

Hendren was awarded a Doctorate of Laws for his outstanding service. He had not yet finished his B.A. degree; the awarding of an honorary doctorate in such a case, however, is not without a long and distinguished precedent.

A $65,000 gift from the Synod of the Pacific, one of the largest gifts ever received from the Presbyterian Church, was tangible evidence of a rejuvenated interest by the church in Idaho's oldest college and helped further stimulate positive feelings that 1983-84 would indeed be a good year. Additional financial support came from the second consecutive "Phone-a-thon." The 1983 solicitation netted pledges amounting to $36,343, an increase of 61 percent over the 1982 effort of $22,560.

Familiar names appear on the roster of new faculty and staff for 1983-84. Helen Washburn replaced Jane Sherman as Director of Graduate Studies; Helen later moved east to become president of Cottey College in Nevada, Missouri. Ellen Batt joined the faculty as part-time instructor of German, and Mary Higdem, who had been coordinating the Idaho Department of Energy's campus extension center, was engaged to conduct the College's geology program. Jan Boles '65 turned to teaching photography part-time for the Art Department, having served from 1969-1972 as Director of Publications and Information and as staff photographer. Dorothy Gerber became the College's Study Skills Coordinator. All continue to serve the College; others who were hired the same time have moved on and so are not identified here.

Contributing to the elements making 1983-84 a banner year was a gift from Trustee Warren E. McCain and Bernice McCain (Mrs. Warren) of a full pay scholarship to a qualified graduate of Payette High School, from which both Warren and Bernice graduated. Part of the reason for establishing the scholarship was the gratitude the McCains felt toward the Payette community and the school and faculty it made available to Payette students. Mary Alice Pierce, '28, of Payette's English faculty had been a much loved teacher of McCain.

Intellectually, the campus was stimulated by a symposium engineered by Professor Orville Cope, a program on bio-ethics. Speakers included Dr. Robert Blank of the University of Idaho, political scientist, and Dr. Diana Axelson, chair of the Philosophy Department of Spelman College, Atlanta, Georgia. Professors Sheri Robison, Biology, and Terry Mazurak, Philosophy, were C of I presenters.

Other bits of information from this year include the formation of a committee to discuss organizing a law alumni society. The steering committee was composed of Paul Street '70, Warren Jones '65, Ed Lodge '57, and Professor Cope. Additionally, approximately thirty Treasure Valley medical alumni met

The year 1984 saw the restoration and conversion of the Blatchley Little Theater into the David and Blanche Rosenthal Gallery of Art. Following the ribbon cutting ceremony, Linda and Arthur DeRosier shared a congratulatory hug with Mrs. Rosenthal and her daughter Ann Weers.

to form a Medical Alumni Association, led by Gene Sullivan '59, Chairman; James W. Smith, '64, Chairman elect; and Arthur C. Jones III, '70, the Society's representative on the Alumni Association Board of Directors. President DeRosier's commitment to increasing alumni activity was real.

As the school year drew toward its close, activities and events seemed to increase in inverse proportion to the time remaining. A renovated Blatchley Hall and Gallery was dedicated on Friday, May 25, to the applause of a goodly crowd. The mansion had been placed on the National Register of Historic Places in 1980, and monies available for its restoration had to be matched one-to-one. A long-time friend of the College and a personal friend of Robert Smylie, Blanche Rosenthal, provided the necessary match, and Blatchley Hall resumed her former glory as Caldwell's showplace. The David and Blanche Rosenthal Gallery of Art made an appropriate home for the College's permanent collection, including works of William Hogarth, Marc Chagall, and Pablo Picasso, among others. Arthur A. Hart, former C of I faculty member and for a number of years Director of the Idaho State Historical Society, informed the crowd about the historical and esthetic value of the building. Mrs. Rosenthal, who since 1954 has provided scholarship assistance for qualified graduates of Wood River High School in Hailey, was quoted as saying of the occasion,

> It is one of the most exciting things ever to happen to me. There was only one other time in my life when I have been speechless, and that was when I met the Pope (*Bulletin*, Summer 1984).

Commencement is always an opportunity for the College to put its best foot forward and bask in the glory reflected by students going from undergraduate into post-graduate education, into professional school, into the classroom and the world of work to take their part in the life of community, state, nation, and world. An international flavor was provided for the 1989 commencement by Jack E. Morpurgo. Dr. DeRosier characterized Morpurgo's presentation as "the finest commencement address I believe I have ever heard" (*Bulletin*, Summer 1984). While it is not possible to identify all recipients of honorary degrees, the Class of 1984 was particularly noteworthy: Morpurgo; Blanche Rosenthal; Janet Hay, one of Idaho's singularly accomplished legislators and a former biology assistant at the College; and George Crookham. Crookham was the original and creative soul who designed and built the mill whose revolving arms lowered Viola Evans in the stunning Beale production of *The Red Mill*.

Morpurgo returned to Caldwell to serve as scholar-in-residence for part of the semester, and he and Mrs. Morpurgo, a product of the Royal Academy of Dramatic Art, treated patrons of the Fine Arts Series to an evening of readings of English poetry: he possesses one of the richest speaking voices west of the prime meridian. In his autobiography (*Master of None*: Carcanet Press, 1990), Dr. Morpurgo admits that it came as something of a surprise to him to learn that there were excellent schools besides Oxbridge and the Ivy League and mentions Elmira College and The College of Idaho as two of them.

The year ended on two high notes—the election of new members to the Board of Trustees, including Governor Cecil Andrus, and a reception in the J. R. Simplot home in Boise for C of I alumni. Additionally, Trustee Raymond Smelek, General Manager of the Boise Division of Hewlett Packard, was elevated to the chairmanship of the Board, and Lee Abercrombie, Jr., Vice President for Finance and Treasurer of Morrison-Knudsen, was named vice chairman. The reception was attended by upwards of two hundred guests, who were greeted by Mr. and Mrs. Simplot and entertained by the Boise Philharmonic String Quartet. The writer for the *Bulletin* (Summer 1984) said, "It was truly an elegant Sunday afternoon."

Indeed, 1983-84 was a bright year...with the one exception, underscored in the Minutes of the Fall meeting of the Board (September 20, 1983), a report from Lee Abercrombie's Finance and Audit Committee: "Unless the goal for fund raising is increased or other sources of funds identified, the committee will have to reduce expenses to achieve a balanced budget." Surely, the Trustees murmured, the old pattern will not repeat itself.

At the November 16, 1983, Fall session, the President said to the trustees:

> We struggle every day to make ends meet and budgets balance. Progress is being made but the irony is that it is also a time of great frustration. One-half of my administration and one-third of the faculty were not here when the College was at death's door; they did not experience those years. Now that the College appears to be on a sound financial footing the deferred frustrations relating to past problems are surfacing in the form of salary increase requests, a need for more faculty and staff and improved library holdings, and equipment maintenance and replacement.

One issue about which opinions differed was the question of what to do with unrestricted bequests and gifts of property or land. The Board, in its mission to restore the integrity of the endowment and increase its worth, had placed such gifts "into a separate interim interest bearing account until action is taken by the Board of Trustees, to accept the funds and to decide whether the funds go into endowment or current fund accounts [current budget]" (Attachment A, "Study and Recommendations," November 16, 1983). The president and the fundraisers, while not indifferent to the need to restore and enhance the endowment, viewed such funds with a proprietary eye, for who was to say for what purpose the gifts had been made? In striving to balance the 1983-84 budget, which was facing a shortfall of $197,000, Abercrombie moved the following resolution:

> WHEREAS, there has been a breakdown in communications between staff and committees on the application of certain resolutions passed by the Trustees regarding disposition of undesignated estate gifts between the endowment fund and the current fund:

> AND WHEREAS, the Finance and Audit Committee has been unable to arrive at a balanced budget for FY 1983-84 without a significant carry over from FY 1982-83;

> BE IT RESOLVED that the Board of Trustees suspend the resolution passed at the September 21, 1983 Board of Trustees meeting reinstating endowment funds from unrestricted estate gifts and quasi-endowment until such time as the budget for 1983-84 is balanced, and the Trustees restore to the current fund the sum of $215,750 for FY 1982-83 from endowment funds....

> BE IT RESOLVED that to produce a balanced budget for FY 1983-84, the Trustees raise the goal for gifts, other than endowment gifts and restricted gifts for future years, from $1,150,000 to $1,200,000.

The ongoing expenses of the institution had to be met; before an individual or an institution can anticipate an old age, survival in the short run must be secured but another element appears here, a discomfiting one to a certain cast of mind. If spending seems out of line with revenue, an easy solution is to expect more from the fund raisers. The budget, then, becomes balanced—on paper—through the expectation that more work, harder work, and greater success by the development staff will produce, in the specific example cited, $50,000.

On September 25, 1983, Nixon L. Terteling, a trustee of the College for thirty years (1953-1983), died. His contributions to the institution are noted every day by those who enter his library, and he is also remembered for his enduring efforts to provide a science facility—efforts that must have cost him considerable anxiety. Terteling was memorialized in a resolution approved by the Executive Committee on December 8, 1983.

On November 4, 1983, Dean Miller, counsel for the Board of Trustees, also died. Miller was not only the Board's attorney but the prime force in the establishment of the Claud E. and Ethel M. Whittenberger Foundation. The

Board memorialized his death and his contributions in a formal resolution, also at the December meeting.

Mention has been made before of strategic planning and long-range-goal setting under the leadership of Trustee Paul Corddry. The success of Project 90 began to point toward life beyond the centennial for the College. Stratagems, shifts, and evasions; belt-tightening, credit, and the appearance of the magical helper from time to time: perhaps now the school could and should create its future. President Shearer had had such a notion, but reality and human limitations outstripped his resolve and he resigned. The reality was the absence of a significant endowment and the presence of debts to the U.S. government; one of his human limitations has been identified.

But circumstances were different now. An energetic and capable president working with as good a board of trustees as existed for any college anywhere might make things happen. Corddry's committee consisted of the following members: Former Acting President Margaret Boone; President Arthur DeRosier; Trustees Robert Hendren, William Eberle, Ray Smelek, Nancy Symms, Eugene Thomas, Thomas Wright; Faculty Lance Jarvis, Terry Nagel, Richard Widmayer; Ex-Officio member Martin Thomas. During part of the planning, former Trustees Richard Christensen and Eugene Dorsey assisted, as did former faculty member Jane Sherman.

Although space will not permit more than a brief discussion of the committee's work and its report, a few statements will indicate something of the scope and significance thereof. All substantive references are to *The College of Idaho Strategic Plan 1983-1988.*

The planning process was intended to find out where the College is, to ascertain where it wants to be, to identify the means of getting there, and to monitor the strategies employed in the process of getting there. In attempting to discover where the College is, nine categories emerged as pertinent to the problem: student body, curriculum, administration, faculty, physical plant, extra-curricular, alumni, external, and financial. Enrollment records; the Spring 1982 Institutional Self-Study and Accreditation Report; Committee members' impressions; and finally the opinions of students, faculty members, alumni, and high school counselors, were all examined for their pertinence in the matter of the College's status.

In summing up the study, Corddry said in effect that if it had been a marketing survey to discover how a product was doing he would be tremendously encouraged. People generally liked and believed in The College of Idaho. The institution needed more students, the physical facilities needed attention (with a physical education building-swimming pool taking high priority), extracurricular activities needed developing, and there was a continuing problem with name identification: "institution has confusing name."

The study concluded, among other things, that non-graduating students believe the ideal college in comparison to the C of I has "more social activities, more sports, less academic challenge, a more impersonal student group, less faculty contact, and broader [less rigorous] admissions standards." Further, "many dropouts have received a college degree—most from Boise State University or [the] University of Idaho." These dropouts nevertheless claimed that the experience at the C of I "contributed to their lives, would recommend to their children, 1/5 have donated money to The College of Idaho, not to other schools." The process of long range planning is still going on, and by Commencement of 1991 its result will be available to the College community.

The Winter 1984 meeting of the Board produced four pieces of information of considerable interest, the first a report on a merit-pay proposal. As might be expected the proposal generated extensive debate, and a motion to approve was made, seconded, and withdrawn as a consequence of airing of convictions. Finally, the proposal was approved with the passage of the following amendment: "The report is adopted subject to the further report and recommendation of the appropriate committee of the Board as it views the merit plan in action and the dollars associated with merit reward." As I understand the action, it means approved in principle but suspended in practice. However, the Board was unequivocal in lending its support to the concept of comparability. Merit pay, the Board concluded, means little until C of I salaries can be compared favorably with the salaries of institutions with which we compare ourselves. Comparability set a realistic goal, and its achievement was declared a high-priority item.

The third piece of information was contained in a report from Abercrombie's Finance and Audit Committee. The College, he noted, was "running a deficit of income over expenses which compares unfavorably with a budgeted surplus."

And Lyman Wilbur, "in reference to the Endowment Task Force stated that an ultimate endowment goal of $50,000,000 was needed with an intermediate goal of $5,000,000 by 1990...raised without interfering with the $1¼ to 1½ million to be raised for current funds."

Fifty million dollars for The College of Idaho? Could it be done?

May, 1985: Trustees Warren McCain and Idaho Governor Cecil Andrus flank President Arthur DeRosier.

CHAPTER EIGHTEEN

Endowment, Income,

and Students

The year 1983-84 seemed determined to end with a deficit of $129,000; the Minutes of the Executive Committee for April 18, 1984, say, "When compared with the budgeted surplus of $481,000 [the deficit] produces a negative variance of $621,000." By the time of the spring meeting of the Board on May 26, Lee Abercrombie had to report that the fiscal condition had deteriorated just during the month of April to the tune of $106,000: "The deficit of $501,000, when compared to the budgeted surplus of $235,000 produced a negative variance of $736,000." The report continues: "The special fund solicitation from Mr. Simplot and Mr. Albertson creating $225,000 in new funds to help solve our deficit problem was booked in May." It was hoped that holdbacks and expense cutting would reduce the budgeted deficit from $202,000 to $90,000 by year end. In an effort to make funds available for paying bills, the Trustees approved "borrowing" from the Endowment Fund and were prepared to authorize borrowing from the banks up to $335,000 to finance the College through the summer, "at which time revenues will permit retirement of the debt." More dismal news came in Wilbur's report for the Investment Committee. The endowment of $1,878,347.56 had produced $139,397.69 instead of $2,065,040.39 (or $2,265,040.39, a discrepancy or a typographical error in the Minutes) producing $155,936.04.

At the May meeting of the trustees, Ray Smelek replaced Bob Hendren as chairman. In an interview with the editor of the *Bulletin*, Ron Pisaneschi,

Chairman Smelek spoke on a variety of subjects. Their dialogue is instructive; part of it is quoted here:

Bulletin:

> When board chairman Robert L. Hendren, Jr. and president DeRosier took over the leadership...four years ago the school was in terrible financial trouble and their #1 goal was to begin improving its fiscal position and fiscal integrity. Do you have a five year goal?

Smelek:

> Yes. I think the five year goal has to include two things: one part of the goal has to be to continue to develop financially.... The other side of the coin is to make sure that we meet our enrollment goals....

Bulletin:

> Many people say that the future of the school lies in building a large endowment.

Smelek:

> I think that is certainly true.... If you look back a few years, the endowment of the College was virtually dissipated....

Much of this story of the College seems concerned with fiscal matters. The story of The College of Idaho is in a real sense a story of a heroine on a quest for a dowry or, in collegiate terms, an endowment.

The year 1984-85 and the remaining tenure of President DeRosier were marked by this lifelong institutional inadequacy respecting an endowment. An additional source of distress and a loss to the College's fiscal management was the death of Lee Abercrombie, memorialized by Board action on October 17, 1984.

At this same meeting, figures comparing enrollment for 1983 with 1984 were given: 1983—516 full-time, 105 part-time, 621 headcount, 552 full-time equivalent, units generated 7152; 1984—584 full-time, 92 part-time, 676 headcount, full-time equivalent 614, units generated 8034. Enrollment was improving, and careful attention directed to the endowment began to pay off: Wilbur could report that the endowment was worth about $2,000,000. If that fund could be increased, then the persistent problem of budget overrun might finally be resolved.

The FY budget, for example, was $5,337,900; however, as of October 15, 1984, a known budget overrun of $264,038 existed. That figure when reduced by a larger than expected September income made it likely that something approaching a deficit of $164,038 would be on the books. Yet another year of an unbalanced budget.

Lyman Wilbur moved a resolution that formally raised the target amount of Smylie's earlier resolution ($25,000,000) to $50,000,000 in recognition of the absolute necessity for a healthy institution to have a healthy endowment. The date by which the endowment campaign was to be concluded was the "end of the College's 100th anniversary in 1992." By December 13, 1984, the endowment, according to Minutes of the Executive Committee of that date, had experienced both a dramatic market gain and a major gift of stock and stood at the all-time high of $4,851,946.18, as of November 30, 1984. Maybe the centennial goal in Smylie's resolution was feasible!

The new year began on a hopeful note: as of January 31, 1985, the endowment stood at $5,762,749.01. This amount was sufficient to generate an income of about $370,079. Add to that the men's and women's ski teams' success in capturing the NCSA Championship—a national championship—and DeRosier was moved to declaim (Minutes of the Executive Committee March 20, 1985)," [It was] the school's greatest moment in the athletic sun." The presence of Tom Wicker, Associate Editor of the *New York Times*, gained some national publicity for the Spring Symposium, and the hopeful note continued.

However, the Finance and Audit Committee's report to the Executive Committee (March 20, 1985) modulated that cheerful note into a minor key. "Financial reports have improved for this period; we are still looking at a projected accumulative deficit of 1.2 million at the end of June." How many more Project 90s would The College of Idaho have to bring to pass before the school could manage to keep income and expenditures in balance?

An additional development was announced at the March 20 meeting of the Executive Committee. The first dean of the J. A. Albertson School of Business was leaving. Dean Kelly had been eager for the school to be accredited by the AACSB; but such accreditation would have placed impossible demands on an already overburdened budget, and Kelly's frustrated ambitions led to his departure. This in no way compromised the College's accreditation by the Northwest Association, nor did it work to the detriment of business graduates who wished to continue at the graduate level at institutions of their choice. Kelly was replaced by Dean Benson. At the Saturday, June, 1985 meeting of the Board, Ray Smelek passed to Cecil Andrus the chairmanship of the Board. Thus the former governor of the State and head of its public schools became the head of Idaho's oldest institution of higher learning, which happened to be a private establishment.[*] He was also one of the College's staunchest supporters. The same meeting saw termination of the contract with the Port of Hope, thus restoring Anderson Hall to its wonted use as a college dormitory—this time an honors residence hall.

When Board Chairman Andrus opened his first Executive Committee meeting on July 19, 1985, he was greeted by the good news that in October of 1985 The College of Idaho would be listed among the 221 colleges featured in *The Best Buys in College Education* by Edward B. Fisk of the *New York Times*. The continuing fiscal bad news, however, concerned gift income, which was $297,000 short of the 1984-85 goal, and the year-end deficit of $189,300. At this meeting Coach Holly announced that Cisco Limbago '72 had been hired to coach women's tennis and Tim Mooney to coach baseball, the field of dreams to be restored to the Caldwell campus in a most successful way in 1986-87. But grim news was in store for the Executive Committee meeting October 18, 1985: the auditors could give only a qualified audit in view of a $1,775,000 current fund deficit, with borrowing from the endowment increasing to $850,000 as of June 30, 1985. Added to that news was the bitter pill that enrollment was down, partly because states like Nevada and California were awarding grants to entice their students to stay in state and also because the C of I was reducing its financial aid. Undergraduate enrollment had dropped by nineteen students from 1984. It was reported that "the Paul Smith estate will be valued over $1 million," but no one saw fit to question the assertion.

If undergraduate enrollment was declining, the graduate program appeared to be flourishing. In a memo of October 18, 1985, to faculty and staff, included in his report to the Executive Committee of the Board, President DeRosier reported as follows:

> To date, 283 different people have enrolled in graduate courses; last year's total was 277 (+2.1%).

> Last year, we had 326 total enrollments in graduate courses; this year the number is already 406 (an increase of 24.5%), and it will probably go to 491 (an increase of 50.1%).

---

[*]   He was subsequently re-elected governor.

Last year, we generated 790 graduate units; this year we have already generated 873 (+10.5%) and will generate many more from those yet to register.

The hairsbreadth-crisis management-nick of time- characteristic of the life of the College brings to the attention of the reader how similar in many respects are the fairy tale and the melodrama. Both make interesting reading, as conscienceless editors of scandal sheets know well, but those who are actually living in and through the events find them stressful. Whose budget will be frozen this month? How much can be borrowed from the endowment? What interest should be paid on that amount? Dare we beg yet another gift from x or y or z? Can the students endure yet another tuition rise? What will a tuition increase do to enrollment? Yes, it will decline (it usually does), but by how much? Will the College accreditation survive with yet another qualified audit? The century-long history of this heroine struggling for her endowment emerges as just that—a struggle. At the Fall 1985 meeting of the Board of Trustees, when Chairman Andrus reminded the Trustees of the auditors' report of October that the College would end fiscal year 1985 with a qualified financial report, he could also report a gift from the Albertsons of 100,000 shares of Albertson stock, "directed to the endowment in a manner making it possible to remove the debt to the endowment, to computerize the campus, and to allow for salary increase to faculty and staff, [erasing] the C of I's indebtedness and also [diminishing] the shortfall of $160,000 in our current operating budget reported at the October meeting."

Mr. Lou Henry, the representative of Touche Ross, who presented the audit to the Trustees, "issued the warning that Mr. and Mrs. Albertsons most recent contribution was a 'life-saving gift' but until the endowment is in place, the annual fund drive must be the most critical item on the Board agenda." The point was well taken. The Albertsons' gift made possible a $300,000 line of credit with Idaho First National Bank to meet cash flow requirements, indicating that the C of I's credit had been restored.

In the comprehensive and detailed report by the auditors, two items deserve scrutiny. The first concerns the bonds payable to the U.S. Department of Housing and Urban Development (HUD). The total amount still owed—*not* paid for by Project 90 and not paid for by subsequent generous gifts—on the Student Union (Bond Series A and B) and on dormitories and dining facilities (Bond Series A, B, C, D, and E) came to $1,640,000 with the next yearly payment figured at $116,000. This indebtedness was to be met from student fees and cafeteria and housing charges; if enrollment sagged or if a dormitory had to be closed the payments nevertheless had to be made.

The second item refers to the Boone Science Center. Because it represents an accurate synopsis of that tangled financial arrangement, I quote the audit at this point:

> During the year ended June 30, 1979, the owners of the Boone Science Building [the Terteling Organization] sold a 10% interest in the building to the College for $500,000 and gifted an additional 34% interest in the building to the College. During the current year, an additional 35% interest was gifted to the College. The owners of the residual balance have agreed to gift their remaining 21% interest to the college within 15 years from the date of the agreement. Future gifts will be recorded at the fair market value of the gift when received. At June 30, 1980, the latest valuation date, the fair value of the remaining 21% interest was approximately $1,050,000.

A final note from this meeting refers to a report from the Board's Investment Committee to the full Board, submitted by Lyman Wilbur. "Concerned about the manner in which gifts to the endowment fund and endowment earnings...are handled," the Committee requested the implementation of five procedures and detailed two other recommendations by which such gifts would be approved and earnings understood by the Trustees. Included was a recommendation coupling the interest rate on borrowings from the endowment to the rate earned by the endowment fund, approximately, on its money market funds. Wilbur's report set the value of the endowment at $6,610,023 as of October 31, 1985.

At the December meeting of the Executive Committee (December 13, 1985), Wilbur reported that the total endowment stood at $6,701,666, an increase of $91,643 during November. Trustee Tom Wright, zealous concerning the buildings and grounds, reported that Finance and Audit agreed with him that a maintenance building was essential—especially in view of the higher use to which Blatchley Hall would be put, forcing maintenance to be housed elsewhere. To that end, Finance and Audit agreed to expend $2,000 for seed money for the maintenance building.

These regular and serious meetings of the Trustees, in either full committee or in various subcommittees, resulted in what? Simply put, they resulted in the continuing heartbeat of the institution. In Fall Semester 1985, that meant an Oktoberfest, the President's Trust Dinner (at which guests first learned of the 100,000 shares of Albertsons—$3,000,000—given by J. A. and Kathryn Albertson), a fall convocation at which Rhodes Scholar and University of Idaho philosopher Dr. Marvin Henberg spoke. Henberg had been a member of the same class of Rhodes Scholars to which the C of I's Jim Roelofs belonged. It was at this convocation that Thurlow "Stub" Bryant received the Distinguished

Service Award for his long and faithful service to the College. It may well be that Bryant is the last staff member to have served under Dr. Boone; with the death of Sara Rankin, there are no surviving Boone faculty.

Those sometimes tiresome volunteer trustee chores also meant that students like Sarah Wallace of Caldwell and Dan Semmens of Helena, Montana (both English majors), could be sufficiently well prepared to win Rotary International Scholarships, Wallace to France and Semmens to England.

On November 21, 1985, Dr. Leslie V. Brock, Professor Emeritus of History, who had served the College for thirty-four years, died at the age of eighty-two. Dr. Ralph Sayre's eulogy deserves to be quoted; I offer this one paragraph from the *Bulletin*, Spring 1986:

> As a scholar, Leslie has left an important and lasting contribution [*The Currency of the American Colonies, 1700-1764*]. As a colleague, Leslie was the steadfast defender of the liberal arts and of high standards for the College. As a friend Leslie was sympathetic and understanding, but at the same time highly entertaining. He was the rarest of storytellers.

From this same *Bulletin* came news of Richard Widmayer's literary field trip to London, news of a Trustee-adopted long-term loan program for students, and the stirring news that Caldwell native and C of I alumnus Steve Maughan, Class of 1985 with majors in history and chemistry, was named a Mellon Fellow in the Humanities. One of a highly select group to be funded through the Ph.D. degree, Maughan chose to undertake post-graduate work in history at Harvard.

Additional items from this issue of The College of Idaho *Bulletin* refer to Ed Bonaminio's brain child, the Nifty-Fifties reunion planned for July 18-20 (a highly successful reunion, incidentally, and a model and inspiration for the Fabulous Forties reunion of the following year), and to an NEH challenge grant of $337,500 to be matched three to one that, when matched, would supply money for much needed library resources, for faculty development, and for an endowed chair in the Department of English. The humanities would thus receive some of the financial support that the National Science Foundation had extended to the Division of Natural Sciences over a score or more years. A disquieting piece of news was Dr. Gabbard's health problem on the choir tour; alumnus Bob Chilman '66 stepped in to substitute for Dr. Gabbard until laboratory tests gave him clearance to continue the tour.

Finally, it was with much pleasure that the alumni Association recognized the contributions of George and Martha (Uyematsu) Nishitani, Barry Fujishin, and Warren Taylor, by giving them appropriate awards.

343

In the next issue of the *Bulletin* (Autumn 1986), a serious President DeRosier looks earnestly at the reader from page two, his photograph accompanying the regular feature "The President's Message." The seriousness of his mien matches the seriousness of his message—challenges, work, contentment only momentary, lights and shadows, time slipping away. In this year three long-time faculty members retired, representing more than three-quarters of a century of service. Dr. Peggy Gledhill, English, had joined the faculty in 1965, becoming full-time in 1968; Dr. Joseph Dadabay, Sociology, had come to the College in 1958; and Professor Richard Elliott, Librarian, had arrived also in 1958.

Elliott had helped plan the College's primary material intellectual resource, the superb Terteling Library, and had masterminded the transfer of more than 65,000 volumes from old Strahorn Library to the new facility, using a shelf-numbering system devised by Assistant Librarian Stan Ruckman. Students and faculty formed a "carton brigade" and passed boxes of books along this human chain to their new home. It took about five hours and was accomplished so effectively, according to *Bulletin* contributor Dora Morley, that the "N. L. Terteling Library was open for business the next day."

During the summer of 1986, Ray Gabbard won an apprenticeship with the Des Moines Metro Opera Company, the beginning of a promising musical career for this son of Jim and Virginia Gabbard. The Music Department continued to produce sterling musicians in spite of limited numbers of students and declining performance scholarships with which to compete for talented high school students.

One of the highlights of the Fall Semester of 1986 was the appearance of Jack Morpurgo as Scholar-in-Residence. Faculty were reminded of the two earlier visits—one in the late 1940s, the other in the 1960s—of the church historian F. Roland Bainton and of similar visits by other widely recognized scholars, writers, and musicians, and their value to the College community.

The grim reaper continued his task, taking Eldon Marsh, long time business manager; Anna Jensen, '30, member of the family that had lived across the alley from Dr. Boone and had sent many fine students and athletes to the College over two generations, including Dr. Robert Jensen and his and Charlotte's two sons, Rob and Rick; and Florence Sinclair Marshall, from a family whose roots are deeply sunk in the College's story—the family of Margaret and Bess Sinclair Weaver, of Steve Marshall, of Catherine Marshall, of Joseph Marshall. Outstanding football quarterback (a Little All-American) and highly successful Caldwell Coach Charlie Alvaro, '60, died of a heart attack, and the deaths of

Harold Willmorth, '26, and Canzada (Mrs. Robert R.) McCormick, '17, are recorded in the *Bulletins* for the Fall and Winter of 1986.

At the May 1986 meeting of the Board of Trustees, it was noted that honorary degrees had been awarded to a distinguished group—Pulitzer Prize novelist and first College of Idaho Writer-in-Residence A. B. Guthrie, Jr. (in absentia); James A. McClure, Idaho native and U.S. Senator; John A. Young, President and Chief Executive Officer of Hewlett Packard and commencement speaker; and Klara Hansberger, devoted trustee and corporation president. Honored by resolution were retiring trustees and alumni Barry Fujishin and J. L. Scott and trustee Nancy Symms.

At this same meeting board counsel William Gigray reported that the College's gain from the Paul Smith estate was closer to $90,000 than to the larger anticipated amount.

Some years before, the editor of the Idaho *Press-Tribune*, of Nampa, had submitted his own name as a candidate for the Board of Trustees, a submission on which the Trustees wisely withheld action. Whether the editor felt aggrieved over their decision, or whether he had been attacked by the journalistic fever of investigative reporting, or perhaps for some other reason, he permitted a story to appear in that paper on May 30, 1986—the day before commencement—which contained a litany of innuendos and inaccurate statements, complaints by Dr. Benson, the recently discharged dean of the Business School. It was a clever ruse on the part of a disgruntled former employee to embarrass his ex-employer. There was no major negative consequence, although some indignant letters were written to the publisher and some subscriptions were cancelled.

Dean Benson, however, seemed bent on anticlimax and refused to submit both grade book and final grades. When faced with legal action, he changed his mind, surrendered the necessary material, and left. He was temporarily replaced by alumnus Jim Wolcott, retired business executive.

The Academic Year 1985-86 included a letter from Vice President for Finance and Administration Pepper Reese that read in part:

> I wish the news were better but it was impossible... to make up the loss of $921,000 or 14.5 percent of our budgeted revenue.... The consequences of booking another deficit would be costly. This is the third straight year of deficit which will surely result in a re-visit by the accreditation team and possibly a performance bond on our HUD bonds.

The calendar year 1987 began with an executive session of the Executive Committee of the Board of Trustees (January 16, 1987) at which it was decided that a gift of one million dollars from Albertsons, Inc. to the College's endowment would not be the subject of any public announcement. Besides this gift, another positive note was sounded when Trustee Tom Wright reported that the sorely needed maintenance building was nearly finished.

On the negative side was the alarming statistic showing how inadequate was the book fund for the library: in 1985-86, the College added 750 new books; five schools not dissimilar had added an average of 4,448. Indeed, the library holdings had fallen to such a state over a fifteen-year period, according to a memorandum from Librarian Dale Corning dated January 16, 1987, that the deficiencies could not be made up through a one-year program. Since all departments had shared equally in library reductions over that decade and a half, a sustained remedial program was required. It was a blow at the very heart of the College. A palliative, however, might be available, but it was unknown at this time and it would not be forthcoming until next month. In the meantime, at this executive session of January 16, 1987, President DeRosier announced another extraordinary accomplishment: Michael Woodhouse, senior English major from Oakley, Idaho, had won a Rhodes Scholarship. Not only was this aerodynamic error of a bumblebee, this college with a minuscule endowment, flying, it was producing young people as bright as any produced anywhere.

The Rhodes Scholarship for Michael Woodhouse was a high-water mark for the administration of President DeRosier, who had helped to restore the confidence of the public in an institution whose history is nearly a continuing story of the consequences of an inadequate endowment. Part of the credit for Project 90 and for securing significant gifts must, however, go to the trustees, whom DeRosier had stimulated to become more active than heretofore in the grunt work of actually raising money for the College, and to one of the trustees in particular whose energy and aggressiveness paid off time after time.

Probably the **kairos** moment had come for Dr. Rosier, that moment of fulfillment or the fullness of time. A report by Michael Born on the annual fund solicitation makes this clear. The fourth paragraph of the "Report on Annual Fund Giving," (January 12, 1987) includes the following:

> In late August, the College was notified by the Anderson Foundation that the College would no longer be receiving funds due to the dispute over accepting federal funds several years ago [the HUD bonds]. This resulted in the elimination of $65,000 which always came in December. Also, some $10,000 of December gifts came in as restricted or for the

endowment when in 1985-86 they had been unrestricted. This included in part $5,000 from Mrs. Myrtle Symms and $2,000 from Mr. William Moore. The Anderson Foundation decision and the changes of gifts from unrestricted to restricted and endowment giving are major factors in a reduction of unrestricted December giving of approximately $100,000 from last year.

Again, Born writes:

> There is a serious question as to how much can be accomplished toward the $400,000 goal with only six months left in the 1986-87 fiscal year and considering that only $1,400 has been raised in the past six months. [Surely there is a typographical error here, but if Mr. Born really meant $114,000 or $140,000, there was still a problem of the first magnitude.]

> An additional problem in the last few months, which has impacted on fund raising, is the role of the President. Starting in November, the question of the President's future at The College of Idaho began to surface among many in the local community. In previous years, the President worked regularly on major donors, but in November this effort seemed to falter relating to the uncertainty of the President remaining at the College. There remains a pressing need for the Board of Trustees to clear up the uncertainty. It is vital to many of the major fund raising goals of the College that a strong leader be in the President's position as soon as possible.

Leadership desperate to present black ink to the trustees at the end of a fiscal year was prone to look everywhere for money with which to balance the budget. Into that black hole went money from various accounts, irrespective of whether there had been wishes of the grantors of the funds. In the present instance, some of the money raised for the Smith-Stanford Chair was appropriated and sucked into the operating budget—not, however, the monies from the sale of the Caldwell Hospital, for that amount was held inviolate for the purposes for which it was given and will be the corpus for the restoration of the amount used for budgeting purposes so that the Chair can be truly endowed.

What good is an endowed chair in a defunct institution? When survival is at stake, sacrifices have to be made in the interests of the organism. But the reflexive question then arises of how many of its arms and legs an organism can lose and still live. Surely the line walked by the officers of the school was more nearly a tightrope whose one end was secured in life, the other in death. Even so, the insistence of the Investment Committee on the inviolability of the endowment had brought that fund from a negative to an astonishing multi-million dollar figure, even before the gift of thirteen million dollars from Joe and Kay Albertson reported at the meeting of the Trustees on March 20, 1987.

So the administration of Arthur DeRosier, a brisk and lively time, ended, and the energetic New Englander by way of the South announced on January 27, 1987, that he was accepting the presidency of a small school in the Big Sky State: "With most of the goals I set in mid-1980 met, it is time for me to step aside and allow another to take the helm, develop his/her list of goals, and take the next step forward" (*Bulletin* Spring 1987).

It is appropriate to conclude this era with a few paragraphs from the Resolution of March 20, 1987, by the Board of Trustees:

RESOLUTION

Whereas, Dr. Arthur H. DeRosier, Jr. came to The College of Idaho in June, 1980, to serve as the institution's eighth President and that he fulfilled the duties of ceremonial and administrative leader of the College until his resignation, effective in February, 1987;

Whereas, under President DeRosier's leadership the college opened the J. A. Albertson School of Business, expanded the curriculum, and became a leader among liberal arts colleges in the use of academic microcomputers;

Whereas, under President DeRosier's leadership the academic programs of the college were successful in producing scholars of excellence, including a Rhodes Scholar, a Mellon Fellow in the Humanities, five Rotary International Scholars, two NAIA Academic All-Americans (basketball), a National Hispanic Scholar and a Harry S. Truman Scholar;

Now, therefore, be it resolved, that the members of the College's Board of Trustees, in the name of the College's administration, faculty and students—past and present—offer their heartfelt thanks and appreciation to Arthur H. DeRosier, Jr. for contributions that will be remembered for generations to come;

Adopted this twentieth day of March, 1987.

Part IX

℞ Renaissance: Robert L. Hendren, Jr.,

February 1987-

Fall, 1990: Venerable Kirkpatrick Gymnasium serves as the venue for the press conference announcing the gift to the College from J. A. and Katherine Albertson of $13.5 million for the construction of two major buildings.

CHAPTER NINETEEN

In Midstream

In Chapter eighteen an unidentified trustee was mentioned as a particularly energetic and aggressive fund-raiser. By implication he was also one of the most vocal of the College's supporters. When the trustees were faced with the task of choosing the ninth president of The College of Idaho, their deliberations must have been somewhat like the following.

In the first place, they were faced with a mid-year resignation and departure. The departing chief executive was not present to tie up loose ends nor available for the transfer of power. There is a widely accepted assumption that philanthropies view with considerable alarm all institutions where rapid turnover in chief executives occurs. The longer it takes to replace a president, the longer it takes for the institution to get back on their lists, even in last place.

So there was some merit in calling for a quick response.

But while rapid replacement held advantages, careless replacement might result in inept leadership, and that the trustees and the College could not endure. What to do? It was decided not to constitute a broadly based search committee as had operated rather ineffectively heretofore, but to form a committee from the trustees, choose the best candidate available, and quickly get on with the business of trying to develop the best liberal arts college in the Intermountain West, one of the best anywhere.

The trustee who had participated with vigor and effectiveness in raising money, had served as chairman of the Board of Trustees and knew the intimate details of its finances, was an experienced administrator. Not only that, but he was a successful and respected businessman whose opinions were frequently sought by Boiseans. A fourth consideration that made Bob Hendren a serious candidate was his recent experience as a college student. He had attended the

University of Idaho after the war but had left without taking his degree, promising Merlyn they would both finish their education later. Both returned to school and did, indeed, finish their degrees at The College of Idaho—Merlyn as an English major and Bob in philosophy.

But the final reason why Hendren went after the job was supplied by a donor who was ready to make a major gift, provided, "a president with wide business experience be found.... The donor then asked: 'Why don't you do it?' Mr. Hendren recalls. In fact, Mr. Hendren says, the donor's words were: 'Take it or leave it'" (Monaghan, "With Help...a Turnabout...," *The Chronicle of Higher Education*, January 16, 1991).

Rather than select an unknown quantity, the board concurred that an excellent candidate was available, and Robert L. Hendren, Jr., was called to the presidency. For the second time in the school's history it had a president who knew all the nooks, crannies, pitfalls, bogs, and sloughs of despond of its finances. There would be no honeymoon period; no business manager would have to mediate among creditors, the Board of Trustees, and a neophyte chief executive. Not since President Boone had there been this situation. Added to all this was the fact that the new president had a vision for the institution which he saw sustained by a growing and healthy endowment. As a merchant whose reputation had been established by dealing in quality merchandise, he foresaw enrollment growth simply as a function of quality. The best students will want

The ninth president of the College, Robert L. Hendren, Jr., and Mrs. Hendren greet trustee Walter Minnick at a Blatchley Hall reception.

to attend the best of institutions. If the best library, laboratories, equipment, and faculty signify anything, they mean magnetic attraction to the best of students.

Some faculty believed that to bypass them, not to set up a formal search process (committee and all), was a serious breach of protocol if not worse. Some of the Caldwell community felt old jealousies and hostilities toward a product of the capital city. Some students believed that the Ph.D. degree was *sine qua non* to holding the office of president, not knowing a great deal about the real world of higher education, and a few faculty nursed imagined grievances against the new president while dreaming that the administration of Dr. DeRosier had been prelapsarian Eden. Ruffled faculty feelings were smoothed by an address by Bill Chalker, who told Faculty-Staff Association of the realities of previous fund-raising efforts and spoke confidently of the quality of mind of the new president. Caldwell residents ceased gradually to talk about "the Boise mafia," and students were gradually weaned away from their false beliefs about requirements for a Ph.D. degree. No argument is quite so persuasive as results, and President Hendren had begun producing them as a trustee. The thirteen-million-dollar gift from Joe and Kay Albertson had resulted from the

Dr. Robert Steunenberg, '47.

Mary Shaw Shorb, '28.

donors' confidence in him, as had the additional million dollar gift from Albertsons, Inc., through the action of trustee Warren McCain.

The *Bulletin* of Spring 1987 offered a slice of life to its readers. DeRosier left January 23; before February 20, Hendren had been named to succeed him. Those events aside, what other things were happening on campus?

On February 26, Dr. Robert Steunenberg, '47, "co-holder of sixteen patents and author of more than two hundred scientific papers and reports," and Dr. Wayne Myers, Associate Dean for Regional Affairs, University of Washington Medical School, were honored. The new edition of *Rugg's Recommendations on Colleges* listed the C of I among four hundred top schools; two other national guides also recommended the college—*Peterson's Guide to College and Universities* and *Best Buys in College Education.* Mark Montgomery, 1984-85, and Chuck Blackhurst, 1985-86, were NAIA Academic All-American basketball players. Sal Gomez, 1983-84, had been designated a National Hispanic Scholar. Dr. Wallace A. Lonergan, '50, was named to head the J. A. Albertson School of Business. Dr. Mary Shaw Shorb, '28, was nominated to the Maryland Women's Hall of Fame by the American Association of University Women. And on August 14-16 the Fabulous Forties Reunion would take place. It, too, would prove to be a big success and would bring back to the campus the veteran men and women from the war years...the big war years...including people like Kay Chaffey, who had flown for the Army Air Corps ferrying military aircraft. Graduation time, 1987, was a triumph, featuring a baccalaureate sermon by retiring Dr. Chalker, recognition of the Thomas family at baccalaureate, and a commencement address by Alvin Josephy. The Thomas family merit more space than is available, for these six brothers and sisters are among the brightest luminaries produced by the College. They stand here for all the families whose multiple members attended this institution. They are doctors, teachers, business people, citizens, and community builders. Louis, Mary, Lorraine, Weldon, Elmer, C. Lloyd—a roster of distinction. Dr. Louis B. Thomas spoke as follows:

> A person, Orma J. Smith, and an institution, The College of Idaho, played crucial roles in my life.... [Dean Smith] inspired us with the belief that we could go to college if we really wanted to. And there was The College of Idaho...with more spirit than money and with a faculty of dedicated men and women taking a personal interest in the lives, hopes, and aspirations of their students (*Bulletin*, Summer 1987).

Another important development was the hiring of Dr. Nancy Hazelwood as Academic Vice President and Provost. Thus competent people were established at the two cornerstones of the College—development and fund raising by the president and the curriculum and academics by the vice president and provost.

Walter Cerveny, teacher of violin and member of the Department of Music for thirty-five years, retired; he had joined the faculty in 1952, two years into the Pitman era. And finally, in this year of great change, the baseball team won the Timber-Prairie League Championship and six singles players and three doubles teams—District Two Champions—represented the College in the NAIA women's tennis competition in Kansas City.

What would happen in 1987-88 to equal all these accomplishments?

For one thing, a former Professor of English at Yale University—who, after serving that institution as its president, left academe for major league baseball, first directing the National League and then becoming baseball's commissioner, agreed to appear on campus and speak in connection with the inauguration of President Hendren. A. Bartlett Giamatti was another of those many speakers who, over the years, have made convocations well worth the time and effort expended in putting them together.

For another thing, the *Bulletin* for Winter, 1987, carried a news item of considerable interest to those who remembered the enduring saga of the HUD bonds, that indebtedness that had hung around the College's neck since the days of Tom Shearer. On October 29, 1987, that indebtedness was removed in a symbolic mortgage burning presided over by President Hendren, Joe Albertson, Jack Simplot, Warren McCain, and Governor Andrus. The *Bulletin* states: "HUD nearly closed the College by declaring it in default on the $2 million still owed for expansion of housing, dining and student services facilities...."

A new chair had been created late in the summer, the Esther Becker Simplot Chair in Performing and Fine Arts, and Dr. James L. Murphy named its holder. This development at once recognized a loyal supporter and benefactor and published the new divisional structure that put the departments of art and music together and subsumed programs in dance and theater. Humanities was thereafter comprised of the departments of English, Modern Languages, and Philosophy and Religion.

The Spring 1988 issue of the *Bulletin* updated the entire matter of endowed chairs, and readers of this issue saw on its cover the faces of holders of endowed chairs. Professor Franklin Specht had been named to the John P. Weyerhaeuser Chair of History, succeeding Dr. DeRosier. The NEH Chair of English, secured by funds from an Albertson gift offered in match of National Endowment Funds, seemed an inappropriate designation. As the first holder of this chair, I suggested it be re-named to honor two people who had invested their lives in the institution: Professor Anna Smyth Eyck, who had been my major professor, and Professor Ralph Berringer, Chair of the Department when I first began teaching here for summer sessions in 1954 and 1955. It is thus the Anna Smyth Eyck—Ralph W. Berringer Chair in English. The third was the Esther Becker Simplot Chair held by Professor Murphy.

While the skiers in 1987-88 did not bring the accolades to which College supporters had grown accustomed, they did not fare badly (women's and men's teams won sixth and seventh places at the March National Nordic competition.) The baseball team did well, winning the Eastern Washington University Invitational, and the tennis players did well. The basketball team was no longer among the "first outs" at the tournament in Kansas City, winning their first two games before losing in overtime by three points to the team that took the national title. And C of I graduates were making news. Professor Mary Stoner Wald, '66, teacher of risk management at Temple University, wrote *Controlling Your Money.* George Venn, Professor of English, teaching writing and literature at Eastern Oregon State College, published a collection of essays, fiction, and poetry entitled *Marking the Magic Circle,* his fourth book. The work contains seven photographs by C of I classmate and fellow English major Jan Boles.

President Robert L. Hendren, Esther Simplot, and Dr. James L. Murphy announcing the endowment of the Esther Becker Simplot Chair in Performing and Fine Arts, 1988.

These items, pleasant to read and satisfying to the soul, lose none of their character when linked to the report from Lyman Wilbur's Investments Committee, in the July 22, 1987, Minutes of the Executive Committee, that "as of June 30, 1987, the total endowment is $21,007,421." The figure included the fourteen-million-dollar gift from the Albertsons and Albertsons Inc. secured by President Hendren in a permanent and binding way for the endowment as long as the institution remained.

In the Fall of 1988, the *Bulletin* became The College of Idaho *Quest*, edited by alumnus Larry Gardner '63, winner of the President's Distinguished Service Award in October 1985. A Professional Journalism Fellow at Stanford in 1976, Gardner was the incarnation of the oft-repeated truth that to write for any medium, the prerequisite is competence in writing, not a degree in journalism. Gardner had been an outstanding English major in college and had honed his skills by writing for Professors Berringer, Boone, and Brock.

For his first *Quest*, Gardner interviewed alumna, former trustee, professor emeritus—she had held nine different administrative posts at the College, including Acting President!—Margaret Boone. Her memories of her father and of an earlier time in Caldwell and on the campus, added to her insights into a college education that is more concerned with living a life than with making a living, resulted in a timely feature article.

But the bright prospects for a glorious new year—with academics the new year begins in September, not January—were dimmed by the death of one of the pillars of the Department of Music and the College as a whole. Dr. James Gabbard, choral director for twenty-five years and Chair of the Department of Music for four of those years, was another who died in the service of the College before he could retire and look back with satisfaction upon his career. He died of pancreatic cancer, which may have been the same affliction that took Payne Boulton so many years before. The vacancy left by his too early passing was like that left by other fine C of I faculty who died in service; it, too, would never be filled, though others would come along to create their own niches. The Department of Music had suffered two crippling losses in a brief span, for it was still reeling from the death the Dick Skyrm. Dr. Murphy and Dr. Greg Detweiler will create their own niches. Such transitions are never easy; Ian Morton's replacing of F. F. Beale created more than a little resentment from Beale partisans, who were inhospitable to Professor Morton's attachment to such fine music as that of "Palestrino," [sic] as one critic spelled it in an angry letter to Morton, the new chairman.

Fiscal conditions had continued to improve during 1988. The Executive Committee of the Board of Trustees had been informed at its August 24

357

meeting that $1,250,000 would be distributed to the unrestricted account of the College, a 49 percent increase over the year before. This amount represented earnings allowable for distribution rather than being returned to the endowment—which had gained some $3 million to bring it to approximately $25 million, or half of the centennial goal.

Additional information shared at this meeting concerned the Strategic Plan "which [was] progressing through all departments and review by the faculty," according to Dr. Lonergan. For what might have been the first time in ninety-eight years, it appeared that a plan might (in the trite language of business) be the engine driving the College and its curriculum instead of the College and curriculum being driven by what money could be begged or borrowed.

Professor Richard Widmayer gave the annual Liberal Arts Lecture and resigned his position, after a score of years of fine teaching, to try his hand at academic administration by becoming academic vice president for Arthur DeRosier.

At the meeting of the Executive Committee of the Board on December 14, 1988, it was announced that two long-time faculty members would be retiring in the spring, alumna and Professor of Botany Pat Packard and Frank Specht holder of the Weyerhaeuser Chair of History.

At the annual meeting of the Board on May 27, 1989, Governor Cecil Andrus passed the gavel of leadership to Walter Minnick; Phil Obenchain, who was filling many posts, including that of Dean of Enrollment Services, noted that 71 percent of the students accepted for fall were honor students, including four national Merit Scholar finalists and three with National Merit commendations; and Coach Holly gave an extended report on accomplishments by C of I scholar athletes—extended because the soccer, ski, basketball, baseball, and tennis teams had done so well. Perhaps a summary is justified: men's soccer, second in District; combined women's and men's alpine championship; in basketball, the one school out of 512 to make the final eight at the NAIA championship games in the past two years; tennis team, 17th in the nation; baseball, second in the district and in the top 20 in the national polls, for the first time.

Commencement this year was again a happy time, a time when students—and not a few faculty—looked back across their years at the College to which the ceremony marked finis and also looked ahead, for a new life was commencing. The traditional and welcome address was given by President Emeritus of Stanford University Richard Lyman, Dr. Chalker received an honorary degree, as had former professor and dean Ralph Sayre at Spring Convocation some four months earlier. And at the afternoon portion of the

Trustees' meeting, the portion that traditionally follows the luncheon after the commencement, the Investment Committee reported as follows: "We will be distributing $1,365,000 which reflects for the first time that the College has not used all of the excess."

Original inscription found in the catacombs in Rome by a centurion in the 4th century.

Excess? In the story of The College of Idaho? Would the heroine really come into her dowry after all?

Centenary Celebration

1891–1991

Evolution of the official seal of The College of Idaho.

How sweet it is! Burning the HUD mortgage, left to right, J. A. Albertson, Warren McCain, Robert L. Hendren, Jr., Cecil Andrus, and Jack Simplot.

CHAPTER TWENTY

The Renaissance, New Style

Students, visitors, and even a few older faculty (those in their midforties) sometimes look at the official seal of the College and ask, "Lux? Dux? Rex? Lex? What do they mean?" Bob Smylie once said that some of his contemporaries answered the query with, "It's a lucky duck that sees the right light." Others have seen in the seal a challenge to their creative impulses. Professor of Modern Languages and Registrar William Wallace committed the following **aubade** (a reference to its 4 a.m. composition) above a drawing of one of our ubiquitous pigeons:

> This bird upon her LEX stands bold,
> and leaves our attics perfect REX.
> The scholar DUX, his blood runs cold,
> but she LUX out and lays her ex.

An unsigned feature in Gardner's third number of The College of Idaho *Quest* (Spring 1989 which, incidentally carries an interview with Myrtle Smith Symms) offers "A Centenary Reflection." It is the fullest treatment of the College seal that I have seen.

> At some time in that distant past a centurion found an inscription on the walls of the catacombs under the city of Rome. The device we show here and the meaning scholars have ascribed to it [are] essentially the message and format yet carried on The College of Idaho seal in this time closing out the second millennium, a.d.

"O Lord, be to me my Savior,

my King, my Law,

my Light,

my Leader."

Dr. William Judson Boone took the message and its meaning and made it a part of the official seal of the College. Dr. Boone designed it with the help of some early believer who had drawn an inscription on the wall, in those dark and secret tunnels where early Christians worshipped and studied...and buried their dead.

So, across the centuries from some unknown artisan, believer, seeker of light...from some learned one comes the Latin, the "living" language, with a sign to us that has as much meaning today as it did when it was scratched into the wall perhaps 2,000 years ago.

LUX for light...DUX for leader...LEX for law...REX for king...each carrying both a secular and a Christian meaning. Dr. Boone illustrated each with representations of the sun for light, a flag and sword for leader, a book for law and a crown and scepter for king.

It has perhaps been best described by Dr. Paul Pitman, fourth president of the College, who said of it during chapel services on October 25, 1950: "The ideals which gave birth to the College, the values it seeks to serve, stand at the very heart of the American way of life, at the very center of our democratic society. They constitute the foundation of Western civilization.

"These ideals were epitomized in the character and life of Dr. Boone. Through him, and the men and women he trained, these ideals and values have been woven into the warp and woof of the College we love."

Thus a 2,000-year-old inscription from ancient Rome has become the focus of the official seal of The College of Idaho.

The academic year 1989-1990 began well. "The Newcomen Society of the United States honored The College of Idaho with its first ever recognition dinner in Idaho on September 26, 1989," ran a story in the Fall 1989 *Quest*, "[marking] only the second Idaho institution and 211th private college in the nation honored by the Society." The non-profit corporation's stated purpose is the support, promotion, and interpretation of "the nation's free enterprise system by recognizing achievement in American business and the society it serves."

It was appropriate to bring the College within that context, for although private support has not always been forthcoming to the degree the institution has deserved, still enough support has been marshalled—often in the nick of time—to preserve the institution and to enable it to take the next step toward its destiny. President Hendren gave the obligatory address to a full house at the Red Lion Riverside in Boise, reminding the audience of the history of the College and outlining some of the goals to which this private school remains dedicated. The Society's recognition, it was hoped, might help remind private benefaction of its essential role in the tripartite support upon which private institutions rest.

New board chairman Walter Minnick made two observations in the *Quest* (Summer 1989) that bear repeating:

> I think until you get a $50 million minimum endowment there simply is not the financial wherewithal to provide the level of excellence that has always been the school's traditional role.

> [The new] trustees have unique and extraordinary backgrounds and each has things to bring to the school that will greatly help us. I think if you look at the existing trustees, that's been uniformly a characteristic.

Minnick further said,

> I don't think it's going to be easy, but it's not impossible.... It just requires a lot of effort, a lot of pulling together, and a little bit of luck.

The College of Idaho Athletic Hall of Fame, long overdue, was finally established in October. Of the many superior candidates for inclusion, the Hall of Fame Committee chose to honor athletes Edwin "Josh" Lowell and R. C. Owens and coach Eddie Cole. At the recognition banquet of October 14, held in the Simplot Dining Hall and filled to capacity, these three were recognized, their careers highlighted, and the audience treated to their modest and humble responses. Two of Josh's teammates, "Bud" Brown and Jim Lyke (themselves logical contenders for the Hall of Fame along with their coach Anson Cornell), shared with the audience a few of the athletic distinctions won by this remarkable man. Owens' accomplishments were sufficiently recent that even the youngest alumnus connected him with a remarkable career as a premier receiver of passes thrown by Y. A. Tittle. The "alley oop" catch was his trademark.

At the Alumni Banquet a day earlier, alumnus Bob Wolcott was given the Distinguished Alumni award and Ward Tucker the Alumni Service award.

A stirring feature of this issue of the College's new outlet was an essay by Jim Wolcott on the Orma J. Smith Museum of Natural History, a study of the restoration of that collection of artifacts and specimens named after its first curator and director. Add to that the Harold Tucker Herbarium and the Mexican Herbarium (more than 40,000 specimens in the two), and to that the Evans Gem and Mineral Collection, and it is easy to see why these facilities are visited annually by about 5,000 people—including school children of all grade levels. Without the donated labor of people like Assistant Director Bill Clark (honored by the Alumni Association for his tireless efforts in behalf of the Museum), Midori and Jim Furushiro, Gene Mooney, Martha Hagen (widow of Professor Larry Hagen), and Sid Wint, the Museum's rebirth would not have been possible. Now, in Clark's words,

> We are a valuable research collection. We have made loans of mate-
> rial—mostly in entomology—all over the world. I process many loans
> of specific taxa to specialists on a regular basis.

Another collection gaining recognition and conferring merit upon the College and likewise highlighted in the Fall issue of *Quest* is the art collection. Bill Carter, a photo illustrator and grandson of William Judson Boone, gave to the College a gift of money for the preservation and enhancement of its permanent collection. Some of the Hogarth works, according to this item, "are currently on loan to the Museum of Art at Washington State for an exhibit called the 'Art of Satire—Goya, Daumier, and Hogarth.'"

Recognition reflecting brightly upon the College came when the Idaho Music Teachers Association honored Fern Nolte Davidson with a lifetime membership and at the same time dedicated its 32nd annual convention to her. These encomia were added to her honorary doctorate from the C of I, her distinguished alumna award from Vennard College, a Distinguished Citizen award from the *Idaho Statesman*, and the Governor's Award for Excellence in the Arts.

In another interview Larry Gardner provided Dr. Albert M. Popma the opportunity to celebrate private education and to review some of his experience as Chairman of the Board of Trustees, beginning in the Shearer administration.

The launching of The College of Idaho Foreign Studies Program, announced in the Fall issue of *Quest*, represented a commitment by the institution to expand the College's vision to one of global dimensions. This program and its natural ally, the Department of Modern Foreign Languages, will expand under the leadership of Jim Wolcott and Professor Starr Ackley.

A final indication of renaissance was the publication of a collection of short stories, the syndication of weekly essays (one on Idaho appeared internationally, an admirer sending along a copy of a Vancouver, B.C., daily which featured the Idaho essay), and continuing assignments from *Travel and Leisure* and other widely circulated and respected journals—all redounding to the credit of Visiting Professor of English John Rember and to the College for having had the good sense to hire him. Rember had done his freshman year at the College and finished his B.A. (*cum laude*) at Harvard as an English major. His M.F.A. from the University of Montana put him on the list of graduates from one of the three or four best writing programs in the United States.

New faculty added to the upbeat tempo of the academic year. Plans and reforms initiated in part by a trustee-faculty committee and partly by Vice President and Provost Dr. Hazelwood resulted in extended and extensive meetings. The new critical posture found expression in remarks by Professor Howard Berger, latest holder of the John P. Weyerhaeuser Chair of History, as recorded in the Spring 1990 *Quest*:

> Berger says the decline in American education began in the mid-1970's when "educators turned into counselors instead of teachers. That's when American educational theorists became preoccupied with the theory that stresses popular psychology at the expense of course content."

> "It's not a matter of liberal or conservative politics.... It's an issue of installing expectations in students and seeing that they're met...."

> A return to a superior education system could occur quickly, Berger believes: "It will happen as soon as teachers begin to teach instead of just caring."

Within this posture of critical analysis, the strategic plan belongs as visible evidence of two conditions. The first is the necessity to plan for a future beyond next year and the year after, in the historic continuum of crisis management and cliff-hanging annual budget anxieties. To an institution whose story has been that of day to day survival, this is a strange new world where plans can be made for the next five years. The second condition is related to the first: the school must adjust and adapt to a curriculum-driven educational process and a position of growth.

Some of the thinking reflected in the strategic plan is instructive. Strategic Plan II 1985-89 is a thirty-one page document describing rather specifically the background of the plans and an analysis of that background, a statement of current institutional strengths and weaknesses, an assessment of influences external to the institution that affect it, nine objectives of the strategic plan, and actions to be taken to realize those objectives. A few of these components stand forth. A strategic objective states that the student body should achieve an optimum level of between nine hundred and twelve hundred students (FTE). More rigorous admissions standards should be set. More minority students should be recruited. The College should expand and diversify library holdings, and it needs to improve the quality and quantity of intellectual activities outside the classroom. More chairs should be endowed. Facilities for athletic and recreational opportunities need to be developed.

Add to the above the process of curriculum revitalization instituted by Vice President Hazelwood and a comprehensive strategic plan emerges. Strategic plans are always in process and subject to change as circumstances and new knowledge dictate alteration. In a memorandum of November 14, 1989, Dr. Hazelwood outlined some five stages to this revitalization process and summarized tentative faculty expectations of the kind of graduate the College ought to produce. I quote from the memorandum, reminding the reader again of its tentative nature and its submission to alteration with changed circumstances and new knowledge.

FACULTY STATEMENT OF EDUCATIONAL INTENT

In order for our students to prepare for their future in which they may achieve personal goals, lead fulfilled lives, and contribute to the good of society, The College of Idaho intends that students experience the widest possible variety of ways to examine and interpret their world. In three major areas—Knowledge, Skills, and Values—students become part of our community of learning, our pursuit of excellence, our vision of the future, our preservation of past heritage.

The student who graduates from The College of Idaho should possess: I. An intellectual foundation, both broad and deep, II. An understanding of our world and the ability to communicate that understanding, III. A coherent, mature perspective.

Specifically, the first category requires analytic, logical, and creative thought enabling the graduate to make judgments and evaluations. From those intellectual functions, it follows that the graduate will have a certain flexibility, will be able to work independently, and will gain a thorough competence in at least one field by virtue of immersion in an academic major. The second category is concerned in part with a command of skills in communication, mathematics, and computers. Understanding refers to the development of ethical values and the awareness of connections between the individual and society. An understanding of science and technology and an appreciation of cultural pluralism are further expectations under this category. Finally, under the last category are those aspects of the educated mind that have to do with perspective, the ability to perceive connections among the academic disciplines, the ability to connect one's life to moral and ethical values, the ability to perceive life-long learning and the creative use of leisure time as functions of education. Physical, mental, spiritual, moral, and ethical wholeness are part of this perspective.

This renaissance from which the present chapter takes its title is both broad and deep, affecting students, alumni, faculty, trustees, donors, indeed the entire spectrum of what might be called The College of Idaho community. It will obviously and in ways unpredictable affect unborn generations, and that is a prospect of awesome implications.

A further look at the Spring 1990 *Quest* shows direct evidence of this rebirth. Trustee Warren McCain, then Chairman and CEO of Albertsons, Inc., donated $500,000 for an endowed chair in the humanities in honor of his wife. The Bernie McCain Chair in the Humanities, (held by Professor of Philosophy Terry Mazurak), McCain said, "Not only reflects my commitment to The College of Idaho and the private liberal arts education the school so ably provides, but it also represents the strong support of the McCain family members who have attended the C of I."

In addition to the excitement created by the processes of long-range planning and curriculum reform, student athletes were generating considerable national publicity, including exposure on national television, by winning another set of national ski titles—men's and women's alpine-combined championships in competition in Waterville Valley, New Hampshire, "the first time in NCSA history," according to this issue of *Quest*, "that one school earned both major titles in the same year."

As if in answer to the question of what long-standing need ought to be met next, Joe and Kathryn Albertson, '29, in a press conference in Kirkpatrick Gymnasium, announced a $13.5 million gift to their alma mater for siting and constructing two major facilities: a new J. A. Albertson School of Business and International Studies, and the J. A. Albertson Activities Center. The former will contain a 100-seat lecture hall, an auditorium, classrooms, seminar rooms, a computer center, a study area, a student advising center, a resource library with four audio rooms, faculty and administrative offices, a faculty lounge, and a conference room. The planned 25,000-square-foot brick structure will harmonize with the many other brick buildings on campus.

The second building is a response to the work of committee after committee drawn from trustees, students, faculty, and alumni over more than a twenty-year period, all begging for a facility with a swimming pool, weight rooms, and areas for intramural and interscholastic athletic competition. The 75,000 square-foot activities center will contain 2,400 bleacher seats with room for 1,600 temporary seats, with the finest of contemporary sound systems, a resource where commencement could be held. Classrooms, offices, lockers, and conference rooms are also included in the plan for the brick structure.

But something else was going on, essential to conclusion of these buildings: the campus was expanding. Because of previous transactions, the large campus had steadily shrunk until it occupied scarcely more than thirty acres. To provide land on which to site these buildings, property was acquired: some two and a half blocks, which, with the streets involved, amounted to slightly more than six acres. Both new buildings will be located on or adjacent to the Blatchley block.

The excitement of celebrating the College's first hundred years continues to build, and the rebirth of its old vitality can be indicated in ways other than these, not so dramatic as these gifts, granted, but significant.

A connection with Duane Dagley Associates, enrollment management consultants, appears to have paid off. Statistics for Fall Semester 1990 show an increase of just over 20 percent for new students (211), a retention of more students than had been anticipated, and an enrollment total up more than 8 percent for a student body of 511 FTE the highest since 1987. New students arrived with an average GPA of 3.3. The endowment at the opening of school in September stood at $29 million, of which $24 million produces income.

The student of history will recall that the Reformation was one of the significant consequences of the first Renaissance. It was significant in the life of this institution that the faculty chose to reorder the scope and size and reform the function of "that bloated and power hungry" group, the Academic Council. Restored to its original function as a steering committee of Faculty Assembly, Academic Council will no longer make of the Assembly a rubberstamp for Council decisions. Debate will be restored to faculty meetings, and one of the expected outcomes of this restoration is the wider sharing of knowledge of what is happening on the campus. The absence of news sharing has been frequently lamented by faculty and others. This move to return curricular matters directly to the faculty should restore communications.

Further evidence of the recovery of vitality, consistent with goals of the strategic plan, is the conference planned by some of the new faculty in English, notably Dr.

Dean Bethea, Modern Languages, and Philosophy and Religion. Scheduled for April 25-27 (and consequently part of the historical record by the time this book is in print) is an international humanities conference titled "Vision/Re-vision: Radical Post-structuralist Theory and the Liberal Arts." Scheduled to participate are Dr. Stanley Fish of Duke University, Dr. Jerome McGann of the University of Virginia, and Dr. Robert Scholes of Brown University.

Speakers chosen for baccalaureate and commencement for 1990 are further evidence of rebirth. The Reverend Benjamin Weir, held captive by Shiite Moslems for sixteen months, spoke at the traditional baccalaureate services, and Dr. Lauro Cavazos, U.S. Secretary of Education, gave the commencement address.

On April 26, 1990, Faculty Assembly convened and in the course of its business unanimously approved a resolution honoring its ninth president. It was an act of profound gratitude for a leader with a vision, energy, the confidence of the Board of Trustees, and a will to be second to none. That resolution from a faculty sparing in its praise but generous with criticism helps conclude this work.

RESOLUTION

April 26, 1990

> WHEREAS The College of Idaho's position of leadership in regional higher education has been secured through the recently announced major gifts from J. A. and Kathryn Albertson; and

> WHEREAS, those gifts were obtained through the untiring and devoted labor of the President of The College of Idaho, as he ever sought the dawn of a future for it which its founders had truly dreamed but which had provided elusive and as illusory as a dream;

> NOW THEREFORE BE IT RESOLVED that a grateful Faculty Assembly of The College of Idaho extend to its president, Robert L. Hendren, Jr., its most sincere appreciation for his concern for this institution, a concern which first declared itself by his acceptance of an invitation to serve as a trustee; by his subsequent service as Chairman of the Board of Trustees; and by his ever-during and successful efforts to secure funds for this institution; that this resolution be spread upon the pages of the minutes of this assembly; and that a copy of this resolution be sent by the secretary to President Hendren.

Groundbreaking ceremonies for the new buildings were held on October 12, 1990. Bids for the activities center had been let on September 12, 1990, and the contract in the amount of $7,790,000 was awarded on November 2, 1990, to S. D. Deacon. Bids for the J. A. Albertson School of Business and International Studies were let on October 12 and the contract was awarded to Jordan-Wilcomb for $2,193,000 on November 19, 1990. By the time this history is in press, those handsome buildings will be much more than drawings and architects' projections; no historian can predict what other buildings and developments will be revealed by the time the anniversary is here. Additional good news was the distinction conferred upon the College by the well-known weekly magazine *U.S. News and World Report* when, in October, that journal announced that in its forthcoming book *1991 America's Best Colleges* The College

Velma Morrison hits the switch that powers up the Centennial Carillon for its first public performance.

of Idaho would be identified as the second best up-and-coming regional liberal arts college in the West.

"Well, Mr. President, what other Visions and Re-visions have been imagined by those who dream and plan?" Dr. Hendren was asked. And quicker than I could write, he answered, "We want an esplanade leading into a fine and performing arts center. We want honor student housing. We want a humanities building. We must expand the student body. And we want to enter the 21st Century with an endowment that will enable us to become one of the best colleges anywhere. We want to offer competitive salaries and expand the library and bring and keep our science and computer equipment up to date. We must restore the three aging but graceful architectural gems that at the time of their construction must have captured the attention of all. It is hard to think of The College of Idaho without thinking of the queen and her attendants—Sterry Hall and Finney and Voorhees" (September 19, 1990).

In front of the William Judson Boone Science Center on a five-foot sandstone base stands a nine-foot statue of the College's first president. From that vantage point, President Boone's statue will gaze for generations to come over the domain he shaped and sustained. Between Sterry Hall and the William Judson Boone Science Center a modest brick and limestone tower contains the Velma Morrison Centennial Clock and Carillon, recognition extended by Trustee Morrison on the occasion of the College's centennial. A school that is a hundred years old ought to boast a clock tower and carillon, a daily and hourly reminder of how far it has come, through many dangers, toils, and snares, and how bright is its future, secured by faith...and a grand endowment.

Dedication of the Velma Morrison Centennial Clock and Carillon, November, 1990

371

Commencement ceremonies in front of Boone Hall, spring 1989.

Afterword

Three professors—Margaret Sinclair, a colleague whose identity I can't recall, and I—noted the slow and painful headway a handicapped student was making toward Strahorn Hall and his next class. We stood near the SUB, and in Margaret's hands were the results of her morning quest for litter. "Coors cans by more than four to one," she said. As her attention returned once again to the student, she said, "When I see that boy who has to labor for every step he takes, a boy for whom a college education means sacrifice, and then when I think of those others who take money, health, and this campus for granted and don't seem to care what they do with it, it just makes me angry." Her eyes snapped. "Let them come," Boone had said. "Let them all come and we'll see what they can do." Although he might have needed assistance to kneel and drink from the well prepared by others, a sunny Ron Pirnie, '71, would rise by himself. It is time, after a hundred years, to recognize and memorialize those whose care and concern passed on a legacy to hands they cannot see, even though I cannot name them all. This present work is at least a beginning, a first step toward those ends. It is reassuring to believe that the one who will write the bicentennial history will find some of the ground covered, some facts gathered, and some people celebrated . . . a hundred years' worth, in fact.

It is appropriate to identify some who have benefitted from that legacy. The list does not include the names of scholars recognized after graduation by such awards as Fulbright grants, nor does it list graduates who received institutional awards enabling them to pursue post-graduate work at various institutions.

HONORS SCHOLARS

FROM THE OFFICE OF NANCY HAZELWOOD AUGUST 28, 1990

FIVE RHODES SCHOLARS

Erling Skorpen	1954
Ted Wills	1960
Tom McFadden	1968
Jim Roelofs	1969
Michael Woodhouse	1987

ONE MELLON FELLOW IN THE HUMANITIES

Steven Maughan	1985

TWO MARSHALL SCHOLARS

Nancy Miller Okimoto	1964
Barry Fujishin	1972

THREE NATIONAL SCIENCE FOUNDATION FELLOWS

Rose Marie Holt McFarland	1977
Kent Holsinger	1978
Robert Cordova	1979

FOUR DANFORTH FELLOWS

Elden E. Jacobson	1958
Jonathan W. Perry	1961
Charles Rearick	1964
Brent Fry	1973

SEVEN ROTARY INTERNATIONAL SCHOLARS

Patrick Thompson Gillespie	1976
Zoe Rayborn	1982
Tad Martin	1984
Dan Semmens	1985
Sarah Wallace	1985
Jane Gregory (awarded '86)	1988
Derek Schulz	1990

ONE TRUMAN SCHOLAR

Elizabeth Van Veldhuizen	1984

FIVE FULBRIGHT SCHOLARS

Janean Walsh Wilske	1956
Loy Maugh Vail	1958
James Weed	1960
Margaret Burk Dietrich	1962
Kathleen Von Bargen	1965

ONE WOODROW WILSON SCHOLAR

Robert Snider	1959

ONE NATIONAL HISPANIC SCHOLAR

Salomon Gomez	1985

Finally, as I look over the story of this modest institution, a story that I have worked on for two years, I find gaps. I'm sure the reader will find more. It may be that some will be offended that I have omitted Professor Henry's record of successful proposals for funding to the National Science Foundation, the Murdock Foundation, and the EESA, bringing in well over $600,000 to the Division of Science and Mathematics and making that division a leader in the teaching of teachers of mathematics and science in the state. Professors Higdem and Anderson have written proposals whose funding has enhanced the College's computer holdings. Space will not permit the inclusion of all feats of grantsmanship.

Nor have I discussed the Spanakos Brothers, those championship boxers from Erling Skorpen's home borough of Brooklyn...nor the exceptional Japanese nationals Yasuaki Tanaka, whose knowledge of English grammar set him apart, and Giusuke "Gus" Tomoda, whose mastery of judo won him championships in NCAA competition. *The Boyfriend* and *Little Mary Sunshine* delighted capacity audiences as collaborations between the drama and music programs.

The writing of this history must stop somewhere, and printing deadlines impose an effective if arbitrary halt. The ski teams acquitted themselves with distinction in the regional and national meets, not quite at the championship level but well ahead of many larger schools. Individual All-American team titles went to Tiffan Rowe, Linda Evans, Tom Lyman, Alain Paquette, and Dave Rothman. The basketball team won the NAIA district championship, won the first game in the play-offs in Kansas City—in double overtime—with John Hilliard and Bill Perkins receiving several accolades, Perkins an honorable mention All-American and Hilliard the first All-American since Elgin Baylor, 1955. The baseball and women's tennis teams are performing well. Under the leadership of former national Alumni President Helen von Dach and Alumni Director, June Fitzgerald, the Margaret Sinclair Alumni Walk became a reality. The project involved the planting of two rows of trees, one on either side of the long promenade between the Morrison Clock Tower and Sterry Hall. The Walk will eventually appear as an avenue of trees, giving the small campus an appearance of spaciousness as the eye of the beholder catches the depth of the extensive east-west axis. Finally, the C of I *Coyote* has been reborn—*Canis latrans redux*—and appears once again to be an organ for reporting the life of the school; indeed the information on athletics came from pages four and five of the *Coyote* of April 5, 1991, edited by Eric Ellis.

Some may note my failure to mention Professor Siemsen's efforts through which the College and the Caldwell Public Schools are cooperating in our first Cross-Age Tutoring program. And for some, failure to identify all the boards of trustees will be a cardinal sin of omission. In the spring of 1990, it should be noted, Greg Koller replaced Larry Gardner as Director of Communications.

Modern technology no longer requires the presses to stop to insert an important development, but a gift of $2,000,000 from Gladys Langroise, Boise, to enhance the College's music department nearly invoked the old cry. The money will be held in endowment, income from which will support a joint venture of the College and the Boise Philharmonic Orchestra. It is another bright spot in this Centennial Year.

I have said the writing of history is selective. I hope the reader has found these selections worthwhile and that something of the hope and good cheer and belief in progress so real to the founders in the bright April springtime of 1891 has been recovered in this administration, making the Centennial truly an occasion for celebration.

Sources

Future historians may find useful a few brief comments about some of the sources used for this book. It is my fervent hope that well before the College's bicentennial there will be an archives, a real one. The present repository serving that function is a small room in the basement of Terteling Library into which in as orderly a fashion as possible archival materials are stored. The room is not humidity and temperature controlled. Flooding from lawn irrigation is not unknown. Materials stored there are not identified by accession number. It is not an archives, but it is the best we have. Many materials may be there that would have been helpful to the History, but I cannot be sure.

Professor Bollinger's paper may be in the archives; he gave me the copy I have.

Ed Bonaminio's paper is catalogued in Terteling Library with other graduate eduction seminar papers.

President Boone's diary—it is a journal or day book—is extremely useful. There are typewritten transcriptions of all the extant handwritten volumes, but the typist occasionally misspells a name or guesses at a word. There should be corrected copies made.

The Cox, Eastman, Hall, and Hayman materials are in Terteling.

University of Denver News is in my possession. Chancellor Daniel L. Ritchie's remarks deserve wide dissemination.

James L. Martin's autobiography has not been published. The portion of it pertinent to the College is in my possession, through Dr. Martin's courtesy.

Robert McCormick's transcript is in the archives.

The McGrath essay was brought to my attention by Jim Roelofs.

Peter Monaghan's long account in the *Chronicle* is an upbeat publication. It is in Terteling.

William G. Phelps' history of the military presence at the College during part of WWII, written with advice from Merle Wells, is a full account of that presence and is a valuable resource. It is in the archives.

Mimi Soran's fine paper is now in the archives in a slightly edited form, together with taped interviews.

Wilson's book on Charles Eastman is in Terteling and is an excellent source of information on a remarkable man.

The Reavis thesis is in Terteling Library.

The newspapers are widely available in their original form or on microfilm.

The Petersen book and the Edwards essay in *PNQ* are both in Terteling. Both are helpful for shedding light on early educational matters in the Northwest.

The Cowley report of October 8, 1949, is in the office of the president of the College.

Carrie Adell Strahorn's book, with illustrations by Charles M. Russell is in the archives in a first edition. It has since been reissued by the University of Nebraska, edited by Judy Austin.

Leslie Brock's article on Lawrence Henry Gipson in the Terteling collection of *Idaho Yesterdays* is important as a study of the early years of Idaho's first Rhodes Scholar.

Warren Knox's *Eye of the Hurricane* is in Terteling and is generally available.

Robert Davidson's transcribed talk is a valuable resource in pointing out the responsibilities of Boards of Trustees, responsibilities not always met in some instances.

Statistics on higher education appear in various publications of the American Council on Education.

Two other classes of publication require additional discussion. These are the periodic publications emerging from the campus—the school newspaper, the catalog, the alumni bulletin, and the school annual, making up one large category. The other category is the minutes—the official record of proceedings of trustees, faculty assembly, faculty association, and the like.

About the first category, I must note that the *Coyote* and the *Trail*, while varying in quality from year to year as strong or weak editors were in charge, generally constitute the most faithful record of the life of the institution. Some of the writing is superb. The early practice of failing to identify people in photographs was finally overcome by editors of both publications. These are available in the archives. However, the usefulness of both publications began to decline in the late 1960s, and about that time the *Coyote* staff no longer saw to it that bound copies were given to the library for archival purposes. There may be copies subsequent to 1965-66 in publication offices, but accessibility is a problem. Although there are complete issues of the *Trail*, the College annual, that publication's usefulness is severely compromised by the practice of not identifying people or events in photographs in recent editions.

378

Ralph Sayre's lengthy essay on Tom E. Shearer published in *The Fairfield Ledger* is in my possession. Both descriptive and analytic, the essay is a study of this complex man by a fellow Iowan who knew him, advised him, worked for him.

Finally, although reading minutes of meetings requires some assiduity, they are important sources of official information. Copies of Minutes of the Board of Trustees are in the office of the president. Minutes of the meetings of other organizations are in the archives.

American Council on Education, *Higher Education and National Affairs,* Washington, D.C., XXVI, 29, July 29, 1977.

W. LaMar Bollinger. The Development of Business and Economics Program at The College of Idaho, 1910-1982.

Edward Bonaminio. *The Football Program at The College of Idaho.* Education Seminar paper, 1966.

William Judson Boone. Diary

Leslie V. Brock. "Lawrence Henry Gipson, Historian: The Early Idaho Years," *Idaho Yesterdays,* 22, 2 Summer 1978.

W. H. Cowley. "Report to the Committee Seeking a President for The College of Idaho," October, 8, 1949.

Thomas Cox. *The Park Builders: A History of State Parks in the Pacific Northwest,* Seattle; Univ. of Wash., 1988.

Robert T.H. Davidson. "The College of Idaho from a Foundation Executive's Viewpoint," a talk to the Board of Trustees of The College of Idaho, Boise, Idaho, September 22, 1979.

Elaine Goodale Eastman. *Sister to the Sioux: The Memoirs of Elaine Goodale Eastman,* 1885-91. Lincoln: University of Nebraska, 1978.

G. Thomas Edwards. "Pioneer President Alexander Jay Anderson and the Formative Years of the University of Washington and Whitman College," *Pacific Northwest Quarterly,* 9, 2, April, 1988.

William Webster Hall, Jr. *The Small College Talks Back: An Intimate Appraisal.* New York: Richard R. Smith, 1951.

H.H. Hayman. *That Man Boone.* The College of Idaho, Caldwell, ID. 1948.

HB 1182, Yes! *University of Denver News,* 28, 2 Summer, 1990.

Warren Barr Knox. *Eye of the Hurricane: Observations on Creative Educational Administration.* Corvallis: Oregon State University Press, 1973.

James L. Martin. *An Autobiography.* Vol. I, 1917-1957, June, 1990.

Robert McCormick. *The Excitement of Building a College* Typescript n.d.

Earl James McGrath. *Values, Liberal Education, and National Destiny,* 1975.

Peter Monaghan. With Help from Philanthropists, Alumni, Politicians, and Business Leaders, A Turnaround at [The] College of Idaho; *The Chronicle of Higher Education*, A33, January 16, 1991.

Keith C. Petersen. *This Crested Hill: An Illustrated History of the University of Idaho.* Moscow, Idaho: University of Idaho Press, 1987.

William G. Phelps. *History of [the] 311th College Training Detachment* (Aircrew) n.d.

C. Ben Reavis. *Profile of The College of Idaho.* Unpublished thesis. Utah State Agricultural College. 1957.

Ralph L. Sayre. "Tom Shearer: an independent spirit," *The Fairfield Ledger*, Parsons Reunion Edition, June 22, 1989.

Mimi Soran. "The Frederick Fleming Beale School of Music," paper. May 22, 1989.

Carrie Adell Strahorn. *Fifteen Thousand Miles by Stage: A Woman's Unique Experience During Thirty Years of Pathfinding and Pioneering from the Missouri to the Pacific and from Alaska to Mexico.* Lincoln: University of Nebraska, 1988.

Raymond Wilson. *Ohiyesa: Charles Eastman, Santee Sioux.* Urbana: University of Illinois, 1983.

Boise *Capital News*

Caldwell *News-Tribune*

Caldwell *Tribune*

Evening Capital News (Boise)

Idaho *Statesman*

Minutes of the Board of Trustees

Minutes of the Faculty Assembly

Minutes of the Faculty Association

Minutes of the Faculty-Staff Association

Minutes of the President's Cabinet

COLLEGE PUBLICATIONS

The Bulletin (*Quest* after 1989)

The Coyote

The Catalog

The Renaissance

The Trail

Index of Photographs

Illustration

Acknowledgements

Many photographers have helped document the history of The College of Idaho. The first, of course, was Dr. William Judson Boone. Subsequent workers include Robert McCormick '17, Harold Tucker '23, Margaret Sinclair '27, Omar Fricke '58, Dr. Robert Bratz, Bill Rankin '41, Earl F. Brockman '52, Dr. John Wilmorth, Jan Boles '65, Ron Pisaneschi, Steve Grant, plus any number of anonymous contributors to the *Trail* and *Coyote*. Caldwell photographic businesses such as the Snodgrass Studio, Welchel-Milliner Studio, and others now long gone are represented in the College archives. Generous alumni and friends of the College have donated other photos that help round out the visual history. The picture on p. 336 is by Keith Book of the Idaho *Press-Tribune*, and is used with his permission. The 1891 map of Idaho is provided courtesy of the Idaho Historical Society Library and Archives.

Index

Y

Z